Annual Editions: U.S. History,
Volume 2: Reconstruction
Through the Present, 22/e

Larry Madaras
Robert James Maddox

http://create.mcgraw-hill.com

ISBN-10: 0078097541   ISBN-13: 9780078097546

Contents

Unit 5 117

5. From the Cold War to 2010 118

Unit 6 169

6. New Directions for American History 170

Preface

This volume covers the 155+ years between the end of the Civil War and the present. The United States at the start of the period was a very different world from the one we live in today. Revolutionary changes have taken place in virtually every area. Following the development of automobiles, people were able to travel in hours distances that would have previously taken days. Airplanes have put any place on the globe within reach. Radio, television, and computers have vastly changed the transmission of knowledge, earlier restricted to word of mouth or the printed page. Still, many of the problems we face today have echoes in the past: race relations, gender roles, domestic terrorism, and environmental problems to name just a few. At least one new epidemic—AIDS—has become a scourge just as smallpox once was. We can all profit from the study of history, not to get solutions for specific problems, but to discover in the past some guidelines for our own time.

The study of history has changed over the years. Someone once said that historians wrote about "chaps," meaning white males who enjoyed positions of power or influence. Older history books tended to concentrate on presidents, titans of industry or finance, and military leaders. Women usually were mentioned only in passing, and then primarily as the wives or lovers of important men. Minority groups were treated, if at all, as passive objects of social customs or legislation. Mention of sexual orientation was simply out of the question.

Now virtually everything that has happened is considered fit for study. Books and articles tell us about the lives of ordinary people, about groups previously ignored or mentioned only in passing, and about subjects considered too trivial or commonplace to warrant examination. History "from the bottom up," once considered innovative, has become commonplace. Welcome as these innovations are, they often are encumbered by two unfortunate tendencies: many are freighted down with incomprehensible prose, and many are produced to advance agendas the authors try to fob off as scholarship.

Traditional history is still being written. For better or worse, there *have* been men and women who have exercised great power or influence over the lives and deaths of others. They continue to fascinate. Presidents such as Woodrow Wilson and Franklin D. Roosevelt had to make decisions that affected enormous numbers of people at home and abroad. The Wright brothers opened a new era in human history with their invention of a practical airplane. And the relatively unknown Belva Lockwood, who never held elected office, caused quite a stir in her day.

Annual Editions: American History, Volume 2, constitutes an effort to provide a balanced collection of articles that deal with great leaders and great decisions, as well as with ordinary people, at work, at leisure, and at war.

Practically everyone who uses the volume will think of one or more articles he or she considers would have been preferable to the ones actually included. Some readers will wish more attention had been paid to one or another subject, others will regret the attention devoted to matters they regard as marginal. That is why we encourage teachers and students to let us know what they believe to be the strengths and weaknesses of this edition.

Annual Editions contains a number of features designed to make the volume "user friendly." These include a *Topic Guide* to help locate articles on specific individuals or subjects; and the *Table of Contents abstracts* that summarize each article with key concepts in boldface. The essays are organized into topical units. Each unit includes an overview that provides background information, and every reading is framed with Learning Outcomes, Critical Thinking questions, and additional Internet References for further exploration.

There will be a new edition of this volume in two years, with approximately half the readings being replaced by new ones. Please let us know if you have suggestions for new readings or improving the format.

Larry Madaras, Robert James Maddox
Editors

Academic Advisory Board

Members of the Academic Advisory Board are instrumental in the final selection of articles for Annual Editions books and ExpressBooks. Their review of the articles for content, level, and appropriateness provides critical direction to the editor(s) and staff. We think that you will find their careful consideration reflected here.

Maribeth Andereck
University of Southern Mississippi

Elaine M. Artman
Mercer University

Frank Aycock
Appalachian State University

Julia Ballenger
Texas Wesleyan University

Felicia Blacher-Wilson
Southeastern Louisiana University

Sally Blake
University of Memphis

Christopher Boe
Pfeiffer University

Beverly Bohn
Park University

Betty Brown
University of North Carolina–Pembroke

Correlation Guide

The *Annual Editions* series provides students with convenient, inexpensive access to current, carefully selected articles from the public press. **Annual Editions: United States History, Volume 2: Reconstruction through the Present, 22/e** is an easy-to-use reader that presents articles on important topics such as *culture, diplomacy, labor,* and many more. For more information on *Annual Editions* and other *McGraw-Hill Create*™ titles, visit www.mcgrawhillcreate.com.

This convenient guide matches the units in **Annual Editions: United States History, Volume 2, 22/e** with the corresponding chapters in two of our best-selling McGraw-Hill Education History textbooks by Brinkley and Davidson et al.

Annual Editions: United States History, Volume 2, 22/e	The Unfinished Nation: A Concise History of the American People, 7/e by Brinkley	Experience History: Interpreting America's Past, 8/e by Davidson et al.
Unit: Reconstruction and the Gilded Age	**Chapter 15:** Reconstruction and the New South	**Chapter 18:** The New South & the Trans-Mississippi West 1870–1914
Unit: The Emergence of Modern America	**Chapter 16:** The Conquest of the Far West **Chapter 17:** Industrial Supremacy **Chapter 18:** The Age of the City **Chapter 19:** From Crisis to Empire	**Chapter 19:** The New Industrial Order 1870–1914 **Chapter 20:** The Rise of an Urban Order 1870–1914 **Chapter 21:** The Political System under Strain at Home and Abroad 1877–1900
Unit: From Progressivism to the 1920s	**Chapter 20:** The Progressives **Chapter 21:** America and the Great West **Chapter 22:** The New Era	**Chapter 22:** The Progressive Era 1890–1920 **Chapter 23:** The United States and the Collapse of the Old World Order 1901–1920 **Chapter 24:** The New Era 1920–1929
Unit: From the Great Depression to World War II	**Chapter 23:** The Great Depression **Chapter 24:** The New Deal **Chapter 25:** The Global Crisis, 1921–1941 **Chapter 26:** America in a World at War	**Chapter 25:** The Great Depression and the New Deal 1929–1939 **Chapter 26:** America's Rise to Globalism 1927–1939
Unit: From the Cold War to 2010	**Chapter 27:** The Cold War **Chapter 28:** The Affluent Society **Chapter 29:** Civil Rights, Vietnam, and the Ordeal of Liberalism **Chapter 30:** The Crisis of Authority **Chapter 31:** From the "Age of Limits" to the Age of Reagan	**Chapter 27:** Cold War America 1945–1954 **Chapter 28:** The Suburban Era 1945–1963 **Chapter 29:** Civil Rights & Uncivil Liberties 1947–1969 **Chapter 30:** The Vietnam Era 1963–1975 **Chapter 31:** The Conservative Challenge 1976–1992 **Chapter 32:** The United States in a Global Community, 1989–Present
Unit: New Directions for American History	**Chapter 32:** The Age of Globalization	**Chapter 32:** The United States in a Global Community, 1989–Present

Topic Guide

This topic guide suggests how the selections in this book relate to the subjects covered in your course. You may want to use the topics listed on these pages to search the Web more easily.

All the articles that relate to each topic are listed below the bold-faced term.

African Americans
Baseball's *Noble* Experiment
The American Civil War, Emancipation, and Reconstruction on the
   World Stage
The Forgotten Radical History of the March on Washington

Bush, George W.
The Rove Presidency

Carnegie, Andrew
Gifts of the "Robber Barons"

Chief Joseph
The Nez Perce Flight for Justice

Clinton, Bill
The Tragedy of Bill Clinton

Cody, William
How the West Was Spun

Cold war
The Key to the Warren Report
The Real Cuban Missile Crisis: Everything You Think You Know Is
   Wrong
Soft Power: Reagan the Dove
Why Truman Dropped the Bomb

Culture
Baseball's *Noble* Experiment
Becoming Us
How the West Was Spun
Remember the Roaring '20s?
The Spirit of '78, Stayin' Alive
Where the Other Half Lived

Depression, the great
15 Minutes that Saved America
A New Deal for the American People
Labor Strikes Back
When America Sent Her Own Packing
Why the Money Stopped

Diplomacy
Soft Power: Reagan the Dove
To Make the World Safe for Democracy

Environment
Between Heaven and Earth: Lindbergh: Technology and
   Environmentalism
Father of the Forests
Global Warming: Who Loses—and Who Wins?

Ford, Henry
The $5 Day

Government
15 Minutes that Saved America
Father of the Forests
Global Warming: Who Loses—and Who Wins?
Good Health for America?
Lockwood in '84
Losing Streak: The Democratic Ascendancy and Why It Happened
The Key to the Warren Report
The Rove Presidency
The American Civil War, Emancipation, and Reconstruction on the
   World Stage
The Tragedy of Bill Clinton
Why the Money Stopped

Immigrants
Becoming Us
What Happened at Haymarket?
When America Sent Her Own Packing
Where the Other Half Lived

Kennedy, John F.
The Key to the Warren Report
The Real Cuban Missile Crisis: Everything You Think You Know Is
   Wrong

Labor
A Day to Remember: March 25, 1911: Triangle Fire
Labor Strikes Back
The $5 Day

Lockwood, Belva
Lockwood in '84

Mellon, Andrew
Gifts of the "Robber Barons"

Military
Meuse-Argonne: America's Bloodiest Single Battle Occurred in the
   Forests and Fields of Eastern France during World War I
Why Truman Dropped the Bomb

Morgan, J. Pierpont
Upside-Down Bailout

Native Americans
A Day to Remember: December 29, 1890
The Nez Perce Flight for Justice
What Do We Owe the Indians?

Obama, Barack
Good Health for America?
Losing Streak: The Democratic Ascendancy and Why It
   Happened

Panama Canal
Theodore Roosevelt, the Spanish-American War, and the Emergence
   of the United States as a Great Power

Unit 1

UNIT

Reconstruction and the Gilded Age

Abraham Lincoln had wanted to reunite the nation as quickly as possible after four years of war. During the last months of his life, he had instituted simple procedures through which Southern states could resume their positions within the union. Only a few high-ranking Confederate officials were prohibited from participating. Where did this leave the former slaves? Lincoln's version of reconstruction would result in the South being ruled by essentially the same people who had brought about secession. Those who became known as "Radical" or "Extreme" Republicans refused to abandon Freed People to their former masters. They wished to use the power of the federal government to ensure that blacks enjoyed full civil and legal rights. At first they thought they had an ally in Vice President Andrew Johnson, who assumed the presidency after Lincoln's assassination. When this proved untrue, a grueling struggle ensued that resulted in Johnson's impeachment and the Radicals in command of reconstruction. The South was divided into five military districts and federal troops were sent to protect the rights of Freed People. White Southerners used every means possible to keep blacks "in their place." This section, among other things, analyzes the ultimate failure of Radical Reconstruction.

Historians used to debate whether business leaders during the latter part of the nineteenth century should be regarded as "industrial statesmen" or "robber barons." Most of them were both. Without denying the shady business practices these men often employed, they and others like them did much to create a modern industrial society.

William "Buffalo Bill" Cody's Wild West shows provided plenty of excitement. There were shootouts, daring rescues, and cavalry charges, among other things. They justified Indian removal in the name of progress and reassured whites that, however civilized they might be, they could "beat the braves and bullies of the world at their own game."

In 1884, at a time when women could not even vote, Belva Lockwood ran for the presidency on the Equal Rights Party ticket. She was regarded as a gadfly by some and resented by others. Many women suffragists, for instance, regarded her candidacy as harmful to their cause because they incorrectly believed that the Republican Party provided the best hope for attaining the vote.

The treatment of American Indians constitutes a sordid chapter in this nation's history. Time after time tribes were pushed off their ancestral lands, often with violence or the threat of violence. Frequently they were promised that if only they moved to this or that area they would be permitted to live in peace thereafter. Such promises usually lasted only until whites decided they wanted those lands, too.

Article

The American Civil War, Emancipation, and Reconstruction on the World Stage

EDWARD L. AYERS

Learning Outcomes

After reading this article, you will be able to:

- Describe the importance of the U.S. Civil War and the Reconstruction from a world perspective.
- Explain how the white South, claiming to be victims, affected the Reconstruction effort.

Americans demanded the world's attention during their Civil War and Reconstruction. Newspapers around the globe reported the latest news from the United States as one vast battle followed another, as the largest system of slavery in the world crashed into pieces, as American democracy expanded to include people who had been enslaved only a few years before.[1]

Both the North and the South appealed to the global audience. Abraham Lincoln argued that his nation's Civil War "embraces more than the fate of these United States. It presents to the whole family of man, the question, whether a constitutional republic, or a democracy . . . can, or cannot, maintain its territorial integrity." The struggle, Lincoln said, was for "a vast future," a struggle to give all men "a fair chance in the race of life."[2] Confederates claimed that they were also fighting for a cause of world-wide significance: self-determination. Playing down the centrality of slavery to their new nation, white Southerners built their case for independence on the right of free citizens to determine their political future.[3]

People in other nations could see that the massive struggle in the United States embodied conflicts that had been appearing in different forms throughout the world. Defining nationhood, deciding the future of slavery, reinventing warfare for an industrial age, reconstructing a former slave society—all these played out in the American Civil War.

By no means a major power, the United States was nevertheless woven into the life of the world. The young nation touched, directly and indirectly, India and Egypt, Hawaii and Japan, Russia and Canada, Mexico and Cuba, the Caribbean and Brazil, Britain and France. The country was still very much an experiment in 1860, a representative government stretched over an enormous space, held together by law rather than by memory, religion, or monarch. The American Civil War, played out on the brightly lit stage of a new country, would be a drama of world history. How that experiment fared in its great crisis—regardless of what happened—would eventually matter to people everywhere.

More obviously than most nations, the United States was the product of global history. Created from European ideas, involvement in Atlantic trade, African slavery, conquest of land from American Indians and European powers, and massive migration from Europe, the United States took shape as the world watched. Long before the Civil War, the United States embodied the possibilities and contradictions of modern western history.

Slavery was the first, most powerful, and most widespread kind of globalization in the first three centuries after Columbus. While colonies came and went, while economies boomed and crashed, slavery relentlessly grew—and nowhere more than in the United States. By the middle of the nineteenth century, the slave South had assumed a central role on the world stage. Cotton emerged as the great global commodity, driving factories in the most advanced economies of the world. The slaves of the South were worth more than all the railroads and factories of the North and South combined; slavery was good business and shrewd investment.

While most other slave societies in the hemisphere gradually moved toward freedom, the American South moved toward the permanence of slavery. Southerners and their Northern allies, eager to expand, led the United States in a war to seize large parts of Mexico and looked hungrily upon the Caribbean and Central America. Of all the slave powers—including the giants of Brazil and Cuba, which continued to import slaves legally long after the United States—only the South and its Confederacy fought a war to maintain bondage.[4]

Ideas of justice circulated in global intercourse just as commodities did and those ideas made the American South increasingly anomalous as a modern society built on slavery. Demands for universal freedom came into conflict with ancient traditions of subordination. European nations, frightened by revolt in Haiti and elsewhere and confident of their empires' ability to prosper without slavery, dismantled slavery in their colonies in the western hemisphere while Russia dismantled serfdom.

Black and white abolitionists in the American North, though a tiny despised minority, worked with British allies to fight the acceptance of slavery in the United States. A vision of the South as backward, cruel, and power-hungry gained credence in many places in the North and took political force in the Republican party. The global economy of commodities and ideology, demanding cotton while attacking slavery, put enormous and contradictory strains on the young American nation.[5]

Meanwhile, a new urge to define national identity flowed through the western world in the first half of the nineteenth century. That determination took quite different forms. While some people still spoke of the universal dreams of the French and American Revolutions, of inalienable attributes of humankind, others spoke of historical grievance, ethnic unity, and economic self-interest. Many longed for new nations built around bonds of heritage, imagined and real.[6]

White Southerners, while building their case for secession with the language of constitutions and rights, presented themselves as a people profoundly different from white Northerners. They sought sanction for secession in the recent histories of Italy, Poland, Mexico, and Greece, where rebels rose up against central powers to declare their suppressed nationhood, where native elites led a "natural, necessary protest and revolt" against a "crushing, killing union with another nationality and form of society."[7]

As the South threatened to secede, the Republicans, a regional party themselves, emphasized the importance of Union for its own sake, the necessity of maintaining the integrity of a nation created by legal compact. It fell to the United States, the Republicans said, to show that large democracies could survive internal struggles and play a role in world affairs alongside monarchies and aristocracies.[8]

Once it became clear that war would come, the North and the South seized upon the latest war-making strategies and technologies. From the outset, both sides innovated at a rapid pace and imported ideas from abroad. Railroads and telegraphs extended supply lines, sped troop reinforcements, and permitted the mobilization of vast armies. Observers from Europe and other nations watched carefully to see how the Americans would use these new possibilities. The results were mixed. Ironclad ships, hurriedly constructed, made a difference in some Southern ports and rivers, but were not seaworthy enough to play the role some had envisioned for them. Submarines and balloons proved disappointments, unable to deliver significant advantages. Military leaders, rather than being subordinated by anonymous machinery, as some expected, actually became more important than before, their decisions amplified by the size of their armies and the speed of communication and transport.[9]

The scale and drama of the Civil War that ravaged America for four years, across an area larger than the European continent, fascinated and appalled a jaded world. A proportion of the population equal to five million people today died and the South suffered casualties at a rate equal to those who would be decimated in Europe's mechanized wars of the twentieth century.

The size, innovation, and destructiveness of the American Civil War have led some, looking back, to describe it as the first total war, the first truly modern war. Despite new technologies and strategies, however, much of the Civil War remained old-fashioned. The armies in the American Civil War still moved vast distances on foot or with animals. The food soldiers ate and the medical care they received showed little advance over previous generations of armies. The military history of the Civil War grew incrementally from world history and offered incremental changes to what would follow. Although, late in the war, continuous campaigning and extensive earthen entrenchments foreshadowed World War I, Europeans did not grasp the deadly lesson of the American Civil War: combining the tactics of Napoleon with rapid-fire weapons and trenches would culminate in horrors unanticipated at Shiloh and Antietam.[10]

Diplomacy proved challenging for all sides in the American crisis. The fragile balance of power on the Continent and in the empires centered there limited the range of movement of even the most powerful nations. The Confederacy's diplomatic strategy depended on gaining recognition from Great Britain and France, using cotton as a sort of blackmail, but European manufacturers had stockpiled large supplies of cotton in anticipation of the American war. British cartoonists, sympathetic to the Confederacy, ridiculed Abraham Lincoln at every opportunity, portraying him as an inept bumpkin—until his assassination, when Lincoln suddenly became sainted. Overall, the North benefited from the inaction of the British and the French, who could have changed the outcome and consequences of the war by their involvement.[11]

Inside the United States, the change unleashed by the war was as profound as it was unexpected. Even those who hated slavery had not believed in 1861 that generations of captivity could be ended overnight and former slaves and former slaveholders left to live together. The role of slavery in sustaining the Confederacy through humbling victories over the Union created the conditions in which Abraham Lincoln felt driven and empowered to issue the Emancipation Proclamation. The Union, briefly and precariously balanced between despair and hope, between defeat and victory, was willing in 1862 to accept that bold decision as a strategy of war and to enlist volunteers from among black Americans.[12]

The nearly 200,000 African Americans who came into the war as soldiers and sailors for the Union transformed the struggle. The addition of those men, greater in number than all the forces at Gettysburg, allowed the Union to build its advantage in manpower without pushing reluctant Northern whites into the draft. The enlistment of African Americans in the struggle for their own freedom ennobled the Union cause and promised to set a new global standard for the empowerment of formerly enslaved people. The world paid admiring attention to the brave and disciplined black troops in blue uniforms.[13]

The destruction of American slavery, a growing system of bondage of nearly four million people in one of the world's most powerful economies and most dynamic nation-states, was a consequence of world importance. Nowhere else besides Haiti did slavery end so suddenly, so completely, and with so little compensation for former slaveholders.[14] Had the United States failed to end slavery in the 1860s the world would have felt the difference. An independent Confederate States of America would certainly have put its enslaved population to effective use in coal mines, steel mills, and railroad building, since industrial slavery had been employed before secession and became more common during wartime. Though such a Confederacy might have found itself stigmatized, its survival would have meant the evolution of slavery into a new world of industrialization. The triumph of a major autonomous state built around slavery would have set a devastating example for the rest of the world, an encouragement to forces of reaction. It would have marked the repudiation of much that was liberating in Western thought and practice over the preceding two hundred years.[15]

Driven by the exigencies of war, Northern ideals of color-blind freedom and justice, so often latent and suppressed, suddenly if briefly bloomed in the mid-1860s. The Radical Republicans sought to create a black male American freedom based on the same basis as white male American freedom: property, citizenship, dignity, and equality before the law. They launched a bold Reconstruction to make those ideals a reality, their effort far surpassing those of emancipation anywhere else in the world. The white South resisted with vicious vehemence, however, and the Republicans, always ambivalent about black autonomy and eager to maintain their partisan power, lost heart after a decade of bitter, violent, and costly struggle in Reconstruction. Northern Democrats, opposing Reconstruction from the outset, hastened and celebrated its passing.[16]

If former slaves had been permitted to sustain the enduring political power they tried to build, if they had gone before juries and judges with a chance of fair treatment, if they had been granted homesteads to serve as a first step toward economic freedom, then Reconstruction could be hailed as a turning point in world history equal to any revolution. Those things did not happen, however. The white South claimed the mantle of victim, of a people forced to endure an unjust and unnatural subordination. They won international sympathy for generations to follow in films such as *Birth of a Nation* (1915) and *Gone With the Wind* (1939), which viewed events through the eyes of sympathetic white Southerners. Reconstruction came to be seen around the world not as the culmination of freedom but as a mistake, a story of the dangers of unrealistic expectations and failed social engineering. Though former slaves in the American South quietly made more progress in landholding and general prosperity than former slaves elsewhere, the public failures of Reconstruction obscured the progress black Southerners wrenched from the postwar decades.[17]

When the South lost its global monopoly of cotton production during the Civil War, governments, agents, and merchants around the world responded quickly to take the South's place and to build an efficient global machinery to supply an ever-growing demand in the world market. As a result, generations of black and white sharecroppers would compete with Indian,

Brazilian, and Egyptian counterparts in a glutted market in which hard work often brought impoverishment. The South adapted its economy after the war as well. By the 1880s, the South's rates of urban growth, manufacturing, and population movement kept pace with the North—a remarkable shift for only twenty years after losing slavery and the Civil War—but black Southerners were excluded from much of the new prosperity.[18]

As the Civil War generation aged, younger men looked with longing on possible territorial acquisitions in their own hemisphere and farther afield. They talked openly of proving themselves, as their fathers and grandfathers had, on the battlefield. Some welcomed the fight against the Spanish and the Filipinos in 1898 as a test of American manhood and nationalism. The generation that came of age in 1900 built monuments to the heroes of the Civil War but seldom paused to listen to their stories of war's horror and costs.

The destruction of slavery, a major moral accomplishment of the United States Army, of Abraham Lincoln, and of the enslaved people themselves, would be overshadowed by the injustice and poverty that followed in the rapidly changing South, a mockery of American claims of moral leadership in the world. Black Southerners would struggle, largely on their own, for the next one hundred years. Their status, bound in an ever-tightening segregation, would stand as a rebuke to the United States in world opinion. The postwar South and its new system of segregation, in fact, became an explicit model for South Africa. That country created apartheid as it, like the American South, developed a more urban and industrial economy based on racial subordination.

Americans read about foreign affairs on the same pages that carried news of Reconstruction in the South. Even as the Southern states struggled to write new constitutions, Secretary of State William Henry Seward purchased Alaska in 1867 as a step toward the possible purchase of British Columbia. President Grant considered annexation of Santo Domingo, partly as a base for black Southern emigration; he won the support of black abolitionist Frederick Douglass, who wanted to help the Santo Domingans, but was opposed by Radical Republican Senator Charles Sumner.

Americans paid close attention to Hawaii in these same years. Mark Twain visited the islands in 1866, and Samuel Armstrong—the white founder of Hampton Institute, where Booker T. Washington was educated—argued that Hawaiians and former slaves in the South needed similar discipline to become industrious. At the same time, Seward signed a treaty with China to help supply laborers to the American West, a treaty that laid the foundation for a large migration in the next few decades. In 1871, American forces intervened militarily in Korea, killing 250 Korean soldiers. The leaders of the Americans admitted they knew little about their opponents, but brought the same assumptions about race to the conflict that they brought to their dealings with all non-Europeans everywhere, Koreans—like Hawaiians, Chinese, American Indians, and African Americans—needed to be disciplined, taught, and controlled.

No master plan guided Americans in their dealings with other peoples. In all of these places, the interests of American businessmen, the distortions of racial ideology, and hopes for partisan political advantage at home jostled with one another. As a result, the consequences of these involvements were often unclear and sometimes took generations to play out. Nevertheless, they remind us that Americans paid close attention to what was happening elsewhere, whether in the Franco-Prussian War (1870–1871), where the evolution of warfare continued to become more mechanized and lethal, or the Paris Commune (1871), where some thought they saw the result of unbridled democracy in chaos and violence—and wondered if Reconstruction did not represent a similar path.

Some people around the world were surprised that the United States did not use its enormous armies after the Civil War to seize Mexico from the French, Canada from the English, or Cuba from the Spanish. Conflict among the great powers on the European Continent certainly opened an opportunity and the United States had expanded relentlessly and opportunistically throughout its history. Few Americans, though, had the stomach for new adventures in the wake of the Civil War. The fighting against the American Indians on the Plains proved warfare enough for most white Americans in the 1870s and 1880s.[19]

The United States focused its postwar energies instead on commerce. Consolidated under Northern control, the nation's economy proved more formidable than ever before. The United States, its economic might growing with each passing year, its railroad network and financial systems consolidated, its cities and towns booming, its population surging westward, its mines turning out massive amounts of coal and precious minerals, its farms remarkably productive, and its corporations adopting new means of expansion and administration, became a force throughout the world. American engineers oversaw projects in Asia, Africa, and Latin America. American investors bought stock in railroads, factories, and mines around the globe. American companies came to dominate the economies of nations in Latin America.[20]

Americans became famous as rich, energetic, and somewhat reckless players amid the complexity of the world. As the Civil War generation aged, younger men looked with longing on possible territorial acquisitions in their own hemisphere and farther afield. They talked openly of proving themselves, as their fathers and grandfathers had, on the battlefield. Some welcomed the fight against the Spanish and the Filipinos in 1898 as a test of American manhood and nationalism. The generation that came of age in 1900 built monuments to the heroes of the Civil War but seldom paused to listen to their stories of war's horror and costs.

The American Civil War has carried a different meaning for every generation of Americans. In the 1920s and 1930s leading historians in a largely isolationist United States considered the Civil War a terrible mistake, the product of a "blundering generation." After the triumph of World War II and in the glow of the Cold War's end, leading historians interpreted the Civil War as a chapter in the relentless destruction of slavery and the spread of democracy by the forces of modernization over the forces of reaction. Recently, living through more confusing times, some historians have begun to question straightforward stories of the war, emphasizing its contradictory meanings, unfulfilled promises, and unintended outcomes.[21]

The story of the American Civil War changes as world history lurches in unanticipated directions and as people ask different questions of the past. Things that once seemed settled now seem less so. The massive ranks, fortified trenches, heavy machinery, and broadened targets of the American Civil War once seemed to mark a step toward the culmination of "total" war. But the wars of the twenty-first century, often fought without formal battles, are proving relentless and boundless, "total" in ways the disciplined armies of the Union and Confederacy never imagined.[22] Nations continue to come apart over ancient grievances and modern geopolitics, the example of the United States notwithstanding. Coerced labor did not end in the nineteenth century, but instead has mutated and adapted to changes in the global economy. "A fair chance in the race of life" has yet to arrive for much of the world.

The great American trial of war, emancipation, and reconstruction mattered to the world. It embodied struggles that would confront people on every continent and it accelerated the emergence of a new global power. The American crisis, it was true, might have altered the course of world history more dramatically, in ways both worse and better, than what actually transpired. The war could have brought forth a powerful and independent Confederacy based on slavery or it could have established with its Reconstruction a new global standard of justice for people who had been enslaved. As it was, the events of the 1860s and 1870s in the United States proved both powerful and contradictory in their meaning for world history.

Notes

1. For other portrayals of the Civil War in international context, see David M. Potter, "Civil War," in C. Vann Woodward, ed., *The Comparative Approach to American History* (New York: Basic Books, 1968), pp. 135–451; Carl N. Degler, *One Among Many: The Civil War in Comparative Perspective*, 29th Annual Robert Fortenbaugh Memorial Lecture (Gettysburg, PA: Gettysburg College, 1990); Robert E. May, ed., *The Union, the Confederacy, and the Atlantic Rim* (West Lafayette, IN: Purdue University Press, 1995); Peter Kolchin, *A Sphinx on the American Land: The Nineteenth-Century South in Comparative Perspective* (Baton Rouge: Louisiana State University Press, 2003). My view of the workings of world history has been influenced by C. A. Bayly, *The Birth of the Modern World, 1780–1914: Global Connections and Comparisons* (Malden, MA: Blackwell, 2004). Bayly emphasizes that "in the nineteenth century, nation-states and

contending territorial empires took on sharper lineaments and became more antagonistic to each other at the very same time as the similarities, connections, and linkages between them proliferated" (p. 2). By showing the "complex interaction between political organization, political ideas, and economic activity," Bayly avoids the teleological models of modernization, nationalism, and liberalism that have dominated our understanding of the American Civil War.

2. Lincoln quoted in James M. McPherson, *Abraham Lincoln and the Second American Revolution,* reprint (New York: Oxford University Press: 1992, 1991), p. 28.

3. The seminal work is Drew Gilpin Faust, *The Creation of Confederate Nationalism: Ideology and Identity in the Civil War South* (Baton Rouge: Louisiana State University Press, 1988). For an excellent synthesis of the large literature on this topic, see Anne S. Rubin, *A Shattered Nation: The Rise and Fall of the Confederacy, 1861–1868* (Chapel Hill: University of North Carolina Press, 2005).

4. For a useful overview, see Robert W. Fogel, *Without Consent or Contract: The Rise and Fall of American Slavery* (New York: W. W. Norton, 1989).

5. David Brion Davis, *Slavery and Human Progress* (New York: Oxford University Press, 1984); Davis, *The Problem of Slavery in the Age of Revolution, 1770–1823* (Ithaca, NY: Cornell University Press, 1975); and Davis, *Inhuman Bondage: The Rise and Fall of Slavery in the New World* (Oxford University Press, 2006).

6. For helpful overviews of the global situation, see Steven Hahn, "Class and State in Postemancipation Societies: Southern Planters in Comparative Perspective," *American Historical Review* 95 (February 1990): 75–98, and Hahn, *A Nation Under Our Feet: Black Political Struggles in the Rural South From Slavery to the Great Migration* (Cambridge, MA: Belknap Press of Harvard University Press, 2003).

7. Quoted in Faust, *Creation of Confederate Nationalism,* p. 13.

8. There is a large literature on this subject, not surprisingly. A useful recent treatment is Susan-Mary Grant, *North Over South: Northern Nationalism and American Identity in the Antebellum Era* (Lawrence: University of Kansas Press, 2000). Peter Kolchin also offers penetrating comments on nationalism in *A Sphinx on the American Land,* pp. 89–92.

9. Brian Holden Reid, *The American Civil War and the Wars of the Industrial Revolution* (London: Cassell, 1999), pp. 211–13; John E. Clark Jr., *Railroads in the Civil War: The Impact of Management on Victory and Defeat* (Baton Rouge: Louisiana State University Press, 2001); Robert G. Angevine, *The Railroad and the State: War, Politics, and Technology in Nineteenth-Century America* (Stanford, CA: Stanford University Press, 2004).

10. For a range of interesting essays on this subject, see Stig Forster and Jorg Nagler, eds., *On the Road to Total War: The American Civil War and the German Wars of Unification, 1861–1871* (Washington, DC: The German Historical Institute, 1997).

11. See D. P. Crook, *The North, the South, and the Powers, 1861–1865* (New York: Wiley, 1974); R. J. M. Blackett, *Divided Hearts: Britain and the American Civil War* (Baton Rouge: Louisiana State University Press, 2001); James M. McPherson, *Crossroads of Freedom: Antietam* (Oxford: Oxford University Press, 2002); Robert E. May, ed., *The Union, the Confederacy, and the Atlantic Rim;* and Charles M. Hubbard, *The Burden of Confederate Diplomacy* (Knoxville: University of Tennessee Press, 1998).

12. See Allen C. Guelzo, *Lincoln's Emancipation Proclamation: The End of Slavery in America* (New York: Simon and Schuster. 2004).

13. See Joseph T. Glatthaar, *Forged in Battle: The Civil War Alliance of Black Soldiers and White Officers* (New York: Free Press, 1990).

14. See Leon Litwack, *Been in the Storm So Long: The Aftermath of Slavery,* 1st Vintage ed. (New York: Vintage, 1980, 1979) and the major documentary collection edited by Ira Berlin, Leslie S. Rowland, and their colleagues, sampled in *Free At Last: A Documentary History of Slavery, Freedom, and the Civil War* (New York: The New Press, 1992).

15. See Davis, *Slavery and Human Progress,* for a sweeping perspective on this issue.

16. The classic history is Eric Foner, *Reconstruction: America's Unfinished Revolution, 1863–1877* (New York: Harper and Row, 1988), I have offered some thoughts on Reconstruction's legacy in "Exporting Reconstruction" in *What Caused the Civil War? Reflections on the South and Southern History* (New York: W. W. Norton, 2005).

17. On the legacy of Reconstruction, see David W. Blight, *Race and Reunion The Civil War in American Memory* (Cambridge, MA: Belknap Press of Harvard University Press, 2001).

18. For a fascinating essay on the South's loss of the cotton monopoly, see Sven Beckert, "Emancipation and Empire: Reconstructing the Worldwide Web of Cotton Production in the Age of the American Civil War," *American Historical Review* 109 (December 2004): 1405–38. On South Africa: John W. Cell, *The Highest Stage of White Supremacy: The Origins of Segregation in South Africa and the American South* (Cambridge: Cambridge University Press, 1982) and George M. Fredrickson, *White Supremacy: A Comparative Study in American and South African History* (New York: Oxford University Press, 1981).

19. See the discussion in the essays by Robert E. May and James M. McPherson in May, ed., *The Union, the Confederacy, and the Atlantic Rim.*

20. For the larger context, see Eric J. Hobsbawm, *The Age of Empire, 1875–1914* (New York: Pantheon, 1987) and Bayly, *Birth of the Modern World.*

21. I have described this literature and offered some thoughts on it in the essay "Worrying About the Civil War" in my *What Caused the Civil War?*

22. Reid, *American Civil War,* p. 213.

Bibliography

Surprisingly, no one book covers the themes of this essay. To understand this era of American history in global context, we need to piece together accounts from a variety of books and articles. For recent overviews of different components of these years, see Jay Sexton, "Towards a Synthesis of Foreign Relations in the Civil War Era, 1848–1877," *American Nineteenth-Century History* 5 (Fall 2004): 50–75, and Amy Kaplan, *The Anarchy of Empire in the Making of U.S. Culture* (Cambridge, MA: Harvard University Press, 2002).

Robert E. May, in the introduction to the book he edited, *The Union, the Confederacy, and the Atlantic Rim* (West Lafayette, IN: Purdue University Press, 1995), provides a useful summary of the larger context of the war. Though it is older, the perspective of

D. P. Crook, *The North, the South, and the Powers, 1861–1865* (New York: Wiley, 1974) brings a welcome worldliness to the discussion. On the crucial debate in Britain, see Howard Jones, *Union in Peril: The Crisis Over British Intervention in the Civil War* (Chapel Hill: University of North Carolina Press, 1992) and R. J. M. Blackett, *Divided Hearts: Britain and the American Civil War* (Baton Rouge: Louisiana State University Press, 2001).

James M. McPherson offers characteristically insightful, and hopeful, analysis in several places. Perhaps the single best focused portrayal of the interplay between events in the United States and in the Atlantic World is in his *Crossroads of Freedom: Antietam* (Oxford: Oxford University Press, 2002). McPherson's essay, " 'The Whole Family of Man': Lincoln and the Last Best Hope Abroad," in May, ed., *The Union, the Confederacy, and the Atlantic Rim,* makes the fullest case for the larger significance of the war in encouraging liberal movements and belief around the world.

Peter Kolchin's, *A Sphinx on the American Land: The Nineteenth-Century South in Comparative Perspective* (Baton Rouge: Louisiana State University Press, 2003), offers an elegant and up-to-date survey that puts the conflict in the larger context of emancipation movements. A useful overview appears in Steven Hahn, "Class and State in Postemancipation Societies: Southern Planters in Comparative Perspective," *American Historical Review* 95 (February 1990): 75–98.

Another pioneering work is Drew Gilpin Faust, *The Creation of Confederate Nationalism: Ideology and Identity in the Civil War South* (Baton Rouge: Louisiana State University Press, 1988). Faust changed historians' perspective on nationalism in the South, which had been considered largely fraudulent before her account. Building on Faust are two recent books that offer fresh interpretations: Anne S. Rubin, *A Shattered Nation: The Rise and Fall of the Confederacy, 1861–1868* (Chapel Hill: University of North Carolina Press, 2005) and Susan-Mary Crant, *North Over South: Northern Nationalism and American Identity in the Antebellum Era* (Lawrence: University of Kansas Press, 2000).

On the much-debated issue of the relative modernity and totality of the Civil War, see Stig Förster and Jörg Nagler, eds., *On the Road to Total War: The American Civil War and the German Wars of Unification, 1861–1871* (Washington, DC: The German Historical Institute, 1997); the essays by Stanley L. Engerman and J. Matthew Gallman, Farl J. Hess, Michael Fellman, and Richard Current are especially helpful. Brian Holden Reid, in *The American Civil War and the Wars of the Industrial Revolution* (London: Cassell, 1999), offers a concise but insightful portrayal of the war in larger military context.

For a powerful representation of the role of slavery in this history, David Brion Davis's works are all helpful. His most recent account synthesizes a vast literature in an accessible way: *Inhuman Bondage: The Rise and Fall of Slavery in the New World* (Oxford University Press, 2006).

Excellent examples of what might be thought of as the new global history appear in Sven Beckert, "Emancipation and Empire: Reconstructing the Worldwide Web of Cotton Production in the Age of the American Civil War," *American Historical Review* 109 (December 2004): 1405–38; and Gordon H. Chang, "Whose 'Barbarism'? whose 'Treachery'? Race and Civilization in the Unknown United States-Korea War of 1871," *Journal of American History* 89 (March 2003): 1331–65.

Critical Thinking

1. In what ways were the struggles in the United States during the Civil War similar to those in other countries?

2. Do you agree that the failures of the Reconstruction of the South affected the progress of black Southerners? Explain.

Create Central

www.mhhe.com/createcentral

Internet References

Thinkquest.org
http://library.thinkquest.org/J0112391/reconstruction.htm

Sparknotes.com
www.sparknotes.com/history/american/reconstruction/context.html

Smithsonian
http://americanhistory.si.edu/presidency/timeline/pres_era/3_656.html

Library of Congress
www.loc.gov/teachers/classroommaterials/presentationsandactivities/presentations/timeline/civilwar

http://memory.loc.gov/ammem/aaohtml/exhibit/aopart5.html

EDWARD L. AYERS is Dean of the College of Art and Sciences at the University of Virginia, where he is also the Hugh P. Kelly Professor of History. He has published extensively on nineteenth-century Southern history, his most recent publication being *In the Presence of Mine Enemies: War in the Heart of America, 1859–1863* (2003), which received the Bancroft Prize. An earlier book, *The Promise of the New South* (1992), was a finalist for both the Pulitzer Prize and the National Book Award. In addition, Ayers has created and directs a prize-winning Internet archive, "Valley of the Shadow: Two Communities in the American Civil War," containing original sources related to two towns at either end of the Shenandoah Valley, one in Virginia and the other in Pennsylvania.

Ayers, Edward L. From *OAH Magazine of History*, January 2006, pp. 54–60. Copyright © 2006 by Organization of American Historians. Reprinted by permission via the Copyright Clearance Center.

Article

The Nez Perce Flight for Justice

W. David Edmunds

Learning Outcomes

After reading this article, you will be able to:

- Describe the journey of the Nez Perce, from compliance to flight.
- Discuss the reasons for the political tension between the U.S. government and Native American tribes.

The charismatic Indian leader Chief Joseph stood on the bank of the Snake River, looking across the water to Idaho and beyond to his people's new home, the Nez Perce reservation in the Clearwater Valley. With him were several hundred men, women, and children, many on horses, dragging their belongings behind them on travois. These Northern Plateau Indians, who called themselves Nee-Me-Poo (The People) or Iceyeeye Niim Mama'yac (The Children of the Coyote), were deeply unhappy about being turned out of the Wallowa Valley of northeastern Oregon, where their people had lived for centuries. But federal officials had given Chief Joseph and his people an ultimatum only six months earlier, forcing them to join other Nez Perce who had signed a treaty more than a decade before and moved to the reservation.

Until 1877 the Nez Perce had prided themselves on their friendship with Americans, beginning when they welcomed the Lewis and Clark Expedition in September 1805. In the decades that followed, as the young republic pushed west, increasing numbers of settlers trespassed on their lands. Even so, the Nez Perce had patiently avoided any open conflict.

In 1877 Chief Joseph was 37 years old, strikingly handsome, married, and the father of several children, all of whom, except one daughter, Kapap Ponmi, or "Brook Song," had died in infancy. He was a skilled negotiator but had little left to work with. Worried about his people's future, Joseph distrusted the U.S. officials but believed he had little choice and reluctantly agreed to relocate his people.

Swollen with late spring snowmelt, the Snake River moved fast, its strong currents largely hidden below its rippled surface. When the Nez Perce started to cross, things went wrong almost immediately. Several of their livestock were torn away down river and lost to sight. Joseph directed the rescue effort, which scattered the people all along the bank. In the midst of this confusion, some frontier ne'er-do-wells took advantage of the situation to raid the Nez Perce's stock of fine Appaloosas. Hours later, the now exhausted and angry Nez Perce had gathered up their animals and set up camp just south of the reservation. They dug up camas bulbs for food and brooded about their forced expulsion.

Tensions had long simmered between white incomers and the Indians already pressed onto the reservation. On June 13 a few young warriors from Chief White Bird's village killed four settlers whom they believed had mistreated their kinsmen. When news reached Joseph, he counseled caution, but fearing reprisal, the new arrivals withdrew to White Bird Canyon, near present-day Grangeville, Idaho. On June 18 scouts reported the approach of a large party of U.S. troops and local volunteers commanded by Capt. David Perry.

Joseph sent out a negotiating party under a white flag, but the volunteers fired upon them, setting off the Battle of White Bird Canyon. Although outnumbered two to one and poorly armed, the Nez Perce inflicted a devastating defeat on Perry's party, killing 34 soldiers before the army retreated. Meanwhile, Nez Perce war parties raided neighboring ranches, killing 14 civilians.

White Bird Canyon thrust Joseph onto the horns of a dilemma. The U.S. Army still reeled from its defeat at the Little Big Horn and the death of George Armstrong Custer the year before. Joseph understood that federal officials would act decisively to suppress any acts of resistance. He still preferred to negotiate, or at least to retreat back to the Wallowa Valley and mount a defense among familiar surroundings. But the other chiefs believed that while negotiations were no longer possible, the U.S. army at least would never pursue them over the mountains into Montana. The Nez Perce fled into the rugged country between the Salmon, Snake, and Clearwater rivers.

Gen. Oliver Howard, commander of the Department of the Columbia, turned his attention to Chief Looking Glass's village. While Looking Glass had not taken part at White Bird Canyon, Howard, mistakenly believing that he was actively recruiting for the "hostiles," ordered Capt. Stephen Whipple and two companies of cavalry to arrest him. While Howard and the rest of his command pursued Joseph into the mountains, Whipple attacked Looking Glass's village on July 1, killing mostly women and children. The chief and most of his people escaped, although losing many of their horses.

Whipple's attack drove Looking Glass, a skilled military leader well versed in the mountain trails leading into Montana, into Joseph's camp, along with all his followers, increasing the "hostile" ranks to approximately 300 warriors and 500 women and children. Looking Glass added his voice to those urging a retreat to Montana, and Joseph reluctantly agreed.

While Looking Glass, White Bird, and other war chiefs directed the defense, Joseph focused his efforts upon the formidable task of ensuring that the refugees had food and adequate transportation. The route across Idaho passed through a challenging topography of towering mountains and canyons blocked by deadfalls, and made use of narrow trails that would tax the endurance even of seasoned warriors. Most of the refugees were tribal elders, women, and children, many riding horses, but some walking along the steeper trails, gasping for air at the higher altitudes. Some women and children led horses dragging travois or packed with hides for small tepees or other shelters, while others searched for roots and berries. Hunting parties scoured the route for game and slaughtered stray livestock but were hard-pressed to fill their cooking pots.

In late July, Joseph led the Nez Perce over the treacherous Lolo Pass in the Bitterroot Mountains, then around a barricade U.S. soldiers had built across the trail and into the Bitterroot Valley. Footsore and short of provisions, but well ahead of their pursuers, they stopped along the Big Hole River near modern Wisdom, Montana, in early August to hunt and rest their mounts.

None realized that Col. John Gibbon and about 175 troopers from Fort Shaw in western Montana had approached. Shortly before dawn on August 9, 1877, Gibbon's men opened fire on the sleeping Indians. The warriors rallied, forced the soldiers to retreat, and captured a mountain howitzer. When night fell, Joseph led the way south and up the Big Hole Valley. The Nez Perce escaped at a cost of 30 warriors killed, along with at least 60 women and children. The U.S. forces' casualties totaled 29 dead and 40 wounded.

Shortly before dawn, Gibbon's men opened fire on the sleeping Indians.

The hard-beset band crossed Bannock Pass into Idaho, then turned eastward along the Lemhi Valley. Howard followed, but on August 20, while Joseph hurried the main party toward Wyoming, Nez Perce scouts captured or scattered so many of Howard's horses at the Camas Meadows that the general postponed his pursuit until he could recapture or recoup his livestock. By late August the weary Nez Perce had crossed what is now Yellowstone Park and descended Clark's Fork of the Yellowstone. In September they eluded Col. Samuel Sturgis and the remnants of the 7th Cavalry until they were overtaken by, and threw back, Sturgis's force at Canyon Creek on September 13. By mid-September the Nez Perce had spent three months fleeing and fighting off pursuers across 1,000 miles of steep mountains, rocky trails, and raging rivers.

On September 17 Sturgis turned his troopers back, but Joseph and what remained of the Nez Perce trekked on. Leaving the Missouri, they skirmished with a wagon train and a small party of volunteers from Fort Benton, then stopped on September 25

on the northern fringe of the Bear Paw Mountains to catch their breath and rest their exhausted horses. Scouts reported that both Howard's and Sturgis's commands lay far behind. Only 40 miles separated them from Canada, but the weather had turned cold and blustery. While some did not want to stop, Looking Glass assured them that they had several days to rest, hunt, and restock their larders, before heading north.

Again the chiefs underestimated their enemies. Howard had telegraphed Col. Nelson Miles at Fort Keogh in southeastern Montana, prompting Miles and 400 troopers to ride northwest, guided by Lakota and Cheyenne scouts. Undetected, on the morning of September 30 they swept in on the Bear Paw encampment. When the first shots rang out, Joseph and his daughter were outside the camp tending their horses. Galloping back, Joseph rallied a party of warriors who repulsed two cavalry charges. When a third foray penetrated the village, he led a counterattack that again drove the troops to retreat, but meanwhile the Lakota and Cheyenne had scattered or captured many of the Nez Perce horses. The surviving Nez Perce took refuge on a ridge overlooking the encampment. The battle continued throughout the day. As night fell, a blizzard swept in from the northwest.

Still not contemplating surrender, Joseph and the other chiefs argued over the next move. Realizing the hopelessness of their situation, Joseph stated his willingness to negotiate a settlement, but not an unconditional capitulation. White Bird feared that they would hang should they surrender. Looking Glass, who believed that Sitting Bull would send assistance from Canada, took a sniper's bullet on October 3 and died.

Two days later, Howard arrived with reinforcements at the battlefield. After conferring, Miles and Howard sent a messenger to Joseph guaranteeing him that if the Nez Perce surrendered they could return to Idaho; if not, the assault would be renewed. For Joseph the choice was clear. Burdened with women, children, and tribal elders, he could not escape to Canada. On the afternoon of October 5 he rode forward, reluctantly met with Miles and Howard, and delivered his famous speech: "I am tired. My heart is sick and sad. From where the sun now stands, I will fight no more forever." Chief Joseph and about 400 of his followers surrendered. Another 300 Nez Perce led by White Bird slipped through the American lines and eventually joined the Sioux in Canada under Sitting Bull.

While Miles was sincere in his promises, federal officials refused to honor them. Joseph and his people were shipped first to Kansas, then south to Indian Territory. After Joseph journeyed to Washington and repeatedly pled for their return to the Northwest, in 1884 they were finally placed on the Colville Reservation in Washington, where Chief Joseph died in 1904. Yet the epic of undaunted resolution struck a responsive chord, even among their enemies. Howard and Miles united in praising their bravery, military ability, and perseverance. Journalists lionized Chief Joseph, and for many readers the handsome, eloquent chieftain and his people emerged as the embodiment of the "noble red man's" justifiable resistance to heavy-handed U.S. Indian policy. Regardless of stereotypes, their flight and resistance remain remarkable epics of American history, while today the modern Nez Perce people play a viable part in the American nation.

Critical Thinking

1. Why did Chief Joseph agree to relocate to the Nez Perce reservation?
2. Were Miles and Howard to be trusted? Explain.

Create Central

www.mhhe.com/createcentral

Internet References

NezPerce.org
www.nezperce.org/index.html

PBS.org
www.pbs.org/lewisandclark/native/nez.html

U.S. Army
www.army.mil/article/28124/The_Nez_Perce_War_of_1877

HistoryNet.com
www.historynet.com/nez-perce-war.htm

Edmunds, W. David. From *American Heritage*, Fall 2008, pp. 36–39. Copyright © 2008 by American Heritage, Inc. Reprinted by permission of American Heritage Publishing and W. David Edmunds.

Article

How the West Was Spun

Buffalo Bill Cody heralded the closing of the frontier by reassuring Americans that they would never be too civilized to beat the braves and bullies of the world at their own game.

STEPHEN G. HYSLOP

Learning Outcomes

After reading this article, you will be able to:

• Describe the premise of Buffalo Bill Cody's Wild West Show.

• Discuss how Sitting Bull's presence in the show illustrated the harsh reality Indians faced at the closing of the frontier.

When fabled bison hunter William "Buffalo Bill" Cody first staged his Wild West show in 1883, he needed more than heroic cowboys, villainous Indians, teeming horses and roaming buffalo to transform it from a circus into a sensation. He needed star power. And there was one man who guaranteed to provide it: the Sioux chief widely blamed for the uprising that overwhelmed George Armstrong Custer's 7th Cavalry at the Battle of Little Bighorn only a decade earlier. "I am going to try hard to get old Sitting Bull," Cody said. "If we can manage to get him our ever lasting fortune is made."

It took two years, but Cody finally got his man. In June 1885, Sitting Bull joined the Wild West show for a signing bonus of $125 and $50 a week—20 times more than Indians who served as policemen on reservations earned. Buffalo Bill reckoned his new star would prove to be an irresistible draw. With the Indian wars drawing to a close, and most Plains Indians confined to reservations, Buffalo Bill set the stage for a final conquest of the frontier. Since accompanying an army patrol as a scout shortly after the Battle of Little Bighorn and scalping the Cheyenne warrior Yellow Hair, he was known as the man who took "the first scalp for Custer." As the man who now controlled Sitting Bull, he symbolically declared victory in the war for the West and signaled a new era of cooperation with the enemy. Cody excluded the chief from acts in which other Indians made sham attacks on settlers and then got their comeuppance from heroic cowboys. All Sitting Bull had to do was don a war costume, ride a horse into the arena and brave an audience that sometimes jeered and hissed.

Sitting Bull's mere presence reinforced the reassuring message underlying Cody's Wild West extravaganza, as well as the Western films and novels it inspired, that Americans are generous conquerors who attack only when provoked. At the same time, Cody's vision of the West spoke to the fiercely competitive spirit of an American nation born in blood and defined by conflict on the frontier, where what mattered most was not whether you were right or wrong but whether you prevailed. The lesson of his Wild West was that sharpshooting American cowboys like Buffalo Bill could be as wild as the Indians they fought and match them blow for blow. The real frontier might be vanishing, but by preserving this wild domain imaginatively and reenacting the struggle for supremacy there, he gave millions of Americans the feeling they were up to any challenge.

Buffalo Bill's Wild West depended on Cody's ability to draw shrewdly on his frontier experiences to make himself a commanding figure. He earned his nickname, he claimed, by killing 4,280 buffalo during an 18-month stint for the Kansas Pacific Railroad in the late 1860s. Indiscriminate hunting was encouraged by the army as part of a campaign to wipe out buffalo herds that gave subsistence to free-roaming Plains Indians. The Indians did not take well to having this food supply annihilated. Cody told of being chased once by 30 Indians on horseback. Cavalry guarding the tracks came to his aid, and together they killed eight "redskins," he said, expressing sympathy only for a horse one of the warriors was riding, killed by a shot from his trusty rifle Lucretia: "He was a noble animal, and ought to have been engaged in better business."

Later in life Cody mused that Indians deserved better. But his early exploits on the Plains and his autobiographical account of those feats, designed to portray him as a classic frontier enforcer, came first. His crowning claim involved the rescue of a white woman from the clutches of Indians. In July 1869, he was serving as a scout for the 5th Cavalry when it surprised hostile Cheyennes in an encampment at Summit Springs, Colorado

Territory, where one white woman held captive was killed in the ensuing battle and one rescued. Official records give credit for locating the camp to Pawnee scouts—who volunteered to serve the army against their traditional tribal foes—and make no mention of Buffalo Bill. But Cody boasted of killing Cheyenne Chief Tall Bull during the engagement after creeping to a spot where he could "easily drop him from the saddle" without hitting his horse, a "gallant steed" he then captured and named Tall Bull in honor of the chief.

This fabricated tale demonstrated Cody's knack for translating the grim realities of Indian fighting into rousing adventure stories in which he symbolically appropriated the totemic power of defeated warriors by claiming their scalp, horse or captives, much as Indians did in battle. But he took care to distinguish his bravery from the bravado of warriors who refused to fight fair and targeted women and children. Left unmentioned in his account of the Battle of Summit Springs—which, like the Battle of Little Bighorn, he incorporated as an act in his Wild West show—was that women and children were among the more than 70 Cheyennes killed or captured.

After returning with the cavalry from Summit Springs to Fort Sedgwick in Colorado, Buffalo Bill met Edward Judson, who was looking for Western heroes to celebrate in the dime novels he wrote under the name Ned Buntline. His fiction did so much to create and inflate the reputation of Buffalo Bill that actors were soon playing him on stage. "I was curious to see how I would look when represented by some one else," Cody recalled, so while visiting New York in 1872 he attended a performance of *Buffalo Bill: The King of the Border Men* and was called on stage. He soon realized that he could succeed in the limelight simply by being himself, or by impersonating the heroic character contrived by Buntline.

"I'm not an actor—I'm a star," he told an interviewer soon after making the transition from frontier scout to itinerant showman. Crucial to his ascent to stardom was his awareness that he needed to become something more than a stereotypical Indian fighter or "scourge of the red man." He never renounced that role and continued to bank on it throughout his career, but his genius as an entertainer lay in softening his own image— and that of the Wild West—just enough to reassure Americans that the conquest he dramatized was a good clean fight that had redeeming social value without robbing this struggle for supremacy of its visceral appeal.

Buffalo Bill's first appearance on stage in Chicago gave little hint of the bright future that awaited him in show business. He and other ornery frontiersmen blasted away at Indians ludicrously impersonated by white extras in a murky plot concocted by Buntline. One reviewer called the acting "execrable" and concluded that such "scalping, blood and thunder, is not likely to be vouchsafed to a city a second time, even Chicago." Nonetheless, the show proved commercially successful, and Buffalo Bill made $6,000 over the winter, substantially improving his take in seasons to come by forming his own troupe called the Buffalo Bill Combination.

For several years, he combined acting with summer stints as a scout or guide, honing his skills as an entertainer by conducting wealthy dudes from the East and European nobility on hunting expeditions and diverting them with shows of skill that sometimes involved Indians hired for the occasion. Buffalo Bill enjoyed "trotting in the first class, with the very first men of the land," and came away convinced that a Wild West spectacle involving real cowboys and Indians could appeal to all classes and become, as it was later billed, "America's National Entertainment."

Other showmen of the era tried to mine that same vein by mounting Wild West themed circuses in which sharpshooters and bronco-busters demonstrated their skills. But when Buffalo Bill launched his Wild West show in 1883, he set his aim higher. He wanted an epic production with theatrical flair that defined the West and drew viewers into it. After a lackluster first season, marred by his drunken escapades with a fellow sharpshooter and business associate named Doc Carver, he teamed with Nate Salsbury, a shrewd theater manager, and hired director Steele MacKaye to make the production more than a series of stunts by creating a show within the show called *The Drama of Civilization.* First staged in the winter of 1886 in New York's Madison Square Garden, where it was viewed by more than a million people, the pageant was set against painted backdrops and included four acts that purported to represent the historical evolution of the West from "The Primeval Forest," occupied only by wild Indians, to "The Prairie," where civilization appeared with the arrival of wagon trains, setting the stage for further progress in the form of "The Cattle Ranch" and "The Mining Camp."

Buffalo Bill wanted a high-toned epic production with theatrical flair and elaborate staging that defined the West and drew viewers into it.

The elaborate staging fulfilled Buffalo Bill's stated goal of offering "high toned" entertainment, but the acts themselves suggested that the coming of the white man had done little to tame the Wild West. The climactic mining camp episode included a duel between gunfighters and an attack on the Deadwood Stagecoach by bandits, playing much the same role as that performed by marauding Indians in other performances. In the grand finale, the mining camp was blown away by a cyclone, suggesting that if wild men did not defeat those trying to civilize the West, wild nature surely would.

At heart the Wild West extravaganza was less about the triumph of civilization than ceaseless struggle in which "barbarism and civilization have their hands on each other's throat," as one observer put it. Cody could not afford to become so high toned that he robbed the show of the smoke and thunder that many came to see, and he surely welcomed notices like that from a reviewer who promised the public that "Buffalo Bill's 'Wild West' is wild enough to suit the most devoted admirer of western adventure and prowess." At the same time, Cody promoted the show as family entertainment, suitable for women and children. By hiring Annie Oakley, whom Sitting Bull nicknamed "Little Sure Shot," Cody graced his cast with a deadly shot who was so demure and disarming that spectators who might otherwise have been scared away by gunplay were as eager to attend as those for whom fancy shooting was the main draw.

European blue bloods also found the show enchanting. In 1887 Buffalo Bill and an entourage of 100 whites, 97 Indians, 180 horses, 18 buffalo, 10 elk, 5 Texan steers, 4 donkeys and 2 deer traveled to England to help celebrate the Jubilee Year of Queen Victoria. In addition to staging twice-a-day shows during a five-month stay in London for crowds that averaged around 30,000, the Wild West troupe gave a command performance for the queen in which the Prince of Wales and the kings of Belgium, Greece, Saxony and Denmark rode around the arena in a stagecoach with Buffalo Bill fending off marauding Indians from the driver's seat. In the process, Buffalo Bill's pop interpretation of the American frontier was validated as high culture and for the next five years the Wild West toured the major capitals of Europe.

Despite his warm reception throughout Europe, when Buffalo Bill brought the show home in 1893 he was shunned as too commercial by the organizers of the Columbian Exposition in Chicago, a grandiose celebration of civilization in America that featured 65,000 exhibits in an array of gleaming Beaux Arts buildings dubbed the White City. Undeterred, Buffalo Bill camped out across the street and drew an audience that summer of more than 3 million people, including a group of historians who took a break one afternoon from a conference at the exposition to see the Wild West show and later that evening heard their colleague Frederick Jackson Turner deliver his landmark essay "The Significance of the Frontier in American History."

Turner portrayed the settling of the West as a largely peaceful process, in which the availability of "free land" on the frontier served as a safety valve, releasing social tensions by providing fresh opportunities for Americans who might otherwise have been stifled in their ambitions for a better life. But Cody, for all the historical distortions in his show, hit on a fundamental truth that eluded the erudite Turner: There was no free land. Everything that American settlers claimed, from the landing at Jamestown to the closing of the frontier in 1890, was Indian country, wrested from tribal groups at great cost. Buffalo Bill's Wild West remains with us to this day because he recognized that fierce competition and strife had as much to do with the making of America as the dream of liberty and justice for all.

Ultimately, it was Indians who lent an air of authenticity to Buffalo Bill's Wild West. He could not hire Indians without the government's permission and faced scrutiny and criticism from officials who argued that his show displayed Indians as bloodthirsty warriors while the government was trying to convert them to a peaceful, productive existence. But he was keenly aware of their importance to the production and tried to ensure they were well treated. Luther Standing Bear, a Sioux who served as chief of the Indian performers on one European tour, expressed gratitude for the support Buffalo Bill showed when he complained that Indians were being served inferior food. "My Indians are the principal feature of this show," he recalled Buffalo Bill telling the dining steward, "and they are the one people I will not allow to be misused or neglected."

Black Elk, whose dictated reminiscences to poet John Neihardt were published in 1932 under the title *Black Elk Speaks,* shared Luther Standing Bear's appreciation for the way he and other performers were treated by Buffalo Bill, or Pahuska (Long Hair). When Black Elk wearied of life on tour and said he was "sick to go home," Buffalo Bill was sympathetic: "He gave me a ticket and ninety dollars. Then he gave me a big dinner. Pahuska had a strong heart."

But Black Elk's memories of the show itself were more ambivalent. "I liked the part of the show we made," he said, "but not the part the Wasichus [whites] made." Like other Sioux hired by Buffalo Bill, he enjoyed commemorating their proud old days as mounted warriors but seemingly recognized that their role was defined and diminished by what whites made of it. Describing the command performance of Buffalo Bill's Wild West for Queen Victoria, he recalled that she spoke to Indian performers after they danced and sang for her and told them something to this effect: "All over the world I have seen all kinds of people; but today I have seen the best-looking people I know. If you belonged to me, I would not let them take you around in a show like this." Whether or not she spoke such words, Black Elk evidently felt that "a show like this" did not do his people great honor.

The show relegated Indians to the vanishing world of war bonnets and scalp dances—the only Indian culture many whites recognized.

The willingness of proud warriors who once resisted American authority to join Cody's show demonstrated that they were capable of adapting to the modern world. Yet the conventions of the Wild West relegated them to the past, a vanishing world of tepees, war bonnets and scalp dances that was the only Indian culture many whites recognized. One chief who toured with Cody, Iron Tail, was said to be a model for the Indian Head nickel, with a bonneted warrior on one side and a buffalo on the other—icons that became cherished as distinctively American only when the way of life they represented was on the verge of extinction.

Sitting Bull, whose appearance in the show prompted many other Sioux to join the traveling troupe, epitomized the wide gulf between the myth perpetuated by Buffalo Bill's Wild West and the harsh reality Indians faced with the closing of the frontier. By all accounts he got on well with Cody. But he hated the hustle and bustle of Eastern cities and only stayed with the show for four months. In the years that followed, government officials grew concerned about the emergence of the Ghost Dance, a messianic religious movement on the reservations that promised Indians who joined in the ritualistic dance eternal life in a bountiful world of their own, where they would be reunited with their lost loved ones and ancestors. Reports in late 1889 that Sioux who joined this movement were wearing "ghost shirts," which they believed would protect them from bullets, increased fears among authorities that the movement would turn violent. When Sitting Bull began encouraging the Ghost Dancers, Maj. Gen. Nelson Miles called upon Buffalo Bill to find him and bring him in, hoping that the chief would yield peacefully to a man he knew and trusted.

Cody headed west to Bismarck, N.D., in December 1890 and reportedly filled two wagons with gifts before setting off in his showman's outfit to track down Sitting Bull on the Standing Rock Reservation. The escapade is clouded in legend and it remains unclear whether or not Cody was serious about trying to arrest Sitting Bull. In any case he got waylaid by two scouts working for the Indian agent James McLaughlin, who wanted credit for corraling Sitting Bull himself. This was no longer Cody's show, and it would play out as a reminder of the grim realities that underlay his rousing performances.

On December 15, McLaughlin sent Indian police to arrest Sitting Bull. A struggle ensued, and shots were fired. Sitting Bull was killed instantly. His son, six of his supporters and six policemen also died. Two weeks later, fighting erupted at nearby Wounded Knee Creek on the Pine Ridge Reservation between a band of Sioux caught up in the Ghost Dance movement and troops of Custer's old regiment, the 7th Cavalry, after soldiers grappled with a deaf young Indian who refused to hand over his gun. When the shooting stopped, 25 soldiers and about 150 Sioux, many of them women and children, lay dead. In the words of Charles Eastman, a mixed-blood Sioux physician who searched among the victims for survivors, Wounded Knee exposed the lurking "savagery of civilization."

The massacre marked the tragic end of the real Indian wars.

Critical Thinking

1. In what ways did Cody's show misrepresent and do a disservice to the reality of life in the West?

2. Why did Cody feel it was important to have Sitting Bull in his show?

Create Central

www.mhhe.com/createcentral

Internet References

PBS.org
www.pbs.org/wgbh/americanexperience/features/general-article/oakley-show

Exploring the Old West
www.exploretheoldwest.com/sitting_bull_and_buffalo_bill's_wild_west.htm

authentichistory.com
www.authentichistory.com/diversity/native/hb5-wwshow/index.html

Article

Gifts of the "Robber Barons"

JAMES NUECHTERLEIN

Learning Outcomes

After reading this article, you will be able to:

- Describe how "robber barons" of the industrial era, Carnegie and Mellon, are complex individuals whose lives need to be considered in whole in order to truly understand their impacts on society.

- Discuss both the differences and similarities between Andrew Carnegie and Andrew Mellon and their legacies.

Even those who consider American history one long triumphal march tend to pass quickly over the decades of industrial expansion and consolidation between the Civil War and the early years of the 20th century. Industrialization was a necessary prelude to mass prosperity; but in America, as elsewhere, it often made for a dispiriting spectacle—pollution, urban blight, glaring material inequalities, ethnic and class conflict, moral dislocation.

To observers at the time, modern America's coming of age often seemed like an unraveling of the social fabric. Because so much had changed so quickly, precise explanations were hard to come by, but the responsibility for what had gone wrong settled quickly on those who had most obviously benefited. If, broadly speaking, industrialization was the problem, the men who ran the system—and who often got enormously rich doing so—had to be made to answer for its shortcomings.

Thus was born the notion of the "robber barons," and it has had a long historical shelf life. Until well into the second half of the 20th century, historians of post-Civil War industrial capitalism echoed contemporary observers both in their emphasis on the system's costs and in their indictment of those in charge.

In recent decades, a measure of economic sophistication has crept into accounts of the era, and the tendency to dwell on personal or institutional villainy has abated. For all its unlovely aspects, the period was one of dynamic economic growth, and those at the top must have been doing at least some things right. They may have gained disproportionately from economic progress, but most workers found their own real wages on the upswing. Industrial development was not the zero-stun game that progressive historians imagined it to be, nor is the concept of "robber barons" an adequate rubric to summarize either the men or the age to which it refers.

Evidence for this view abounds in two outstanding new biographies—David Nasaw's *Andrew Carnegie*[1] and David Cannadine's *Mellon: An American Life*.[2] Nasaw teaches at the Graduate Center of the City University of New York, Cannadine at the Institute of Historical Research, University of London. Neither author ignores or minimizes the flaws in his subject's behavior. But by offering portraits in the round, both resist historical reductionism. Readers may not come away admiring Andrew Carnegie or Andrew Mellon, but they will know better than simply to relegate them to historical pigeonholes.

That is particularly the case with Carnegie, a force of nature and, as Nasaw makes clear, a figure of fascinating complexity. In his business operations, he was sometimes a robber baron, sometimes an enlightened industrial statesman. More significantly, his life was about much more than business, and in his various non-business ventures he fit into no consistent analytical category. As a man, he was devious, deceptive, egomaniacal, and occasionally ruthless; he was also kindly, generous, dutiful, and possessed of an encompassing curiosity that suggested broad human sympathies. He defies convenient summing-up.

Carnegie's career was the American Dream personified. He was born in 1835 in Dunfermline, Scotland, to a poor, none-too-industrious weaver and his ambitious and resourceful wife. The family emigrated to America in 1848, settling near relatives and friends just outside Pittsburgh. Andrew, who had next to no formal education, went immediately to work as a bobbin boy in a cotton mill. Dissatisfied with the physical drudgery, he became a telegraph messenger, taught himself Morse code, and soon became the private telegraph operator and chief assistant to Thomas A. Scott, head of the Pennsylvania Railroad in the Pittsburgh region.

Bright, energetic, and personable—his inveterately optimistic and positive disposition attracted people to him all his life—Carnegie rose quickly in the railroad and considerably augmented his income with investments on the side, especially in oil.

After leaving the company at age thirty, he continued to work with Scott and the railroad's president, J. Edgar Thomson, in a number of joint ventures, contracting with the Pennsylvania and other railways to supply raw materials and grade crossings, and manufacture rails, bridges, and rolling stock of all varieties. He was already a rich man when he expanded from iron to steel in the early 1870's. By the time he retired in 1901, his share of the proceeds from the sale of Carnegie Steel to J. P. Morgan came to almost $120 billion in today's currency, making him the richest man in America, quite possibly the world.

Carnegie considered himself a businessman of probity and integrity and, by the standards of the day, he was. Attacks on his character genuinely baffled and appalled him. Nonetheless, as Nasaw notes, over the course of his career he engaged in activities that included sweetheart deals with corporate cronies, profiting from inside information, the floating of overvalued bonds, stock speculation, and involvement in pools to set minimum prices and allocate market shares. Carnegie operated in an intensely competitive and lightly regulated business environment. Although he acted decently enough by the lights of the day, those lights appear somewhat dim in retrospect.

The greatest blemish on Carnegie's reputation was the notorious lockout and strike at the Homestead steel works near Pittsburgh in July 1892. Carnegie considered himself a friend of the working man—he referred proudly to his family's involvement in the radical Chartist movement in Britain in the 1830's and 40's—but the theoretical rights of workers gave way when they came in conflict with his companies' profit margins. His operating partner Henry Clay Frick attempted to break the Homestead strike by bringing in Pinkerton men, but workers were there to block them. Violence broke out, and by the time order was restored there were dead and wounded on both sides. For the rest of his life, Carnegie, who was vacationing in Scotland at the time of the strike, disavowed responsibility for Homestead, but Nasaw shows that he had prior knowledge of Frick's intentions—they kept in contact by cable—and cites instances of earlier labor conflicts in which Carnegie employed similar tactics.

Still, Carnegie's image as an industrialist of generally enlightened opinions was not without substance. A member of the GOP's progressive wing—he had first been drawn to the party for its antislavery sentiments—he favored establishment of the Interstate Commerce Commission, backed Theodore Roosevelt on railroad regulation, and spoke in favor of a government commission to regulate prices. He defended the progressive income tax and proposed stiff levies on inherited fortunes. He was even known to speak favorably, if vaguely, of a possible socialist future. In foreign policy he was a fervent anti-imperialist, a strong internationalist, and a near fanatical advocate of world peace.

When he was just thirty-three, Carnegie determined that he would no longer preoccupy himself with material gain. "The amassing of wealth," he wrote in a personal memo, "is one of the worst species of idolatry." He began to work only three or four hours a day, spending the rest of his time at intellectual pursuits, philanthropy, and leisure. Much of his effort was devoted to self-education. More than anything else, Carnegie wanted recognition as a man of letters, and to a considerable degree he attained it. He moved in distinguished literary circles in America and Britain (Matthew Arnold and Samuel Clemens were among his close associates), published in fashionable journals of ideas, and wrote the best-selling *Triumphant Democracy* (1886), which, as its title suggests, was an extended celebration of the achievements wrought by America's political and economic institutions.

For Carnegie, America's moral and material progress showed it to be in conformity with the scientific imperatives of Herbert Spencer's Social Darwinism, under whose influence he himself had converted from "theology and the supernatural" to "the truth of evolution." Evolutionary progress was not, to be sure, without its conundrums. "In particular," he wrote, "I don't at all understand the mysterious law of evolution, according to which the higher forms of life live upon the lower, rising through slaughter and extinction. That is profoundly, tragically obscure and perplexing." Still, the evolutionary consolation by which he overcame all doubts remained: "All is well, since all grows better."

Evolutionary theory provided, among other things, an argument for the social utility of millionaires like himself. Beginning in the 1880's, Carnegie elaborated that argument in a series of articles, later gathered into a book, that created the catchphrase with which his name is enduringly associated: the Gospel of Wealth. The simplest defense for great wealth was that it was a necessary byproduct of modern development. Earlier societies were restricted to the household or workshop method of manufacture and provided goods of uneven quality at high prices. Modern industrial society might generate greater inequalities of income, but it also produced dependable products at prices so low that now the poor could enjoy a style of material life available in the past only to the rich. Complex industrial society required as its leaders men with a special talent for organization and management; such men were relatively rare, and so could command a high level of compensation.

As Carnegie saw it, the emergence of the millionaire class resulted from the workings of immutable economic laws that societies ignored at their peril. Those in doubt about this "beneficent necessity," he explained, need only look about them: desperately poor nations like India, China, and Japan had few if any millionaires; as one went up the economic scale, from Russia to Germany to England, the incidence of millionaires proportionately increased. But none of these societies produced anything like America's abundant supply of the very rich, and in America—here, for Carnegie, was the clincher—the income of the many far surpassed that achieved anywhere else. The wealth gap was not a problem to be solved; it was an essential element in a system that worked to the good of all.

Another boon offered to society by millionaires was the proper use of the riches they accumulated that exceeded their personal needs. "The duty of the man of wealth," Carnegie said, is "to consider all surplus revenues which come to him simply as trust funds, which he is called upon to administer . . . in the manner which, in his judgment, is best calculated to produce the most beneficial results for the community."

That duty followed from the fact that, while the wealthy surely earned their riches, wealth itself came ultimately from the community. It was only the growth in the size and needs of the population that created the context in which business leaders could exercise their superior talents. In that sense, Carnegie noted, "the *community* created the millionaire's wealth."

Not all of his fellow millionaires, Carnegie conceded, did what duty required. Some left their fortunes not to the community but to their children, a practice Carnegie condemned as both self-regarding and, in the end, no favor to the children, for whom unearned wealth often turned out to be more blight than blessing. (Thus his support for steep inheritance taxes. Carnegie himself did not marry until he was past fifty, and he had only one child, a daughter.) Others earned Carnegie's rebuke by leaving their estates to be administered, often badly, by lesser men after their deaths. "It is well to remember," Carnegie warned, "that it requires the exercise of not less ability than that which acquired it to use wealth so as to be really beneficial to the community." Then there were those who gave their money away in their lifetimes but did so unwisely. Better to toss money into the sea, Carnegie thought, than to spend it "to encourage the slothful, the drunken, the unworthy." It was philanthropy that was needed, not heedless charity.

Whatever one thinks of his rationale, Carnegie was indeed serious about his philanthropic responsibilities. He did not quite succeed in his intention of giving away all of his money before his death in 1919, but he did disburse vast amounts and left the remainder (minus relatively modest bequests to his wife and various employees and friends) in a charitable trust.

His giving was diverse and sometimes idiosyncratic: it included, inter alia, thousands of community library buildings and endowments in America and Britain, thousands more organs for churches (to introduce parishioners to classical music), pensions for college professors, free tuition for students in Scottish universities, a scientific research institution in the nation's capital, a peace endowment, and a library, music hall, art gallery, and natural-history museum in Pittsburgh.

Carnegie's philanthropy was not motivated—as was the case with so many of his fellow millionaires—by guilt, religious convictions, or a desire to affect public opinion. He felt no pangs of conscience concerning his wealth, harbored no Calvinist or other theological beliefs, and settled on giving away his money long before he became a prominent target of public criticism. He surrendered his fortune because he thought it the right thing to do.

Carnegie had hoped that his retirement would be committed primarily to philanthropic activities. As it turned out, however, philanthropy became subordinate to the cause that consumed his final decades: world peace. He took a major role in opposing Britain's Boer War in South Africa and America's war with Spain and subsequent conflict with rebel forces in the Philippines. But his broader target was war itself, which he considered a moral anachronism among nations in the same way dueling had once been among individuals. The progress of civilization had eliminated the latter evil; that same progress, in combination with the increasing economic interdependence of nations, would do away with the former.

In this case, of course, what Nasaw terms his subject's "almost intolerable self-confidence" failed him. In his incessant, imperious, often condescending badgering of political leaders in Washington, London, and Berlin, he finally made himself "slightly ridiculous." Teddy Roosevelt bore more or less patiently with Carnegie's importunities in public, but referred to him privately as the leader of a "male shrieking sisterhood."

The outbreak of war in 1914 shattered, at least in the short run, Carnegie's naive faith that the ultimate result of the various policies he urged—bilateral arbitration treaties, international disarmament conferences, a permanent world court, a league of peace with enforceable powers—would be the cessation of armed conflict among nations. But if the Great War shook his pacifist dreams, it did not entirely destroy them. One of his last public acts was to write to Woodrow Wilson congratulating the President on his decision in 1917 to enlist America in what both of them believed would be the war to end war.

David Cannadine's biography of Andrew Mellon suffers in comparison with Nasaw's masterful work, but that has to do more with the book's subject than with its author. The historian Burton J. Hendrick, who wrote biographies of both Carnegie and Mellon (the latter was never published) and was thus uniquely positioned to offer a comparative judgment, concluded succinctly that "Mr. Mellon lacks the personal qualities that made Mr. Carnegie so attractive a subject, nor, in other ways, was he so great a man." Mellon's career was less interesting than Carnegie's, his mind less lively and original, his personality less compelling, his impact less memorable. Still, as Cannadine notes, his range of experience in business, politics, art collecting, and philanthropy has no equivalent among those commonly classed as robber barons, and it is well past time that he received full-scale treatment.

Cannadine concedes that he began his research prejudiced against his subject. At the outset, he says, he found Mellon "an unsympathetic person with unappealing politics." Mellon is best known to history as Secretary of the Treasury in the 1920's in the conservative administrations of Warren Harding, Calvin Coolidge, and Herbert Hoover. Cannadine, who is English (though he has studied and taught in the U.S.), admits that had he been an American during that period he would have voted against the Presidents whom Mellon served and thereafter in favor of Franklin D. Roosevelt. Nonetheless, he assures us that he has tried to remain evenhanded in his judgments, and he does scrupulously attempt to provide a comprehensive account of his subject that might satisfy both admirers and detractors. It does not, however, take a terribly perspicacious reader to conclude that the author's final estimation differs little from the one with which he began.

Mellon's career had none of the rags-to-riches romance of Carnegie's. He was born into comfortable circumstances in Pittsburgh in 1855; his father Thomas, whose Ulster Scots family had come to America in 1818 when he was five years old, had prospered as a lawyer, judge, businessman, and banker. Andrew inherited his father's aptitude for business, and already by 1882 had assumed control of T. Mellon and

Sons Bank. Through the bank he gradually acquired interests in a broad range of enterprises: real estate, utilities, transportation, coal, steel, chemicals, oil, aluminum. By the turn of the century T. Mellon and Sons had become Mellon National Bank, and its head was now a very rich and powerful industrial financier.

Wealth and power did not translate into fame. Of the great industrialists of the age, Mellon was, until his entry into national politics in the 1920's, the least known. He was associated with no one major business, worked behind the scenes, and avoided publicity. He had none of Carnegie's flair and no desire for his notoriety. (The two men, twenty years apart in age, knew each other but were never close. In his dealings in steel, Mellon carefully avoided competition with Carnegie.) From childhood Mellon had been, even among his several siblings, a shy loner, remote and self-sufficient. He achieved his success through intellect and shrewd judgment, not force of personality.

Mellon's only experience in the public spotlight prior to the 1920's had been embarrassing and personally disastrous. He delayed marriage until 1901 when he was forty-six. He had met Nora McMullen on a cruise three years earlier, when she was nineteen, and had, for the first and only time in his life, fallen immediately and hopelessly in love. The two were utterly mismatched, their marriage a failure from the start. (Cannadine compares the union to that of Prince Charles and Diana Spencer.) Within a few years Nora had entered into a flagrant affair, and by 1912 the marriage was over, its dissolution marked by ugly, protracted, and widely publicized divorce proceedings that titillated the public and left the Mellons' two young children, Ailsa and Paul, with psychological scars that never entirely healed.

After the divorce, Mellon turned his attention not just to work but to the avocation of art collecting, which he had taken up in the late 1890's. Over the years, making his purchases through the prominent art dealers Roland Knoedler and Joseph Duveen, he built a magnificent personal collection. His greatest coup came in 1930–31, when he secretly purchased 21 of the finest paintings from the Hermitage collection in the Soviet Union for some $7 million, an acquisition—Cannadine calls it "the sale of the century"—made possible by Stalin's need for cash in his efforts to modernize the Soviet economy.

B y 1920, Mellon was sixty-five and thinking about retirement. He was instead about to enter on a new career in national politics. Long active behind the scenes in the Republican party, he was particularly involved in the 1920 presidential campaign, pleased with the conservative turn in the party and nation that resulted in the nomination and landslide election of Warren Harding. His generous contributions and success at money-raising brought him to the attention of party leaders, and his name was put forward by conservatives to join Harding's cabinet as Secretary of the Treasury, in part to offset the presumed progressive influence of the incoming Secretary of Commerce, Herbert Hoover.

Mellon would serve under three Presidents, from 1921 to 1932. His major policies included reductions in interest rates and the national debt, cuts in taxes and government spending, and settlement of the huge debt that the European allies had incurred with the U.S. to finance their war efforts. On all these matters he achieved, over time, considerable success, and with the return of national prosperity he became a highly regarded figure. Mellon was hailed as "the greatest Secretary of the Treasury since Alexander Hamilton" and was even mentioned as a possible presidential candidate in 1928. This, of course, was before the stock-market crash of 1929 and the onset of the Great Depression, when praise turned to condemnation.

Examining Mellon's stewardship through the prism of the Depression, historians have more often than not been highly critical of his policies, even those prior to 1929. Cannadine, though a liberal in his politics and often disdainful of his subject's views, concludes that Mellon's tenure in the cabinet deserves "a more sympathetic appraisal than it has generally received." He defends in particular Mellon's tax policies, which have frequently been dismissed as special favors for the rich.

In cutting rates at the top, in fact, Mellon wanted to induce the wealthy to pay more in taxes, not less. The high wartime federal rates had prompted the wealthy to concentrate their investments in state and municipal bonds, which were tax-exempt. Mellon rightly supposed that lower income taxes would redirect investment from bonds, where returns were low, to taxable industrial stocks whose generally higher returns would offset the tax bite. Mellon, Cannadine notes, consistently held to the principle that payment of federal taxes should be proportionate to income. His reduction in top rates meant that the rich paid more than they had before, while his elimination of taxes for the first several thousand dollars of income meant that most Americans paid nothing.

Nor, Cannadine thinks, could Mellon have done much either to prevent the crash or to restore the economy in its aftermath. The government's monetary and fiscal tools were inadequate to both tasks. All in all, he concludes, "most of what happened in America between 1929 and 1932 would probably have happened regardless of who had been running the Treasury."

Where Cannadine *is* critical of Mellon concerns his practice, despite public denials, of continuing to look after his personal business interests while in office. There is no evidence of corrupt dealings, but there were times when Mellon urged policies that had favorable implications for companies he was involved in, like Gulf Oil and Alcoa. As Cannadine puts it, Mellon "simply never understood or accepted the notion of conflict of interest." Nor was this the first time that Mellon had cut ethical corners. Like Carnegie, Mellon thought of himself as a businessman of probity and honor, and by prevailing standards, he mostly was. On occasion, though, he indulged in practices that were similar to Carnegie's and that similarly would not pass muster today.

The triumph of Franklin Roosevelt and the New Deal turned Mellon's world upside down. As Cannadine writes, the new President considered Mellon "the embodiment of everything in the pro-business Republican world before 1932 that [he] loathed and was determined to destroy." Immediately upon assuming office in 1933, the administration ordered the Bureau of Internal Revenue to audit Mellon's income-tax returns during his last years in office. When the investigation found nothing amiss (the bureau's agents in fact recommended that Mellon be granted a refund for 1931) the administration, in an action Cannadine calls "wholly without precedent," turned the matter over to the Justice Department for criminal prosecution.

In May 1934, a grand jury unanimously refused to indict Mellon for knowingly filing a false return. But, instead of dropping the matter, the administration turned to a civil suit before the federal Board of Tax Appeals. Cannadine's careful analysis shows that Mellon had not, knowingly or unknowingly, violated the law. He died of bronchial pneumonia on August 26, 1937, some three months before the tax board announced its decision vindicating him.

W hat adds peculiar irony to this unsavory episode is that while the administration was proceeding in its political vendetta against Mellon, it was also negotiating with him about an extraordinary philanthropic gift he intended for the nation. For many years, Mellon had been planning to deed his art collection to "the people of the United States" and to build a gallery in the nation's capital in which that collection might be housed. In December 1936, after the tax board had concluded its hearings in his case, he made a formal offer to the President. Whatever his personal feelings toward Mellon, Roosevelt accepted the offer in a cordial meeting that proceeded as if the tax case did not exist.

Thus was born the National Gallery of Art, a philanthropic contribution that, in Cannadine's estimation, is without "precedent or parallel in the nation's history." The final worth of the gift, including the art, the building, and a substantial endowment, came to some $60 million in 1936 dollars. Mellon's gesture was self-effacing as well as generous: in an effort to encourage other patrons to make their own gifts of art to expand the collection, he stipulated that his name not appear on the building. Mellon's philanthropy, Cannadine makes clear, was as straightforward in motivation as Carnegie's had been: he felt no guilt for his fortune, was only nominally religious, and had always been disdainful of public opinion.

Cannadine devotes the final pages of his book to weighing Mellon's life in the balance. Though he attempts to do his subject justice, his own expressed support for the New Deal makes it difficult for him fully to comprehend Mellon's conservative political and social views, about which he offers frequent denigrating comments. Mellon should have been more critical of the social order in which he grew up, Cannadine suggests, and more sympathetic toward a Roosevelt who, he says again and again, was only striving to preserve capitalism. Thus he characterizes Mellon's antipathy to the New Deal as "imprudent, unimaginative, chilling." That anachronistic criticism, one feels sure, would utterly have baffled Andrew Mellon.

Cannadine is even harder on Mellon's personality than on his politics. He consistently places the overwhelming burden of blame on Mellon for his troubled relations with his wife and children, a judgment that appears to discount evidence of ambiguities and mutual misunderstandings that Cannadine himself presents. His sweeping condemnations of Mellon—"one of the

most famously cold, taciturn, and repressed men of his generation"; "a hollow man, with no interior life"—seem imposed and gratuitous, unwarranted extrapolations from a life that, in the author's own account, sounds more complicated than the conclusions he puts forward about it.

None of this is to belittle Cannadine's achievement in writing an absorbing, intelligent, well-researched biography. But David Nasaw's approach seems preferable to me. While describing and analyzing Andrew Carnegie in brilliant detail, and offering occasional critical comments along the way, Nasaw does not attempt to characterize him. He says to his readers, in effect: here is a fascinating and multifaceted man, make of him what you will. Nasaw's own political views are decidedly liberal—as I discovered by stumbling across an op-ed piece he recently wrote—but they do not intrude on his narrative.

C arnegie and Mellon were very different creatures, but both of their lives bring into question the stereotype of the robber baron. Two men do not an era make, of course, but other recent biographical studies of industrial titans—Ron Chernow on John D. Rockefeller and Jean Strouse on J. P. Morgan, for example—point in the same direction.

In one key respect, however, the accounts of Nasaw and Cannadine do not support the efforts of an earlier generation of revisionists. In the 1950's, for instance, Allan Nevins defended John D. Rockefeller in part by arguing that he brought necessary order out of the chaos of the oil industry in the immediate post-Civil War period. Similar cases have been made for leaders in other industries. In this view, early industrial competition—cut-throat and frequently corrupt—had led to an untrustworthy boom-and-bust economy that undermined national prosperity. Against the backdrop of a reigning laissez-faire philosophy that precluded effective government intervention, the great industrial oligopolists supplied a measure of rough-and-ready economic stability that preceded the more formal controls on industry provided by Progressive and New Deal reforms.

Neither Cannadine nor Nasaw tries to make this case. Cannadine does not raise the issue, and Nasaw says quite explicitly that "the source materials I have uncovered do not support the telling of a heroic narrative of an industrialist who brought sanity and rationality to an immature capitalism plagued by runaway competition, ruthless speculation, and insider corruption." ("Nor," he immediately adds, "do they support the recitation of another muckraking exposé of Gilded Age criminality.")

Ultimately, the most persuasive way to rebut the robber-baron school of thought is to step back from its emphasis on the actions and intentions of particular individuals. Critics have presupposed that during this era the rich became rich at the expense of the general population. But (as I noted at the outset) this supposition flies in the face of the evidence of rising real wages. Indeed, as Milton Friedman once observed: "There is probably no other period in history, in this or any other country, in which the ordinary man had as large an increase in his standard of living as in the period between the Civil War and the First World War, when unrestrained individualism was most rugged." If Friedman is correct—or even anywhere near correct—the robber barons stand rehabilitated.

More precisely, they may be somewhat beside the point. Friedman did not mean to suggest that, but for specific men, the greatest economic boom in human history would not have occurred. Carnegie and Mellon were players—not interchangeable, of course, but also not indispensable—in an epic economic story whose outcome they only incidentally determined. Just as they were neither creators nor despoilers of general economic abundance, so too were they neither heroes nor villains in the roles they played. Like the rest of us, Carnegie and Mellon were made of mixed stuff, and were morally accountable as individuals, not as members of a class.

In that perspective we can appreciate the biographies of David Nasaw and David Cannadine without worrying whether they help to make or unmake a thesis. The stories they tell are not without larger significance; but the best stories, and the people who inhabit them, have never been reducible to neat moral and ideological categories.

Notes

1. Penguin, 878 pp., $35.00.
2. Knopf, 779 pp., $35.00.

Critical Thinking

1. Do you believe tycoons such as Mellon and Carnegie have a responsibility to give back to society? Explain.

2. Is it necessary to try to understand the complexities of the whole person in those who leave behind public legacies, or is the legacy itself enough?

Create Central

www.mhhe.com/createcentral

Internet References

PBS.org
  www.pbs.org/wgbh/amex/carnegie/peopleevents/pande01.html
History.com
  www.history.com/topics/andrew-carnegie
Brittanica.com
  www.britannica.com/EBchecked/topic/374012/Andrew-W-Mellon
Biography.com
  www.biography.com/people/andrew-mellon-9405176

JAMES NUECHTERLEIN, a former professor of American studies and political thought at Valparaiso University, is a senior fellow of the Institute on Religion and Public Life.

Article

Prepared by: Larry Madaras, *Howard Community College*

Upside-Down Bailout

H. W. BRANDS

Learning Outcomes

After reading this article, you will be able to:

- Explain why and how J. P Morgan was the most powerful person in America from 1890–1914.

- Explain what caused the depression of the 1890s and what effect it had on the American Worker.

- Explain why President Cleveland was reluctant to use him to solve the treasury's shortage of gold reserves.

- Explain how the economic crisis of September 2008 differed from the Panic of 1893.

P resident Grover Cleveland was getting desperate. The economy had been hemorrhaging jobs since the Panic of 1893; 18 months later, millions of Americans pounded the streets looking for work, huddled around fires in hobo camps against the winter cold, and wondered where they would find food for their crying children. Across the street from the White House, the United States Treasury was on the verge of collapse. Worries among investors that paper dollars would soon be worthless had triggered a run on the Treasury's gold reserves. Within days, the gold would be gone. The government would be bankrupt. And Cleveland would be blamed.

One man could save the day, but Cleveland shuddered at the thought of accepting his help. John Pierpont Morgan was not only the most powerful banker in the country, but also the most despised. His visage alone made babies wail and adults recoil: Chronic rosacea inflamed and deformed his nose, till persons who met him could neither look nor look away. Morgan's mastery of Wall Street was even more frightening. His command of capital put whole industries in thrall to his whims; ordinary citizens had difficulty believing that anyone so wealthy and powerful could be other than malign. Nonetheless, Morgan's Midas touch drew Cleveland irresistibly toward him. With the condition of the Treasury growing more dire each day, the president didn't see how he could avoid making a deal with the financial Gorgon who was the embodiment of the oppressive power of Wall Street.

In the absence of a central banking authority, Morgan was the country's lender of last resort. Cleveland's decision to kowtow to him saved the dollar and averted the demise of federal credit. It also provoked an uproar that led to a takeover of Cleveland's Democrats by the populist wing of the party. Anger toward Morgan was rekindled when he again operated as America's de facto central banker in the financial panic of 1907, prompting the progressive heirs of the populists to train the withering light of public scrutiny on his practices. Neither Morgan nor his practices survived.

More than a century later, when the subprime mortgage mess plunged America into a deep recession, Washington politicians again felt that they had no choice but to make a deal with the bankers on Wall Street. Only this time, the circumstances were flipped. In Morgan's day, he put up tens of millions of dollars to save the government and economy. In our day, Washington poured billions into propping up the banks and financial institutions that had brought the economy to its knees. But one thing didn't change. As the financial panic began to lift, the resentment and hatred of Wall Street was palpable.

"The banker's calling is hereditary," Walter Bagehot, the founding editor of London's *Economist* weekly, asserted after examining the banking dynasties of Britain. "The credit of the bank descends from father to son; this inherited wealth brings inherited refinement." J. P. Morgan inherited the banker's calling from his father and grandfather, who had constructed a financial fiefdom that spanned the Atlantic, with principal offices in New York and London. Morgan apprenticed with a firm associated with his father's; in the wake of the Panic of 1857 he displayed a boldness that shocked his seniors but earned Morgan a fortune and convinced him he had a gift for the money trade. During the Civil War he speculated in commodities and gold, proceeding from coup to coup until his income reached $50,000 a year, at a time when a skilled laborer might earn $500.

After the war Morgan entered the burgeoning railroad business, underwriting stock issues for the new roads crisscrossing the country. He took a commission on the transactions but also something more: In partial payment he insisted on seats on the boards of directors of the roads. At a time when corporate information was considered proprietary and was commonly withheld even from shareholders, Morgan's inside position gave him a vantage available to few others. He quickly became the country's expert on railroads.

He turned the information to good use. Morgan, like many other successful men, perceived a consonance between his personal interests and those of the larger community. Morgan believed he could make money reorganizing the nation's railroads, but he believed as well that the nation would benefit. Duplication entailed enormous waste as rail companies built lines almost side-by-side and waged rate wars that destabilized the industry and disrupted transportation. Morgan hosted periodic rail summits at his New York mansion. Amid the smoke of cigars and the acrimony of executives with lesser clout, Morgan would orchestrate truces in current wars and extract promises not to aggress in the future. Financial reporters staked out Morgan's home; they listened at windows and bribed servants to obtain details from the inner sanctum. They rarely succeeded, but the gist was clear enough, and it inspired a typical headline after one summit: "Railroad Kings Form a Gigantic Trust."

Morgan detested the publicity. He resented the reporters' inquisitiveness, and he loathed their cameras, which cast his ugly nose before the smirking gaze of the world. When he could, he insisted that photographers reconstruct his nose with their airbrushes; when he couldn't, he paid to destroy the negatives. He believed, moreover, that his business was *his* business, however much it might suit the public interest. Let others do with their money what they chose, and leave him to do with his what *he* chose.

The distinction between the private and the public became harder to defend after the Panic of 1893 triggered the worst depression in American history to that date. "Men died like flies under the strain," Henry Adams, a great-grandson of John Adams, wrote of the period. "Boston grew suddenly old, haggard, and thin." Wage cuts triggered strikes at Homestead, Pa., where steelworkers battled Pinkerton detectives for control of the Carnegie Steel works, and Pullman, Ill., where workers initiated a labor action that paralyzed the country's rail system. Jacob Coxey led an army of the unemployed in a march to Washington. Graybeards recalled the dark period before the Civil War and wondered if America could hold together. "In no civilized country in this century, not actually in the throes of war or open insurrection, has society been so disorganized as it was in the United States during the first half of 1894," an editor asserted a short while later. "Never was human life held so cheap. Never did the constituted authorities appear so incompetent to enforce respect for law."

No one could say just what had precipitated the panic or was causing the depression to persist. But all explanations noted the declining price level the country had experienced since the 1870s. Falling prices pinched farmers and other debtors, since the relative value of the dollars they owed their creditors increased with each passing year, and hence required greater effort to earn. Farmers' organizations demanded that the government re-level the playing field by expanding the money supply. The Treasury, after a war-induced fling with unsecured paper dollars, clung to the gold standard, promising to redeem the American currency with the yellow metal upon the bearer's demand. But the farmers' advocates pointed out that the American economy had grown much faster than the supply of gold. With so many goods vying for so little gold, prices were bound to keep falling. The proposed solution: Supplement gold with silver. The slogans of the silverites were "free silver" and "16 to 1,"

by which they meant the free coinage of silver at a ratio of 16 ounces of silver to 1 ounce of gold. If effected, this would have dramatically expanded the American money supply, and reversed the falling prices.

But the mere thought of such inflation terrified creditors, who benefited from the falling prices—which was to say, the strengthening dollar—to the same degree the debtors suffered. Many were tempted to trade their dollars for gold ahead of the feared devaluation; more than a few succumbed to the temptation. As they did so the Treasury's gold reserve declined. By law and custom the Treasury was expected to maintain $100 million in gold, usually a sufficient cushion against the quotidian buffets of supply and demand. But the extraordinary circumstances after the 1893 panic suggested this wasn't enough. During 1894 the Treasury's reserve flirted with the $100 million floor; by year's end the hoard was barely above the mark. The new year briefly slowed the drain, but at mid-month the pressure on the Treasury resumed. On January 24, 1895, the gold reserve fell to $68 million; one week later it was $45 million.

As large dollar-holders converged on the Treasury and scrambled to convert their paper to gold, the panic resembled runs that had brought down thousands of commercial banks since the depression began. But now the imperiled institution was the federal government. The solvency of the republic was at risk.

The danger to the dollar overwhelmed Morgan's reluctance to show himself in public. He left the comfort and security of New York, where he was respected, if not exactly loved, and headed for Washington, where his enemies clustered. He traveled by private railcar, to avoid the hostile glares as long as possible.

Grover Cleveland learned he was coming. The president hadn't invited the banker; even as the country approached the brink, Cleveland hoped something would occur to spare him the ignominy of turning to Morgan. And when Morgan reached the capital, Cleveland tried to keep him at a distance. He sent his secretary of war and closest confidant, Daniel Lamont, to intercept Morgan at Union Station. Lamont said the president would not meet with Morgan; he would find another solution to the problem.

The panic resembled runs that had brought down thousands of banks. But now the solvency of the republic was at risk

Morgan refused to be put off. There was no other solution, he said. And having ventured this far into enemy territory, he wasn't going to retreat without accomplishing his mission. "I have come down to see the president," he told Lamont. "And I am going to stay here until I see him." He climbed into a cab and drove to a hotel near the White House.

All that evening Cleveland agonized. Morgan's journey to Washington had been reported in the papers; his presumed intervention heartened investors and diminished the pressure on the Treasury. The president wondered if he could somehow capture the financial benefits of Morgan's proximity without paying the political costs. Lamont brought word of Morgan's determination to remain in Washington; Cleveland considered riding out the siege.

Morgan affected nonchalance. Reporters circled his hotel, swarming the entryways and infiltrating the lobby. He remained inside, silent and unseen. His few friends in the capital dropped by to visit; he greeted them one by one. After the last visitor left, he stayed up playing solitaire. Hotel workers later told reporters that the light in his room didn't go out till after 4 a.m.

But the next morning by 9:00, he was shaved and ready for breakfast. He received with his juice the first reports of the opening of business in New York, and learned that the run on the Treasury had resumed. He hadn't even lit his post-breakfast cigar when a messenger arrived from the White House. The president would see him.

Dark clouds threatened snow as Morgan hurried across Lafayette Square, shielding his face from the wind—and from reporters—with the upturned collar of his coat. He was shown to Cleveland's office.

The president's discomfort was obvious. He spoke of the crisis in terms suggesting he still hoped to avoid a Morgan rescue. Morgan listened briefly, then brought the matter to a head. His sources had told him that the Treasury's reserve was around $9 million. Other sources revealed that a single investor held a draft of $10 million against the Treasury's gold. "If that $10 million draft is presented, you can't meet it," Morgan declared. "It will be all over before three o'clock."

Cleveland realized he had no choice. "What suggestion have you to make, Mr. Morgan?"

Officials at the Treasury had been considering a public bond offering; Morgan declared this method too slow. A private sale was necessary, he said. He would gather a syndicate that would take the government bonds and give the Treasury the gold it needed to stay afloat.

Cleveland questioned whether this was legal. Morgan asserted that it was, citing a Civil War statute—number "four thousand and something," he said—that had authorized President Lincoln to sell bonds privately in emergencies. The law had never been repealed.

Cleveland looked at his attorney general, Richard Olney, and asked if this was so. Olney said he would have to check. He disappeared and then returned, bearing a volume of the Revised Statutes. He handed the book to Treasury Secretary John Carlisle, who read to the group: "The Secretary of the Treasury may purchase coin with any of the bonds or notes of the United States . . . upon such terms as he may deem most advantageous to the public interest." Carlisle turned to Cleveland. "Mr. President," he said, "that seems to fit the situation exactly."

Cleveland asked Morgan how large a transaction he had in mind. One hundred million, Morgan replied. Cleveland groaned. To the public it would appear that Morgan wasn't simply rescuing the Treasury but taking over the place. The president said $60 million would have to do.

He then asked the critical question. "Mr. Morgan, what guarantee have we that if we adopt this plan, gold will not continue to be shipped abroad, and while we are getting it in, it will go out, and we will not reach our goal? Will you guarantee that this will not happen?"

Morgan didn't hesitate. "Yes, sir," he said. "I will guarantee it during the life of the syndicate, and that means until the contract has been concluded and the goal has been reached."

Morgan was as good as his word, and his word was as good as gold—quite literally. As soon as news of the rescue flashed along the telegraph lines to New York and London, the gold that the Morgan syndicate pledged to deliver was almost superfluous. The fact that Morgan had become a cosigner on the federal debt was what impressed the markets. Within days the Treasury's condition stabilized; within weeks the dollar's danger had passed.

But Cleveland's troubles were only beginning. Presidents rarely get credit for disasters averted, which the skeptical and partisan can argue would never have happened anyway. The left wing of Cleveland's party excoriated him for handing control of public finances to a private syndicate headed by the very symbol of capitalist power. Morgan didn't help Cleveland's case by stonewalling efforts to make him reveal the profit he had made on the rescue. "That I decline to answer," Morgan told congressional investigators. "I am perfectly ready to state to the committee every detail of the negotiation up to the time that the bonds became my property and were paid for. What I did with my own property subsequent to that purchase I decline to state."

Democratic populists didn't have the votes to compel Morgan, and so turned their wrath against Cleveland. At the Democratic convention the following year they rallied to William Jennings Bryan, who lumped Cleveland with Morgan in the camp of those crucifying mankind on a "cross of gold." Cleveland, who had led the party out of its post-Civil War wilderness, could only watch in dismay as Bryan led the party back into the wilderness, losing not once—in 1896—but thrice—in 1900 and 1908, as well.

Morgan's demise took longer. The Treasury rescue burnished his reputation among capitalists, who in 1901 watched in awe as he fashioned the first billion-dollar corporation in American history, the United States Steel trust. Wall Street marched to Morgan's orders as he stepped into the breach amid the financial panic of 1907, when the nation's chronic gold shortage triggered a run on undercapitalized trust banks.

With President Theodore Roosevelt off shooting game in Louisiana for two weeks, Morgan, then 70, operated as a self-appointed financial crisis manager from his Madison Avenue brownstone. He saved the New York Stock Exchange by demanding that New York bankers float it a $24 million loan. He organized another $30 million loan to keep New York City from defaulting on its payroll and debt obligations. As two major trust companies teetered on the brink of failure, Morgan summoned some 50 bank presidents to his library on a Saturday night and closed the door. He didn't let them out until dawn on Sunday, after stipulating how much each would have to contribute to a $25 million bailout package.

Morgan's efforts kept the financial system from disintegrating. Nonetheless, his critics maintained their hostile fire. After the progressives—the heirs to the populists—seized control of Congress in the 1910 elections, they launched a probe of what they called the "money trust." Morgan was summoned to testify, but offered only the vaguest answers to queries as to how he made decisions to provide or withhold credit. He denied that he or anyone else exerted inordinate influence on American finance. He declared that the most important thing in business was not money or property, but character. A man might have all the collateral in the world, but without character he wouldn't get a loan—at least not from Morgan. "I have known a man to come into my office," Morgan said, "and I have given him a check for a million dollars when I knew he did not have a cent in the world."

Morgan declared that the most important thing in business was not money or property, but character

The committee wasn't buying, and its resulting report delineated a network of interlocking directorates among the country's banks, with J. P. Morgan & Co. at the center. The report decried the monopoly power this afforded Morgan and his associates, and warned of future crises worse than those of the recent past, concluding, "The peril is manifest."

Morgan slipped out of the country amid the furor and steamed to Europe in the spring of 1913 for an annual art-buying holiday. His traveling companions noted that he seemed unusually anxious and depressed. In Italy he contracted a fever that abruptly proved fatal. His physicians expressed puzzlement, but his colleagues blamed the death on the weight of public opprobrium.

Morgan's death neatly marked the passing of an age in American banking. The exposé of his financial power provided grist for the mills of reform, which in December 1913 produced the Federal Reserve Act, wresting control of banking and the nation's money supply from the likes of Morgan and delivering it to the new Federal Reserve System.

In the first decade of the 21st century, when panic again seized the financial markets, it was the Fed that rode to the rescue with a massive monetary stimulus. The world had changed since Morgan towered like a colossus over Wall Street. But one thing remained the same. If Morgan had lived to see the political flogging Fed chief Ben Bernanke was forced to endure for his decisive action on behalf of the bankers, he would have smiled knowingly.

Critical Thinking

1. Explain the techniques used by J. P. Morgan to prop up the national government's gold reserves.
2. Explain what Morgan meant when he said the most important thing in business was not money or property, but character.
3. How did Morgan's rescue of the government's gold reserves in 1895 and 1907 lead to the creation of the Federal Reserve System?
4. Explain how the rescue of the American financial system differed in September 2008 from 1895 and 1907.

Create Central

www.mhhe.com/createcentral

Internet References

International Institute of Social History
This site focuses on business and labor history.
   www.socialhistory.org
World Wide Web Virtual Library
This site focuses on labor and business history. As an index site, this is a good place to start exploring these two vast topics.
   www.iisg.nl/~w3vl

H. W. BRANDS, Professor of History at Texas A & M, is the author of a dozen books including *The Money Men* and *American Colossus: The Triumph of Capitalism.*

Article

Lockwood in '84

In 1884, a woman couldn't vote for the president of the United States, but that didn't stop activist lawyer Belva Lockwood from conducting a full-scale campaign for the office. She was the first woman ever to do so, and she tried again for the presidency in 1888. It's time we recognized her name.

JILL NORGREN

Learning Outcomes

After reading this article, you will be able to:

- Describe how Belva Lockwood overcame sexism to become the first woman to campaign for the presidency of the United States.

- Discuss the irony in a system in which a woman can campaign for president yet not be allowed to vote.

In 1884, Washington, D.C., attorney Belva Lockwood, candidate of the Equal Rights Party, became the first woman to run a full campaign for the presidency of the United States. She had no illusion that a woman could be elected, but there were policy issues on which she wished to speak, and, truth be told, she welcomed the notoriety. When challenged as to whether a woman was eligible to become president, she said that there was "not a thing in the Constitution" to prohibit it. She did not hesitate to confront the male establishment that barred women from voting and from professional advancement. With the spunk born of a lifelong refusal to be a passive victim of discrimination, Lockwood told a campaign reporter, "I cannot vote, but I can be voted for." Her bid for the presidency startled the country and infuriated other suffrage leaders, many of whom mistakenly clung to the idea that the Republican Party would soon sponsor a constitutional amendment in support of woman suffrage.

In the last quarter of the 19th century, Lockwood commanded attention, and not just from the columnists and satirists whom she led a merry chase. Today she is virtually unknown, lost in the shadows of the iconic suffrage leaders Elizabeth Cady Stanton and Susan B. Anthony. That's an injustice, for Belva Lockwood was a model of courageous activism and an admirable symbol of a woman's movement that increasingly invested its energies in party politics.

Lockwood was born Belva Ann Bennett in the Niagara County town of Royalton, New York, on October 24, 1830, the second daughter, and second of five children, of Lewis J. Bennett, a farmer, and Hannah Green Bennett. Belva was educated in rural schoolhouses, where she herself began to teach at the age of 14. In her first profession she found her first cause. As a female instructor, she received less than half the salary paid to the young men. The Bennetts' teenage daughter thought this treatment "odious, an indignity not to be tamely borne." She complained to the wife of a local minister, who counseled her that such was the way of the world. But bright, opinionated, ambitious Belva Bennett would not accept that world.

From her avid reading of history, Belva imagined for herself a life different from that of her mother and her aunts—the life, in fact, of a great man. She asked her father's permission to continue her education, but he said no. She then did what she was expected to do: On November 8, 1848, she married Uriah McNall, a promising young farmer. She threw herself into running their small farm and sawmill, wrote poetry and essays, and determined not to let marriage be the end of her individuality. She wanted to chart her own course, and tragedy gave her an opportunity to do so. In April 1853, when she was 22 and her daughter, Lura, three, Uriah McNall died.

The young widow had a second chance to go out into the world. She resumed her teaching and her education. In September 1854, she left Lura with her mother and traveled 60 miles east to study at the Genesee Wesleyan Seminary in Lima. The seminary shared a building with the newly coeducational Genesee College, which offered a more rigorous program. Belva transferred to the college (becoming its third woman student), where she took courses in science and politics. She graduated with a bachelor's degree (with honors) on June 27, 1857, and soon found a position teaching high school in the prosperous Erie Canal town of Lockport. Four years later, she took over a small school in the south-central New York town of Owego.

In 1866, Belva McNall traveled to Washington and began to reinvent herself as an urban professional. She was neither flamboyant nor eccentric. Indeed, had she been a man, it would have been apparent that her life was following a conventional 19th-century course: Talented chap walks off the farm, educates himself, seeks opportunities, and makes a name. But because Belva strove to be that ambitious son of ordinary people who rises in the world on the basis of his wits and his work, she was thought a radical.

In Washington, Belva taught school and worked as a leasing agent, renting halls to lodges and organizations. She tutored herself in the workings of government and the art of lobbying by making frequent visits to Congress. In 1868 she married Ezekiel Lockwood, an elderly dentist and lay preacher who shared her reformist views. We do not know precisely when she fell in love with the law. In antebellum America the profession belonged to men, who passed on their skill by training their sons and nephews and neighbors' boys. After the Civil War a handful of women, Lockwood among them, set out to change all that. She believed from her reading of the lives of great men that "in almost every instance law has been the stepping-stone to greatness." She attended the law program of Washington's National University, graduated in 1872 (but only after she lobbied for the diploma male administrators had been pressured to withhold), and was admitted to the bar of the District of Columbia in 1873 (again, only after a struggle against sex discrimination). When the Supreme Court of the United States refused to admit her to its bar in 1876, she single-handedly lobbied Congress until, in 1879, it passed, reluctantly, "An act to relieve the legal disabilities of women." On March 3, 1879, Lockwood became the first woman admitted to the high Court bar, and, in 1880, the first woman lawyer to argue a case before the Court.

From her earliest years in Washington, Lockwood coveted a government position. She applied to be a consul officer in Ghent during the administration of Andrew Johnson, but her application was never acknowledged. In later years, she sought government posts—for women in general and for herself in particular—from other presidents. Without success. When Grover Cleveland passed over Lockwood and appointed as minister to Turkey a man thought to be a womanizer, she wrote to compliment the president on his choice: "The only danger is, that he will attempt to suppress polygamy in that country by marrying all of the women himself." A year later, in 1886, in another communication to Cleveland, she laid claim to the position of district recorder of deeds and let the president know in no uncertain terms that she had a "lien" on the job. She did not give up: In 1911 she had her name included on a list sent to President William Howard Taft of women attorneys who could fill the Supreme Court vacancy caused by the death of Justice John Marshall Harlan.

W**hat** persuaded Lockwood that she should run for the highest office in the land? Certainly, she seized the opportunity to shake a fist at conservatives who would hold women back. And she was displeased with the enthusiasm for the Republican Party shown by suffrage leaders

Susan B. Anthony and Elizabeth Cady Stanton. More than that, however, campaigning would provide an opportunity for her to speak her mind, to travel, and to establish herself on the paid lecture circuit. She was not the first woman to run for president. In 1872, New York City newspaper publisher Victoria Woodhull had declared herself a presidential candidate, against Ulysses Grant and Horace Greeley. But Woodhull, cast as Mrs. Satan by the influential cartoonist Thomas Nast, had to abandon her campaign barely a month after its start: Her radical "free love" views were too much baggage for the nascent women's movement to bear, and financial misfortune forced her to suspend publication of *Woodhull & Claflin's Weekly* at the very moment she most needed a public platform.

Years later, Lockwood—and the California women who drafted her—spoke of the circumstances surrounding her August 1884 nomination, their accounts colored by ego and age. Lockwood received the nod from Marietta Stow, a San Francisco reformer who spoke for the newly formed California-based Equal Rights Party, and from Stow's colleague, attorney Clara Foltz. Foltz later insisted that Lockwood's nomination amounted to nothing more than a lighthearted joke on her and Stow's part. But Stow's biographer, Sherilyn Bennion, has made a strong case that the nomination was, in fact, part of a serious political strategy devised by Stow to deflect attention from the rebuff given suffrage leaders that year at the Republican and Democratic conventions, and to demonstrate that "the fair sex" could create its own terms of engagement in American party politics. Women were becoming stump speakers, participants in political clubs, candidates for local office, and, in a handful of places, voters. (By 1884 the Wyoming, Utah and Washington Territories had fully enfranchised women, who in 14 states were permitted to vote in elections dealing with schools.) Marietta Stow began the Equal Rights Party because she had long been interested in matters of public policy and because readers of her newspaper, *The Women's Herald of Industry,* had expressed an interest in a "new, clean, uncorruptible party."

In July 1884 Stow urged Abigail Scott Duniway, an Oregon rights activist and newspaper editor, to accept the Equal Rights Party's nomination. But Duniway declined, believing, as Bennion writes, that "flaunting the names of women for official positions" would weaken the case for equal rights and provide "unscrupulous opponents with new pretexts and excuses for lying about them." Undiscouraged, Stow continued her search for a candidate. In August, she hit her mark.

Belva Lockwood, *Women's Herald* reader, had already begun to think of herself as a standard-bearer. On August 10 she wrote to Stow in San Francisco and asked rhetorically, and perhaps disingenuously, "Why not nominate women for important places? Is not Victoria Empress of India? Have we not among our country-women persons of as much talent and ability? Is not history full of precedents of women rulers?" The Republicans, she commented, claimed to be the party of progress yet had "little else but insult for women when [we] appear before its conventions." (She had been among those rebuffed that summer by the Republicans.) She was exasperated with the party of Lincoln and maddened by Stanton and Anthony's continuing faith in major-party politics: "It is quite time that we had our own party, our own platform, and our own nominees. We shall never have equal rights until we take them, nor respect until we command it."

Stow had her candidate! She called a party convention on August 23, read Lockwood's letter to the small group, and proposed her as the party's nominee for president of the United States, along with Clemence S. Lozier, a New York City physician, as the vice presidential nominee. Acclamation followed, and letters were sent to the two women. The dispatch to Lockwood read as follows: "Madam: We have the honor to inform you that you were nominated, at the Woman's National Equal Rights Convention, for President of the United States. We await your letter of acceptance with breathless interest."

Lockwood later said that the letter took her "utterly by surprise," and she kept it secret for several days. On September 3, she wrote to accept the nomination for "Chief Magistrate of the United States" from the only party that "really and truly represent the interests of our whole people North, South, East, and West. . . . With your unanimous and cordial support . . . we shall not only be able to carry the election, but to guide the Ship of State safely into port." Lockwood went on to outline a dozen platform points, and her promptness in formulating policy signaled that she (and the party) intended to be taken seriously about matters of political substance.

Forecasters in '84 were predicting another close presidential race. Four years earlier, James Garfield had defeated Winfield Hancock by just 40,000 votes (out of nine million cast), and people were again watching the critical states of New York and Indiana. The nearly even division of registered voters between the two major parties caused Democratic candidate Grover Cleveland and Republican candidate James G. Blaine to shy away from innovative platforms. Instead, the two men spent much of their time trading taunts and insults. That left the business of serious reform to the minor parties and their candidates: Benjamin Butler (National Greenback/Anti-Monopoly), John St. John (Prohibition), and Samuel Clarke Pomeroy (American Prohibition). Butler, St. John, and Pomeroy variously supported workers' rights, the abolition of child and prison labor, a graduated income tax, senatorial term limits, direct election of the president, and, of course, prohibition of the manufacture, sale, and consumption of alcohol. Lockwood joined this group of nothing-to-lose candidates, who intended to promote the public discussion of issues about which Blaine and Cleveland dared not speak.

The design of Lockwood's platform reflected her practical savvy. The platform, she said, should "take up every one of the issues of the day" but be "so brief that the newspapers would publish it and the people read it." (She understood the art of the sound bite.) Her "grand platform of principles" expressed bold positions and comfortable compromise. She promised to promote and maintain equal political privileges for "every class of our citizens irrespective of sex, color or nationality" in order to make America "in truth what it has so long been in name, 'the land of the free and home of the brave.'" She pledged herself to the fair distribution of public offices to women as

well as men, "with a scrupulous regard to civil service reform after the women are duly installed in office." She opposed the "wholesale monopoly of the judiciary" by men and said that, if elected, she would appoint a reasonable number of women as district attorneys, marshals, and federal judges, including a "competent woman to any vacancy that might occur on the United States Supreme Bench."

Lockwood's views extended well beyond women's issues. She adopted a moderate position on the contentious question of tariffs. In her statement of September 3, she placed the Equal Rights Party in the political camp that wanted to "protect and foster American industries," in sympathy with the working men and women of the country who were organized against free trade. But in the official platform statement reprinted on campaign literature, her position was modified so that the party might be identified as middle-of-the-road, supporting neither high tariffs nor free trade. Lockwood urged the extension of commercial relations with foreign countries and advocated the establishment of a "high Court of Arbitration" to which commercial and political differences could be referred. She supported citizenship for Native Americans and the allotment of tribal land. As was to be expected from an attorney who earned a substantial part of her livelihood doing pension claims work, she adopted a safe position on Civil War veterans' pensions: She argued that tariff revenues should be applied to benefits for former soldiers and their dependents; at the same time, she urged the abolition of the Pension Office, "with its complicated and technical machinery," and recommended that it be replaced with a board of three commissioners. She vowed full sympathy with temperance advocates and, in a position unique to the platform of the Equal Rights Party, called for the reform of family law: "If elected, I shall recommend in my Inaugural speech, a uniform system of laws as far as practicable for all of the States, and especially for marriage, divorce, and the limitation of contracts, and such a regulation of the laws of descent and distribution of estates as will make the wife equal with the husband in authority and right, and an equal partner in the common business."

Lockwood's position paper of September 3 was revised into the platform statement that appeared below her portrait on campaign flyers. The new version expanded on certain points, adopted some sharper rhetoric, and added several planks, including a commitment that the remaining public lands of the nation would go to the "honest yeomanry," not the railroads. Lockwood stuck to her radical positions of support for women's suffrage and the reform of domestic law, but, in a stunning retreat, her earlier promises of an equitable allotment of public positions by sex and any mention of the need for women in the judiciary were absent from the platform.

Armed with candidate and platform, the leaders and supporters of the Equal Rights Party waited to see what would happen. A great deal depended on the posture adopted by the press. Fortunately for Lockwood and the party, many of the daily newspapers controlled by men, and a number of weeklies owned by women, took an interest in the newest contender in the election of '84. A day after she accepted the nomination, *The Washington Evening Star* made her candidacy front-page news and reprinted the entire text of her acceptance letter and platform of September 3. The candidate told a *Star* reporter that she would not necessarily receive the endorsement of activist women. Indeed, leaders of the nation's two top woman suffrage associations had endorsed Blaine, and Frances Willard had united temperance women with the Prohibition Party. "You must remember," Lockwood said, "that the women are divided up into as many factions and parties as the men."

On September 5, an editorial in the *Star* praised Lockwood's letter of acceptance: "In all soberness, it can be said [it] is the best of the lot. It is short, sharp, and decisive. . . . It is evident that Mrs. Lockwood, if elected, will have a policy [that] commends itself to all people of common sense." Editor Crosby Noyes rued the letter's late appearance: Had it existed sooner, "the other candidates might have had the benefit of perusing it and framing their several epistles in accord with its pith and candor." Newspaper reporting elsewhere was similarly respectful.

Abigail Duniway's warning that women candidates would meet with "unpleasant prominence" and be held up "to ridicule and scorn" proved correct, but Lockwood actually encountered no greater mockery than the men in the election. She had to endure silly lies about hairpieces and sham allegations that she was divorced, but Cleveland was taunted with cries of "Ma, Ma Where's My Pa" (a reference to his out-of-wedlock child). Cartoonists for *Frank Leslie's Illustrated* and *Puck,* mass-circulation papers, made fun of all the candidates, including Lockwood. This was a rite of passage and badge of acceptance. *Leslie's* also ran an article on Lockwood's campaign and contemplated the entrance of women into party politics with earnest good wishes: "Woman in politics. Why not? . . . Twenty years ago woman's suffrage was a mere opinion. Today, it is another matter."

After establishing campaign headquarters at her Washington home on F Street, Lockwood wrote to friends and acquaintances in a dozen states asking that they arrange ratification meetings and get up ballots containing the names of electors (as required by the Constitution) pledged to her candidacy. This letter to a male friend in Philadelphia was a typical appeal: "That an opportunity may not be lost for the dissemination of Equal Rights principles, cannot, and will not the Equal Rights Party of Philadelphia hold a ratification meeting for the nominee, put in nomination a Presidential Elector, and get up an Equal Rights ticket? Not that we shall succeed in the election, but we can demonstrate that a woman may under the Constitution, not only be nominated but elected. Think of it."

Closer to home, party supporters organized a ratification meeting in mid-September at Wilson's Station, Maryland. (They bypassed the District to make the point that, under federal law, neither men nor women could vote in the nation's capital.) Lockwood delivered her first speech as a candidate at this gathering of about 75 supporters and journalists, and two Lockwood-for-president electors were chosen.

She did not disclose at the rally that Clemence Lozier had declined the nomination for vice president—and not until September 29 did Marietta Stow decide to run in the second spot and complete the ticket.

Throughout September the national press spread the story of the Equal Rights Party and its candidate, and letters poured in to the house on F Street. They contained "earnest inquiries" about the platform, nasty bits of character assassination, and, from one male admirer, the following poem, which so amused Lockwood that she gave it to a reporter for publication:

O, Belva Ann!

Fair Belva Ann!

I know that thou art not a man;

But I shall vote,

Pull off my coat,

And work for thee, fair Belva Ann.

For I have read

What thou hast said,

And long I've thought upon thy plan.

Oh no, there's none

Beneath the sun

Who'd rule like thee, my Belva Ann!

The letters also brought invitations to speak in cities across the East and the Midwest. In late September, Lockwood prepared to go on the stump, her expenses covered by sponsors. Many of the lectures she gave were paid appearances; indeed, she claimed to be the only candidate whose speeches the public paid to hear. She was a widowed middle-class woman (her second husband, who was more than 30 years her senior, had died in 1877), and her livelihood depended on the earnings of her legal practice. So the time she devoted to politics had to pay. When the election was over, she told reporters that she had a satisfaction denied the other candidates: She had come out of the campaign with her expenses paid and "$125 ahead."

Lockwood took to the field in October. She made at least one full circuit in October, beginning in Baltimore, Philadelphia, and New York. Mid-month she delivered speeches in Louisville and in Cleveland, where she appeared at the Opera House before 500 people. In a loud and nasal voice, she attacked the high-tariff position of the Republicans on the grounds that it would injure American commerce. But she also assailed the free-trade policy of the Democrats, arguing that they were "willing to risk our manufacturing interests in the face of the starving hordes of pauper labor in other countries." She applauded the good that capital had done and said that "capital and labor did not, by nature, antagonize, and should not by custom."

If the people who came to hear Lockwood expected nothing but women's rights talk, they were disappointed. She and her party colleagues believed that the Equal Rights Party should not run a single-issue campaign. Of course, the platform introduced "feminist" ideas. But it also allowed Lockwood to address many other issues that preoccupied Americans. So she directed only a small part of her talk to describing how women had helped to make the country "blossom as a rose." She intended her candidacy to make history in the largest sense—by demonstrating that the Constitution did not bar women from running in elections or serving in federal elective office.

People who saw her for the first time said that her campaign photographs did not do her justice: The lady candidate had fine blue eyes, an aquiline nose, and a firm mouth, and she favored fashionable clothes. The cartoonists naturally focused on her sex, and the public had its own fun by creating dozens of Belva Lockwood Clubs, in which men meaning to disparage Lockwood paraded on city streets wearing Mother Hubbard dresses, a new cut of female clothing with an unconstructed design that freed movement and was considered improper to wear out of doors.

On November 3, the day before the election, Lockwood returned from a campaign tour of the Northwest. She had stayed "at the best hotels; had the best sleeping berths." Her last stop was Flint, Michigan, and she told a Washington reporter that 1,000 people had attended her (paid) talk there, a larger number than Ohio congressman Frank Hurd drew the following night. When asked on November 4 where she would await the election news, she replied that her house would be open throughout the evening, "the gas will be lighted," and reporters were welcome to visit. The historic first campaign by a woman for the presidency of the United States had ended, though in politics, of course, nothing is ever over.

When the ballots were tallied, Cleveland was declared the winner, with an Electoral College vote of 219 to 182. In the popular vote, he squeaked by with a margin of 23,000.

In 1884 the United States had yet to adopt the "Australian" ballot, which has the names of all candidates for office printed on a single form. The system then in effect, dating from the beginning of the Republic, required that each political party in a state issue ballots that contained the names of that party's slate and the electors pledged to them. A supporter cast his vote by depositing the ballot of his chosen party in a box. Some states required that voters sign the back of their ballot, but the overall allocation of ballots was not controlled by polling place officials, and stuffing the box was not impossible. It was also possible for officials in charge of the ballot boxes to discount or destroy ballots. And that, Lockwood claimed, is precisely what happened.

In a petition sent to Congress in January 1885, she wrote that she had run a campaign, gotten up electoral tickets in several states, and received votes in at least nine of the states, only to determine that "a large vote in Pennsylvania [was] not counted, simply dumped into the waste basket as false votes." In addition, she charged that many of the votes cast for her—totalling at least 4,711—in eight other states ("New Hampshire, 379 popular votes; New York, 1,336; Michigan, 374; Illinois, 1008; Iowa, 562; Maryland, 318; California, 734 and the entire Electoral vote of the State of Indiana") had been "fraudulently and illegally counted for the alleged majority candidate."

She asked that the members of Congress "refuse to receive the Electoral returns of the State of New York, or count them for the alleged majority candidate, for had the 1,336 votes which were polled in said state for your petitioner been counted for her, and not for the one Grover Cleveland, he would not have been awarded a majority of all the votes cast at said election in said state." (Cleveland's margin of votes in New York was 1,149). Lockwood also petitioned Congress for the electoral vote of Indiana, saying that at the last moment the electors there had switched their votes from Cleveland to her. In fact, they had not; it was all a prank by the good ol' boys of Indiana, but either she did not know this or, in the spirit of political theater, she played along with the mischief and used it to her advantage.

The electoral votes of New York (36) and Indiana (15) had been pivotal in the 1880 presidential race. With her petition and credible evidence, Lockwood—perhaps working behind the scenes with congressional Republicans—hoped to derail Cleveland's victory and keep him from becoming the first Democratic president since James Buchanan in 1856. She failed when the legislators ignored her petition, which had been referred to their Committee on Woman Suffrage. On February 11, Congress certified the election of New York governor Grover Cleveland as the 22nd president of the United States.

Subsequent interviews suggest that Lockwood was satisfied with the campaign, if not with the vote counting. The U.S. Constitution had betrayed women in the matter of suffrage, but it did not, as she said, prohibit women's speech and women's candidacies. As a celebration of the First Amendment, Lockwood's campaign was a great success. It served the interests of women (though it angered Susan B. Anthony), the candidate, and the country. Lockwood ran as an acknowledged contender and was allowed to speak her mind. American democracy was tested, and its performance did not disappoint her.

After the election, while maintaining her law practice, Lockwood embarked on the life of travel that she had long sought—and that she continued until her early eighties. Not unlike 21st-century politicians, she capitalized on the campaign by increasing her presence on the national lecture circuit; she even made at least one product endorsement (for a health tonic). She had long worked as a pension claims attorney, and, while traveling as a lecturer, she used the publicity surrounding her appearances to attract clients who needed help with applications and appeals. In 1888, the Equal Rights Party again nominated her as its presidential candidate. She ran a more modest campaign the second time around, but she still offered a broad domestic and foreign policy platform and argued that "equality of rights and privileges is but simple justice."

Lockwood always spoke proudly of her campaigns, which were important but not singular events in a life that would last 87 years. She was a woman of many talents and interests. Blocked from political office or a high-level government position because of her sex, she sought new realms after the campaigns of 1884 and 1888 where she might raise questions of public policy and advance the rights of women. Representing the Philadelphia-based Universal Peace Union, she increased her work on behalf of international peace and arbitration at meetings in the United States and Europe. She participated in an often-interlocking network of women's clubs and professional organizations. And she maintained a high profile in the women's suffrage movement, which struggled throughout the 1890s and the first two decades of the 20th century to create a winning strategy. In the spring of 1919, the House of Representatives and the Senate acted favorably on legislation to amend the Constitution to give women the right to vote; the proposed Nineteenth Amendment went out to the states in a ratification process that would not be completed until August 1920. But Belva Lockwood never got the right to vote. She died in May 1917.

Lockwood remains the only woman to have campaigned for the presidency right up to Election Day. (In 1964, Senator Margaret Chase Smith of Maine entered several Republican primaries and received 27 delegate votes; in 1972, Representative Shirley Chisholm of New York ran in a number of Democratic primaries and won 151 delegates.) In 1914 Lockwood, then 84 years old, was asked whether a woman would one day be president. The former candidate answered with levelheaded prescience and the merest echo of her former thunder: "I look to see women in the United States senate and the house of representatives. If [a woman] demonstrates that she is fitted to be president she will some day occupy the White House. It will be entirely on her own merits, however. No movement can place her there simply because she is a woman. It will come if she proves herself mentally fit for the position."

Critical Thinking

1. In what ways did Belva Lockwood put steps in place for a political career long before she ran for office?

2. What factors exist today that prevent many qualified people from running for the office of president of the United States?

Create Central

www.mhhe.com/createcentral

Internet References

National Archives
    www.archives.gov/publications/prologue/2005/spring/belva-lockwood-1.html

Biography.com
    www.biography.com/people/belva-lockwood-9384624

About.com
    http://womenshistory.about.com/od/publicofficials/tp/ran_for_president.htm

JILL NORGREN, a former Wilson Center fellow, is professor of government and legal studies at John Jay College and the University Graduate Center, City University of New York. She is writing the first full biography of Belva Lockwood, to be published in 2003. Copyright © 2002 by Jill Norgren.

Norgren, Jill. From *Wilson Quarterly*, August 2002, pp. 12–20. Copyright © 2002 by Jill Norgren. Reprinted by permission of the author.

Article

A Day to Remember: December 29, 1890

CHARLES PHILLIPS

Learning Outcomes

After reading this article, you will be able to:

- Explain how Ghost Dancing became the catalyst for the Wounded Knee Massacre.

- Discuss how assumptions on the part of both agents and Miles led to Sitting Bull's death and the surrender of the Sioux.

The intermittent war between the United States and the Plains Indians that stretched across some three decades after the Civil War came to an end on December 29, 1890, at the Pine Ridge Reservation in South Dakota. The events leading up to its final act—the Wounded Knee Massacre—had been building since the late 1880s, when the son of a Paiute shaman named Wovoka had first introduced a series of new beliefs and practices to the Indian reservations of the West.

Fundamentally peaceful, Wovoka's movement envisioned the coming of a new world populated solely by Indians living on the Great Plains where buffalo were again plentiful. Generation upon generation of Indians slain in combat would be reborn into this new world, and all—the living and the formerly dead—would live in bliss, peace and plenty. U.S. Indian authorities claimed that in the hands of the defeated and embittered leaders of the Teton Sioux—men like Short Bull, Kicking Bear and eventually Sitting Bull himself—Wovoka's peaceful religion had taken on the militant overtones of a millennial uprising. Wovoka had created a ceremony called the Ghost Dance to invoke the spirits of the dead and facilitate their resurrection. The Sioux apostles of the Ghost Dance purportedly preached that it would bring about a day of deliverance—a day when they were strong enough again to wage all-out war against the whites. They had fashioned "ghost shirts," which they claimed white bullets could not penetrate. In any case, Ghost Dancing had quickly become the rage of the Western reservations such as Pine Ridge and Rosebud.

"Indians are dancing in the snow and are wild and crazy," an anxious Pine Ridge Reservation agent, Daniel F. Royer, telegraphed Washington in November 1890. "We need protection and we need it now. The leaders should be arrested and confined at some military post until the matter is quieted, and this should be done at once."

The Indian Bureau in Washington quickly branded the Ghost Dancers "fomenters of disturbances" and ordered the Army to arrest them. On November 20, cavalry and infantry reinforcements arrived at the Pine Ridge and Rosebud reservations, but their arrival did not intimidate the Sioux followers of Short Bull and Kicking Bear. Quite the contrary, it seemed to galvanize their resolve. A former Indian agent, Dr. Valentine McGillycuddy, advised Washington to call off the troops: "I should let the dance continue. The coming of the troops has frightened the Indians. If the Seventh-Day Adventists prepare their ascension robes for the second coming of the savior, the United States Army is not put in motion to prevent them. Why should the Indians not have the same privilege? If the troops remain, trouble is sure to come."

About 3,000 Indians had assembled on a plateau at the northwest corner of Pine Ridge in a nearly impregnable area that came to be called the Stronghold. Brigadier General John R. Brooke, commander of the Pine Ridge area, quickly dispatched emissaries to talk with the "hostiles." Brooke's commanding officer, hard-nosed Civil War veteran and Indian fighter Maj. Gen. Nelson A. Miles, did not approve of such parleys. He saw in them evidence of indecision, and, furthermore, believed the Indians would interpret talk as a sign of weakness. Miles decided to prosecute the campaign against the Ghost Dancers personally and transferred his headquarters to Rapid City, S.D.

While Miles was preparing this move, Sitting Bull—the most influential of all Sioux leaders—began actively celebrating the Ghost Dance and its doctrine at the Standing Rock Reservation that straddled the North and South Dakota border. The agent in charge there, James McLaughlin, weighed his options. He did not want to repeat the hysterical mistake of his colleague at Pine Ridge by telegraphing for soldiers. He decided instead to use reservation policemen—Indians—to effect the quiet arrest and removal of the old chief.

Unfortunately, General Miles would not accept it. For Miles, the arrest of Sitting Bull would be a momentous act in a great drama. It should not be left to Indians, and it should not be done secretively; if anything, it called for showmanship. Miles contacted the greatest showman the West had ever known: William "Buffalo Bill" Cody. As everybody in the country probably knew—Buffalo Bill had seen to that himself—he and Sitting Bull were friends, or, at least, Sitting Bull held Cody in high regard. Sitting Bull, after all, had been a star attraction in

Buffalo Bill's Wild West Show. If any white man could convince Sitting Bull to step down, it would be Buffalo Bill.

Agent McLaughlin was aghast at the notion of carting in the likes of Buffalo Bill Cody to carry out what should be done quietly and without publicity. He was convinced that Buffalo Bill's presence would only inflame tempers and transform the proceedings into a circus or something worse. Accordingly, when Cody arrived at Standing Rock on November 27, McLaughlin saw to it that the celebrity was glad-handed and subtly shanghaied by the commanding officer of nearby Fort Yates, Lt. Col. William F. Drum. Drum entertained Cody all night at the officers' club while McLaughlin worked feverishly behind Miles' back to have the showman's authority rescinded. It was a desperate plan, and McLaughlin had missed one crucial fact: The man capable of drinking Buffalo Bill Cody under the table had yet to be born. Come morning, Cody was bright eyed and ready to set out for Sitting Bull's camp. McLaughlin hastily arranged for additional delays—just long enough for the arrival of orders canceling Cody's mission. The old entertainer seethed but boarded the next train back to Chicago. He had not set eyes on Sitting Bull.

But the situation at Pine Ridge Reservation was heating up. Word reached McLaughlin that Short Bull and Kicking Bear had formally invited Sitting Bull to leave Standing Rock and join them and their people at the Stronghold on the reservation. The time had come to act. McLaughlin dispatched 43 reservation policemen on December 15 to arrest Sitting Bull before he set out for Pine Ridge. Officers surrounded the old chief's cabin as Lieutenant Bull Head, Sergeant Red Tomahawk and Sergeant Shave Head entered it.

The chief awoke from slumber, and, seeing the men, asked, "What do you want here?"

"You are my prisoner," said Bull Head. "You must go to the agency."

Sitting Bull asked for a moment to put his clothes on. By the time the reservation police officers emerged with their prisoner, a crowd had gathered. A warrior named Catch-the-Bear called out, "Let us protect our chief!" and he leveled his rifle at Bull Head. He fired, hitting him in the side. The wounded policeman spun around with the force of the impact. His own weapon discharged, perhaps accidentally, perhaps intentionally. A round hit Sitting Bull, point blank, in the chest. Then policeman Red Tomahawk stepped into the fray and shot Sitting Bull in the back of the head.

McLaughlin had hoped to avoid a circus. As the reservation police officers scuffled with Sitting Bull's followers, the slain chief's horse—which Buffalo Bill had presented to him back when he was part of the Wild West Show—was apparently stimulated by the familiar noise of a crowd, and performed his repertoire of circus tricks.

Miles had not intended that Sitting Bull be killed, but it had happened, and the general accepted it as he would any casualty in the fog of war. Just now he had yet another Ghost Dancer to arrest, and that's where he focused his attention. Chief Big Foot was leader of the Miniconjou Sioux, who lived on the Cheyenne River. Unknown to Miles, Big Foot had recently renounced the Ghost Dance religion, convinced that it offered nothing more

than desperation and futility. Miles was also unaware that Chief Red Cloud, a Pine Ridge leader friendly to white authorities, had asked Big Foot to visit the reservation and use his influence to persuade the Stronghold party to surrender. All Miles knew—or thought he knew—was that Big Foot was on his way to the Stronghold, and it was up to the Army to prevent him from joining Short Bull, Kicking Bear and the others. Miles dispatched troops across the prairies and badlands to intercept any and all Miniconjous, especially Big Foot.

On December 28, 1890, a squadron of the 7th Cavalry located the chief and about 350 Miniconjous camped near a stream called Wounded Knee Creek. Big Foot was in his wagon, huddled against the bitter winter. He was feverish, sick with pneumonia. During the night of the 28th, additional soldiers moved into the area, so that by daybreak on the 29th, 500 soldiers, all under the command of Colonel James W. Forsyth, surrounded Big Foot's camp. Four Hotchkiss guns, small cannons capable of rapid fire, were aimed at the camp from the hills around it. The mission was to disarm the Indians and march them to the railroad, where a waiting train would remove them from the "zone of military operations."

As the Indians set up their tepees on the night of the 28th, they saw the Hotchkiss guns on the ridge above them. "That evening I noticed that they were erecting cannons up [there]," one of the Indians recalled, "also hauling up quite a lot of ammunition." The guns were ominously trained on the Indian camp. A bugle call woke up the Indians the next morning. The sky was clear and very blue as the soldiers entered the camp. Surrounded by bluecoats on horses, the Indians were ordered to assemble front and center. The soldiers demanded their weapons. Outraged, medicine man Yellow Bird began dancing, urging his people to don their sacred shirts. "The bullets will not hurt you," he told them. Next, Black Coyote, whom another Miniconjou called "a crazy man, a young man of very bad influence and in fact a nobody," raised his Winchester above his head as the troopers approached him to collect it. He began shouting that he had paid much money for the rifle, that it belonged to him and that nobody was going to take it. The soldiers, annoyed, crowded in on him and then began spinning him around and generally roughing him up.

A shot rang out. Instantly, troopers began firing indiscriminately at the Indians. "There were only about a hundred warriors," Black Elk reported. "And there were nearly five hundred soldiers." The warriors rushed to where they had piled their guns and knives. Hand-to-hand fights broke out, and some of the Indians started to run. Then the Indians heard the "awful roar" of the Hotchkiss guns. Shells rained down, almost a round a second, mowing down men, women and children—each shell carrying a two-pound charge, each exploding into thousands of fragments. The smoke was thick as fog; the Indians were running blind. Louise Weasel Bear said, "We tried to run, but they shot us like we were buffalo." Yellow Bird's son, just 4 years old at the time, saw his father shot through the head: "My father ran and fell down and the blood came out of his mouth." Those who fled the camp were chased down by soldiers. Rough Feathers' wife remembered: "I saw some of the other Indians running up the coulee so I ran with them, but the soldiers kept shooting at us and the bullets flew all around us. My father, my grandfather, my older brother and my younger brother were all killed. My son who was two years old was shot in the mouth that later caused his death." Black Elk added: "Dead and wounded women and children and little babies were scattered all along there where they had been trying to run away. The soldiers had followed them along the gulch, as they ran, and murdered them in there." In one of the gulches, "two little boys" who had found guns were lying in ambush, and "they had been killing soldiers all by themselves."

An hour later the guns stopped. The place was silent. Trails of blood trickled along the ground heading out of camp toward the gulches. Hundreds of Indians lay dead or dying on the frosted earth alongside a score of soldiers, hit mostly by the fire of their own Hotchkisses. Clouds filled the sky, and soon a heavy snow began to fall. Three days later, New Year's Day 1891, after the blizzard had passed, a burial party was sent to pull the frozen Indians from beneath the blanket of snow and dump them in a long ditch, "piled one upon another like so much cordwood, until the pit was full." Many of the corpses were naked because soldiers had stripped the ghost shirts from the dead to take home as souvenirs.

General Miles scrambled to distance himself from what public outrage there was over the massacre at Wounded Knee. He relieved Forsyth of command and convened a court of inquiry, which exonerated the colonel. Miles protested, but his immediate superior, General John M. Schofield, together with Secretary of War Redfield Proctor, eventually reinstated Forsyth's command.

In the meantime, the massacre at Wounded Knee caused "hostile" and "friendly" Sioux factions to unite. Even though Chief Red Cloud protested and repudiated his people's participation, on December 30, Sioux under Kicking Bear attacked the 7th Cavalry near the Pine Ridge Agency along White Clay Creek. At first it looked like it might be another Custer debacle, but black troopers of the 9th Cavalry rode to the rescue and drove off the Indians.

General Miles acted quickly to assemble a force of 8,000 troops, deploying them to surround the Sioux, who had returned to the Stronghold. This time Miles was careful, acting slowly and deliberately to contract the ring—almost gently—around the Indians. As he did this, he urged them to surrender, and he pledged good treatment. Whether anyone believed Miles or not, it had become clear that what the Ghost Dance foretold was a hope forlorn. The Sioux laid down their arms on January 15, 1891, bringing decades of war to an end. While lives were lost on both sides at White Clay Creek and in other skirmishes here and there, the massacre at Wounded Knee is generally considered to be the last major engagement of the Indian wars.

Critical Thinking

1. Agents Royer and McGillycuddy had opposite reactions to the Ghost Dancing. What cultural issues today present similar controversial viewpoints?

2. What can be learned from this tragedy that may prevent us from repeating such mistakes with other diverse cultural groups?

Create Central

www.mhhe.com/createcentral

Internet Resources

History.com
www.history.com/topics/wounded-knee

USHistory.org
www.ushistory.org/us/40e.asp

Encyclopedia of the Great Plains
http://plainshumanities.unl.edu/encyclopedia/doc/egp.war.056

PBS.org
www.pbs.org/weta/thewest/resources/archives/eight/wklakota.htm

Phillips, Charles. From *American History*, December 2005, pp. 16, 18, 20, 68. Copyright © 2005 by Weider History Group. Reprinted by permission.

Unit 2

UNIT

The Emergence of Modern America

The United States underwent enormous changes during the 1880s and 1890s. Millions of people continued to live on family farms or in small towns. Millions of others flocked to the cities in search of a better life. It was a period of much immigration, most of which landed in the poorer parts of cities. Most of these people came from Southern and Eastern Europe, and became known as the "new" immigration (previous waves had come from Ireland and Germany). Because their dress, their languages, and their customs differed so markedly from native born Americans, they were seen by many as inferior peoples. Some of these people had to endure incredible poverty and crowded conditions.

Small- and medium-sized businesses continued to exist, but corporations on a scale previously unheard of came to dominate the marketplace. Though the gross national product increased dramatically, the gap between rich and poor steadily widened. Corporate leaders, on the one hand, amassed unprecedented fortunes on which they paid no income taxes. Urban working families, on the other hand, often lived in unhealthy squalor even though all their members—including young children—worked in some shop or factory. Depressions, one beginning in 1873 and another in 1893, threw more people out of work than ever before. Farmers had to sell what they produced in markets that fluctuated widely, but had to purchase equipment and other necessities at prices often fixed by the large companies. Minority groups, such as Indians and blacks, continued

to suffer socially and economically through good times as well as bad.

Working conditions during this period often were abominable, and laborers usually had no choice but take whatever wages were offered. Indeed, for most companies labor was just another cost of doing business. It should be purchased as cheaply as possible and exploited to the utmost without regard for human consequences. Workers' efforts to create unions to give them some protection were vigorously fought, often with violence.

Conditions under which people had to work were miserable. In 1909 employees of the Triangle Waist Company had joined in a strike led by the Women's Trade Union League, calling for better pay, shorter hours, and improvement of miserable working conditions. They gained little from the strike, and the company management continued to impose the most degrading working conditions. A fire at Triangle in 1911 cost the lives of 146 women and brought to public attention the squalid and dangerous circumstances that existed there and in other sweatshops. Blocked exits and leaky fire hoses caused many unnecessary deaths.

The Wright Brothers are best known for successfully completing the first powered, manned flight at Kitty Hawk, North Carolina in 1903. That flight, however, covered only 872 feet and lasted 59 seconds. It was not until 1905 that they developed an airplane that could be "flown reliably over significant distances under the pilot's complete control." Crouch discusses the significance of this achievement.

Article

Where the Other Half Lived

The photographs of Jacob Riis confronted New Yorkers with the misery of Mulberry Bend—and helped to tear it down.

VERLYN KLINKENBORG

Learning Outcomes

After reading this article, you will be able to:

- Describe the circumstances that led to the transformation of Mulberry Bend from an overcrowded immigrant neighborhood to a park.

- Discuss the sociopolitical situation of immigrants in Mulberry Bend in the 19th century.

A block below Canal Street in lower Manhattan, just a few hundred yards from City Hall, there is a small urban oasis called Columbus Park. Early on a spring morning, the sun rises over an irregular threshold of rooftops to the east of the park—a southern spur of Chinatown—and picks out details on the courthouses and state office buildings looming over the west side of the park. Carved eagles stare impassively into the sunlight. Incised over a doorway on the Criminal Courts Building is a strangely senseless quotation from Justinian. "Justice is the firm and continuous desire to render to every man his due," it says, as though justice were mainly a matter of desire.

Beneath the sun's level rays high overhead, Columbus Park seems almost hollow somehow, and since it is open ground—open playground, to be accurate—it exposes the local topography. The land slopes downward from Bayard Street to Park Street, and downward from Mulberry to Baxter. At the north end of the park, temporary fencing surrounds an ornate shelter, the sole remnant of the park's original construction in 1897, now given over to pigeons. Plane trees lean inward around the perimeter of the asphalt ball field, where a tidy squadron of middle-aged and elderly Asian women stretches in unison, some clinging to the chain-link fence for balance. One man wields a tai chi sword to the sound of Chinese flutes from a boom box. A gull spirals down out of the sky, screeching the whole way. All around I can hear what this city calls early morning silence, an equidistant rumble that seems to begin a few blocks away.

I watch all of this, the tai chi, the stretching, the old men who have come to sit in the cool spring sunshine, the reinforced police vans delivering suspects to the court buildings just beyond it all, and as I watch I try to remember that Columbus Park was once Mulberry Bend. Mulberry Street still crooks to the southeast here, but the Bend proper is long gone. It was the most infamous slum in 19th-century New York, an immeasurable quantity of suffering compacted into 2.76 acres. On a bright April morning, it's hard to believe the Bend ever existed. But then such misery always inspires disbelief.

The Bend was ultimately torn down and a park built on its site in 1897 after unrelenting pressure from Jacob Riis, the Danish-born journalist and social reformer. In *How the Other Half Lives,* an early landmark in reforming literature whose title became a catchphrase, Riis provides some numbers for Mulberry Bend, which he obtained from the city's Registrar of Vital Statistics. In 1888, he wrote, 5,650 people lived on Baxter and Mulberry streets between Park and Bayard. If Riis means strictly the buildings within the Bend, as he almost certainly does, then the population density there was 2,047 persons per acre, nearly all of them recent immigrants.

By itself, that's an almost meaningless figure. But think of it this way: In Manhattan today, 1,537,195 persons live on 14,720 acres, a density of slightly more than 104 per acre. (In 1890, the average density within the built-up areas of Manhattan was about 115 per acre.) If Manhattan were peopled as thickly today as the Bend was in 1888, it would have more than 30 million inhabitants, an incomprehensible figure, the equivalent of nearly the whole of California jammed onto a single island. To put it another way, if the people who live in Manhattan today were packed as tightly as the immigrants in Mulberry Bend were, they could all live in Central Park with room to spare. But these are suppositions, imaginary numbers. The truly astonishing figure, of course, is 5,650 persons—actual human beings, every one of them—living in Mulberry Bend, among the highest population density ever recorded anywhere.

Now consider a final set of numbers: According to Riis and the city statistician, the death rate of children under five in Mulberry Bend was 140 per 1,000, roughly 1 out of 7. This is likely to be an underestimate. (Citywide, the number was just under 100 per 1,000 and falling fast.) Today, Mulberry Bend would rank between Lesotho and Tanzania in under-five mortality and worse than Haiti, Eritrea, Congo, and Bangladesh. Last year, the under-five mortality rate for the United States was 8 per 1,000, or 1 out of 125.

Numbers, even numbers as striking as these, do not do a good job of conveying horror. But when the horror is literally fleshed out, it begins to make an impression, as it did on Riis himself. After coming to America in 1870, at age 21, and enduring a vagrant existence for a few years, he found work at the *New York Tribune* as a police reporter and was sent to the office at 303 Mulberry Street, a few blocks north of the Bend and across from police headquarters. Night after night, Riis visited the Bend, sometimes in police company, often not, and he reported what he saw—especially the extreme overcrowding—to the Board of Health. "It did not make much of an impression," Riis wrote in *The Making of an American.* "These things rarely do, put in mere words."

So Riis put them in pictures. With a flashgun and a handheld camera, invented just a few years earlier, Riis began to take photographs of what he found in the Bend. "From them," he wrote, "there was no appeal." They made misery demonstrable in a way that nothing else had. No political or economic or cultural theory could justify the crowding his photographs document. There was no explaining away the sense of oppression and confinement they reveal. In picture after picture you see not only the poverty and the congestion of the Bend—the stale sweatshops and beer dives and five-cent lodging houses—but the emotional and psychological consequences of people living on top of each other.

Since the mid-20th century, Riis has been considered one of the founders of documentary photography. Over the years, his photographs of Mulberry Bend and other New York slums have become a part of the city's conscience. But his approach to photography was flatly utilitarian. "I had use for it," Riis wrote of the camera, "and beyond that I never went." Printing technology at the time meant that in books and articles his pictures had to be redrawn as wood engravings, considerably reducing their impact. The actual photographs were seen only in lantern slides accompanying his lectures. What mattered was not aesthetics but what the pictures showed. Riis had a similar use for words and statistics. They were merely tools to persuade New Yorkers to witness what was right in front of their eyes.

In one of his many articles on tenement housing, Riis printed a map of the Bend drawn from overhead, a silhouette showing the proportion of open space to buildings. Looking at that map is like looking at an old-fashioned diagram of a cell, a hieroglyphic of dark and light. It's hard to know what to call the spaces depicted by the white areas on Riis's map. *Yard* is too pastoral and *air shaft* too hygienic. Riis calls them "courts" and "alleys," but even those words are too generous. What the white spaces really portray are outdoor places where only a single layer of humans could live, many of them homeless children who clustered in external stairwells and on basement steps. In the tenements of the Bend—three, four, and five stories each—families and solitary lodgers, who paid five cents apiece for floor space, crowded together in airless cubicles. "In

a room not thirteen feet either way," Riis wrote of one midnight encounter, "slept twelve men and women, two or three in bunks set in a sort of alcove, the rest on the floor."

For reformers, Riis included, the trouble with the Bend wasn't merely the profits it returned to slumlords and city politicians, nor was it just the high rents that forced tenants to sublet floor space to strangers. The problem was also how to portray the Bend in a way that conveyed its contagious force, the absence of basic sanitation, of clean water and fresh air, the presence of disease, corruption, and crime, the enervation and despair. It was, for Riis, the problem of representing an unrepresentable level of defilement. The power of his silhouette map, for instance, is flawed by its white margins, which falsely imply that conditions improved across the street, when, in fact, the entire Sixth Ward was cramped and impoverished. Even the grimmest of Riis's photographs show only a few people, at most, in the back alleys and basement dives. Powerful as they are, these pictures fail to convey the simple tonnage of human flesh in those dead-end blocks.

But the problem of Mulberry Bend was also how to interpret it. On a bright spring morning in the 1880s or early 1890s, a New Yorker—curiosity aroused, perhaps, by one of Riis's articles—might have strolled over to Mulberry or Baxter Street to see for himself. What he found there would depend on his frame of mind. It might have been, as photographs suggest, a bustling streetfront crowded with people going rather shabbily about the ordinary sorts of business, much as they might in other neighborhoods. Such a New Yorker—disinclined to push through to the dark inner rooms a few flights up or to the dismal courts and alleys behind or to the dank beer dives below—might conclude that perhaps Riis had exaggerated and that perhaps all there was to see here was a people, immigrants nearly all of them, who were insufficiently virtuous or cleanly or hardworking or American. It would be possible for such a person to blame Mulberry Bend on the very people who were its victims. But when the tenements were condemned and their inhabitants moved into decent housing, particularly in Harlem, they blended imperceptibly into the fabric of the city.

Riis has been faulted for his glib descriptive use of racial and ethnic stereotypes, a convention of his time that sounds raw and coarse to us now. In his defense, he came to understand that the power of a place like Mulberry Bend was enough to corrupt its residents, no matter who they were, as it had the Irish, and then the Italians who were their successors in the Bend. No iniquity within the Bend was as great, to Riis, as the political and financial iniquity that sustained the tenements there.

But the tragedy of Mulberry Bend isn't only that it came to exist and, once in existence, to be tolerated. It was also that when the city finally tore down the Bend and at last built the park that Calvert Vaux had designed for the site, a kind of forgetfulness descended. A New Yorker coming to the newly built Mulberry Bend Park in 1897, or to its renaming in 1911, or merely to watch the sun rise on a bright spring morning in 2001, might never know that there had been such a place as the Bend. The park that stands in its place is some kind of redemption, but without memory no redemption is ever complete. And without action of the kind that Riis undertook, justice remains only a matter of desire.

Critical Thinking

1. Riis used new technology—photography—to illustrate his point in a way not seen before. Is there a similar way in which today's technology is being used to open people's minds to understanding complex issues? Explain.

2. What does the author mean by "without memory, no redemption is ever complete"? Do you agree? Why or why not?

Create Central

www.mhhe.com/createcentral

Internet References

Virginia.edu

http://xroads.virginia.edu/~ma01/davis/photography/riis/reporter.html

wikipedia.org

http://en.wikipedia.org/wiki/Mulberry_Bend

nytimes.com

http://topics.nytimes.com/topics/reference/timestopics/people/r/jacob_riis/index.html

Article   Prepared by: Larry Madaras, *Howard Community College*

What Happened at Haymarket?

JOHN J. MILLER

Learning Outcomes

After reading this article, you will be able to:

- Describe the conventional view of the Haymarket Square Riot of May 4, 1886.
- Describe the evidence Professor Timothy Messer-Kruse uncovered to challenge the traditional view of the riot.

TIMOTHY MESSER-KRUSE doesn't remember her name, but the question she asked in his college classroom a dozen years ago changed his career—and now it may revolutionize everything historians thought they knew about a hallowed event in the imagination of the American Left. "In my courses on labor history, I always devoted a full lecture to Haymarket," says Messer-Kruse, referring to what happened in Chicago on the night of May 4, 1886. He would describe how a gathering of anarchists near Haymarket Square turned into a fatal bombing and riot. Although police never arrested the bomb-thrower, they went on to tyrannize radical groups throughout the city, in a crack-down that is often called America's first Red Scare. Eight men were convicted of aiding and abetting murder. Four died at the end of a hangman's noose. Today, history books portray them as the innocent victims of a sham trial: They are labor-movement martyrs who sought modest reforms in the face of ruthless robber-baron capitalism.

As Messer-Kruse recounted this familiar tale to his students at the University of Toledo in 2001, a woman raised her hand. "Professor," she asked, "if what it says in our textbook is true, that there was 'no evidence whatsoever connecting them with the bombing,' then what did they talk about in the courtroom for six weeks?"

The question stumped Messer-Kruse. "It had not occurred to me before," he says. He muttered a few words about lousy evidence and paid witnesses. "But I didn't really know," he recalls. "I told her I'd look it up." As he checked out the standard sources, he failed to find good answers. The semester ended and the student moved on, but her question haunted him. "My interest grew into an obsession." As Messer-Kruse began to look more closely, he started to wonder if the true story of Haymarket was fundamentally different from the version he and just about everybody else had been told.

The 49-year-old Messer-Kruse now teaches at Bowling Green State University in Ohio. His father was a minister, so he moved around a lot as a kid, eventually winding up in Oshkosh, Wis., where he graduated from high school. After that came the University of Wisconsin–Madison, but he needed nearly seven years to earn his undergraduate degree because he kept taking time off to make money as a taxi driver. These days, he prefers jogging to driving, and he has qualified to compete in the Boston Marathon this April. He posts running times on his office door. Messer-Kruse is in many ways an ordinary academic liberal. He mentions anti-poverty activist Michael Harrington as an inspiration, calls himself a "social democrat," and says he voted twice for Barack Obama.

In 1986, when he was a senior in Madison, a buddy suggested that they drive down to Chicago for the weekend. "I just wanted to hang out with friends," says Messer-Kruse. His companion also proposed a side trip to a cemetery, where labor activists planned to commemorate the centenary of the Haymarket protest. "I had been aware of Haymarket in passing," says Messer-Kruse. "But I didn't have any special knowledge or appreciation." He doesn't remember much about the day, which featured a roster of speakers including populist author Studs Terkel. Yet the number of young people in attendance and their passion for working-class causes affected him. "The whole day made a deep impression," he says. It stayed with him as he entered graduate school and specialized in labor history. A framed poster for the event now decorates the wall of his cramped office at Bowling Green. "Partly because of that experience, I became a labor historian," he says. Haymarket lit a fire in the mind of the young scholar, but Messer-Kruse devoted his doctoral dissertation to a completely different topic. "I assumed that there wasn't anything new to research or write about Haymarket," he says.

He also accepted a version of events that had been written into the history books long ago. The details vary, but the broad strokes of the story are the same. A group of workers, most of them German-speaking immigrants, assembled near Haymarket Square to appeal for an eight-hour workday. Many called themselves anarchists, but they were mainly a peace-loving bunch who simply wanted to improve their wretched conditions. As police arrived to bust up the crowd, someone tossed a bomb. No one knows who did it—perhaps an anarchist agitator or, as Howard Zinn suggests in *A People's History of the United*

States, perhaps "an agent of the police, an *agent provocateur.*" Regardless of the culprit's identity, police panicked and opened fire, accidentally killing several of their fellow officers. The incident left seven cops and a handful of protesters dead. In a fit of xenophobic hysteria, authorities rounded up political radicals, showing little regard for civil rights or criminal evidence. At a trial with hostile jurors and a biased judge, eight defendants who could not be connected to the bombing were nevertheless declared guilty. Seven received death sentences. One committed suicide in prison. Four went to the gallows. The other three eventually were pardoned.

Ever since, Haymarket has occupied a central place in progressive lore. The international labor movement honors May Day as its holiday in part because of its proximity on the calendar to Haymarket's anniversary. In the United States, Haymarket ranks alongside the cases of Sacco and Vanzetti, Alger Hiss, and the Rosenbergs as a fable of anti-radical persecution. Well into the 20th century, its notoriety provoked violent rage. In 1969, Bill Ayers and an accomplice from the Weather Underground engaged in their own Haymarket terror, bombing a statue that honored the fallen policemen of 1886. "This is too good—it's us against the pigs, a medieval contest of good and evil," wrote Ayers of the affair in his memoir, *Fugitive Days.*

The Haymarket legend became more than a preoccupation of red-diaper babies. It entered mainstream education. A common college textbook—*America: A Concise History,* by James A. Henretta and David Brody—says the Haymarket defendants were "victims of one of the great miscarriages of American justice." Another textbook—*American Stories,* whose authors include best-selling historian H. W. Brands—claims that there was "no evidence of their guilt." Worst of all, the episode was thought to have exposed the nation's highest ideals as gross hypocrisies: "The Haymarket case challenged, like no other episode in the nineteenth century, the image of the United States as a classless society with liberty and justice for all," wrote James Green in *Death in the Haymarket,* a popular account published in 2006.

"I believed all of this," says Messer-Kruse. "I had drunk the Kool-Aid." Then his student asked her vexing question: If the trial was a sham, what did everyone talk about for week after week? Driven by curiosity, Messer-Kruse wanted to find out.

His first step was to consult the conventional scholarship—works published by labor historians Henry David in 1936 and Paul Avrich in 1984. "I thought it would be easy to learn what happened," he says. Yet neither account satisfied him. Then the Internet came to the rescue: Messer-Kruse discovered that the Library of Congress and the Chicago Historical Society had just digitized a large collection of material on Haymarket, including a transcript of the trial. He slogged through thousands of pages, consulting other primary documents to gain a sharper picture of what lay buried in the historical record. Along the way, he realized that earlier researchers had not consulted this

transcript. Instead, they had relied on an abstract of the trial prepared by defense lawyers, drawing their conclusions from a flamboyantly prejudiced account of the bombing and its aftermath. "The best source had been hiding in plain sight," says Messer-Kruse.

Here was a scholar's dream: untapped evidence about a landmark moment in history. Messer-Kruse looked at Haymarket from brand-new angles, embarking on the *CSI: Haymarket* phase of his research. The trial transcript made him question the claim that friendly fire was at least as deadly to the police as the actual bomb, so he consulted old maps and built a scale-model diorama in his basement. Cardboard cutouts represented buildings. Plastic green soldiers stood in for police and protesters. One time, his wife came down the steps to find him fixated on his miniature scene. "A beautiful mind," she said before turning around and heading back up, in an allusion to the then-current movie about John Nash, a brilliant professor who sinks into madness. "I was just trying to understand the evidence," says Messer-Kruse.

This unusual approach seems to have paid off: Messer-Kruse believes that although it's impossible to rule out lethal friendly fire, several policemen were probably shot by armed protesters—a fact that chips away at the belief that the anarchists were peaceful. Messer-Kruse also worked with chemists to study the forensic remains of Haymarket's violence. He determined that the original trial experts brought in to study the bomb and bullet fragments had done their jobs well. He furthermore concluded that one of the Haymarket defendants—Louis Lingg, who killed himself before authorities could carry out his death sentence—almost certainly built the bomb.

These findings made their way into Messer-Kruse's first formal work of scholarship on Haymarket: a 2005 paper printed in *Labor,* a top academic journal. Around the same time, Messer-Kruse organized a symposium on his work at an annual labor-history conference at Wayne State University, in Detroit. "I expected skepticism," he says. "Instead, I encountered utter and complete denial of the evidence." The standing-room-only crowd refused to question what had become an article of faith in left-wing mythology. "They seemed to think that our purpose as historians was to celebrate Haymarket, not to study it or challenge it," he says. The most provocative attack came a year later, when Bryan D. Palmer of Trent University, in Canada, published a rebuttal to Messer-Kruse. The Haymarket anarchists, he wrote, were "humane, gentle, kindly souls." Evildoers oppressed them: "The state, the judiciary, and the capitalist class had blood on their hands in 1886–87," he wrote. Those of us who "drink of this old wine adorned with the new label of Messer-Kruse . . . may end up with the sickly sweet repugnance of blood on our lips."

These fighting words convinced Messer-Kruse that he needed to continue his work. He envisioned a magnum opus on Haymarket—a large book that would ask hard questions and exploit new sources. "A lot of labor historians think they must be deeply engaged with the prospects and agenda of labor unions," says Messer-Kruse. "But we have an obligation to represent as best we can the objective reality of the past."

For several years, Messer-Kruse toiled away. He produced a thick manuscript, only to find that publishers didn't want a big book on the subject. They feared a commercial flop. So he broke it into three parts, delivering his reinterpretation of Haymarket in a long academic paper and two peer-reviewed books: *The Trial of the Haymarket Anarchists,* published by Palgrave-Macmillan in 2011, and *The Haymarket Conspiracy,* published by the University of Illinois Press last summer.

"My aim is not to prove that the police and the courts were right and the anarchists and their supporters were wrong," writes Messer-Kruse in the introduction to *Trial.* Yet the sum of his work appears to do just that. He shows that Chicago's anarchists belonged to an international network of left-wing militants who believed that only bloodshed could bring social change. They plotted to incite violence at Haymarket. The person who threw the bomb was almost certainly Rudolph Schnaubelt, a close confederate of the defendants. He was never brought to justice because he fled Chicago and vanished from history, though Messer-Kruse suggests that he lived out his days as a farm-equipment salesman in Buenos Aires. The eight men who were arrested received a fair trial by the standards of the day. Finally, most of the blame for their being found guilty lies with a defense team that seemed more committed to political theater than to providing competent legal counsel.

Once again, Messer-Kruse encountered the closed-minded hostility that he had experienced at the Wayne State conference. When a press release for *The Haymarket Conspiracy* appeared on an online discussion board for labor historians in August, within days of Mitt Romney's acceptance of the Republican presidential nomination, Norman Markowitz of Rutgers University delivered this deep thought: "Perhaps Romney will put the book on his reading list." *Dissent,* a left-wing quarterly, attacked Messer-Kruse's work, and most mainstream publications have ignored it. Messer-Kruse even battled Wikipedia editors when he tried to update the entry for Haymarket.

Yet Messer-Kruse is also starting to receive a strange new respect. Last May, the Labadie Collection—the nation's premier archive of anarchist documents, housed at the University of Michigan—asked Messer-Kruse to deliver the keynote address at its centennial exhibit. In August, the academic journal *Labor History* picked *Trial* as its book of the year. In the fall, *Labor,* the scholarly periodical, published a symposium on his work. Colleagues offered criticism, but they also praised his "careful," "well-argued," and "impressively nuanced" scholarship. The January 2013 issue of *Choice,* the professional magazine for college librarians, listed *Trial* as an outstanding academic title.

Even the best revisionist scholarship can take a long time to influence the way teachers and schools treat history, especially when the authors of leading textbooks show little interest in examining new evidence. "I haven't read Messer-Kruse's book and so can't comment," says H. W. Brands. Bryan Palmer, who wrote the blistering "blood on our lips" attack in 2006, says he hasn't read the new material. James Green, author of *Death in the Haymarket,* also demurs.

Yet change is coming, according to Eric Arnesen, a labor historian at George Washington University. "This is going to make people pause when they get to the Haymarket part of their courses," he says. "They won't be able to use their old lecture notes anymore. They'll have to bring up Timothy Messer-Kruse."

Critical Thinking

1. Compare the traditional view of the Haymarket Square Riot with the revisionist view of Professor Messer-Kruse.
2. Explain why pro-labor historians and union supporters are unwilling to challenge the traditional view.
3. Evaluate the evidence Messer-Kruse uses to establish his case.

Create Central

www.mhhe.com/createcentral

Internet References

The Chicago Historical Society contains newspaper articles and transcripts of the trial of the Haymarket Square defendants.
   http://chicagohs.org

International Institute of Social History. This site focuses on business and labor history.
   www.socialhistory.org

World Wide Web Virtual Library. This site focuses on labor and business history. As an index site, this is a good place to start exploring these two vast topics.
   www.iisg.nl/~w3vl

JOHN J. MILLER is a senior editor and national correspondent for *National Review.*

Article   Prepared by: Larry Madaras, *Howard Community College*

Father of the Forests (Gifford Pinchot)

T. H. WATKINS

Learning Outcomes

After reading this article, you will be able to:

- Understand why the conservation movement began in the late nineteenth century.

- Distinguish between the preservationists, conservationists, and the utilitarian conservationists.

- Evaluate the successes and failures of Chief Forester Gifford Pinchot as a utilitarian conservationist.

- Evaluate the political successes and failures of Pinchot in his relationships with Presidents Roosevelt and Taft.

L ike most public officials, Gov. Gifford Pinchot of Pennsylvania could not answer all his mail personally. Much of it had to be left to aides, but not all of these realized the character of their boss. When a citizen wrote in 1931 to complain angrily about one of the governor's appointments, Pinchot was not pleased to find the following prepared for his signature: "I am somewhat surprised at the tone of your letter. . . . It has been my aim since I became Governor to select the best possible person for each position. . . . I hope time will convince you how greatly you have erred."

The governor was not given to such mewlings and forthwith composed his own letter: "Either you are totally out of touch with public sentiment, or you decline to believe what you hear. . . . To say that I was not attempting to do right when I made these appointments is nonsense. I was doing the best I knew how, and my confidence that I did so is by no means impaired by your letter." That was more like it—and more like the man too.

Gifford Pinchot passed through nearly six decades of American public life like a Jeremiah, the flames of certitude seeming to dance behind his dark eyes. "Gifford Pinchot is a dear," his good friend and mentor Theodore Roosevelt once said of him, "but he is a fanatic, with an element of hardness and narrowness in his temperament, and an extremist."

The complaint was legitimate, but the zealot in question also was the living expression of an idea shared by much of an entire generation (indeed, shared by Roosevelt himself): the conviction that men and women could take hold of their government and shape it to great ends, great deeds, lifting all elements of American life to new levels of probity, grace, freedom, and prosperity. The urge was not entirely selfless; the acquisition and exercise of power have gratifications to which Pinchot and his kind were by no means immune. But at the forefront was a solemn and utterly earnest desire that the lot of humanity should be bettered by the work of those who were equipped by circumstance, talent, and training to change the world. It had something to do with duty and integrity and honesty, and if it was often marred by arrogance, at its best it was just as often touched by compassion.

And the world, in fact, was changed.

I have . . . been a Governor, every now and then, but I am a forester all the time—have been, and shall be, all my working life." Gifford Pinchot made this pronouncement in a speech not long before his death at the age of eighty-one, and repeated it in *Breaking New Ground,* his account of the early years of the conservation movement and his considerable place in it. It was true enough, but it could just as legitimately be said of him that he had been a forester every now and then but was a politician, had been and would be, all his working life.

It could also be said that it was forestry that taught him his politics. Pinchot was born on August 11, 1865, into the sort of environment that would normally have pointed him in the direction of nothing more exotic than law or one of the other gentlemanly persuasions. His father, James, a self-made man of the classic stripe, had acquired so much money as a dry goods merchant in New York City that he had been able to retire to the pursuit of good works at the age of forty-four. His mother, Mary, was the daughter of Amos Eno, a Manhattan real estate tycoon whose Fifth Avenue Hotel was so valuable a property that his estate was able to sell it after his death for the staggering figure of $7,250,000.

The Pinchots figured prominently, if sedately, in society and traveled ambitiously in England and on the Continent. Gifford, his younger brother, Amos, and their sister, Antoinette, all grew up able to speak French and snatches of German at early ages, and Antoinette, in fact, would become Lady Johnstone, wife of the British consul in Copenhagen.

Altogether it seemed an unlikely background for a man who was to spend much of his adult life with trees. There was not at the time a single American-born man and precious few men of any nationality in this country practicing anything that could remotely be described as forestry. Nevertheless, "How would you like to be a forester?" Pinchot's father asked him in the summer of 1885, as the young man prepared to enter Yale. "It was an amazing question for that day and generation," he remembered, "how amazing I didn't begin to understand at the time." In his travels the elder Pinchot had become an admirer of the kind of scientific forestry practiced in France, Germany, and Switzerland and had even written a few articles on the subject.

The son proved open to his father's enthusiasm. From childhood Pinchot had been active in the outdoors, fond of hiking, camping, and, especially trout fishing. Since there was nowhere yet in the United States to study his chosen profession, after graduating from Yale he took himself back to Europe, where for more than a year he studied forest management at the French Forestry School in Nancy and put in a month of fieldwork under Forstmeister ("Chief Forester") Ulrich Meister in the city forest of Zurich, Switzerland.

Back in this country he was hired by George W. Vanderbilt in 1892 to manage the five-thousand-acre forest on his Biltmore estate in North Carolina, a ragged patchwork of abused lands purchased from numerous individual farmers. While nursing this wrecked acreage back to health, the young forester persuaded Vanderbilt to expand his holdings by an additional one hundred thousand acres of nearly untouched forest land outside the estate. This new enterprise became known as the Pisgah Forest, and it was there in 1895 that Pinchot introduced what were almost certainly the first scientific logging operations ever undertaken in this country.

By then the young man had made a secure reputation in the field; indeed, he *was* the field. In December 1893 he opened an office in Manhattan as a "consulting forester." Over the next several years, while continuing his work for Vanderbilt in North Carolina, he provided advice and research work on forest lands in Michigan, Pennsylvania, and New York State—including the six-million-acre Adirondack Park and Forest Preserve, established in 1895 as the largest state-owned park in the nation. He could—and doubtless did—take satisfaction from a description given of him by a newspaper columnist as early as 1892: "Contrast the career of this Yale graduate with that of certain young men of Gotham who flatten their noses against club windows in the morning, and soften their brains with gossip, champagne and the unmentionables at other periods of the day and night."

There was nothing soft in this graduate's brain, and since he lived most of his time at home with his mother and father, there was even less that could be called unmentionable in his behavior or experience (his first fiancée died in 1894, an event that so devastated him he did not marry until twenty years later, after his mother's own death). By the turn of the century he was fully equipped by temperament and experience to assume the task that would soon be given him: the intelligent management of more forest land than had ever been placed in the control of any single individual.

It would be difficult to find a more convenient symbol for the dark side of American enterprise than the state of the nation's forest lands in the last quarter of the nineteenth century. Restrained only by the dictates of the marketplace, the timber industry had enjoyed a free hand for generations, and the

wreckage was considerable. Most of the best forest land east of the Mississippi had long since been logged out—sometimes twice over—and while generally humid conditions had allowed some of the land to recover in second and third growth, erosion had permanently scarred many areas. Unimpeded runoff during seasonal rains had caused such ghastly floods as that leading to the destruction of Johnstown, Pennsylvania, in 1889.

The land of the Mississippi and Ohio valleys was almost entirely privately owned; west of the Mississippi most of the land belonged to the nation. It was called the public domain, its steward was the federal government, as represented by the General Land Office, and for years it had been hostage to the careless enthusiasm of a tradition that looked upon land as a commodity to be sold or an opportunity to be exploited, not a resource to be husbanded. About two hundred million acres of this federal land were forested, and much of it, too, had been systematically mutilated. In addition to legitimate timber companies that consistently misused the various land laws by clear-cutting entire claims without even bothering to remain around long enough to establish final title, many "tramp" lumbermen simply marched men, mules, oxen, and sometimes donkey engines onto an attractive (and vacant) tract of public forest land, stripped it, and moved out, knowing full well that apprehension and prosecution were simply beyond the means or interest of the understaffed, over-committed, and largely corrupt General Land Office. As early as 1866 such instances of cheerful plunder had gutted so many forests of the public domain that the surveyors general of both Washington Territory and Colorado Territory earnestly recommended to the General Land Office that the forest lands in their districts be sold immediately, while there was something left to sell.

The forests were not sold, nor did they vanish entirely, but they did remain vulnerable to regular depredation. It was not until 1891 and passage of an obscure legislative rider called the Forest Reserve Clause that the slowly growing reform element in the executive branch was enabled to do anything about it. Armed with the power of this law, President Benjamin Harrison withdrew thirteen million acres of public forest land in the West from uses that would have been permitted by any of the plethora of lenient land laws then on the books, and at the end of his second term, President Grover Cleveland added another twenty-one million acres. Since there was virtually no enforcement of the new law, however, withdrawal provided little protection from illegal use; at the same time, it specifically disallowed legitimate use of public timber and grasslands. In response to the howl that arose in the West and to give some semblance of protection and managed use, Congress passed the Forest Organic Act of June 1897, which stipulated that the forest reserves were intended "to improve and protect the forest . . . for the purpose of securing favorable conditions of water flow, and to furnish a continuous supply of timber for the use and necessities of citizens of the United States."

Gifford Pinchot, the young "consulting forester," was the author of much of the language of the act. In the summer of 1896 he had distinguished himself as the secretary of the National Forest Commission, a body formed by President Cleveland to investigate conditions in the nation's public forests and to recommend action for their proper use and protection, and it was the commission that had put forth the need for an organic act. No one knew more about American forests than Pinchot did, and he seemed the only logical choice to head the Department of Agriculture's Forestry Division when the position of director fell vacant in May 1898.

On the face of it, Pinchot's new post was less than prestigious. The Forestry Division was housed in two rooms of the old red-brick Agriculture Building on the south side of the Mall in Washington, D.C. It enjoyed a total of eleven employees and an annual appropriation of $28,500. And since the forest reserves remained under the jurisdiction of the Interior Department, the Forestry Division had little to do beyond advising private landowners on the proper management of their wood lots and forests. This was anathema to an activist like Pinchot, and he was soon honing the skills that would make him one of the most persistent and effective lobbyists who ever prowled the cloakrooms and cubbyholes of Congress.

His ambition was not a small one: He wanted nothing less than to get the forest reserves transferred to Agriculture and placed under his care in the Forestry Division and then to build the division into the first effective agency for the management and conservation of public lands in the history of the nation. It did not hurt his chances when he became intimate with another early American conservationist— Theodore Roosevelt.

Roosevelt had spent much of his youth killing and stuffing birds and was to spend much of his adult life shooting bigger and better animals, which he had other people stuff for him. Nevertheless, when he assumed the Presidency in 1901, he became the first Chief Executive to play an informed and active role in the conservation movement. With George Bird Grinnell (editor of *Forest and Stream* magazine) he had been a cofounder of the Boone and Crockett Club, an exclusive gathering of conservation-minded hook-and-bullet men whose influence had gone a long way toward preserving the wildlife in Yellowstone National Park and toward slowing the wholesale commercial slaughter that had exterminated the passenger pigeon and was well on its way toward wiping out several other species. During his Presidency Roosevelt would establish the first federal wildlife refuges, support the expansion of the national park system, back passage of the Reclamation Act of 1902, and use the full power of the Antiquities Act of 1906 to designate no fewer than eighteen national monuments, including the Grand Canyon, in Arizona.

Nor was Roosevelt indifferent to forests. "The American had but one thought about a tree," he once wrote, "and that was to cut it down." While governor of New York, he had sought forestry advice from Pinchot, and they had hit it off from the start. "There has been a peculiar intimacy between you and Jim [James R. Garfield, his Secretary of the Interior] and me," Roosevelt wrote Pinchot in later years, "because all three of us have worked for the same causes, have dreamed the same dreams, have felt a substantial identity of purpose as regards many of what we three deemed the most vital problems of today." Pinchot's own feelings bordered on adulation, although Roosevelt maintained that the younger man admired his predatory instincts above all else. "He thinks," he told Archie Butt, his personal assistant, "that if we were cast away somewhere together and we were both

hungry, I would kill him and eat him, *and,*" he had added with that carnivore's grin of his, "*I would, too.*"

The two men combined almost immediately in an effort to get the forest reserves into Pinchot's care. The public lands committees of both the House and Senate, however, were dominated by Westerners, many of whom had vested interests in the status quo, and it took more than three years of public campaigning and artful cajolery, Roosevelt himself bringing the full weight of the Presidency to bear on the point, before Pinchot was given his heart's desire: passage of the Forest Transfer Act, on February 1, 1905. In addition to bringing over the forests— which now totaled more than sixty-three million acres—the new law provided for the charging of fees for cutting timber and grazing cattle and sheep, and this was followed by the Agricultural Appropriation Act of March 3, a section of which gave federal foresters "authority to make arrests for the violation of laws and regulations relating to the forest reserves. . . ."

The government was now in the tree business with a vengeance. Shortly the name of the reserves was changed to that of national forests, the Forestry Division to that of the U.S. Forest Service, and Gifford Pinchot was solidly in place as the nation's first chief forester, a position he would hold officially only until his resignation in 1910 but would hold in his heart for the rest of his life.

With his President's blessing, Pinchot crafted the young agency into a public body whose dedication to the ideal of service to the public was nearly unique for its time (or our own, for that matter). It came directly out of Pinchot's own convictions. "It is the first duty of a public officer to obey the law," he wrote in *The Fight for Conservation,* in 1910. "But it is his second duty, and a close second, to do everything the law will let him do for the public good. . . ."

It was an elite corps that Pinchot created, built on merit and merit alone, one in which both competence and stupidity were swiftly rewarded—and little went unnoticed by the chief forester ("I found him all tangled up," Pinchot wrote to a lieutenant about one hapless employee, "and generally making an Ass of himself, with splendid success"). William R. Greeley, one of the twenty-five hundred foresters who served under Pinchot (and who later became chief forester himself), caught the spirit of Pinchot's influence precisely: "He made us . . . feel like soldiers in a patriotic cause."

The system this exemplary body of men administered was carefully structured by the chief forester. Individual forests were divided up into management units, each with its own ranger or ranger force, and administrative headquarters were established in the six districts across the West where most of the forests were grouped, from Missoula, Montana, to Portland, Oregon. Pinchot gave his district supervisors a great deal of autonomy and encouraged them to give their rangers similarly loose reins in the field—whether selecting stands of harvestable trees, supervising a timber sale, regulating the number of cows or sheep that might be allowed on a piece of grazing land, or fighting fires. The first step in proper administration, he said, "was to find the right man and see that he understood the scope and limits of his work, and just what was expected of him"; then "the next step was to give him his head and let him use it."

The chief forester did not remain aloof. He was given to unannounced field trips, poking his prominent nose into every nook and cranny of the system to see what was what, and he maintained a body of field inspectors who reported regularly to him and him alone. "To get results," he remembered, "we had to revise, common-sensitize, and make alive the whole attitude and action of the men who had learned the Land Office way of handling the Reserves. . . . We had to drive out red tape with intelligence, and unite the office and the field. Next . . . we had to bring about a fundamental change in the attitude and action of the men who lived in or near the Reserves and used them. We had to get their cooperation by earning their respect."

That respect did not come easily. Those individuals and corporations that had become accustomed to unrestricted access to Western resources did not remain silent during all this, nor did their politicians. At one point in 1908 the *Rocky Mountain News* featured a cartoon showing "Czar Pinchot and His Cossack Rangers." Others declared that the Forest Service was subverting the pioneering instinct that had built the country. "While these chiefs of the Bureau of Forestry sit within their marble halls," Sen. Charles W. Fulton of Oregon intoned in 1907, "and theorize and dream of waters conserved, forests and streams protected and preserved throughout the ages and the ages, the lowly pioneer is climbing the mountain side where he will erect his humble cabin, and within the shadow of the whispering pines and the lofty firs of the forest engage in the laborious work of carving out for himself and his loved ones a home and a dwelling place."

Despite such cavils, by the time Roosevelt left office in March 1909, the national forest system had been enlarged to 148 million acres, and the Forest Service had become one of the most respected government services in the nation—reason enough for the historian M. Nelson McGeary's encomium of 1960: "Had there been no Pinchot to build the U.S. Forest Service into an exceptionally effective agency, it would hardly have been possible to report in 1957 that 'most' of the big lumber operators had adopted forestry as a policy; or that the growth of saw timber has almost caught up with the rate of drain on forest resources from cutting, fire, and natural losses. . . ."

Nor, it is safe to say, would there have been much left of the forests themselves. The principles Pinchot put to work would inform the management of the public lands throughout most of the twentieth century and become one of the roots of the sensibility we call environmentalism. It was called conservation then, and Pinchot always claimed that he was the first to put that use upon the word. "Conservation," he wrote, "means the wise use of the earth and its resources for the lasting good of men. Conservation is the foresighted utilization, preservation, and/or renewal of forests, waters, lands, and minerals, for the greatest good of the greatest number for the longest time."

Wise use was the cornerstone, and Pinchot and his followers had little patience with the still-embryonic notion that the natural world deserved preservation quite as much for its own sake as for the sake of the men and women who used it. John Muir, a hairy wood sprite of a naturalist whom Pinchot had met and befriended as early as 1896, personified this more idealistic instinct, tracing the roots of his own inspiration back to Henry David Thoreau's declaration that "in Wildness is the preservation of the World." For a time, the two men were allies in spite of their differences, but the friendship disintegrated after 1905, when Pinchot lent his support to the efforts of the city of San Francisco to dam the Hetch Hetchy Valley in Yosemite National Park for a public water-and-power project in order to free the city from a private power monopoly.

Muir, whose writings about Yosemite had brought him a measure of fame, had founded the Sierra Club in 1892 largely as a tool to protect the glorious trench of the Yosemite Valley and other pristine areas in the Sierra Nevada. Among these was the Hetch Hetchy Valley, which these early preservationists maintained was the equal of Yosemite itself in beauty. The reservoir that would fill up behind the proposed dam on the Tuolumne River would obliterate that beauty. But this was exactly the sort of public power-and-water project that spoke most eloquently to the deepest pragmatic instincts of Pinchot and his kind, who argued that every measure of conservation as they understood it would be fulfilled by approval of the project. "Whoever dominates power," Pinchot wrote, "dominates all industry."

Both sides in the argument faced off energetically in this first major conflict between the utilitarian and the preservationist wings of the conservation movement, and it took nearly ten years, the approval of two Presidents, and the passage of special legislation by Congress in 1913 before San Francisco obtained permission to build its dam. "The destruction of the charming groves and gardens, the finest in all California," Muir wrote to a friend, "goes to my heart. But in spite of Satan & Co., some sort of compensation must surely come out of this dark damn-dam damnation." Pinchot had no doubts and no regrets.

P inchot's devotion to the principles of conservation went beyond the immediate question of use versus preservation. Monopoly was evil personified, and monopoly, he believed, stemmed directly from the control of the natural world. "Monopoly of resources," he wrote in *Breaking New Ground*, "which prevents, limits, or destroys equality of opportunity is one of the most effective of all ways to control and limit human rights, especially the right of self-government." With this conviction to guide him, it did not take him long to find his way from the world of conservation to the world of politics, where, like thousands of his class, he found his imagination seized by Progressive Republicanism. . . .

The movement had been distilled from more than forty years of what the historian Howard Mumford Jones called "exuberance and wrath" following the Civil War. Its followers saw themselves and their values caught in a vise: threatened on one side by an increasingly violent and potentially revolutionary uprising on the part of the great unwashed—largely represented by the Democratic party—and on the other by a cynical plutocratic brotherhood—largely represented by the regular Republican party—which brutally twisted and subverted American institutions for purposes of personal greed and power.

Imperfectly but noisily, Theodore Roosevelt had given these people in the middle a voice and a symbol to call their own, and when he chose not to run for a third term in 1908, they felt abandoned. Prominent among them was Gifford Pinchot, and there is some evidence to suggest that he engineered his own dismissal as chief forester by President William Howard Taft, whom Roosevelt had groomed as his own chosen successor. The opportunity came in 1909, when Pinchot learned that Taft's Secretary of the Interior, Richard Ballinger, was determined to honor a number of coal-mining claims on lands in Alaska that Roosevelt had earlier withdrawn from such uses.

When Taft backed his Interior Secretary, Pinchot chose to see it as the beginning of a wholesale repudiation of all that Roosevelt had done to champion the public interest. He made no secret of his conclusions, and Taft was certain that more than bureaucratic integrity was behind Pinchot's loudly voiced concerns. "I am convinced," he wrote his brother, "that Pinchot with his fanaticism and his disappointment at my decision in the Ballinger case plans a coup by which I shall be compelled to dismiss him and he will be able to make out a martyrdom and try to raise opposition against me."

Taft resisted as long as he reasonably could, but when Pinchot violated the President's direct orders to maintain silence by writing an open letter to a Senate committee investigating the Ballinger matter, he decided he had no choice. Calling the letter an example of insubordination "almost unparalleled in the history of the government," Taft fired the chief forester of the United States on January 7, 1910. Pinchot rushed home with the letter of dismissal and waved it at his mother, crying, "I'm fired!" "My Mother's eyes flashed," he remembered, in *Breaking New Ground;* "she threw back her head, flung one hand high above it, and answered with one word: 'Hurrah!'"

Despite these memories of triumph, the most effective and rewarding part of Pinchot's career had come to an end. It certainly would not have seemed so to him at the time, however, as he joined in his friend Roosevelt's 1912 campaign to unseat Taft as a third-party candidate. Pinchot had been promised the State Department if Roosevelt won, but Roosevelt lost and, losing, spilt the Republican party and gave the Presidency to Woodrow Wilson. All Pinchot got was the satisfaction of seeing Taft humiliated—which nonetheless was "something to be proud and happy about," he crowed.

There followed years of politicking, all with his old vigor, but with mixed results and mostly confined to the state of Pennsylvania, where he served a couple of stormy, largely unproductive terms as governor.

It all took him too far from the forests that were his abiding interests. He had never lost sight of them, of course. In 1937, at the age of seventy-two, he undertook a five-thousand-mile trip sponsored by the Forest Service through the national forests of Montana, Idaho, Oregon, and California, sleeping out in the open, flying in Forest Service planes, and generally re-creating the delights of his youthful days on the old Forest Commission. "What I saw gave me the greatest satisfaction," he wrote upon his return. "The service is better than it was when I left and everywhere the forests are coming back. What more could a man ask?"

He was a good deal less mellow when FDR's Secretary of the Interior, his old friend and colleague Harold L. Ickes, opened a campaign to have the national forests taken out of the Department of Agriculture and placed back in Interior—an effort that earlier Interior Secretaries had supported and to which Pinchot had taken predictable umbrage. This time, however, the invective he launched against the idea was more than matched by that of the self-described curmudgeon Ickes, as the two old Progressives attempted to outdo each other in vitriol.

"What is behind all this?" Pinchot asked the assembled members of the Izaak Walton League in April 1937. "The man who has been my friend for more than a quarter of a century has allowed his ambition to get away with his judgement," and Ickes's great power had "bred the lust of greater power." Ickes countered that "Gifford Pinchot, who is a persistent fisherman in political waters, exemplifies more than anyone else in American public life how the itch for public office can break down one's intellectual integrity." The character of the debate between the two men rarely rose above this level until the beginning of World War II rendered the question moot. The forests stayed in the Department of Agriculture.

Appropriately, much of Pinchot's remaining years were spent in the writing of *Breaking New Ground,* which remains one of the central documents of the American conservation movement. That was a legacy worth the offering, and it is a pity that he did not live to see its publication before his death on October 4, 1946.

But the essential legacy of this committed, driven man, this public servant, this prince of rectitude, is the national forests themselves. There are 191 million acres of them now, spreading over the mountain slopes and river valleys of the West like a great dark blanket, still the center of controversy, still threatened and mismanaged and nurtured and loved as they were when the son of a dry goods merchant first walked in an American wood and wondered what could be done to save it for the future.

Critical Thinking

1. Critically analyze the role played by Gifford Pinchot in managing the nation's forest reserves.
2. Critically evaluate the relationship between President Theodore Roosevelt and Chief Forester Gifford Pinchot in the development of effective conservation policies.
3. Compare and contrast the preservationist ethic of John Muir with the utilitarian conservationist policies of Gifford Pinchot.
4. Critically evaluate the struggle between the preservationists and utilitarian conservationists to establish a dam to supply water to San Francisco in the Hetch Hetchy Valley.

Create Central

www.mhhe.com/createcentral

Internet References

Gilded Age and Progressive Era Resources
General resources on the Gilded Age and Progressive Era.
    www2.tntech.edu/history/gilprog.html

T. H. Watkins was the former senior editor of *American Heritage* and the author of 19 books.

Article

"A Machine of Practical Utility"

While lauded for their 1903 flight, the Wright brothers were not convinced of their airplane's reliability to sustain long, controlled flights until October 1905.

TOM D. CROUCH

Learning Outcomes

After reading this article, you will be able to:

- Describe the experimental aircrafts the Wrights designed between 1899 and 1905.

- Discuss the importance of the 1905 Wright Flyer.

O
n the morning of October 5, 1905, Amos Stauffer and a field hand were cutting corn when the distinctive clatter and pop of an engine and propellers drifted over from the neighboring pasture. The Wright boys, Stauffer knew, were at it again. Glancing up, he saw the flying machine rise above the heads of the dozen or so spectators gathered along the fence separating the two fields. The machine drifted toward the crowd, then sank back to earth in a gentle arc. The first flight of the day was over in less than 40 seconds.

By the time Stauffer and his helper had worked their way up to the fence line, the airplane was back in the air and had already completed four or five elliptical sweeps around the field, flying just above the level of the treetops to the north and west. "The durned thing was still going around," Stauffer recalled later. "I thought it would never stop." It finally landed 40 minutes after takeoff, having flown some 24 miles and circled the field 29 times.

The 1905 Wright Flyer was the final link in an evolutionary chain of seven experimental aircraft.

Farmer Stauffer had been watching the goings-on in that Ohio cow pasture for two years, but he had never seen anything like this. Neither had anyone else. The 1905 Wright Flyer was the final link in an evolutionary chain of seven experimental aircraft: one kite (1899); three piloted gliders (1900, 1901, 1902); and three powered airplanes (1903, 1904, 1905). Each

machine was a distillation of the lessons learned and the experience gained with its predecessors. The flight of October 5, 1905, was proof that the Wrights had achieved their goal of developing an aircraft that could be flown reliably over significant distances under the pilot's complete control. Six years of trial and error, discouragement and hope, disappointment and exhilaration, risk to life and limb, and brilliant engineering effort had ended in triumph.

Over a century later, the basic question remains. Why Wilbur and Orville? When the brothers began their aeronautical research in the spring of 1899, they seemed unlikely candidates to achieve the age-old dream of navigating the air. They were not college-educated men. Wilbur, 31, and Orville, 28, were living in their father's house while operating a neighborhood bicycle sales and repair shop, where they had just begun to build cycles, one at a time.

Yet these two apparently ordinary small businessmen were intuitive engineers, possessed of unusual talents, insights, and skills that perfectly suited them to the problem at hand. They had an instinctive grasp of the process of innovation—and a rare ability to imagine a machine that had yet to be built and to visualize how it would function. They could move from the abstract to the concrete with relative ease, as in the fall of 1901, when they designed a pair of wind-tunnel balances as mechanical analogues of the algebraic equations they had to apply to calculate the performance of the aircraft they were designing.

The passion that the brothers brought to solving difficult technical problems was another essential key to their success. It was what got them up in the morning and kept them going when the difficulties seemed impossibly daunting. "Isn't it astounding," Orville wrote to a friend in 1903, "that all of these secrets have been preserved for so many years just so that we could discover them!!"

Their first taste of success came on the morning of December 17, 1903, with four powered and controlled flights made on the sand flats south of Kitty Hawk, North Carolina. Although they had flown, the Wrights realized that their best flight of the day, 872 feet in 59 seconds, would not sound impressive to a world that had waited millennia for a flying machine.

Determined to solve the remaining problems, they transferred operations to a borrowed cow pasture eight miles east of their home in Dayton, where they flew for the next two years with scarcely anyone noticing. Without the steady winds and the long, sandy slopes of the Outer Banks, however, progress was slow. Finally learning to catapult themselves to flying speed, they began to stretch their time in the air, improve the design of their aircraft, and build their piloting skills.

As their flights grew ever longer in September and October 1905, local citizens and area journalists finally realized that something extraordinary was taking place in the sky over Torrence Huffman's pasture. Satisfied, the Wrights decided to stop flying altogether, worried that public demonstrations would reveal too much of their technology to potential rivals. They did not fly again until the spring of 1908, by which time they had a valid patent and contracts in hand for the sale of their machine. That August Wilbur stunned Europeans with his first public flights at the Hunaudières racetrack near Le Mans, France. A month later Orville demonstrated their machine to U.S. Army authorities at Fort Myer, Virginia.

Doubts about the Wright claims that had circulated during the years they had spent on the ground were immediately swept away. Wilbur and Orville Wright emerged as two of the first heroes of the new century. They were the inventors of the airplane in a much truer sense than Alexander Graham Bell can be said to have invented the telephone or Thomas Edison the motion picture.

Critical Thinking

1. How does the Wrights' background inspire the idea of true American ingenuity?

2. What were the implications of such a machine to the U.S. Army in 1908?

Create Central

www.mhhe.com/createcentral

Internet References

Smithsonian National Air and Space Museum
    http://airandspace.si.edu/exhibitions/wright-brothers/online
About.com
    http://inventors.about.com/od/wstartinventors/a/TheWrightBrother.htm
The Henry Ford
    www.hfmgv.org/exhibits/wright/#airplane

TOM D. CROUCH, author of *The Bishop's Boys: A Life of Wilbur and Orville Wright* (W. W. Norton 1990), is senior curator of the Division of Aeronautics at the Smithsonian's National Air and Space Museum.

Crouch, Tom D. From *American Heritage*, Winter 2010, pp. 68–70. Copyright © 2010 by American Heritage, Inc. Reprinted by permission of American Heritage Publishing and Tom D. Crouch.

A Day to Remember: March 25, 1911

Triangle Fire

Charles Phillips

Learning Outcomes

After reading this article, you will be able to:

- Discuss the ways in which greed and corruption contributed to the Triangle fire disaster.

- Explain how the 1910 strike was sabotaged by behind-the-scenes politics.

At the end of the work day on March 25, 1911, Isidore Abramowitz, a cutter at the Triangle Waist Company located on the corner of Greene Street and Washington Place in the heart of Manhattan's Garment District, had already pulled his coat and hat down from their peg when he noticed flames billowing from the scrap bin near his cutting table. It was about 4:40 P.M., and within minutes the fire swept through the factory and killed more than 140 of the 500 people who worked there. The conflagration, for some 90 years considered the deadliest disaster in New York City history, would usher in an era of reform with implications far beyond those of mere workplace safety.

The Jewish and Italian immigrants working at Triangle, most of them young women, produced the fashionable shirtwaists—women's blouses loosely based on a man's fitted shirt—popularized by commercial artist Charles Dana Gibson, whose famous "Gibson Girl" had become the sophisticated icon of the times. Beginning in late 1909, these workers participated in a major strike led by the Women's Trade Union League demanding a shorter working day and a livable wage. The garment workers had also protested the deplorable working conditions and dangerous practices of the industry's sweatshops. A large proportion of these firetraps, like Triangle, were located in Manhattan's crowded Lower East Side.

The factory workers had support not only from the left wing of the American labor movement but also among the city's wealthy progressives. Such socially prominent women as Anne Morgan (banker J. P. Morgan's daughter) and Alva Belmont (tycoon William H. Vanderbilt's ex-wife, who married banker Oliver Hazard Perry Belmont) ensured tremendous publicity for the strikers, and they helped stage a huge rally at Carnegie Hall

on January 2, 1910. But they met with adamantine resistance from factory owners, led by Triangle partners Max Blanck and Isaac Harris, who hired thugs from Max Schlansky's private detective agency to break up the strike. The owners in general enjoyed the backing of Tammany Hall boss Charles E. Murphy, which meant not only that the New York police were hostile to the workers but that strikebreakers were also available from the street gangs employed as muscle by Murphy's political machine.

When the strike ended, although the owners had agreed to some minor concessions and the radical newspaper *The Call* declared the strike a victory, little had truly changed, and everyone on the Lower East Side knew it. Certainly the workers at Triangle still put in long hours for penurious wages, without breaks, in an airless factory located on the top three floors of a hazardous 10 story firetrap. Scraps from the pattern cutters piled up in open bins and spilled over at the workers' feet, where the higher paid cutters, often men, dropped the ashes or even tossed the smoldering butts of the cheap cigars they smoked.

Because Blanck and Harris feared pilfering by their employees, access to the exits was limited, despite the city's fire regulations. At closing, workers were herded to the side of the building facing Greene Street, where partitions had been set up to funnel one worker at a time toward the stairway or the two freight elevators before they could leave the building for the day. This allowed company officials to inspect each exiting employee and his or her belongings for stolen tools, fabric or shirtwaists. The stairway and passenger elevators on the opposite side of the building, facing Washington Place, were reserved for management and the public. The only other egress was a narrow and flimsy fire escape on the back side of the building, opposite Washington Place, that corrupt city officials in 1900 had allowed Blanck and Harris to substitute for the third stairway legally required by the city. Access to it was partially blocked by large worktables.

These arrangements all led the disaster when the fire broke out as the result—the fire marshal later ruled—of a match or a smoldering cigarette or cigar tossed into Abramowitz's scrap bin. The loosely heaped scraps of sheer cotton fabric and crumpled tissue paper flared quickly, and the fire was blazing within seconds. Accounts of the chaos that erupted vary greatly, but apparently Abramowitz reached up, grabbed one of the three red fire pails on the ledge above his coat rack, and dumped it on the flames. Other cutters snatched pails and tried in vain to douse the exponentially spreading blaze. Despite their efforts, the fabric-laden old structure, ironically called the Asch Building, began to burn quickly and fiercely.

Factory manager Samuel Bernstein directed his employees to break out the fire hoses, only to find them completely useless. Some claimed the uninspected hoses had rotted through, while others asserted that either the water tanks on the roof were empty or the flow of water from them was somehow blocked. Having lost precious minutes in fruitless attempts to control the blaze, the workers looked for the means of escape.

A few rushed to the solitary, poorly constructed and inadequately maintained fire escape, which descended from the 10th floor to the 2nd, stopping above a small courtyard. Some of the young women who used it fell from one landing to the next; one of the male employees fell from the 8th floor to the ground. Others madly rushed toward the inward-opening doors on the Washington Place side, preventing them from being opened. (Some later claimed these doors were locked.) As more and more workers piled up at the doors, those at the front were nearly crushed. Only with great effort did Louis Brown, a young shipping clerk, bully his way through the pressed bodies and muscle them away from the exit so that he could open the doors. On the opposite side of the building, panicked workers who tried to exit the 8th floor on the Greene Street side were slowed by the funneling partitions, and found the stairway and elevators already jammed with workers fleeing from the 9th and 10th floors.

Afterward, there was much confusion and a lot of debate about which floor the Washington Place passenger elevators visited and when. The elevator operators—Joseph Zito and Gaspar Mortillo—certainly risked their lives by returning to burning floors to carry their co-workers to safety. They probably visited the 8th floor first, saving a lot of lives even as the panic there set in. Then they headed up to the 10th floor, the executive floor. Zito later guessed that they went to 10 twice, dropping off the first group only to find the floor empty on the next trip up.

All 70 workers on the 10th floor managed to escape, as did Blanck (and the two daughters he'd brought to work with him) and Harris, who showed a good deal of bravery in his efforts to save many of his 10th-floor employees. They all got out either by the early elevator trips, by way of the staircases or by ascending to the roof. New York University law students in a taller, adjacent building lowered ladders to the roof of the Asch Building, and the workers inched their way up them to safety.

Of all the Triangle employees, the 260 who worked on the 9th floor suffered the worst fate. According to some accounts, the alert and the fire reached them at the same time. The Greene Street exit was quickly jammed, and the doors to the Washington Place stairwell were found to be locked. Since the elevator car itself was packed with 10th-floor employees, some clambered down the greasy cables of the freight elevator.

Elevator operator Zito peered up the elevator shaft as those left behind faced grim choices. "The screams from above were getting worse," he later reported. "I looked up and saw the whole shaft getting red with fire. . . . They kept coming down from the flaming floors above. Some of their clothing was burning as they fell. I could see streaks of fire coming down like flaming rockets."

Others on the 9th floor wedged their way into the Greene Street staircase and climbed up to the roof. Still others ran to the fire escape, which proved incapable of supporting the weight of so many. With an ear-rending rip, it separated from the wall, disintegrating in a mass of twisted iron and falling bodies. In complete desperation, some 9th-floor workers fled to the window ledges. The firemen's ladders would not reach beyond the 6th floor, so the firefighters deployed a safety net about 100 feet below, and they exhorted the victims to jump. Some of the young women, in terror, held hands and jumped in pairs. But the weight of so many jumpers split the net, and young men and women tore through it to their deaths.

An ambulance driver bumped his vehicle over the curb onto the sidewalk, hoping against hope that jumpers might break their fall by landing on his roof. Deliverymen pulled a tarpaulin from a wagon and stretched it out. The first body to hit it ripped it from their hands. "The first ten [to hit] shocked me," wrote reporter William Gunn Shepherd before he looked up and saw all the others raining down.

Fifteen minutes after the fire started, the firemen—even then New York's finest, the pride of the city—were within moments of bringing the fire on the 8th floor under control. But the 9th was hopeless. On the 9th, the fire took over the entire floor. Later, burned bodies were found piled up in a heap in the loft. A second scorched cluster was discovered pressed up against the Greene Street exit, where they had been caught by the blaze before they could get out. At the time, the crowds watching could see groups of girls trapped in burning window frames, refusing to jump. When they could hold out no longer, they came tumbling through the windows in burning clumps.

Then it was over. The last person fell at about 4:57 P.M., and there was nothing left to do but deal with the dead—146 broken bodies. During the next few days, streams of survivors and relatives filed through the temporary morgue on 26th Street to identify the dead. Eventually, all but six were given names.

Even before the bodies stopped falling, veteran newsman Herbert Bayard Swope had interrupted District Attorney Charles Seymour Whitman's regular Saturday news briefing at his apartment in the Iroquois Hotel to announce the disaster. Whitman immediately rushed to the scene and began looking for somebody to blame. Since he couldn't go after the city itself, he got a grand jury to charge Blanck and Harris with negligent homicide for locking the doors to the back stairway. Defended in a celebrated trial by famed Tammany mouthpiece Max D. Steuer, himself a former garment worker, the "Shirtwaist Kings" were acquitted, much to the outrage of progressives everywhere.

But watching the fire that day was a young woman named Frances Perkins. Perkins happened to be enjoying tea with a friend who lived on the north side of Washington Square. She heard the fire engines and arrived just in time to see the bodies begin to fall. Already a rising star in the progressive firmament, she never forgot what she saw, and she never let it go. Through her efforts, and the efforts of others like her, the horrible images of the Triangle fire brought an anguished outcry for laws to compel heedless, greedy, cost-cutting manufacturers to provide for the safety of employees.

The pre-fire strikes, coupled with the Triangle disaster and its aftermath, unified union organizers, college students, socialist writers, progressive millionaires and immigrant shop workers. Tammany Hall boss Murphy quickly sensed that a transformation of the Democratic Party could take advantage of this new progressive coalition at the ballot box. As a result, he fully supported the New York Factory Investigating Commission, formed three months after the fire, to inspect factories throughout the state. The "Tammany Twins," Alfred E. Smith and Robert F. Wagner, who were the driving force behind the investigation, backed Perkins as she sat on the commission and took the lead in shaping its findings. The commission's report, compiled during $2\frac{1}{2}$ years of research, brought dramatic changes to existing laws and introduced many new ones.

Smith, of course, went on to become governor of New York and the Democratic nominee for the presidency in 1924 and 1928. When Franklin Delano Roosevelt followed in his footsteps and actually won election to the office in 1932, he brought Perkins with him into his New Deal, as the first female Cabinet member (secretary of labor), and Wagner as an adviser who drafted some of the most important progressive legislation in the country's history. In many ways, it is fair to say that the modern American welfare state of the 20th century's middle decades rose from the ashes of the Triangle fire.

Critical Thinking

1. What role did the Triangle fire play in the development of today's welfare system?
2. Why was the acquittal of Blanck and Harris a major blow to workers' reform?

Create Central

www.mhhe.com/createcentral

Internet Reference

Cornell University
www.ilr.cornell.edu/trianglefire

About.com
http://history1900s.about.com/od/1910s/p/trianglefire.htm

New York State Labor Laws
http://law2.umkc.edu/faculty/projects/ftrials/triangle/trianglescodes.html

Phillips, Charles. From *American History*, April 2006, pp. 16, 18, 70. Copyright © 2006 by Weider History Group. Reprinted by permission.

Theodore Roosevelt, the Spanish-American War, and the Emergence of the United States as a Great Power by William N. Tilchin

59

Article

Prepared by: Larry Madaras, *Howard Community College*

Theodore Roosevelt, the Spanish-American War, and the Emergence of the United States as a Great Power

An address presented at the Ninetieth Annual Meeting of the Theodore Roosevelt Association in Tampa, Florida, on October 24, 2009.

WILLIAM N. TILCHIN

Learning Outcomes

After reading this article, you will be able to:

- Explain Theodore Roosevelt's accidental rise to the presidency.

- Explain how Theodore Roosevelt developed a coherent foreign policy.

- Explain the legacy of Theodore Roosevelt's foreign policy today.

It is a common assumption among historians and students of history that the Spanish-American War marked the emergence of the United States as a great power. Particularly significant, they contend, was that the U.S. acquired an overseas empire, most notably the Philippines, as a result of America's decisive defeat of Spain. And indeed, there occurred an alteration in the view of the United States held by governing officials and opinion leaders in foreign capitals. The governments of the major powers across the Atlantic now expected the United States to become a player in the international balance of power and a more formidable rival in international economic competition. They would watch America's behavior closely in order to determine whether a new great power had truly arisen as a result of the U.S. victory over Spain.

The initial signals were ambiguous. While annexing the Philippines and Puerto Rico, the United States had upheld the pledge embodied in the Teller Amendment to support the independence of Cuba. And there was no apparent strategic conception driving U.S. foreign policy. As the distinguished historian Ernest May concludes about America's war against Spain,

"neither [President William McKinley] nor the public had any aim beyond war itself."[1] Very much in the mold of the post-Civil War Presidents who had preceded him, McKinley, to put it simply, was not a strategic thinker.

For the United States unambiguously to play its rightful role as a great power, two requirements would have to be met: (1) a coherent and appropriately ambitious strategic outlook that would guide America's international conduct; and (2) the construction of a powerful modern navy to give credibility to the United States' more active and assertive behavior. But three years after the Spanish-American War ended in August 1898, neither of these requirements was in place.

The chief architect of McKinley's foreign policy, Secretary of State John Hay, did seek to move the United States into a more prominent international role. Hay, a former U.S. ambassador to Great Britain who would continue to head the State Department under President Theodore Roosevelt, had a decided affinity for England, and he endeavored to establish a cooperative Anglo-American relationship. Thus, contrary to the positions of continental European governments and in disregard of American public opinion, Hay persuaded McKinley to provide diplomatic support to Britain during the Boer War in southern Africa, a policy with which Roosevelt fully agreed and which he continued after assuming the presidency. Hay also promoted—on behalf of U.S. business interests and again in tandem with Britain—the Open Door policy in China. But the constricted nature of Hay's view of America's place in the world came sharply into focus when he negotiated with Britain in February 1900 the first Hay-Pauncefote Treaty pertaining to a future trans-isthmian canal. Clearly Hay was *not* intent on attaining U.S. hegemony in the Western Hemisphere, for the terms of this treaty prohibited either the United States or

Britain from fortifying a canal. A key figure in the U.S. opposition that derailed this treaty was New York Governor Theodore Roosevelt, who explained in a letter to his close English friend Cecil Spring Rice that "in the event of our having trouble with Germany or France it would be far better not to have the canal at all than to have it unfortified."[2]

It would only be with Roosevelt's accession to the presidency in September 1901 that the United States would intentionally and effectively assume its role as one of the great powers. In other words, TR would turn America's *potential* international stature into its *actual* international stature. Before proceeding to develop this theme, I would like to step back briefly and zero in on the Spanish-American War as crucial to the United States' emergence as a great power—but from a perspective different from the usual one. For, more than the one-sided U.S. victory over Spain and the resultant acquisition of a diminutive overseas empire, it was the particular saga of Theodore Roosevelt and the Rough Riders that accounts for the emergence of America as a world power in the first decade of the twentieth century.

This is what I mean: If not for his well-publicized courage under fire as commander of the Rough Riders (and TR himself contributed to the publicity by writing a widely read book titled *The Rough Riders*). Theodore Roosevelt almost certainly never would have become President of the United States. Roosevelt had previously held, and performed with distinction in, several positions in local, state, and national government—most recently as assistant secretary of the navy, the post from which he resigned to take up arms against Spain—but new horizons suddenly were now open to him. A popular national hero, particularly in his home state, Roosevelt was handed the 1898 Republican nomination for governor of New York by a scandal-ridden party leadership (that leadership's desire for victory taking precedence over its uneasiness about Colonel Roosevelt's independence), and he defeated his Democratic opponent by a narrow margin. As governor in 1899 and 1900, Roosevelt achieved a very admirable reform record, often acting in defiance of the wishes of Thomas Platt, the state party boss. An exasperated Platt then pushed successfully for Roosevelt's selection as McKinley's running mate in 1900, hoping that vice presidential obscurity would befall the Rough Rider. But when McKinley died from an assassin's bullet on September 14, 1901, Roosevelt became the youngest-ever U.S. President. Unquestionably the crucial first link in this fascinating chain of events was TR's heroism in Cuba. Without it, there would have been no governorship, no vice presidency, no presidency.

As President, one of Roosevelt's highest priorities was increasing the strength and the efficiency of the U.S. Navy. TR would prove to be an extraordinary shepherd of that process. In a recent major book titled *Theodore Roosevelt's Naval Diplomacy*, Henry Hendrix aptly describes Roosevelt as "a self-educated technical expert who sought to change the very design and capabilities of the ships under his command."[3] Despite some limited progress in creating a modern U.S. Navy beginning in the 1880s, U.S. efforts had lagged behind those of numerous other countries, and, Hendrix writes, "the historical record suggests that this condition might have continued indefinitely had Theodore Roosevelt not stepped to the fore."[4] Hendrix details President

Roosevelt's difficult labors on behalf of a stronger American navy and finds approvingly that "by the end of his administration Roosevelt had conquered doctrinal and bureaucratic resistance to create a modern Navy arrayed around a strategic centerpiece, the all-big-gun battleship."[5] While, of course, a modern navy needed to be able to fight and win wars, Roosevelt equally perceived this "big stick" as essential to successful U.S. engagement in great power diplomacy. Now, when he spoke softly, he could be confident that other powerful nations would listen carefully.

As I have contended elsewhere, President Theodore Roosevelt conducted a foreign policy grounded on three precepts, which might be labeled the precept of broadly defined U.S. interests, the precept of U.S. power, and the precept of Anglo-American leadership. Moreover, he implemented these three precepts with exemplary astuteness and adeptness.[6]

Far more than any of his predecessors, Roosevelt involved the United States in the international issues of his day. He had a sophisticated, multidimensional understanding of complex international matters. A powerful American navy and an increasingly close informal U.S. partnership with the British Empire enabled Roosevelt to exercise maximum leverage as he pursued his far-reaching foreign policy objectives.

In the Western Hemisphere, Roosevelt secured a revised Hay-Pauncefote Treaty that permitted U.S. fortification of a future canal, employed his naval forces and his diplomatic talents to induce Germany to stand down during the Venezuela crisis of 1902–1903, acquired the Panama Canal Zone and began building the canal, and boldly proclaimed U.S. hegemony by announcing the Roosevelt Corollary to the Monroe Doctrine. He then proactively prevented outside intervention in the Dominican Republic by taking control of its customs houses through a mutual agreement with the Dominican government.

Roosevelt thought strategically about great power rivalries and about U.S. relations with the other great powers. Based on common values and similar interests, TR viewed Great Britain as a natural and, indeed, an essential partner for the United States. Therefore, he labored assiduously throughout his presidency first to build and then to solidify an Anglo-American special relationship. In sharp contrast, Roosevelt looked upon Germany, Russia, and Japan as potential U.S. enemies. Nevertheless, he skillfully maintained amicable, if at times uneasy, relations with all three. By mediating with great commitment and finesse to bring an end to the Russo-Japanese War in 1905. Roosevelt not only served the cause of great power peace but helped to preserve the Anglo-French entente cordiale, which he viewed as vital to European stability and American interests. He also preserved the Anglo-French entente through adroit diplomacy when Germany tried to destroy it by engineering a crisis over Morocco in 1905 and 1906. And TR resolved tensions between the United States and Japan by sending the Great White Fleet on a world cruise to demonstrate American power, while treating Japan with the utmost respect during the negotiations leading to the Root-Takahira Agreement of November 1908, an agreement that marked the successful culmination of the President's efforts to forge a substantive and genuinely friendly understanding between the United States and Japan.

Theodore Roosevelt, the Spanish-American War, and the Emergence of the United States as a Great Power by William N. Tilchin

61

Throughout the seven-and-a-half years of his presidency. Roosevelt had kept the United States at peace while upholding its vital interests and greatly enhancing its international stature and influence. As I have asserted previously, "it is difficult to imagine the leadership of U.S. foreign policy being passed on to a successor in a more promising condition."[7]

Theodore Roosevelt's diplomacy had established the United States as a leading world power, but for most of the thirty years following his presidency, the United States did not conduct itself like a true great power. The reversal was not a total one, for TR had succeeded brilliantly in institutionalizing U.S. naval power: the nation would never again lose sight of the necessity of maintaining a first-class modern navy. Thus, the transition from battleships to aircraft carriers as the foundation of U.S. naval strength proceeded without serious delay or controversy between the two world wars.

But Theodore Roosevelt's first five successors as President—William Howard Taft, Woodrow Wilson, Warren Harding, Calvin Coolidge, and Herbert Hoover—all lacked strategic sophistication, and they largely set aside TR's guiding foreign policy precepts. During these years, a narrowly selfish economic imperialism, particularly in Latin America, constituted the essence of American international engagement. Even Franklin Roosevelt, who was more in tune with TR's approach to U.S. foreign relations, was reluctant to challenge the country's prevailing isolationist mindset during his first six years as President. Until 1939, therefore, Nazi Germany and Imperial Japan could plan and execute their predatory designs without worrying much about the reaction of the United States, which, despite its formidable, TR-inspired military capacity, simply was not acting in the manner of a responsible great power. As I have observed in a recent article, "it would take the disastrous failure of isolationism and appeasement and the terrible experience of the Second World War to revive TR's way of thinking about U.S. foreign relations and to bring his outlook into the mainstream, where it has been ever since."[8]

So, the Spanish-American War indeed *was* largely responsible for the emergence of the United States as a great power in the early twentieth century, but not primarily for the reasons usually emphasized. Presidential leadership was a significantly more important factor than the acquisition of a small colonial empire. It was Theodore Roosevelt's bravery and heroism in helping to drive the Spanish Army from the San Juan Heights on July 1, 1898, that launched him in the direction of the presidency. And it was the presidency of TR that fundamentally accounts for the behavior of the United States as a great power from 1901 to 1909 and then, after a lengthy lapse and less directly, from 1939 to the present. To reiterate and to conclude, the *potential* was there without TR, but the *realization* of that potential very likely would not have occurred—or, at best, would have been delayed with very serious and very regrettable consequences—in the absence of the presidency of Theodore Roosevelt.

Notes

1. Ernest R. May, *Imperial Democracy: The Emergence of America as a Great Power* (1961; reprint, New York: Harper & Row, 1973), p. 268.

2. Theodore Roosevelt to Cecil Spring Rice, March 2, 1900, quoted in Howard K. Beale, *Theodore Roosevelt and the Rise of America to World Power* (1956; reprint, Baltimore: Johns Hopkins University Press, 1984), p. 104.

3. Henry J. Hendrix, *Theodore Roosevelt's Naval Diplomacy: The U.S. Navy and the Birth of the American Century* (Annapolis: Naval Institute Press, 2009), p. 133.

4. Ibid.

5. Ibid., p. 154.

6. See William N. Tilchin, "For the Present and the Future: The Well-Conceived, Successful, and Farsighted Statecraft of President Theodore Roosevelt," *Diplomacy & Statecraft*, Vol. 19, No. 4, December 2008, pp. 658–670.

7. Ibid., p. 667.

8. Ibid., pp. 667–668.

Critical Thinking

1. Critically analyze three major points of Theodore Roosevelt's foreign policy which gave it a coherent framework that previous presidents had failed to develop.

2. Critically analyze how future presidents built on Theodore Roosevelt's foreign policy.

Create Central

www.mhhe.com/createcentral

Internet References

The Age of Imperialism

During the late nineteenth and early twentieth centuries, the United States pursued an aggressive policy of expansionism, extending its political and economic influence around the globe. That pivotal era in the nation's history is the subject of this interactive site. Maps and photographs are provided.

www.smplanet.com/imperialism/toc.html

Theodore Roosevelt Association

This website contains an abundance of scholarly and popular material pertaining to all aspects of Theodore Roosevelt's multifaceted life.

www.theodoreroosevelt.org

WILLIAM N. TILCHIN is a Professor of History at Boston University, the author of numerous books and articles about Theodore Roosevelt and is the current editor of the *Theodore Roosevelt Association Journal*.

Unit 3

UNIT

From Progressivism to the 1920s

Reform movements in the United States have most often developed in the face of economic dislocation. The Populist crusade in the 1890s and the New Deal in the 1930s are typical. Progressivism was an exception. It developed during a period of relative prosperity. Yet more and more people became dissatisfied with existing conditions. Individuals who became known as "muckrakers" published books and articles that revealed the seamier side of American life. One focused on the terrible working conditions in the meat packing industry, another on corruption and cronyism in the Senate, still another on the "bossism" and "machine politics" he found in a number of cities. The popularity of muckraking in newspapers, journals, and books showed that many segments of the public were receptive to such exposures. The Progressive movement generally was led by white, educated, middle or upper-middle class men and women. They were not radicals, though their opponents often called them that, and they had no wish to destroy the capitalist system. Instead they wanted to reform it to eliminate corruption, to make it function more efficiently, and to provide what we would call a "safety net" for the less fortunate. The reforms they proposed were modest ones such as replacing political appointees with trained experts, having senators elected directly by the people, and conducting referenda on important issues. The movement arose on local levels, then percolated upward to state governments, then into the national arena.

Teddy Roosevelt as president had responded to progressive sentiment through actions such as his "trust busting." He did not seek a third term in 1908, and anointed William Howard Taft as the Republican candidate for the presidency. Taft won the election but managed to alienate both progressives and conservatives during his tenure in office. By 1912, progressivism ran strongly enough that the Democrat Party nominated Woodrow Wilson, who had compiled an impressive record as a reform governor in the state of New Jersey. Roosevelt, now counting himself a full-blown progressive, bolted the Republican Party when Taft was re-nominated and formed the Progressive or "Bull Moose" party. Roosevelt was still popular, but he managed only to split Republican support with the result that Woodrow Wilson won the election with just 42 percent of the popular vote.

The Ford Motor Company shocked the industrial world in January 1914, when it announced that it would double its workers' minimum wage to five dollars per day. Partly this was to encourage loyalty at a time when assembly line production was causing a great deal of absenteeism. The new policy worked in the short-run as workers were reluctant to do without the higher wage. In the long-run, especially after the onset of the Great Depression, it had the unforeseen effect of encouraging labor unions, which Ford fought with everything at his disposal.

What we call "World War I" (contemporaries called it "The Great War") broke out in the summer of 1914. President Woodrow Wilson called upon the American people to remain neutral "in thought and deed" toward the warring powers. By April 1917, however, after Germany had resorted to "unrestricted submarine warfare" against neutral shipping, he asked Congress for a declaration of war.

The 1920s was a decade of great ferment. After a brief postwar recession, the economy became extremely prosperous although not everyone shared in it. Interest in sports grew enormously, and stars such as Babe Ruth, Jack Dempsey, and Red Grange became household names. Prohibition, the "noble experiment," promised to rid the nation of the curse of what was referred to as "Demon Rum." Unfortunately, despite huge expenditures of time and money devoted to enforcing prohibition laws, the experiment failed to produce the results predicted. Bootlegging and home-made beverages made a mockery of what was supposed to be a dry era. Some have argued that the consumption of alcohol actually increased during the period. There can be no question that prohibition contributed to the rise of organized crime. Although there were numerous other factors, the struggle between "wets" and "drys" almost tore the Democrat Party apart.

Charles Lindbergh's highly publicized solo flight across the Atlantic in 1927 made him the most popular man in the world. Boyishly handsome and modest, he represented the ideal American hero. His flight also seemed to epitomize the veritable explosion of technological advances of the time.

Article

The $5 Day

By doubling his workers' salaries, Henry Ford solved his turnover problem—and also unwittingly set the stage for industrial unionism.

ROBERT H. CASEY

Learning Outcomes

After reading this article, you will be able to:

- Explain Ford's reasons for implementing the high pay/low skill wage model.
- Discuss how Ford's wage model led to unionization.

The word spread quickly on January 5, 1914. By 2 A.M. men were gathering outside the employment office of the huge Ford Motor Company plant in Highland Park, Michigan, ignoring the raw weather. Less than 12 hours earlier, the company's two top executives, Henry Ford and James Couzens, had called reporters into the latter's office to announce the company's plan to more than double its minimum wage to $5 for an eight-hour workday. Ten thousand job seekers rushed to the plant at the corner of Woodward Avenue and Manchester Street north of Detroit. The long-term results of this decision, for Detroit and the nation, would be profound and largely unanticipated.

What prompted Ford to adopt such a radical policy? Certainly it represented, at least in part, an effort to deal with his workers' response to the recently developed assembly line, which required little skill but whose mind-numbing repetition and relentless pace resulted in very high worker turnover. Ford hoped better pay would offset these difficulties; but in part his plan was an effort literally to share the wealth. In 1913 Ford Motor Company's net income was $27 million, and its seven stockholders split $11.2 million in dividends. Both Ford and Couzens believed that their employees deserved a bigger share.

The new policy began to unfold early in January 1914, when Ford convened a meeting to discuss production and wages for the coming year. Sources disagree over exactly who attended, but all agree that it concluded with a discussion about a substantial wage raise. Some of those present, including Ford, said Ford pushed the $5 a day idea. Others, including Couzens, claimed that it was Couzens. What's not disputed is that Ford

and Couzens, who held nearly 70 percent of the company stock between them, met with their fellow stockholder Horace Rackham on January 5 and agreed on the new policy. Later that day Ford and Couzens held the news conference that brought the 10,000 job seekers to the plant.

The new policy solved Ford's turnover problem, made his employees the richest factory workers in the country, and elevated Ford to a folk hero. But those were only the short-term consequences. More important, the $5 day redefined the relationship between compensation and skill. Throughout history, workers had increased the price they demanded for their labor by increasing their skill levels. The master craftsman always made more money than the journeyman. Conversely, employers had reduced their labor costs by reducing the skill required to do their work. Thus, mechanizing the textile industry, by reducing the skill level required to spin yarn or weave cloth, reduced the value of spinners' and weavers' labor. But Ford was offering to pay his unskilled workers more, even as he told them he didn't want them to think, only to follow orders.

Other industrialists denounced Ford's new wage policies, but many, in and out of the automobile industry, eventually found it profitable to adopt his mass production and assembly line methods. Inevitably they found it necessary to pay his high wages as well. Rising factory wages made northern industrial cities magnets for foreign immigrants and rural Americans, accelerating existing migration trends. In Detroit, industries that could not pay automobile industry wages left the city, solidifying its status as a one-industry town.

Ford also unwittingly set the stage for industrial unionism. When the Great Depression hit, his and other assembly-line-based companies could no longer pay the prevailing level of wages, making plants fertile ground for union organizers as well as highly vulnerable to labor stoppages. Ford fought the unions with every means possible, legal and illegal, but even he was eventually forced to accept a contract with the United Auto Workers.

But the reversal of the wage/skill relationship turned out not to be permanent. By the 1980s American mass production enterprises found themselves competing with Japanese manufacturers who had learned that actively engaging workers and seeking their ideas improved not only morale but productivity and product quality. Increasingly sophisticated manufacturing technology also required more than manual dexterity and obedience. At the same time competition from lower-cost overseas producers, such as the Chinese, was reducing the number of American manufacturing jobs. By the end of the 20th century what remained of the American manufacturing base paid well, but was open only to those with higher skills. The high wage/low skill era had lasted less than a century.

Critical Thinking

1. What caused the collapse of the high pay/low skill model?
2. How are unions faring today? Explain.

Create Central

www.mhhe.com/createcentral

Internet References

Michigan.gov
www.michigan.gov/dnr/0,4570,7-153-54463_18670_18793-53441–,00.html

RenewAmerica.com
www.renewamerica.com/columns/bates/060103

Forbes.com
www.forbes.com/sites/timworstall/2012/03/04/the-story-of-henry-fords-5-a-day-wages-its-not-what-you-think

ROBERT H. CASEY, author most recently of *The Model T: A Centennial History* (Johns Hopkins University 2009), is the John and Horace Dodge Curator of Transportation at The Henry Ford in Dearborn, Michigan.

Article

Prepared by: Larry Madaras, *Howard Community College*

Meuse-Argonne: America's Bloodiest Single Battle Occurred in the Forests and Fields of Eastern France during World War I

Edward G. Lengel

Learning Outcomes

After reading this article, you will be able to:

- Describe the lack of training and preparation for modern warfare experienced by the American soldiers in World War I.

- Describe the importance of the American troops in shifting the balance of power in favor of the allies during the Meuse-Argonne offensive in eastern France in October, 1918.

- Describe the role played by the Lieutenants and non-commissioned officers who fought the battle in the trenches.

On October 11, 1918, late in the afternoon, a platoon of American doughboys marched to the front in eastern France, passing shattered villages, forests reduced to matchsticks, and water-filled shell craters. At every step the Americans struggled to free their boots from the slopping mud. Icy wind and rain slashed at their clothing, and water poured in steady streams from the rims of their helmets, somewhat obscuring the devastation. They were already exhausted, some literally asleep on their feet, little aware that they soon would find themselves fighting the bloodiest single battle in U.S. history.

As the platoon slogged north, it skirted the summit of a craggy hill named Montfaucon, the slopes studded with burnt-out German pillboxes, and tripped over the sparse ruins of the village of Nantillois, hardly one brick standing on another, then moved through a copse of wildly leaning, fog-draped trees toward the edge of a small ravine. Rolling hills covered by well-plowed fields and small stands of oak covered much of this region of northeastern France. The German defensive positions exploited ridges, ravines, dense forests, and small rivers to maximum effect. Enemy shellfire increased, and the men dropped to a crouch or crawled.

Nearby lay the smoking remnants of a Salvation Army canteen. Less than an hour before, two cheery young American women had been distributing gallons of coffee and mountains of doughnuts to weary soldiers. Now their bodies lay ripped open in the mud, surrounded by doughnuts and coffee tins.

Lt. Samuel Woodfill, a tall, robust, 17-year Army veteran from lower Indiana, led the platoon past even more awful horrors. Unlike his doughboys, most of whom were poorly trained rookies, Woodfill had grown up with a gun in his hand, joining the Army at 18, fighting guerrillas in the Philippines, and then transferred—at his request—to Alaska, where he had hunted moose and grizzly bear in his spare time.

Woodfill hadn't thought much about the outbreak of World War I in August 1914. Less than three years later, however, Germany declared unrestricted submarine warfare and at the same time made a clumsy attempt to convince Mexico to attack the United States. As a result, Woodrow Wilson asked for a declaration of war in April 1917. Congress complied and then set about trying to build an army out of millions of untrained volunteers and draftees. Woodfill was promoted to lieutenant and assigned to Company M, 60th Regiment, 5th ("Red Diamond") Division.

American troops began arriving in France in large numbers in spring 1918, tasked to join French and British troops against the Germans, who had launched a massive offensive in March and come close to taking Paris. By May and early June, when American soldiers and Marines went into action at places such as Cantigny and Belleau Wood, the Germans were still struggling to break the Allied lines in France and end the war. That summer Americans joined the Allied effort in increasing numbers and helped to roll back the German advance.

Woodfill's outfit hadn't seen any action in those summer campaigns. Now, caught in the clammy grip of October, he led his men out of the shattered copse, down the slope of an open ravine, and into action for the first time. German machine-gun fire opened up a murderous volley, sending wounded or frightened doughboys toppling head over heels downslope. Reaching the bottom of the ravine, Woodfill dove for cover in a shallow depression near some partially buried scraps of corrugated iron. His overstuffed backpack bulged into sight, and the Germans pumped it full of bullets.

Adding insult to injury, a louse, or "cootie," began marching slowly down his spine. Scratching was impossible. Nor could he return fire as bullets ricocheted off the corrugated iron. The enemy barrage moved steadily forward, plopping one after another, closer and closer to his position. Woodfill drew a photograph of his wife from his pocket and scribbled on its back his home address and the following words: "please forward this picture to my Darling Wife. And tell her that I have fallen on the field of Honor, and departed to a better land which knows no sorrow and feels no pain. I will prepair a place and be waiting at the Golden Gait of Heaven for the arrival of my Darling Blossom."

The bombardment finally stopped, and Woodfill and his men crawled from their cover, eyeing each other sheepishly, each struggling not to betray his fear. A private who had taken cover near Woodfill tucked a piece of paper into his tunic—he too had written a farewell note.

The platoon traversed the ravine past the ruins of Madeleine Farm and deployed behind the crest of a ridge. "Halt, and dig in!" cried an officer; but there was no time. Instead the men scattered by twos into shell holes half full of water. Darkness fell, and as sight failed other senses grew more acute. The soldiers listened with dread to the grumble of intermittent shell-fire, now far, now near, the crackle of machine guns, muttered curses, and the clank of equipment. The rain intensified.

Woodfill had only a few hours of "rest"—shivering in his shell hole—before a major ordered him to take eight men on a scout into the woods beyond the ridge. On the way back, Woodfill stepped onto a small bridge that the Germans had booby-trapped. A shell planted in a nearby tree burst over his head, and he lost consciousness. When he recovered, he found that blood was pouring from his nose. He felt as if an iron spike had been driven through his temple. Staggering back to his shell hole, he fell asleep, only to be reawakened a few hours later by floating out of the hole, which the rain had turned into a pond.

On September 26, 1918, nine mostly inexperienced American divisions totaling about 600,000 men assaulted well-trenched German positions in a shell-pitted tract just north of Verdun. Thus began the Meuse-Argonne offensive, the largest American campaign of the First World War. During the following six weeks, more than 1.2 million American soldiers in 22 divisions and support formations would assault German positions in northeastern France. More than 120,000 soldiers and Marines would fall wounded: 26,277 would die. Nearly all the casualties—about half of those sustained by the United States during the war—occurred within a three-week period. Some 2,400 artillery pieces fired 4 million shells, more than

the Union army had fired during the entire Civil War. No other single battle in American military history even approaches the Meuse-Argonne in size and cost, yet few know much about it, even though it constituted the most important U.S. contribution to the Allied effort in World War I. Young officers entering the armed forces in the 1930s and 1940s could recite details about the action at Gettysburg but little if anything about the Meuse-Argonne. The reasons for this are many, perhaps the most important being that the doughboys were the first to experience modern industrialized warfare and the horrific large-scale death and destruction that artillery, machine guns, and poison gas could unleash. And perhaps—unlike Pickett's charge, Concord Bridge, or the invasion of Normandy—the First World War's scorched earth, miles upon miles of trenches, and inch-by-inch fighting do not lend themselves to an easy or particularly heroic story line. Yet the heroism that emerged in those bloody days was extraordinary, as inexperienced and untested recruits and draftees went up against the world's best-trained and most formidable army in some of the strongest defensive terrain in France. The battle created heroes of ordinary men, the likes of which America had never seen before. On the darker side, the story is also tragic: military ineptitude and thickheaded nationalism led to thousands of needless deaths. The Meuse-Argonne would also fail to gain traction in the collective American memory because of a mistaken belief that the nation's late entrance into the conflict was merely pro forma, the war essentially being already over.

The American forces in the Meuse-Argonne, a region bordered on the east by the Meuse River and on the west by the dense Argonne Forest, comprised the First Army of the American Expeditionary Force, commanded by Gen. John "Blackjack" Pershing. Their objective was to break through the German defenses for 40 miles to a critical railway junction near Sedan. Supplies for nearly the entire German army in France passed through this junction; its capture would inflict a severe if not catastrophic blow to Germany's military fortunes.

The German forces in the Meuse-Argonne were under orders to stop the Americans at all costs. Four brutal years of combat had severely weakened the German army, which in many parts of France held the lines with young boys and old men; but not in the Meuse-Argonne. Initially outnumbered three or four to one, the Germans reacted to Pershing's offensive by pouring every reserve formation into battle. Their artillery remained the best in the world. Their air formations were strong and vigorous. And they had many thousands of machine guns.

Pershing had expected the initial advance to take no more than 36 hours, but it bogged down almost immediately in the face of determined resistance. That only convinced him to push harder, driving his forces to exert every nerve, every resource. Like President Wilson and his cabinet, Pershing hoped that victory in the Meuse-Argonne would help establish America's right to stand coequal with the old empires of Europe. He also expected his troops to demonstrate the superiority of American initiative and fighting spirit. The individual doughboy, he told them, should not put his faith in trenches, artillery, or machine guns but in his rifle, bayonet, and the will to win. Pershing thus put his boys up against a veteran, well-entrenched enemy with many machine guns and little naïveté about the horrors of war. Later theorists, such as B. H. Liddell Hart, would excoriate Pershing for his inability to "master the requirements of the modern battlefield." And the Americans' lack of training in weapons, tactics, and combined arms had bloody results. But it's too strong to lay it all on Pershing. Many of the problems of Meuse-Argonne resulted from years of unpreparedness and the nation's late entry into the war.

The term "doughboy" has uncertain origins. What's clear is that the doughboys represented all the vigor and variety of American society in the early 20th century. Many were recent immigrants or sons of immigrants and could barely speak English. Thousands were African American, segregated into separate units and constantly persecuted, although they would prove their patriotism in blood. The doughboys came rich, poor, and everything in between, from the city and the country, putting aside work as bankers, farmers, professional baseball players, and gangsters. Poorly trained and unprepared for modern warfare, they were nevertheless determined to prove their mettle.

At dawn the rain ceased, and a dense mantle of fog settled over Madeleine Farm. A runner brought the day's orders, which directed Woodfill to lead a combat reconnaissance of the woods he had scouted the night before and to find the German lines. At 6 a.m. the men of his battalion rose, shivering and sodden with mud, and moved out in skirmish lines, advancing 16 paces apart, bayonets fixed and rifles ready.

After kicking through soaked shrubbery, the doughboys entered another ravine bisected by a light railway line. The fog, which up to this point had covered them, lifted as if on cue, and German mortars and machine guns opened up. Beside Woodfill, a sergeant grunted, moved as if sleepwalking, and then keeled over dead on the railway tracks. Men ran or were hurled by shell blasts in all directions. One teenage soldier screamed and fired wildly until his buddies dragged him down.

Someone had to find the enemy machine guns and take them out. Motioning his men to stay back, Woodfill tore off his pack and dashed ahead. Bullets passed so close to his face that he could feel their heat. A shell hole appeared, and he dove in just in time. After a few moments to catch his breath, he peered over the rim and identified three enemy soldiers: one to his right in an old stable; another hidden in the woods somewhere ahead; and a third in a church tower in the small town of Cunel, about 300 hundred yards to his left.

The church tower and stable came first. Putting his prewar hunting skills to use, Woodfill drew a bead on the tower and downed the enemy gun crew with one clip of bullets. He fired another deadly clip through a gap in the stable boards and, not stopping to savor his success, dashed on into another hole, the third gun's bullets kicking the ground behind him.

After a moment Woodfill leapt up, raced for another hole, and tumbled in. Suddenly he couldn't catch his breath, and his nose, throat, and eyes felt as if they'd been stuffed with horseradish. Gas! He had to get out of that hole, but he searched in vain for another shelter. Spotting a patch of thistles, he crawled out to some open space behind it and lay gasping for air as he waited for the enemy gunner to lose interest.

By 1918 the Germans had developed gas warfare to deadly perfection. After early experiments from 1915 with chlorine and phosgene, they had come up with a new, deadly compound. Mustard gas not only burned a man's lungs but blinded him and left severe burns all over his body. The Americans used gas too, but their techniques lagged far behind those of the Germans. Worse, they had been poorly trained in the use of gas masks and did not appreciate their value. Woodfill, like many others, disdained to use a mask because it limited his scope of vision. The whiffs of gas he received in the Meuse-Argonne would cripple his lungs for the rest of his life.

Woodfill crawled ahead to an old gravel pile. Hearing the German gun just ahead, he carefully laid out his automatic pistol and a clip of rifle ammunition, then pushed the tip of his rifle inch by inch over the gravel's rim, and squinted over the sights. The muzzle of a German Maxim poked out of a thicket just over 10 yards ahead. Gas had brought tears to Woodfill's eyes; he struggled to blink them away. Finally, the outline of an enemy helmet and a grim face came into view. Woodfill fired, and both disappeared.

Another face, equally grim, rose up. Woodfill fired again. The German died, but another took his place. It was like shooting targets in a gallery. Four Germans went down before the two remaining bolted. Woodfill dropped them both, the first with the last bullet in his rifle clip, the second with the .45 pistol he had placed within handy reach.

Moving past the corpse-choked machine-gun nest, he swerved to avoid what looked like a dead enemy officer lying in the mud. As he did so, the German—a huge man—leapt up, grabbed Woodfill's rifle, and hurled it into the brush. Fortunately he had not unholstered his Luger, while the American held his .45 at the ready. Woodfill fired once, then paused briefly to divest the corpse of souvenirs before moving on.

Only now did Woodfill sense the pandemonium surrounding him. Machine-gun and rifle fire echoed through the woods, and shadowy forms dashed from tree to tree among the trailing wisps of fog. As he crawled toward another enemy nest, bullets again splashed the mud only inches from his face. He rolled behind a tree trunk, pinned down. Then, unaccountably, the fire stopped, and he dashed away. Only later did he learn that one of his men had closed with the crew and dispatched it with bayonet and pistol.

Woodfill polished off another enemy nest with his rifle, then happened upon a trio of teenage German ammunition carriers who begged for mercy. He sent them to the rear. Further ahead, he encountered another machine-gun nest. He slid through 10 yards of soupy mud until he could see the top of the German gunner's head. Again, five men went down, one by one.

It had almost been too easy, and for a brief moment Woodfill let down his guard, standing up and walking toward the enemy guns. The air exploded around him as another enemy opened fire, driving him headlong into the apparently vacated trench. He landed on top of an enemy officer with a Luger. The American recovered first and shot the German through the gut. An instant later, another German appeared. When his pistol jammed, Woodfill grabbed the nearest object within reach—a pickax—and swung it down upon the soldier just as he was raising his rifle.

Some instinct told Woodfill to wheel around. Another bullet smacked where he had just stood. The German officer was dying, but he could still use his Luger. Woodfill finished him off with the pickax.

Pulling back to the woods, Woodfill gathered a few of his men and established an outpost amid the storm of steel. Germans seemed to be everywhere. "We might get out and we might not," Woodfill told his men, but "anyway, we could give 'em a hot time before they saw us." Taking cover, they sniped every figure they could identify as German, loading and firing as if in a dream. Finally the woods fell silent. The enemy had withdrawn.

Later that afternoon, Woodfill's remnant herded a gaggle of weary prisoners back to the Red Diamond's front lines. Woodfill's major asked what he had done. "I got a few," he replied. "Yeah," said the major. "I know you did."

On a nearby knoll, Capt. Edward Allworth watched the procession through his binoculars. "Looks like Woodfill's boys are rounding up some prisoners," he shouted to his runner over the rising screech of incoming artillery. "Yes, that's right," he added after a moment. "They're on their way to the rear. Woodfill's having quite a day for himself!"

"Yes sir!" yapped the runner, who looked suspiciously young for his stated enlistment age of 18. "If we could clean out those bastards on the heights, we could mop up this area in a hurry!"

"Just what I was thinking," replied Allworth. "But our artillery has been ordered to lay off this sector until we push the enemy back." Raising himself up for a better look, he provoked a burst of German machine-gun fire that spattered the two with dirt and debris. "For Christ's sake, Captain, keep your head down," screamed the runner, pulling Allworth back down into their shell hole. "That was a little close, eh?" said the captain with a wry grin.

The barrage intensified until the runner felt sure they were doomed. "We've got to get the hell out of here!" he howled. "We'll be blown to bits if we stay here any longer!" As if to confirm his prediction, a shell landed nearby, momentarily lifting the two Americans into the air and partially burying them under mud and stones, as the air came alive with bullets.

"Come on! It's now or never!" cried Allworth, and the two jumped out of their hole and sprinted for what next bit of cover they could find. As they ran, the runner sensed other Americans scrambling around him. Many were cut down, while others sobbed or screamed in panic. "How can anyone live through this hell?" the runner asked himself.

Just as they had seemed to reach safety, another shell barreled in. To the runner it seemed to shriek as no shell had shrieked before, closer and closer until it burst with a terrifying crash. After a moment of oblivion, he opened his eyes and realized he was still alive. "If this is the result of one day, what will it be tomorrow . . . and the next day—and the next?" The runner had never thought in such terms before. He was only 13 years old.

Ernest L. Wrentmore hardly looked like a child. He had a wrestler's build, stood five feet six inches tall, and weighed 145 pounds. A doctor's son from West Farmington, Ohio, he had, like many others, lied about his age in order to enlist; but he got away with much more than most. With his 14th birthday not coming up until November 1918, he was by far the youngest soldier in the American Army. Captain Allworth suspected that Wrentmore was underage, but he couldn't prove it and certainly never imagined that his young charge was only 13. Allworth looked more like a child than Wrentmore did, although the captain had played fullback in college.

Wrentmore and his buddies spent the remainder of that day and the following night scrounging for food—forcing down some moldy bread that tasted like a "haunted house"—and dodging bullets and shells. October 14 found them back at the front, preparing to jump off once more. Soldiers gripped their rifles with white knuckles and stared tensely into the distance. Captain Allworth had confiscated Wrentmore's rifle and ordered him to stay close; but the boy still possessed a small arsenal that he had gathered at various places on the battlefield, including two .45s, two wicked-looking knives, and pocketfuls of ammunition.

Wrentmore shook uncontrollably as H-Hour approached but tried to cover it up with a show of bravado. "Hope none of you guys think I'll turn tail when the chips are down," he told his comrades. "I won't—not as long as I have an ounce of strength left in me!" With that, he gave his pistols a pat and moved off to join his captain.

At 8:30 a.m., Allworth waved and shouted "Forward!" Wrentmore and the other Red Diamonds jumped up, yelling wildly. At first Wrentmore felt like part of an unstoppable avalanche. Then the artillery opened up, killing men in swaths. He felt sick: a million thoughts pulsed through his brain, all variations on the stark certainty that they'd never make it.

Somehow, despite the slaughter, the attack gained momentum. Under covering fire from American heavy machine guns, the infantry pushed across a road and uphill toward Cunel. Corpses and the wounded of both sides lay scattered about; stretcher bearers moved among them with the dreadful slowness of exhaustion. Smoke and poison gas clogged the air, drifting in gray and yellow tufts across a once idyllic countryside that now Wrentmore thought resembled "a scene from the infernal region."

Despite their appalling losses, the Red Diamond doughboys fought on, driving the Germans from the woods adjoining Cunel and burning out their pillboxes. Hand-to-hand fighting swirled around Wrentmore.

He eventually rejoined his captain. The fighting seemed to have gone reasonably well so far, but Allworth's face was grim. To their right, the 3rd Division had lost contact with the Red Diamonds, opening their flank to murderous enfilade. Contact had to be reestablished at all costs—even, Allworth admitted, if it meant Wrentmore's life. No other runners were available. The boy would have to go.

"I understand, sir," answered Wrentmore gamely. "If I don't make it, you'll know that I tried!" But even as he spoke, his insides were turning to jelly. "God be with you," Allworth shouted as Wrentmore leapt out of the hole, passed his buddies, who were still desperately engaged, and moved into a fire-swept no-man's-land, dodging from shell holes to underbrush to shattered tree trunks. Just as he dove behind a tree, bullets cut into the trunk and knocked him cruelly into some bushes.

Pouring with sweat, Wrentmore searched himself frantically for a wound. Not finding any blood, he finally realized that his gas mask had stopped the bullet. "Well, here goes again!" he yelled and then zigzagged frantically, bullets chasing him like bees. Diving through some underbrush, he landed amid a pile of dead Germans.

Eventually he made contact with an officer of the 3rd Division and delivered his message. The gap in the lines was closed up, and the advance resumed. But a raw and bleeding wound had opened in Wrentmore's 13-year-old psyche, one that would never heal. In the following days he witnessed horrors that pushed him to the verge of insanity. "If this don't let up soon," he told a friend, "it'll be curtains for me." Shortly afterward, he was severely gassed while on another mission. Coughing violently, his young body racked with scorching pain, he passed in and out of consciousness.

He awoke in a dressing station under shellfire. Around him lay scores of men on stretchers, one after another screaming "I'm hit! I'm hit!" He passed out again; an ambulance carried him to the rear. Not far away, another ambulance carried Lt. Samuel Woodfill, also gassed. Neither would return to combat.

Woodfill would receive the Medal of Honor, as would Allworth. Wrentmore received no such honors, but he was happy enough just to return home. Their efforts, with those of more than a million other American soldiers, had led to eventual victory in the Meuse-Argonne, as the doughboys finally broke through on November 1 and took all their objectives, helping to hasten the end of the First World War.

American soldiers had fought on a large scale for only the final six months of the war. Yet more than 53,000 men had been killed during that brief period, and more than 200,000 wounded. In the Meuse-Argonne alone, the First Army had killed or wounded 100,000 Germans, taken 26,000 prisoners, and captured 874 artillery pieces and more than 3,000 machine guns. They had experienced combat as intense as any of their countrymen have ever endured. And although their limited training and experience had cost them brutally, they had learned on the job and developed into some of the finest fighting men in the world. The bravery of U.S. soldiers and Marines in the First World War, and especially at the Meuse-Argonne, was acclaimed by everyone who fought alongside them. No other American soldier had ever learned how to fight in such a short period of time. While the First Army had not won the war,

they appreciably hastened its end. But, perhaps most important, the doughboys had shown—more than any number of generals, diplomats, or politicians—that America had an important role to play on the world stage.

The war never truly ended for the doughboys. They returned to families that did not understand and sometimes did not value their sacrifices. Veterans wrestling with post-traumatic stress disorder found it hard to find and keep jobs. Woodfill, returning to the farm where he had grown up, struggled to recover a sense of direction, fell deeply into debt, and relied on the kindness of neighbors to keep him afloat until he died in 1951. Wrentmore served as a colonel in the Army Air Force during World War II, then in the Air Force in the Korean War, but remained frail until his death in 1983. Both were buried at Arlington National Cemetery. But the greatest testament to their unwavering courage was in the shell-scarred woods and fields of the Meuse-Argonne.

Critical Thinking

1. Critically discuss whether the American troops who fought in World War I in 1917 and 1918 shifted the balance of power to the allies and were responsible for the Armistice being declared on November 11, 1918.
2. Critically discuss Professor Lengel's argument that World War I was the first modern war. Would military historians of the Civil War agree or disagree with this assessment?
3. Describe and evaluate the military and post-military careers of Lieutenant Samuel Woodfill and 13-year-old private Ernest L. Wrentmore. How do their experiences reflect a bottom-up rather than a top-down view of World War I?

Create Central

www.mhhe.com/createcentral

Internet References

World War I—Trenches on the Web
Mike Lawrence's interesting site supplies extensive resources about the Great War and is the appropriate place to begin exploration of this topic as regards the American experience in World War I. There are "virtual tours" on certain topics, such as "Life on the Homefront."
    www.worldwar1.com

EDWARD G. LENGEL is an associate professor of history at the University of Virginia and the author of *To Conquer Hell: The Meuse-Argonne, 1918* (Henry Holt and Co., 2008).

Article

To Make the World Safe for Democracy

World War I marked the first time that U.S. soldiers would sail east to decide a major European war.

JOHN LUKACS

Learning Outcomes

After reading this article, you will be able to:

- Describe the catalyst for the U.S. declaration of war on Germany in 1917.
- Explain why many Americans opposed the idea of a League of Nations at the time.

Late on April 2, 1917, President Woodrow Wilson, flanked by a small cavalry escort, drove to the Capitol to address Congress to urge a declaration of war against Germany. He was tired. His speech contained no memorable phrases, save perhaps one: "The world must be made safe for democracy." A few eloquent words were uttered by the opponents of the declaration of war. They were not many; only 50 out of the 435 congressmen and six of the 96 senators stood against it. The Senate voted for war two days later, the House two days after that, on Good Friday.

This was nothing like Fort Sumter or Pearl Harbor. Two months before April 2, Germany had resumed unrestricted submarine warfare, which moved public opinion—and Wilson—toward war. Leading up to this time, the president had often been of two minds. But during the second half of March he convinced himself that he had no choice. April 1917 was a culminating point in the advance of American determination to oppose Germany by war, if it must. And America's subsequent entry into the war would prove one of the most important turning points in U.S. history.

For centuries, European soldiers had crossed the Atlantic from east to west; for the first time American soldiers would sail the other way.

For long centuries, even during the 19th century, European soldiers had crossed the Atlantic from east to west to protect their nations' interests in the Americas. Now, for the first time, two million American soldiers would sail the other way to decide a great European war. A central pillar of the American identity had been its distinctive New World character, independent and distinct from the Old. Now this would change, with the New World becoming involved in the destinies of the Old.

None of this was clear in 1917. Unlike in 1941, the vast economy of the United States was still unprepared for war. The mass of the two million American soldiers did not get to France until a year or more after the declaration of war. They went into combat with the German army after the French and the British, exhausted as they were, halted the last great German drive against Paris in June and July 1918. Still, the American presence in France decided the war.

American troops did not stay long in Europe. For a moment President Wilson seemed to be the leader of the entire world, but he did not have his way either in Paris or, a few months later, with the majority of the American people. They repudiated his version of a League of Nations; indeed, Americans rejected the entire episode of their involvement with Europe. For generations millions of immigrants had been flooding into the United States from the Old World; but a few years after 1917, a series of immigration acts, passed by great majorities in Congress and supported by American public sentiment, put an end to this nearly unrestricted mass movement of peoples. Ten years after 1917 many, if not most, Americans had come to regard the war of 1917–18 as a mistake.

But that too did not last. It was impossible to isolate America. By 1918 the principal financial center of the world had become New York, not London; the almighty dollar replaced the once sovereign pound sterling. In the 1920s European art masterpieces were routinely passing to America, bought by wealthy collectors. The United States was becoming a repository of much that was best in Old World civilization—and the Atlantic was no longer an estranging sea. Twenty years after 1918, Americans were riveted by the horrifying prospect of another world war, which the nation would eventually fight across both of the greatest oceans, bringing down despotic enemies on both sides of the globe. By 1945 the United States had become the strongest and most prosperous country in the world. But so she had been in 1918. Only now an American military presence stayed abroad.

Franklin Roosevelt took up many of Wilson's ideas. The United Nations was meant to be another, grander version of Wilson's League of Nations. Lonely and ill, Wilson had died in February 1924, only 13 days after Vladimir Lenin. But his ideal of national self-determination prevails even now, long after the idea of a proletarian world revolution has disappeared. For a long time many people, including communists as well as anti-communists, believed that the most significant events in 1917 were the Russian Revolution and Russia's withdrawal from the First World War. But it was, in fact, America's entry into the war that was the defining moment.

Critical Thinking

1. Did most Americans agree with the U.S. involvement in WWI?

2. In what ways did immigration play a role in Americans' sentiment about its role in the war?

Create Central

www.mhhe.com/createcentral

Internet References

U.S. Department of State
   http://history.state.gov/milestones/1914-1920/WWI
History.com
   www.history.com/this-day-in-history/america-enters-world-war-i
PBS.org
   www.pbs.org/wgbh/amex/wilson/portrait/wp_league.html
BBC
   www.bbc.co.uk/history/worldwars/wwone/league_nations_01.shtml

---

JOHN LUKACS, winner of the 1994 Pulitzer Prize for *The End of the Twentieth Century and the End of the Modern Age* (Houghton Mifflin Harcourt), is professor of history emeritus at Chestnut Hill College.

Article

Between Heaven and Earth
Lindbergh: Technology and Environmentalism

Glen Jeansonne and David Luhrssen describe how the pioneer aviator Charles Lindbergh was increasingly disturbed by the tension between technology and its impact on the environment. In his later career, in the 1960s, Lindbergh became a spokesman for the embryonic environmental movement as they describe here.

GLEN JEANSONNE AND DAVID LUHRSSEN

Learning Outcomes

After reading this article, you will be able to:

- Explain why Lindberg blamed technology for environmental problems.

- Discuss the ways public sentiment for Lindberg changed after his visit to Germany and his formation of "America First."

The fervour greeting Charles A. Lindbergh on his arrival in Paris on May 21st, 1927, was not unlike the excitement surrounding the first landing on the moon, four decades later. As the first person to pilot an aeroplane solo across the Atlantic, Lindbergh symbolized the triumph of technology over geography and the human spirit over the barrier of space.

Technology was initially Lindbergh's muse. He embraced it like most Americans of his day and became the embodiment of the country's boyish, can-do image, yet he himself soon became ambivalent about it. Crediting his flight to rapid advances in the 'scientific researches that have been in progress for countless centuries', he was uncomfortable that those advances enabled the world to participate in his triumph through radio and radiographs, flashing across the ocean at speeds faster than his plane could travel. The mass media made him the world's most famous person, but he was never entirely comfortable with fame, willing to use it in the cause of American neutrality in the Second World War, yet shrinking from its grip on his private life. He blamed the kidnapping and murder of his two-year-old son in 1932 on the excessive attention of the media.

Lindbergh's ambivalence about technology increased with the years. By the 1960s the man who was once an icon for progress—defined as humanity's conquest of the earth through technology—had become a tireless advocate of nature and aboriginal peoples against the encroachment of civilization.

Perhaps Lindbergh had always carried within himself visions contrary to the onward march of science. Late in life he claimed his ambivalence towards technology had begun in childhood: 'Instinctively I was drawn to the farm, intellectually to the laboratory'. He also claimed in his memoir that misty spectres had followed him on his transatlantic flight years before, writing:

> My visions are easily explained away through reason, but the longer I live, the more limited I believe rationality to be. I have found that the irrational gives man insight he cannot otherwise attain.

Born on February 4th, 1902, Lindbergh spent much of his youth roaming his family's sprawling homestead on the Mississippi River. The family wealth gave Lindbergh first-hand experience of the latest technological advances and their impact on twentieth century life. The Lindbergh's first car with its hand crank was soon replaced by a model with a self-starting engine; machinery supplanted manual farm labour. The social transformation caused by steam turbines, automobiles, electricity and telephones 'confirmed my growing desire to become an engineer and take part in the world's unprecedented progress', as he recalled. Though eloquent and intellectually curious, Lindbergh never enjoyed school and was too much of an individual to conform readily to any curriculum. Bored with his studies, he was expelled in 1922 from the engineering course at the University of Wisconsin for poor grades. He had been thinking of dropping out anyway. Lindbergh wanted to learn how to fly.

The Wright Brothers built and flew the first successful aeroplane less than two years after Lindbergh's birth. Within a short time their rickety invention became a potent weapon. The acceleration of aircraft design spurred by the First World War also raised hopes that the new technology would bring together a world it had helped destroy. With safer, more dependable aircraft, the dream of commercial aviation was becoming reality.

Lindbergh became a 'barnstormer' who entertained paying customers with aerial feats such as wing-walking and flying suspended from the belly of a plane. Envious of the more powerful aircraft being built for the army, Lindbergh enlisted as a reserve officer in 1925 while earning a living by delivering airmail.

Inspired by the much-publicized transpolar flights and other aeronautical adventures, his dreams soon turned to the flight, nonstop from New York to Paris, that would earn him such acclaim. It was a daring journey under the best conditions, given the fragility and limited range of contemporary aircraft. Unruffled by danger, accustomed to altitude and solitude, Lindbergh decided to fly the Atlantic alone.

His plane, *The Spirit of St Louis,* was a feat of engineering, a single-engine monoplane designed to his specifications. Soon after landing in Paris, the young aviator was dubbed 'Lucky Lindy' by the media despite his insistence that the flight represented a triumph for American engineering rather than a trial with fate. Lindbergh found the adulation uncomfortable. He was more concerned with extolling his US-made earth-inductor compass and air-cooled engine than his own act of derring-do. After Lindbergh had completed a whirlwind tour of European capitals, President Calvin Coolidge ordered him home, promoted him to colonel and decorated him in a ceremony listened to by millions on the radio.

In 1929 Lindbergh married Anne Morrow, a shy, intellectually-sophisticated ambassador's daughter, and pushed her to become an independent woman, an early, if perhaps inadvertent, feminist. Anne Lindbergh became a skilled aviator and one of the best-selling female authors of her time, an inspiration to women across America. The Lindberghs were a model modern couple, at the cutting edge of technological developments. Together they pioneered the use of aerial photography as an aid to archaeologists, focusing on Central American sites. When they flew to East Asia in 1931 scouting for US-Chinese air routes, Anne served as co-pilot, navigator and radio operator. The mission was part of Lindbergh's campaign on behalf of commercial aviation. As adviser to Pan American and TWA, he helped choose flight plans and locations for terminals, and became the poster boy for the dawning age of air travel. His flights over several continents sharpened his impression of the Earth's beauty. As early as the 1950s, he was dismayed by the changes visible from the air, the scars on the land, the pollution. Following the kidnap and tragic murder of their first son, the Lindbergh's aversion to publicity and fear that kidnappers might strike at their other children compelled them to leave the United States in 1935. After a sojourn in the United Kingdom where they lived quietly in the Kent countryside in a house rented from the writer Vita Sackville-West, the family moved in 1938 to a remote island off the coast of Brittany. Here Lindbergh worked with a French physician and Nobel Prize winner, Alexis Carrel, with whom he had begun collaborating years before at the Rockefeller Institute, New York. While at the institute, Lindbergh and Carrel perfected the perfusion pump, an apparatus that permitted an organ to live outside the body, making organ transplants feasible.

Lindbergh regretted that aviation, which symbolized the advance of civilization, might lead instead to its destruction.

In 1936 Lindbergh was invited to Germany at the request of the US military attaché in Berlin, Major Truman Smith, who asked him to report on German air power. Following this visit Lindbergh was an honoured guest in Nazi Germany on several other occasions. Profoundly impressed, he pronounced the Luftwaffe as Europe's most powerful air force, though he was concerned about the uses to which it might be put. While his widely-reported remarks may have buttressed the mood of appeasement in Britain and France, Lindbergh took little pleasure from his observations. He regretted that aviation, which symbolized the advance of civilization, might lead instead to its destruction. As political storm clouds gathered over Europe, he began to wonder whether the technology that caused Western civilization to rise would lead to its fall. Lindbergh had first addressed the issue during his first visit to Germany at a lunch in his honour.

After returning home in April 1939, Lindbergh became an advocate of American neutrality, an isolationist adhering to the tradition that the US should stay aloof from foreign wars. Lindbergh was a charter member of the executive committee of America First when the organization was founded in September 1940. America First was an umbrella organization for a disparate group of people who opposed American involvement in the war and Roosevelt's efforts to assist Great Britain. It included liberals, conservatives and socialists, but also attracted a loud contingent of anti-semites and German sympathizers. Lindbergh's visits to Germany and his acceptance of a medal from Luftwaffe commander Hermann Goering tainted his reputation. The rancour between Roosevelt and Lindbergh became noisy after the president hinted publicly that Lindbergh harboured treasonous thoughts. In the aftermath, Lindbergh resigned his military commission. Following Japan's attack on Pearl Harbor (December 7th, 1941), America First disbanded. Lindbergh became a test pilot for military aircraft manufacturers and flew combat missions in the Pacific. Although he was still lionized by the military, the public had become wary of their former hero. The 1942 movie *Keeper of the Flame,* directed by George Cukor, starring Spencer Tracy and Katherine Hepburn, concerned a distinguished American traitor modelled in part on Lindbergh in the minds of many Americans.

Postwar, the cooling of passions enabled Lindbergh's rehabilitation as a national hero. He worked quietly as an advisor to the Strategic Air Command, troubled by the atomic bomb and the growth of weapons technology but fearful of the Soviet Union and the threat of a totalitarian victory in the arms race. He won a Pulitzer Prize for his 1953 bestseller *The Spirit of St Louis,* an account of his transatlantic flight, was appointed an Air Force brigadier general by Dwight D. Eisenhower, invited to the White House under John F. Kennedy, and honoured by

Lyndon B. Johnson for his support of the pioneering work of Robert Goddard, the father of rocketry, on the technology that put man on the Moon. At Lindbergh's recommendation, Goddard was financed during the 1930s by the Guggenheim Foundation at a time when rocketry was often dismissed as science fiction.

During his final years in the 1960s and 70s Lindbergh's thoughts were focused more on the earth than the sky. Stripped of his status as an American idol, Lindbergh enjoyed the privacy he had long sought and was able to pursue his interests outside the public spotlight. As early as the 1930s the Lindberghs had flown to India, ostensibly on behalf of civil aviation but also in search of yogis and mystics. They spent many hours with Alexis Carrel at that time discussing subjects 'beyond conventionally-accepted fields of science'. Lindbergh became fascinated with the Chinese philosophy of Taoism, which emphasized harmony with nature. Perhaps these interests, considered exotic before the 1960s thrust them toward the mainstream, prepared Lindbergh for the final campaign of his career.

I felt revolted by some of the values I had held in the past, and on the martial and material development of science.

'I felt revolted by some of the values I had held in the past, and on the martial and material development of science,' Lindbergh wrote near the end of his life about his postwar reflections. 'I considered renouncing my profession and living far away from modern technology, some place where I could be in touch with nature and the earth'.

By the 1960s he cautiously emerged from seclusion as a champion of the rising environmental movement. Echoing Rachel Carson's *Silent Spring* (1962) and Paul Ehrlich's *The Population Bomb* (1968), books which influenced the rising counterculture, Lindbergh promoted clean air and water and measures curbing pesticides and development. In an article for the *Readers Digest* called 'Is Civilization Progress?' in 1964 he declared: 'Where civilization is most advanced, few birds exist. I realized that if I would have to choose, I would rather have birds than air planes.' During this last period of his life Lindbergh focused on East Asia and the South Pacific. His interest in the latter region was sparked through his association with British cultural anthropologist Tom Harrisson, who had lived among natives in the New Hebrides and Borneo.

The one-time champion of aviation tried to ban US landing rights for the supersonic airliner Concorde, and succeeded in blocking construction of an airbase on the Indian Ocean island of Aldabra, the breeding ground for the giant land tortoise. His name gained him the ear of government and corporate officers who might have ignored the pleas of lesser-known ecological activists.

In 1968 he gave his first public speech since America First, convincing the Alaska legislature to preserve wolves against extinction. He also adopted the cause of the great whales,

persuading the Archer Daniels Midland corporation to reduce harpooning. He became an adviser to the Nixon administration, which proved remarkably eager to extend government regulation of the environment. As a member along with Prince Charles and Prince Bernhard of the Netherlands of the World Wildlife Federation's Committee of 100, Lindbergh lobbied heads of state on behalf of endangered species and habitats. He was especially persuasive with Philippines President Ferdinand Marcos, who he met in 1969 and who established a preserve for the tamarau, a wild buffalo, at his behest. Flying incognito to foreign destinations, Lindbergh was not content simply to remain in the conclaves of the powerful. For example, he embarked on a helicopter trip through the Philippine island of Mindoro to build community support for wildlife conservation. In 1970 Lindbergh became a leader of the Private Association for National Minorities (PANAMIN), a Filipino advocacy group championing tribal peoples against the encroachment of farmers and loggers.

Unlike many celebrity foreigners with a cause to push in the media, Lindbergh largely shunned publicity, lived for months with the tribes he supported and nearly came to blows with unsympathetic local authorities. He was photographed in a peasant's conical hat, brandishing an assault rifle in 1970.

In his final adventure, in 1972, Lindbergh joined an expedition to establish contact with a tiny tribe, the Tasaday, among the last remaining Stone Age people, in the remote Philippines jungle. Lindbergh admired the Tasaday for their ability to exist within nature, but was perplexed by their lack of curiosity over the wider world. He fretted over disturbing their primeval idyll, but ruefully conceded that the Tasaday's time was fast expiring in the age of global travel and communication he had helped advance.

Lindbergh died of cancer on August 25th, 1974, after refusing life support. As a holder of the Congressional Medal of Honor, he was entitled to interment at Arlington National Cemetery in Washington, DC, but chose to be buried in a traditional Hawaiian tomb near his winter home on Maui. Questions about his support for Nazi Germany and public opposition to America's entry to the Second World War continue to darken his reputation even today, while public recognition for his environmental work faded, in part due to his own reluctance to court publicity for it.

At the height of his adulation, many Americans extolled Lindbergh's courage and conviction as the pioneer spirit manifest in the age of air travel. Lindbergh was one of a long line of archetypal American cultural figures, laconic, lonesome and marching to the measure of their own stride. He reflected upon many of the central issues of his age, and his resolute refusal to apologize for mistaken political views from the 1930s and 1940s, a product of the stubbornness that characterized him, was balanced against the actions he took in the 1960s and 1970s. Always in the vanguard, the exponent of technology had become its tireless opponent. An intensely private person, Lindbergh made few efforts to work with the news media to shape his image and agenda and treated reporters with antagonism. As a result, the press came to view him with suspicion. Eventually, he was largely ignored in the media, leaving unsung his accomplishments on behalf of environmentalism and relegating his energetic final years to obscurity.

Further Reading

A. Scott Berg, *Lindbergh* (Putnam's, 1998); Charles A. Lindbergh, *We* (Putnam's, 1927); Charles A. Lindbergh, *Autobiography of Values* (Harcourt Brace Jovanovich, 1978); Joyce Milton, *Loss of Eden: A Biography of Charles and Anne Morrow Lindbergh* (HarperCollins, 1993).

Critical Thinking

1. Why did technology both thrill and upset Lindberg?
2. Besides the personal devastation of losing his first child, in what ways did the kidnapping of his baby affect his public career?

Create Central

www.mhhe.com/createcentral

Internet References

EyeWitnessToHistory.com
www.eyewitnesstohistory.com/volindbergh.htm
wikipedia.com
http://en.wikipedia.org/wiki/Charles_W._Lindberg
CharlesLindberg.com
www.charleslindbergh.com/history

GLEN JEANSONNE is professor of American history at the University of Wisconsin–Milwaukee and the author of *Messiah of the Masses: Huey P. Long and the Great Depression* (Talman, 1995). **DAVID LUHRSSEN** is arts editor of the *Shepherd Express*, Milwaukee's weekly newspaper.

Jeansonne, Glen and David Luhrssen. From *History Today*, January 2008, pp. 55–59. Copyright © 2008 by History Today, Ltd. Reprinted by permission.

Article

Remember the Roaring '20s?

If the crisis is beginning to sound familiar, maybe it rhymes.

ROBERT S. MCELVAINE

Learning Outcomes

After reading this article, you will be able to:

- Describe the similarities between the economic crisis of 1929 and that of today.

- Explain the concept of economic fundamentalism.

"History doesn't repeat itself, but it rhymes." Mark Twain was supposed to have said that, but even if he didn't, there's no denying we're seeing proof of the adage in today's financial crisis.

Consider this statement: "The extraordinary rate of default on residential mortgages forced banks and life insurance companies to 'practically stop making mortgage loans. . . .'" Sounds like 2008, doesn't it? It is in fact a comment from Ben S. Bernanke, current chairman of the Federal Reserve board. But when he wrote those words in 1983, he was talking about the Great Depression.

We've been hearing a lot of comparisons to the Great Depression lately, because today's crisis rhymes with that one to an extraordinary degree. At the most basic level, the cause of the current crisis is simple: Economists, business leaders and policymakers have all been ignoring the lessons learned from that early 20th-century calamity.

I've written extensively about the Great Depression, and in my view, the collapse of the "un-real" estate market of recent years was as predictable as the collapse of the Great Bull Market of the late 1920s. Even though some politicians insist otherwise, the fundamentals of our economy have not been strong, just as they weren't in 1929. And the principal reason is that, just as they were in the period leading up to the Great Depression, economic fundamentalists have been in charge.

It's one of the fascinating coincidences of history that Adam Smith's "The Wealth of Nations" was published in 1776, the year of the United States's birth. America then was seen as an unspoiled paradise, a "New Eden" where humans could return to what they imagined was a "state of nature." There was talk of an "American Adam" who roamed freely in this land where

the "natural economy" of the free market that Smith postulated could operate, well, freely.

Almost from the start, many Americans have operated on the assumption that this American Adam's surname was Smith, and have taken the market as their economic god. The great irony, though, is that a new type of economy was being born in Great Britain at the same time. And industrialism would remove men and women from a state of nature more completely than ever before.

By the 1920s, the industrial economy was mass-producing at a rapid rate, which meant that its survival required the rise of mass consumption. Trying to play by the rules of Adam Smith's pin factory at a time when Henry Ford's massive River Rouge complex was closer to the true nature of the economy was a prescription for disaster. Such huge economic actors don't behave according to the "natural" laws of the simple economy of Smith's day; under modern circumstances, a more visible hand is needed to guide the market onto a course that benefits all. Yet both economists and political leaders of the time maintained their faith in market-god fundamentalism.

The task facing business in the 1920s was replacing the work ethic with a consumption ethic. If the American people were to be made into insatiable consumers, traditional values would have to be undermined and reversed. The means of accomplishing this? Advertising. The Mad Men of the '20s made over the traditional wisdom of "Waste not, want not" into the essential message of the consumption economy: "Waste and want." Bruce Barton of Barton, Durstine & Osborn, for instance, famously portrayed Jesus as the ultimate advertiser and businessman in his 1925 bestseller, "The Man Nobody Knows."

But wanting isn't enough. If the masses are going to be able to buy what they've been persuaded to want, they have to receive a sufficient share of total income to do so. Yet the opposite happened in the '20s. President Calvin Coolidge and his Treasury secretary, Andrew Mellon, drastically reduced

taxes on the highest incomes. Meanwhile, anti-union policies produced less income for worker-consumers. The share
of total national income going to the very richest grew enormously, peaking in 1928, just months before the economy
began to contract in the summer of 1929. The top 10 percent
of American earners then were getting 46 percent of total
income.

Providing large tax cuts for the richest was precisely the
wrong policy. To stimulate consumption, taxes should have
been cut at lower income levels. Cutting taxes on higher
incomes stimulated speculation instead. Sound familiar?

"Don't kill the goose that lays the golden eggs" is one of the
favorite sayings (and warnings) of champions of high profits,
low taxes on the rich, concentrating wealth and income at the
top, and the rest of trickle-down economics. But when profits
become too high and taxes on the very rich too low, the geese
get obese, eventually stop laying eggs and develop coronary
problems.

What the economy needed was an effective weight-loss
program for the monetarily corpulent and a program to help
underweight consumers put on a few pounds (i.e., dollars). Yet
those who argued for such an approach, such as progressive
Republican Sen. George Norris of Nebraska, were ridiculed by
the followers of the god of the unfettered market.

Instead, 1920s financiers gave consumers an injection of the
economic steroid known as credit. And the economy temporarily became extremely robust. Sales of automobiles, radios
and other new products to people who couldn't actually afford
them soared. The ratio of private credit to GDP nearly doubled
between 1913 and 1929. During the '20s, short-term personal
loans from personal finance companies ballooned by more than
1,200 percent.

But a steroid-induced burst of great strength is always likely
to be followed by impotence. Sooner or later the limits of consumer credit are reached—consumers find themselves with
more debt than they can repay, sales decline and banks, left
holding bad loans, begin to fail.

"Sooner or later" arrived in October 1929, as it did again in
September 2008.

Today isn't an exact replay of the 1920s, but it's a pretty
good rhyme. Over the last three decades, top-end tax
rates have been slashed; unions' power has become
diluted; top corporate pay has skyrocketed; the minimum wage
has been allowed to fall in real terms and the average wage
has flatlined. And the credit bubble on which the economy has
been riding in recent years is vastly larger than the one in which
Americans danced the Charleston and drank bathtub gin 80
years ago.

After a long period of less income inequality from the
1940s through the 1970s, inequality began to increase again
in the 1980s and has continued to rise almost continually ever
since. By 2005, income concentration slightly exceeded the
levels of just before the Great Depression: The richest 1 percent of Americans were receiving nearly 22 percent of the

nation's income, and the top 10 percent took in more than
48 percent.

Yet there are some significant differences between the 1920s
and today. Some make our current situation more dangerous.
These include today's huge federal budget deficits (compared
with the more or less balanced budgets of the late 1920s)
and the war in Iraq, which has undermined confidence in the
administration and, along with other policies and the flood of
federal red ink, makes a stimulus through a massive deficit difficult, if not impossible. There's also the trade imbalance: In the
15 years preceding the 1929 collapse, U.S. exports exceeded
imports by $25 billion. Now the trade imbalance is decidedly in
the other direction.

On the other hand, we learned a good deal from what happened in the Great Depression, so the consequences of a major
collapse may be less severe. We came to understand that we live
in an economy far removed from a state of nature and that the
market can't be allowed to rule over us without any restraints.
And although they've been weakened in recent years, we have
in place many regulations and countercyclical programs from
the New Deal, including unemployment insurance and Social
Security.

Here's the main lesson the Great Depression taught us:
Capitalism is the best economic system just as democracy is the best political system, but both contain
inherent dangers that require checks and balances to ensure that
they work properly. One of the most prominent dangers of capitalism is that income will become too concentrated at the top,
undermining the functioning of a consumer-based economy.
The fruits of this lesson were put into effect during the New
Deal through higher taxes on the rich, support for unions to
help working people get a larger share of the national income,
social programs to aid the poor, and such regulatory agencies
as the Securities and Exchange Commission. A system of regulated capitalism was in place and worked very well from World
War II to 1980.

Then economic fundamentalism staged a revival—and once
again got us into a mess. The only thing that can begin to get
us out of it is replacing it with the sort of reasonable, balanced
policies that produced a long period of widespread prosperity
through the middle of the 20th century.

Bottom line: The fundamentalists of the economy are wrong.

Critical Thinking

1. What factors allowed for the economic stability in the
   United States from WWII into the 1980s?

2. What are some of the differences between the 1920s and
   today that make today's economic crisis more dangerous?
   What make it less dangerous?

Create Central

www.mhhe.com/createcentral

Internet References

Encyclopedia2.thefreedictionary.com
http://encyclopedia2.thefreedictionary.com/1929+economic+crisis

CNBC.com
www.cnbc.com/id/46496413

www.france24.com
www.france24.com/en/20081015-19292008-similar-causes-similar
-consequences-financial-crisis

economicshelp.org
www.economicshelp.org/blog/76/economics/wall-street-crash-1929

thebubblebubble.com
www.thebubblebubble.com/1929-crash

ROBERT S. MCELVAINE, a professor of history at Millsaps College, is the author of *The Great Depression* and, most recently, *Grand Theft Jesus: The Highjacking of Religion in America.*

Unit 4

UNIT

From the Great Depression to World War II

After a brief postwar depression, the economy took off during the 1920s. Sales of relatively new products such as automobiles, radios, and telephones mushroomed. Farmers, who sold their goods on a fluctuating market, tended not to fare as well as others but even many of them were purchasing the sundry goods pouring off assembly lines. Successive Republican administrations understandably took credit for this prosperity—attributing it to their wise economic and financial policies. They proclaimed the 1920s as a "New Era." When people ran out of things to buy and still had money left over they dabbled in the stock market in ever-increasing numbers. As stock prices rose dramatically, a kind of speculative mania developed in the latter half of the decade. In the past, most people had bought stocks as long-term investments. That is, they wanted to receive income from the dividends reliable companies would pay over the years. Speculators had no interest in the long run; they bought stocks on the assumption that they would make money when they were sold on the market in a matter of months or even weeks. Rumors abounded, some of them true, about individuals who had earned fortunes "playing" the market.

By the end of the 1920s, stock market prices had soared to unprecedented heights. So long as people were confident that they would continue to rise, they did. There were a few people warning that stocks were overpriced, but they were denounced as doomsayers. Besides, had not the highly regarded President Herbert Hoover predicted that "we are on the verge of a wave of never ending prosperity"? No one can say why this confidence began to falter when it did and not months earlier or later, but on October 24, 1929 the market crashed. "Black Thursday" set off an avalanche of selling as holders dumped their shares at whatever price they could get, thereby driving prices even lower. Some large banks tried to shore up confidence by having representatives appear at the stock exchange where they ostentatiously made large purchase orders. Despite such efforts, prices continued to tumble in the months following.

President Herbert Hoover tried to restore confidence by assuring the public that what had happened was merely a glitch, a necessary readjustment of a market that had gotten out of hand. The economy of America was sound, he claimed, and there was no reason business should not go on as usual. His reassurances met with increasing disbelief as time went on. Businessmen as well as stockholders were worried about the future. In order to protect themselves they laid off workers, cut back on inventory, and put off previous plans to expand or to introduce new products. But their actions, however much sense they made for an individual company, had the collective result of making the situation worse.

Hoover endorsed more federal programs than had any of his predecessors to combat the Depression, but they failed to stop the downward slide. Just as people tend to credit an incumbent when times are good, they also blame him when things go sour. He became the most widely detested man in America: trousers with patches on them were scoffingly referred to as "Hoover" pants and in every city the collection of shacks and shanties in which homeless people lived were called "Hoovervilles." In the presidential election of 1932, Hoover lost by a landside to Democrat candidate Franklin D. Roosevelt. Although Roosevelt had compiled an impressive record as governor of New York state, his greatest asset in the election was that he was not Hoover.

Roosevelt assumed the presidency without any grand design for ending the Depression. Unlike Hoover, however, he was willing to act boldly and on a large scale. His "first 100 days" in office resulted in passage of an unprecedented number of measures designed to promote recovery and to restore confidence. In the first of what became known as Roosevelt's "Fireside Chats," FDR's reassuring manner and his ability to persuade people that he cared about them, went a long way towards restoring confidence.

Massive purchases from abroad and the American preparedness program stimulated the economy as no New Deal legislation had been able to do. Unlike Woodrow Wilson, Roosevelt made no effort to remain neutral when conflict engulfed Europe and Asia. He believed the United States ought to cooperate with other nations to stop aggression, but had to contend with a Congress and public that was deeply influenced by those who thought the United States should remain aloof. After war broke out, Roosevelt took decidedly un-neutral steps when he transferred 50 overage destroyers to Great Britain and later pushed through Congress a "Lend Lease" program providing aid for those nations fighting the Axis Powers. Alarmed at Japan's attempt to conquer China, Roosevelt tried to use economic pressure to get Japan to back off. His efforts only stiffened the will of Japanese hardliners who planned and carried out the raid on Pearl Harbor on December 7, 1941. An aroused Congress almost unanimously approved the declaration of war Roosevelt requested.

Pearl Harbor and Germany's declaration of war against the United States a few days later united Americans in their determination to win the war. For the next six months, the Japanese ran rampant as they inflicted a string of defeats against British and American forces in the Pacific. The British suffered a humiliating setback at Singapore, and though American forces fought with greater determination in the Philippines they too had to surrender. The tide of Japanese expansion was halted during the summer of 1942 by the naval battles at the Coral Sea and at Midway. The United States launched its first offensive operations on Guadalcanal in the Solomon Islands. Though much bitter fighting remained, American military and industrial might rendered Japan's ultimate defeat inevitable.

Roosevelt and his military advisers agreed at the beginning of the war that the European theater should receive top priority. Offensive operations against the Germans and Italians began when U.S. forces invaded North Africa in November 1942, and Sicily and Italy during the next year. Still, the main effort against Germany was put off until June 6, 1944, when Allied forces invaded the French beaches at Normandy.

After tough going against determined German opposition, the invaders broke out across France and began approaching the German border. Hitler launched the last great German offensive in December. In what became known to Americans as "The Battle of the Bulge," the Germans initially made rapid advances but finally were stopped and then pushed back. After more months of fighting, with Germany caught between the western Allies and Soviet armies advancing from the east, Adolf Hitler committed suicide and Germany finally surrendered on May 8, 1945.

Meanwhile, American forces in the Pacific were steadily advancing toward the Japanese homeland. Capture of the Mariana Islands enabled the United States to mount massive air attacks against Japanese cities, and naval actions progressively strangled their war machine. Some historians have argued that President Harry S Truman could have attained a Japanese surrender by the summer of 1945 if only he had assured them that they could retain their sacred emperor. That is incorrect. The Japanese will to resist still ran strong, as the bloody battles of Iwo Jima and Okinawa during the first half of 1945 had shown. Indeed, Japanese generals claimed that they welcomed an invasion of the home islands, where they would inflict such staggering casualties that the United States would settle for a negotiated peace instead of unconditional surrender. The use of atomic bombs against Hiroshima and Nagasaki in August 1945 obviated the need for an invasion as the Japanese surrendered shortly thereafter.

Much has been written about the contributions of women to the war effort. They served in the armed forces as WACS, WAVES, and SPARS, and worked long hours in factories and on farms. This Unit also tells the lesser known story of the Women Airforce Service Pilots, who flew cargo, ferried planes, and towed aerial targets for male pilots. Despite its exemplary record, the organization was disbanded in 1944 and its members were not even officially recognized as veterans until the 1970s.

Why the Money Stopped

JOHN KENNETH GALBRAITH

Learning Outcomes

After reading this article, you will be able to:

• List five flaws in the economy on the eve of the stock market crash in 1929.

• Describe the attempts by President Coolidge and especially President Hoover to stop the depression.

The decade of the twenties, or more precisely the eight years between the postwar depression of 1920–21 and the stock market crash in October of 1929, were prosperous ones in the United States. The total output of the economy increased by more than 50 percent. The preceding decades had brought the automobile; now came many more and also roads on which they could be driven with reasonable reliability and comfort. There was much building. The downtown section of the mid-continent city—Des Moines, Omaha, Minneapolis—dates from these years. It was then, more likely than not, that what is still the leading hotel, the tallest office building, and the biggest department store went up. Radio arrived, as of course did gin and jazz.

These years were also remarkable in another respect, for as time passed it became increasingly evident that the prosperity could not last. Contained within it were the seeds of its own destruction. The country was heading into the gravest kind of trouble. Herein lies the peculiar fascination of the period for a study in the problem of leadership. For almost no steps were taken during these years to arrest the tendencies which were obviously leading, and did lead, to disaster.

At least four things were seriously wrong, and they worsened as the decade passed. And knowledge of them does not depend on the always brilliant assistance of hindsight. At least three of these flaws were highly visible and widely discussed. In ascending order, not of importance but of visibility, they were as follows:

First, income in these prosperous years was being distributed with marked inequality. Although output per worker rose steadily during the period, wages were fairly stable, as also were prices. As a result, business profits increased rapidly and so did incomes of the wealthy and the well-to-do. This tendency was nurtured by assiduous and successful efforts of Secretary of the Treasury Andrew W. Mellon to reduce income taxes with special attention to the higher brackets. In 1929 the 5 percent of the people with the highest incomes received perhaps a quarter of all personal income. Between 1919 and 1929 the share of the one percent who received the highest incomes increased by approximately one-seventh. This meant that the economy was heavily and increasingly dependent on the luxury consumption of the well-to-do and on their willingness to reinvest what they did not or could not spend on themselves. Anything that shocked the confidence of the rich either in their personal or in their business future would have a bad effect on total spending and hence on the behavior of the economy.

This was the least visible flaw. To be sure, farmers, who were not participating in the general advance, were making themselves heard; and twice during the period the Congress passed far-reaching relief legislation which was vetoed by Coolidge. But other groups were much less vocal. Income distribution in the United States had long been unequal. The inequality of these years did not seem exceptional. The trade-union movement was also far from strong. In the early twenties the steel industry was still working a twelve-hour day and, in some jobs, a seven-day week. (Every two weeks when the shift changed, a man worked twice around the clock.) Workers lacked the organization or the power to deal with conditions like this; the twelve-hour day was, in fact, ended as the result of personal pressure by President Harding on the steel companies, particularly on Judge Elbert H. Gary, head of the United States Steel Corporation. Judge Gary's personal acquaintance with these working conditions was thought to be slight, and this gave rise to Benjamin Stolberg's now classic observation that the Judge "never saw a blast furnace until his death." In all these circumstances the increasingly lopsided income distribution did not excite much comment or alarm. Perhaps it would have been surprising if it had.

But the other three flaws in the economy were far less subtle. During World War I the United States ceased to be the world's greatest debtor country and became its greatest creditor. The consequences of this change have so often been described that they have the standing of a cliché. A debtor country could export a greater value of goods than it imported and use the difference for interest and debt repayment. This was what we did before the war. But a creditor must import a greater value than it exports if those who owe it money are to have the wherewithal to pay interest and principal. Otherwise the creditor must either forgive the debts or make new loans to pay off the old.

During the twenties the balance was maintained by making new foreign loans. Their promotion was profitable to domestic investment houses. And when the supply of honest and competent foreign borrowers ran out, dishonest, incompetent, or fanciful borrowers were invited to borrow and, on occasion, bribed to do so. In 1927 Juan Leguia, the son of the then dictator of Peru, was paid $450,000 by the National City Company and J. & W. Seligman for his services in promoting a $50,000,000 loan to Peru which these houses marketed. Americans lost and the Peruvians didn't gain appreciably. Other Latin American republics got equally dubious loans by equally dubious devices. And, for reasons that now tax the imagination, so did a large number of German cities and municipalities. Obviously, once investors awoke to the character of these loans or there was any other shock to confidence, they would no longer be made. There would be nothing with which to pay the old loans. Given this arithmetic, there would be either a sharp reduction in exports or a wholesale default on the outstanding loans, or more likely both. Wheat and cotton farmers and others who depended on exports would suffer. So would those who owned the bonds. The buying power of both would be reduced. These consequences were freely predicted at the time.

The second weakness of the economy was the large-scale corporate thimblerigging that was going on. This took a variety of forms, of which by far the most common was the organization of corporations to hold stock in yet other corporations, which in turn held stock in yet other corporations. In the case of the railroads and the utilities, the purpose of this pyramid of holding companies was to obtain control of a very large number of operating companies with a very small investment in the ultimate holding company. A $100,000,000 electric utility, of which the capitalization was represented half by bonds and half by common stock, could be controlled with an investment of a little over $25,000,000—the value of just over half the common stock. Were a company then formed with the same capital structure to hold *this* $25,000,000 worth of common stock, it could be controlled with an investment of $6,250,000. On the next round the amount required would be less than $2,000,000. That $2,000,000 would still control the entire $100,000,000 edifice. By the end of the twenties, holding-company structures six or eight tiers high were a commonplace. Some of them—the utility pyramids of Insull and Associated Gas & Electric, and the railroad pyramid of the Van Sweringens—were marvelously complex. It is unlikely that anyone fully understood them or could.

In other cases companies were organized to hold securities in other companies in order to manufacture more securities to sell to the public. This was true of the great investment trusts. During 1929 one investment house, Goldman, Sachs & Company, organized and sold nearly a billion dollars' worth of securities in three interconnected investment trusts—Goldman Sachs Trading Corporation; Shenandoah Corporation; and Blue Ridge Corporation. All eventually depreciated virtually to nothing.

This corporate insanity was also highly visible. So was the damage. The pyramids would last only so long as earnings of the company at the bottom were secure. If anything happened to the dividends of the underlying company, there would be trouble, for upstream companies had issued bonds (or in practice sometimes preferred stock) against the dividends on the stock of the downstream companies. Once the earnings stopped, the bonds would go into default or the preferred stock would take over and the pyramid would collapse. Such a collapse would have a bad effect not only on the orderly prosecution of business and investment by the operating companies but also on confidence, investment, and spending by the community at large. The likelihood was increased because in any number of cities—Cleveland, Detroit, and Chicago were notable examples—the banks were deeply committed to these pyramids or had fallen under the control of the pyramiders.

Finally, and most evident of all, there was the stock market boom. Month after month and year after year the great bull market of the twenties roared on. Sometimes there were setbacks, but more often there were fantastic forward surges. In May of 1924 *The New York Times* industrials stood at 106; by end of the year they were 134; by the end of 1925 they were up to 181. In 1927 the advance began in earnest—to 245 by the end of that year and on to 331 by the end of 1928. There were some setbacks in early 1929, but then came the fantastic summer explosion when in a matter of three months the averages went up another 110 points. This was the most frantic summer in our financial history. By its end, stock prices had nearly quadrupled as compared with four years earlier. Transactions on the New York Stock Exchange regularly ran to 5,000,000 or more shares a day. Radio Corporation of America went to 573¾ (adjusted) without ever having paid a dividend. Only the hopelessly eccentric, so it seemed, held securities for their income. What counted was the increase in capital values.

And since capital gains were what counted, one could vastly increase his opportunities by extending his holdings with borrowed funds—by buying on margin. Margin accounts expanded enormously, and from all over the country—indeed from all over the world—money poured into New York to finance these transactions. During the summer, brokers' loans increased at the rate of $400,000,000 a month. By September they totaled more than $7,000,000,000. The rate of interest on these loans varied from 7 to 12 percent and went as high as 15.

This boom was also inherently self-liquidating. It could last only so long as new people, or at least new money, were swarming into the market in pursuit of the capital gains. This new demand bid up the stocks and made the capital gains. Once the supply of new customers began to falter, the market would cease to rise. Once the market stopped rising, some, and perhaps a good many, would start to cash in. If you are concerned with capital gains, you must get them while the getting is good. But the getting may start the market down, and this will one day be the signal for much more selling—both by those who are trying to get out and those who are being forced to sell securities that are no longer safely margined. Thus it was certain that the market would one day go down, and far more rapidly than it went up. Down it went with a thunderous crash in October of

1929. In a series of terrible days, of which Thursday, October 24, and Tuesday, October 29, were the most terrifying, billions in values were lost, and thousands of speculators—they had been called investors—were utterly and totally ruined.

This too had far-reaching effects. Economists have always deprecated the tendency to attribute too much to the great stock market collapse of 1929: this was the drama; the causes of the subsequent depression really lay deeper. In fact, the stock market crash was very important. It exposed the other weakness of the economy. The overseas loans on which the payments balance depended came to an end. The jerry-built holding-company structures came tumbling down. The investment-trust stocks collapsed. The crash put a marked crimp on borrowing for investment and therewith on business spending. It also removed from the economy some billions of consumer spending that was either based on, sanctioned by, or encouraged by the fact that the spenders had stock market gains. The crash was an intensely damaging thing.

And this damage, too, was not only foreseeable but foreseen. For months the speculative frenzy had all but dominated American life. Many times before in history—the South Sea Bubble, John Law's speculations, the recurrent real-estate booms of the last century, the great Florida land boom earlier in the same decade—there had been similar frenzy. And the end had always come, not with a whimper but a bang. Many men, including in 1929 the President of the United States, knew it would again be so.

The increasingly perilous trade balance, the corporate buccaneering, and the Wall Street boom—along with the less visible tendencies in income distribution—were all allowed to proceed to the ultimate disaster without effective hindrance. How much blame attaches to the men who occupied the presidency?

Warren G. Harding died on August 2, 1923. This, as only death can do, exonerates him. The disorders that led eventually to such trouble had only started when the fatal blood clot destroyed this now sad and deeply disillusioned man. Some would argue that his legacy was bad. Harding had but a vague perception of the economic processes over which he presided. He died owing his broker $180,000 in a blind account—he had been speculating disastrously while he was President, and no one so inclined would have been a good bet to curb the coming boom. Two of Harding's Cabinet officers, his secretary of the interior and his attorney general, were to plead the Fifth Amendment when faced with questions concerning their official acts, and the first of these went to jail. Harding brought his fellow townsman Daniel R. Crissinger to be his comptroller of the currency, although he was qualified for this task, as Samuel Hopkins Adams has suggested, only by the fact that he and the young Harding had stolen watermelons together. When Crissinger had had an ample opportunity to demonstrate his incompetence in his first post, he was made head of the Federal Reserve System. Here he had the central responsibility for action on the ensuing boom. Jack Dempsey, Paul Whiteman or F. Scott Fitzgerald would have been at least equally qualified.

Yet it remains that Harding was dead before the real trouble started. And while he left in office some very poor men, he also left some very competent ones. Charles Evans Hughes, his secretary of state; Herbert Hoover, his secretary of commerce; and Henry C. Wallace, his secretary of agriculture, were public servants of vigor and judgment.

The problem of Herbert Hoover's responsibility is more complicated. He became President on March 4, 1929. At first glance this seems far too late for effective action. By then the damage had been done, and while the crash might come a little sooner or a little later, it was now inevitable. Yet Hoover's involvement was deeper than this—and certainly much deeper than Harding's. This he tacitly concedes in his memoirs, for he is at great pains to explain and, in some degree, to excuse himself.

For one thing, Hoover was no newcomer to Washington. He had been secretary of commerce under Harding and Coolidge. He had also been the strongest figure (not entirely excluding the President) in both Administration and party for almost eight years. He had a clear view of what was going on. As early as 1922, in a letter to Hughes, he expressed grave concern over the quality of the foreign loans that were being floated in New York. He returned several times to the subject. He knew about the corporate excesses. In the latter twenties he wrote to his colleagues and fellow officials (including Crissinger) expressing his grave concern over the Wall Street orgy. Yet he was content to express himself—to write letters and memoranda, or at most, as in the case of the foreign loans, to make an occasional speech. He could with propriety have presented his views of the stock market more strongly to the Congress and the public. He could also have maintained a more vigorous and persistent agitation within the Administration. He did neither. His views of the market were so little known that it celebrated his election and inauguration with a great upsurge. Hoover was in the boat and, as he himself tells, he knew where it was headed. But, having warned the man at the tiller, he rode along into the reef.

And even though trouble was inevitable, by March, 1929, a truly committed leader would still have wanted to do something. Nothing else was so important. The resources of the Executive, one might expect, would have been mobilized in a search for some formula to mitigate the current frenzy and to temper the coming crash. The assistance of the bankers, congressional leaders, and the Exchange authorities would have been sought. Nothing of the sort was done. As secretary of commerce, as he subsequently explained, he had thought himself frustrated by Mellon. But he continued Mellon in office. Henry M. Robinson, a sympathetic Los Angeles banker, was commissioned to go to New York to see his colleagues there and report. He returned to say that the New York bankers regarded things as sound. Richard Whitney, the vice-president of the Stock Exchange, was summoned to the White House for a conference on how to curb speculation. Nothing came of this either. Whitney also thought things were sound.

Both Mr. Hoover and his official biographers carefully explained that the primary responsibility for the goings on in New York City rested not with Washington but with the governor of New York State. That was Franklin D. Roosevelt. It was he who failed to rise to his responsibilities. The explanation is far too formal. The future of the whole country was involved. Mr. Hoover was the President of the whole country. If he lacked authority commensurate with this responsibility, he could have requested it. This, at a later date, President Roosevelt did not hesitate to do.

Finally, while by March of 1929 the stock market collapse was inevitable, something could still be done about the other accumulating disorders. The balance of payments is an obvious case. In 1931 Mr. Hoover did request a one-year moratorium on the inter-Allied (war) debts. This was a courageous and constructive step which came directly to grips with the problem. But the year before, Mr. Hoover, though not without reluctance, had signed the Hawley-Smoot tariff. "I shall approve the Tariff Bill. . . . It was undertaken as the result of pledges given by the Republican Party at Kansas City. . . . Platform promises must not be empty gestures." Hundreds of people—from Albert H. Wiggin, the head of the Chase National Bank, to Oswald Garrison Villard, the editor of the *Nation*—felt that no step could have been more directly designed to make things worse. Countries would have even more trouble earning the dollars of which they were so desperately short. But Mr. Hoover signed the bill.

Anyone familiar with this particular race of men knows that a dour, flinty, inscrutable visage such as that of Calvin Coolidge can be the mask for a calm and acutely perceptive intellect. And he knows equally that it can conceal a mind of singular aridity. The difficulty, given the inscrutability, is in knowing which. However, in the case of Coolidge the evidence is in favor of the second. In some sense, he certainly knew what was going on. He would not have been unaware of what was called the Coolidge market. But he connected developments neither with the well-being of the country nor with his own responsibilities. In his memoirs Hoover goes to great lengths to show how closely he was in touch with events and how clearly he foresaw their consequences. In his *Autobiography,* a notably barren document, Coolidge did not refer to the accumulating troubles. He confines himself to such unequivocal truths as "Every day of Presidential life is crowded with activities" (which in his case, indeed, was not true); and "The Congress makes the laws, but it is the President who causes them to be executed."

At various times during his years in office, men called on Coolidge to warn him of the impending trouble. And in 1927, at the instigation of a former White House aide, he sent for William Z. Ripley of Harvard, the most articulate critic of the corporate machinations of the period. The President became so interested that he invited him to stay for lunch, and listened carefully while his guest outlined (as Ripley later related) the "prestidigitation, double-shuffling, honey-fugling, hornswoggling, and skulduggery" that characterized the current Wall Street scene. But Ripley made the mistake of telling Coolidge that regulation was the responsibility of the states (as was then the case). At this intelligence Coolidge's face lit up and he dismissed the entire matter from his mind. Others who warned of the impending disaster got even less far.

And on some occasions Coolidge added fuel to the fire. If the market seemed to be faltering, a timely statement from the White House—or possibly from Secretary Mellon—would often brace it up. William Allen White, by no means an unfriendly observer, noted that after one such comment the market staged a 26-point rise. He went on to say that a careful search "during these halcyon years . . . discloses this fact: Whenever the stock market showed signs of weakness, the President or the Secretary of the Treasury or some important dignitary of the administration . . . issued a statement. The statement invariably declared that business was 'fundamentally sound,' that continued prosperity had arrived, and that the slump of the moment was 'seasonal.' "

Such was the Coolidge role. Coolidge was fond of observing that "if you see ten troubles coming down the road, you can be sure that nine will run into the ditch before they reach you and you have to battle with only one of them." A critic noted that "the trouble with this philosophy was that when the tenth trouble reached him he was wholly unprepared. . . . The outstanding instance was the rising boom and orgy of mad speculation which began in 1927." The critic was Herbert Hoover.

Plainly, in these years, leadership failed. Events whose tragic culmination could be foreseen—and was foreseen—were allowed to work themselves out to the final disaster. The country and the world paid. For a time, indeed, the very reputation of capitalism itself was in the balance. It survived in the years following perhaps less because of its own power or the esteem in which it was held, than because of the absence of an organized and plausible alternative. Yet one important question remains. Would it have been possible even for a strong President to arrest the plunge? Were not the opposing forces too strong? Isn't one asking the impossible?

No one can say for sure. But the answer depends at least partly on the political context in which the Presidency was cast. That of Coolidge and Hoover may well have made decisive leadership impossible. These were conservative Administrations in which, in addition, the influence of the businessman was strong. At the core of the business faith was an intuitive belief in *laissez faire*—the benign tendency of things that are left alone. The man who wanted to intervene was a meddler. Perhaps, indeed, he was a planner. In any case, he was to be regarded with mistrust. And, on the businessman's side, it must be borne in mind that high government office often nurtures a spurious sense of urgency. There is no more important public function than the suppression of proposals for unneeded action. But these should have been distinguished from action necessary to economic survival.

A bitterly criticized figure of the Harding-Coolidge-Hoover era was Secretary of the Treasury Andrew W. Mellon. He opposed all action to curb the boom, although once in 1929 he was persuaded to say that bonds (as distinct from stocks) were a good buy. And when the depression came, he was against doing anything about that. Even Mr. Hoover was shocked by his insistence that the only remedy was (as Mr. Hoover characterized it) to "liquidate labor, liquidate stocks, liquidate the farmers, liquidate real estate." Yet Mellon reflected only in extreme form the conviction that things would work out, that the real enemies were those who interfered.

Outside of Washington in the twenties, the business and banking community, or at least the articulate part of it, was overwhelmingly opposed to any public intervention. The tentative and ineffective steps which the Federal Reserve did take were strongly criticized. In the spring of 1929 when the Reserve system seemed to be on the verge of taking more decisive action, there was an anticipatory tightening of money rates and a sharp drop in the market. On his own initiative Charles E. Mitchell, the head of the National City Bank, poured in new funds. He had an obligation, he said, that was "paramount to any Federal Reserve warning, or anything else" to avert a crisis in the money market. In brief, he was determined, whatever the government thought, to keep the boom going. In that same spring Paul M. Warburg, a distinguished and respected Wall Street leader, warned of the dangers of the boom and called for action to restrain it. He was deluged with criticism and even abuse and later said that the subsequent days were the most difficult of his life. There were some businessmen and bankers—like Mitchell and Albert Wiggin of the Chase National Bank—who may have vaguely sensed that the end of the boom would mean their own business demise. Many more had persuaded themselves that the dream would last. But we should not complicate things. Many others were making money and took a short-run view—or no view—either of their own survival or of the system of which they were a part. They merely wanted to be left alone to get a few more dollars.

And the opposition to government intervention would have been nonpartisan. In 1929 one of the very largest of the Wall Street operators was John J. Raskob. Raskob was also chairman of the Democratic National Committee. So far from calling for preventive measures, Raskob in 1929 was explaining how, through stock market speculation, literally anyone could be a millionaire. Nor would the press have been enthusiastic about, say, legislation to control holding companies and investment trusts or to give authority to regulate margin trading. The financial pages of many of the papers were riding the boom. And even from the speculating public, which was dreaming dreams of riches and had yet to learn that it had been fleeced, there would have been no thanks. Perhaps a President of phenomenal power and determination might have overcome the Coolidge-Hoover environment. But it is easier to argue that this context made inaction inevitable for almost any President. There were too many people who, given a choice between disaster and the measures that would have prevented it, opted for disaster without either a second or even a first thought.

On the other hand, in a different context a strong President might have taken effective preventive action. Congress in these years was becoming increasingly critical of the Wall Street speculation and corporate piggery-pokery. The liberal Republicans—the men whom Senator George H. Moses called the Sons of the Wild Jackass—were especially vehement. But conservatives like Carter Glass were also critical. These men correctly sensed that things were going wrong. A President such

as Wilson or either of the Roosevelts (the case of Theodore is perhaps less certain than that of Franklin) who was surrounded in his Cabinet by such men would have been sensitive to this criticism. As a leader he could both have reinforced and drawn strength from the contemporary criticism. Thus he might have been able to arrest the destructive madness as it became recognizable. The American government works far better—perhaps it only works—when the Executive, the business power, and the press are in some degree at odds. Only then can we be sure that abuse or neglect, either private or public, will be given the notoriety that is needed.

Perhaps it is too much to hope that by effective and timely criticism and action the Great Depression might have been avoided. A lot was required in those days to make the United States in any degree depression-proof. But perhaps by preventive action the ensuing depression might have been made less severe. And certainly in the ensuing years the travail of bankers and businessmen before congressional committees, in the courts, and before the bar of public opinion would have been less severe. Here is the paradox. In the full perspective of history, American businessmen never had enemies as damaging as the men who grouped themselves around Calvin Coolidge and supported and applauded him in what William Allen White called "that masterly inactivity for which he was so splendidly equipped."

Critical Thinking

1. Evaluate the five flaws in the economy in early 1929 listed by Professor Galbraith.
2. Evaluate how the depression could be limited in its damage according to Galbraith.
3. Do some research and analyze how conservative economists disagree with Galbraith's analysis.

Create Central

www.mhhe.com/createcentral

Internet References

The 1920s

This site aims to raise awareness about an amazing time in history, and to serve as a guide to the best sites on the web devoted to aspects of the 1920s.

www.louisville.edu/~ kprayb01/1920s.html

The Roaring 20's and the Great Depression

An extensive anthology of Web links to sites on the Roaring 20's and the Great Depression.

www.snowcrest.net/jmike/20sdep.html

JOHN KENNETH GALBRAITH was America's most popular and widely read economist in the late twentieth century. He taught for many years at Harvard University.

Galbraith, John Kenneth. 1958, pp. 670–680.

Article

15 Minutes that Saved America

How FDR charmed the nation, rescued the banks and preserved capitalism.

H. W. BRANDS

Learning Outcomes

After reading this article, you will be able to:

- Describe the ways in which Franklin D. Roosevelt's first radio address linked the president to the American people.

- Understand how the rise of radio connected people.

- Outline Franklin D. Roosevelt's objectives in his first radio address to the American people.

- Understand the details behind the crisis of the nation's financial sector in early 1933.

Cold weather still gripped most of the country on Sunday, March 12, 1933, as President Franklin Delano Roosevelt prepared to speak to the American people from the White House. The radio networks of the National Broadcasting Company and Columbia Broadcasting System had agreed to suspend regular programming at 10 p.m. Eastern time, and millions of Americans huddled around their radios in kitchens, parlors and living rooms. Forced by hard times to skimp on home heating fuel, they bundled in blankets and overcoats on this late winter night waiting, with everyone else, to hear the president.

Moments before air time, the reading copy of Roosevelt's prepared remarks—triple-spaced and typed by assistant Grace Tully with a special blue ribbon—disappeared. Staff members flew about trying to find it, but Roosevelt calmly retrieved one of the smudged, single-spaced mimeographed copies that had been prepared for the press, and read from that.

Roosevelt spoke quietly, even soothingly. There was no levity in his words, but neither was there obvious gravity.

"I want to talk for a few minutes with the people of the United States about banking," he began. Listeners recognized the voice, but it sounded different tonight. Roosevelt's tenor typically rose when he projected to large crowds; now it retained its conversational tone. He spoke quietly, even soothingly, like a favorite uncle telling a bedtime story. There was no levity in his words or his inflection, but neither was there obvious gravity. A traveler from a distant country, unfamiliar with the crisis facing America, would never have guessed how much hung on Roosevelt's every word as he delivered his first fireside chat to the nation just eight days after his inauguration.

Echoes of the crisis Roosevelt inherited when he took office 75 years ago can be heard today in news reports of home foreclosures and tottering financial institutions. But what resonates more deeply across the decades is an abiding faith in the long-term resilience of the American economy—a faith that Roosevelt helped foster during a brief radio address delivered amid a run on banks that raised troubling questions about credit, the value of the dollar and the future of capitalism. The story of how Roosevelt stopped a nationwide panic and restored Americans' confidence in the banking system is a case study in presidential theatrics and the remarkable power of moral suasion when exercised by a visionary leader.

Presidents had been speaking to the American people since the birth of the republic. The inaugural addresses of every president from George Washington to Warren Harding had been pitched at the entire nation, although they were heard only by those in attendance at the inaugural ceremonies. Presidents' annual messages to Congress functioned similarly: delivered to a discrete audience but intended for Americans at large. Yet during the century between Thomas Jefferson and William Howard Taft, the annual messages had been delivered to the Senate and House in writing and were read to the legislators by clerks. Woodrow Wilson revived the practice of delivering the annual message orally, but even then the American people had to wait to read the speech in their local papers. The president's words were history before they reached their ultimate audience.

The rise of radio created new possibilities for connecting with the people. Calvin Coolidge gave his inaugural address on the radio to a patchwork of stations connected by telephone lines. Yet Coolidge was dubbed Silent Cal for a reason, and neither he nor his successor, Herbert Hoover, seriously explored radio's technological potential.

Nor did they explore radio's psychological potential. Radio continued a shift in the political center of gravity in Washington that had been underway for decades. During the 18th and 19th centuries, the great communicators in American politics had been members of Congress. Listeners swooned at the soaring phrases of Henry Clay, Daniel Webster and John Calhoun, not at the pedestrian utterances of Martin Van Buren, Millard Fillmore and Ulysses Grant. Abraham Lincoln's rare gems—his Gettysburg address, his second inaugural—were the exceptions that proved the rule of executive forgettability in American public speaking.

Things changed under Theodore Roosevelt. The master of the "bully pulpit" understood the moral and emotional power of the presidency, and his speeches sounded like sermons as he lashed the "criminal rich" and "malefactors of great wealth" for conspiring against the public. Wilson sermonized, too, although mostly about foreign affairs. Wilson summoned Americans to war in 1917 in order to make the world "safe for democracy," and he offered his Fourteen Points as a guide to a better future for humanity.

Franklin Roosevelt studied his predecessors closely. During visits to the White House during the presidency of Theodore Roosevelt, his fifth cousin and his uncle by marriage, Franklin mentally tried the residence on for size. FDR patterned his political career on TR's, starting with a stint in the New York legislature, followed by service with the Navy Department and then the governorship of New York. The navy posting afforded Roosevelt a good opportunity to observe the inner workings of the Wilson administration. For 7½ years, as assistant navy secretary, he noted Wilson's successes and failures, and he paid particular attention as Wilson toured the country to enlist popular support for the Treaty of Versailles and the League of Nations. Everywhere Wilson went, he stirred audiences with his vision of American leadership in the world. He might well have forced a skeptical Senate to accept the treaty and the League, but a stroke felled him and his magnificent voice went silent.

Roosevelt was still reflecting on Wilson and the power of presidential words when his own turn came. Not since Lincoln had a president assumed office under such disheartening circumstances. The stock market crash of 1929 had presaged the implosion of the American economy. Industrial production had fallen by half; industrial construction by nine-tenths. The steel industry, long a mainstay of America's might, was staggering along at barely 10 percent of capacity. Unemployment topped 12 million, and even this figure understated the problem, for it ignored those too discouraged to continue seeking work. Commodity prices had collapsed, forcing farmers to struggle ever harder to make ends meet, until the prices fell so far that the farmers couldn't afford to harvest their wheat and corn, and let it rot in the fields.

Hundreds of thousands of families lost their homes; as many as 2 million men, women and children wandered the highways of America seeking shelter. Homeless communities, called Hoovervilles in derision of the Republican president, sprang up in cities all across the country. The shantytowns at first hid under bridges and in gulches but eventually spilled into plain sight. Manhattan's homeless claimed the shore of the Hudson River from 72nd Street to 110th.

Hunger stalked the land, visibly afflicting the crowded shantytowns, invisibly sapping the strength of sufferers on isolated farms and in end-of-the-road hamlets. Some of the starving were reduced to an animal existence; they fought over scraps behind restaurants and in garbage dumps. "We have been eating wild greens," an out-of-work Kentucky coal miner reported unemotionally. "Such weeds as cows eat."

"You could smell the depression in the air," one survivor remembered, before switching metaphors: "It was like a raw wind; the very houses we lived in seemed to be shrinking, hopeless of real comfort." A journalist in Washington remarked at the time: "I come home from the hill every night filled with gloom. I see on the streets filthy, ragged, desperate-looking men, such as I have never seen before."

In the month before Roosevelt's inauguration on March 4, 1933, the crisis centered on the nation's financial sector. The stock market crash had punished many banks, as borrowers defaulted on loans they had used to underwrite speculation, and as speculating banks suffered from their own bad investments. Weak banks dragged stronger ones down when panicked depositors demanded their money, which the banks, having loaned it out, couldn't deliver. Five thousand banks had folded by the time Roosevelt took office, and perhaps 10 million Americans had lost their savings.

In several states the entire banking industry ground to a halt as governors suspended bank operations. The governor of Louisiana locked the bank doors in his state in early February; the governors of Michigan, Maryland, Indiana, Arkansas and Ohio did likewise during the next two weeks. Roosevelt reached Washington 48 hours ahead of his inauguration and took the presidential suite at the Mayflower Hotel; the walls there were festooned with slips of paper detailing the unfolding debacle: "Boise, Idaho: Acting Governor Hill today declared a fifteen-day bank holiday. . . . Salem, Oregon: Governor Meier declared a three-day bank holiday. . . . Carson City, Nevada: A four-day legal holiday. . . . Austin, Texas. . . . Salt Lake City, Utah. . . . Phoenix, Arizona. . . ."

The dollar losses were staggering. The Federal Reserve reported an outflow of more than $700 million in seven days ahead of the inauguration as surviving banks scrambled frantically to meet their depositors' demands. The bleeding escalated to $500 million in the final two days before the inauguration.

Gold grew more precious than ever and scarcer. An all-time record of $116 million of gold was withdrawn from the Fed banks in a single day, as foreign account holders lost faith in the dollar and insisted on the yellow metal. Domestic holders of dollars began to get nervous. They fingered their Federal Reserve notes and wondered whether and how the government would honor the promise engraved on each: "Redeemable In Gold On Demand At The United States Treasury, Or In Gold Or Lawful Money At Any Federal Reserve Bank."

Roosevelt presented a curious mix of reassurance and challenge to the nation in his inaugural address. "The only thing we have to fear is fear itself," he said. Yet he proceeded to catalog some dauntingly real reasons for fear. "The means of exchange are frozen. . . . The withered leaves of industrial enterprise lie on every side. . . . Farmers find no markets for their produce. . . . The savings of many years in thousands of families are gone." Roosevelt likened the nation's dire economic predicament to a war and promised bold action. Americans must operate in unison, he said, "as a trained and loyal army."

Roosevelt then promptly moved to stanch the hemorrhage of gold from the banks by doing what the governors had done but on a broader scale. Inauguration Day was Saturday; on Sunday all the banks were closed. At 1 o'clock on Monday morning, March 6, he issued a decree declaring a national bank holiday. During the suspension, all normal banking operations would be barred. No bank was allowed to "pay out, export, earmark, or permit the withdrawal or transfer in any manner or by any device whatsoever, of any gold or silver coin or bullion or currency."

The move took the country's breath away. Without consulting Congress or, apparently, the Constitution, the president had declared economic martial law. Deposits were frozen; customers of the country's 18,000 banks were prevented from even trying to get their money out. The embargo on gold effectively took the United States off the gold standard, at least for the duration of the bank holiday.

Roosevelt cited an obscure law most people thought had lapsed—the 1917 Trading With the Enemy Act (which gave the president the wartime power to prohibit hoarding gold)—as justification for his diktat. Opinions differed sharply on whether the law was still in force, let alone whether it supported a peacetime stroke of the magnitude Roosevelt had just delivered.

Yet so desperate was the country for decisive action that almost no one in political or business circles seriously challenged the president. Even *The Wall Street Journal* approved. "A common adversity has much subdued the recalcitrance of groups bent upon self-interest," the de facto mouthpiece of the financial sector observed. "All of us the country over are now ready to make sacrifices to a common necessity and to accept realities as we would not have done three months ago."

The bank holiday bought Roosevelt time but only a little. He immediately set his advisers to writing a remedy to the financial panic. William Woodin, the Treasury secretary, led the effort. "We're on the bottom now," Woodin told reporters in a rare break between drafting sessions. This was supposed to be reassuring. "We are not going any lower," he said.

Woodin and the others—including governors of the Federal Reserve, chairmen of private banks, members of key congressional committees, and academic and professional economists—worked until 2 o'clock each morning at the White House. They went home for a few hours' sleep before returning for more of the same. The pressure was tremendous. "We're snowed under, we're snowed under," Francis Await, the comptroller of the currency, muttered. But Woodin kept them on track. "Not once did his grey toupee slip askew in the excitement," a reporter remarked.

Roosevelt wanted to have a bill by Thursday morning, March 9. He had summoned an emergency session of Congress, and he wished to present the lawmakers with a finished product as they gathered that noon. But the myriad intricacies of the money question defied such rapid solution, and when the session convened, the administration's measure was still at the printer's shop. Congress went ahead nonetheless and, employing a folded newspaper as a proxy for the actual bill, approved it on the president's recommendation and that of those lawmakers who had seen a draft of the legislation. The measure stamped retroactive approval on the bank closure and the gold embargo, and it authorized the president to reopen the banks when he deemed appropriate and to reorganize the national banking system to protect strong banks from the weak.

Roosevelt signed the bill that Thursday evening and shortly announced a timetable for reopening the banks. The 12 Federal Reserve banks would open on Monday, March 13, along with the other banks in those 12 cities. Banks in most other cities would open on Tuesday. Banks in small towns and villages would open on Wednesday.

There was less to the bank law than met the eye. Roosevelt had needed to stem the panic, and closing the banks did so. The bank law made the process look legal and planned. But the question on which everything hung—the condition of American finance, the direction of the economy, even the fate of America's distinctive mix of capitalism and democracy—was whether confidence could be restored by the time the banks reopened. If it was restored, the rescue operation would succeed. Prosperity might remain some distance off, but the country could begin moving in that direction.

If confidence was not restored, all the effort would have been wasted. Pessimists noted that democracy was failing in other countries that couldn't solve their economic problems. Germany had installed Adolf Hitler as chancellor a month before Roosevelt was inaugurated. A week before the American inauguration, Nazi agents burned the Reichstag and blamed the German Communists. Hours before Roosevelt closed the American banks, German elections returned a parliamentary majority for Hitler's coalition. Hitler demanded, and quickly received, dictatorial powers from the intimidated legislature.

Roosevelt's foremost objective as he began his first fireside chat on March 12 was to sound a note of calm. Millions had tuned in to his inaugural address, just a week before, but that speech had been delivered to a live audience in Washington, D.C., with the radio listeners merely eavesdropping. Now the radio listeners were the president's sole audience, aside from the few family members and administration officials sitting with him in the Oval Office, as he offered a matter-of-fact explanation of what had precipitated the banking crisis. "Because of undermined confidence on the part of the public, there was a general rush by a large portion of our population to turn bank deposits into currency or gold—a rush so great that the soundest banks could not get enough currency to meet the demand," he said. "The reason for this was that on the spur of the moment it was, of course, impossible to sell perfectly sound assets of a bank and convert them into cash except at panic prices far below their real value."

To remedy the situation, Roosevelt said, he and Congress had taken two important steps. First, he had declared the bank holiday, to give bankers, depositors and everyone else a chance to catch their breath. Second, Congress had approved the bank bill, confirming his authority over the banking system and allowing him to reopen the banks in an orderly fashion.

We have provided the machinery to restore our financial system; it is up to you to support it and make it work.

Roosevelt explained the timetable for the reopenings, and he asked for special patience on the part of depositors. "There is an element in the readjustment of our financial system more important than currency, more important than gold, and that is the confidence of the people," he said. "Confidence and courage are the essentials of success in carrying out our plan. You people must have faith; you must not be stampeded by rumors or guesses. Let us unite in banishing fear. We have provided the machinery to restore our financial system; it is up to you to support and make it work. It is your problem no less than it is mine. Together we cannot fail."

Whether it was his tone of voice, his choice of words, the nature of the medium or a sudden desire on the part of Americans to please their new president, Roosevelt's 15-minute talk evoked a stunningly positive response. Thousands of telegrams poured into the White House overnight. "Created feeling of confidence in me and my family," one said. Another asserted: "Going direct to the people with the facts has inspired every confidence in the reopening of the banks." A third called the talk "a masterpiece in the circumstances and worthy of the historical precedent it established."

Editors and pundits fell over themselves in praise of Roosevelt's performance. *The New York Times* sensed a sudden change in the popular mood: "His simple and lucid explanation of the true function of a commercial bank; his account of what had happened, why it had happened, and the steps taken to correct the mischief were admirably fitted to cause the hysteria which had raged for several weeks before the banks were closed to abate if not entirely to subside."

Will Rogers labeled the speech a "home run" and considered it a model of straightforward eloquence. "Some people spend a lifetime juggling with words, with not an idea in a carload," the popular cowboy humorist observed. "Our President took such a dry subject as banking (and when I say 'dry' I mean dry, for if it had been liquid he wouldn't have had to speak on it at all). Well, he made everybody understand it, even the bankers." Sen. James Lewis marveled at the powerful emotional impact of the president's remarks. "I have never seen within my political life such a real transformation in sentiment from discouragement to encouragement, from despair to complete hope and to immediate new trust and new hope," the Illinois Democrat declared.

Roosevelt was pleased at the praise but cared more for the financial effect of his message. The evidence from this direction was irrefutable. As the banks reopened, the negative currency flows of the previous weeks were reversed: Depositors stopped withdrawing funds and started returning the money they had pulled out. Bank balances began growing again, engendering additional confidence and further deposits. By the time the last banks opened, the crisis had passed.

The expeditious rescue of the banks didn't end the pressure on the larger economy. The grim statistics on national income, production and employment remained as dismal as ever. Central questions about the value of the dollar, the future of gold, the security of deposits and the structure of the industrial system were still to be answered.

But the emergency of the moment had been surmounted by Roosevelt's brilliant act of political theater. Raymond Moley, one of Roosevelt's advisers, later remarked that "capitalism was saved in eight days." He could have been more specific. The essence of the crisis was distilled into the quarter-hour of Roosevelt's fireside chat. Had the president failed to win the confidence of America that Sunday evening, the bank runs would have resumed and the downward spiral would have continued. But he didn't fail, and the banks, and capitalism, were saved.

In the bargain, Roosevelt fashioned a new link between presidents and the American people. *The New York Times,* in the same editorial in which it lauded the efficacy of Roosevelt's words, commented on the method of their delivery: "The President's use of the radio for this purpose is a fresh demonstration of the wonderful power of appeal to the people which science has placed in his hands. When millions of listeners can hear the President speak to them, as it were, directly in their own homes, we get a new meaning for the old phrase about a public man 'going to the country.'" Roosevelt went to the country without leaving the White House, and American politics would never be the same.

Critical Thinking

1. In what ways is Franklin D. Roosevelt's 15-minute radio address important to history?

2. How was this radio address different from the way other presidents before Roosevelt communicated with the American people?

3. Describe Roosevelt's objectives of the fireside chats. How well do you think those objectives were met? Explain.

Create Central

www.mhhe.com/createcentral

Internet References

History
    www.history.com/topics/fireside-chats
United States History
    www.u-s-history.com/pages/h1525.html
Why Guides
    www.whyguides.com/why-were-fireside-chats-important.html

H. W. Brands, Professor of History at Texas A & M, is the author of a dozen books including *The Money Men and American Colossus: The Triumph of Capitalism.*

Brands H. W., From *American History*, October 2008, pp. 36–41. Copyright © 2008 by Weider History Group. Reprinted by permission.

Article

When America Sent Her Own Packing

Fueled by the Great Depression, an anti-immigrant frenzy engulfed hundreds of thousands of legal American citizens in a drive to 'repatriate' Mexicans to their homeland.

STEVE BOISSON

Learning Outcomes

After reading this article, you will be able to:

- Describe the anti-immigrant sentiment that forced Mexican-Americans back to Mexico during the Great Depression.
- Discuss the social-political effects the "Repatriation" had on the immigrants and their children upon return to the United States.

A 9-year-old girl stood in the darkness of a railroad station, surrounded by tearful travelers who had gathered up their meager belongings, awaiting the train that would take her from her native home to a place she had never been. The bewildered child couldn't know she was a character in the recurring drama of America's love-hate relationship with peoples from foreign lands who, whether fleeing hardship or oppression or simply drawn to the promise of opportunity and prosperity, desperately strive to be Americans. As yet another act in the long saga of American immigration unfolds today, some U.S. citizens can recall when, during a time of anti-immigrant frenzy fueled by economic crisis and racism, they found themselves being swept out of the country of their birth.

Emilia Castañeda will never forget that 1935 morning. Along with her father and brother, she was leaving her native Los Angeles. Staying, she was warned by some adults at the station, meant she would become a ward of the state. "I had never been to Mexico," Castañeda said some six decades later. "We left with just one trunk full of belongings. No furniture. A few metal cooking utensils. A small ceramic pitcher, because it reminded me of my mother . . . and very little clothing. We took blankets, only the very essentials."

As momentous as that morning seemed to the 9-year-old Castañeda, such departures were part of a routine and roundly accepted movement to send Mexicans and Mexican-Americans back to their ancestral home. Los Angeles County-sponsored repatriation trains had been leaving the station bound for Mexico

since 1931, when, in the wake of the Wall Street crash of 1929 and the economic collapse and dislocation that followed, welfare cases skyrocketed. The county Board of Supervisors, other county and municipal agencies and the Chamber of Commerce proclaimed repatriation of Mexicans as a humane and utilitarian solution to the area's growing joblessness and dwindling resources. Even the Mexican consul stationed in Los Angeles praised the effort, at least at the outset, thanking the welfare department for its work "among my countrymen, in helping them return to Mexico." The Mexican government, still warmed by the rhetoric of the 1910 revolution, was touting the development of agricultural colonies and irrigation projects that would provide work for the displaced compatriots from the north.

By 1935, however, it was hard to detect much benevolence driving the government-sponsored train rides to Mexico. For young Castañeda's father, Mexico was the last resort, a final defeat after 20 years of legal residence in America. His work as a union bricklayer had enabled him to buy a house, but—like millions of other Americans—his house and job were lost to the Depression. His wife, who had worked as a maid, contracted tuberculosis in 1933 and died the following year. "My father told us that he was returning to Mexico because he couldn't find work in Los Angeles," Castañeda said. "He wasn't going to abandon us. We were going with him. When L.A. County arranged for our trip to Mexico, he and other Mexicans had no choice but to go."

Francisco Balderrama and Raymond Rodríguez, the authors of *Decade of Betrayal,* the first expansive study of Mexican repatriation with perspectives from both sides of the border, claim that 1 million people of Mexican descent were driven from the United States during the 1930s due to raids, scare tactics, deportation, repatriation and public pressure. Of that conservative estimate, approximately 60 percent of those leaving were legal American citizens. Mexicans comprised nearly half of all those deported during the decade, although they made up less than 1 percent of the country's population. "Americans, reeling from the economic disorientation of the depression, sought a convenient scapegoat," Balderrama and Rodríguez wrote. "They found it in the Mexican community."

During the early years of the 20th century, the U.S. Immigration Service paid scant attention to Mexican nationals crossing the border. The disfavored groups among border watchers at the time were the Chinese, who had been explicitly barred by the Chinese Exclusion Act of 1882, criminals, lunatics, prostitutes, paupers and those suffering from loathsome and contagious diseases. In actuality, the Mexican immigrant was often a pauper, but he was not, in the law's language, "likely to become a public charge." Cheap Mexican labor was in great demand by a host of America's burgeoning industries. The railroads, mining companies and agribusinesses sent agents to greet immigrants at the border, where they extolled the rewards of their respective enterprises. Border officials felt no duty to impede the labor flow into the Southwest.

The Mexican population in the United States escalated during the years following 1910. By 1914, according to author Matt S. Meier, the chaos and bloodshed of the Mexican revolution had driven as many as 100,000 Mexican nationals into the United States, and they would continue to cross the border in large numbers legally and illegally. Immigration laws were tightened in 1917, but their enforcement at the border remained lax. While laws enacted in 1921 and 1924 imposed quotas on immigrants from Europe and other parts of the Eastern Hemisphere, quotas were not applied to Mexico or other Western nations. This disparity found its detractors, particularly East Texas Congressman John C. Box, who was a vocal proponent of curtailing the influx from the south.

Though none of Box's proposals became law, his efforts drew favorable coverage in the *Saturday Evening Post* and other journals that editorialized against the "Mexicanization" of the United States. When a Midwestern beet grower who hired Mexican immigrants appeared at a House Immigration Committee hearing, Box suggested that the man's ideal farm workers were "a class of people who have not the ability to rise, who have not the initiative, who are children, who do not want to own land, who can be directed by men in the upper stratum of society. That is what you want, is it?"

"I believe that is about it," replied the grower.

Those who exploited cheap Mexican labor, argued Box and his adherents, betrayed American workers and imperiled American cities with invading hordes of mixed-blood foreigners. Those who railed against quotas should visit the barrios in Los Angeles, wrote Kenneth L. Roberts in the *Saturday Evening Post,* "and see endless streets crowded with the shacks of illiterate, diseased, pauperized Mexicans, taking no interest whatever in the community, living constantly on the ragged edge of starvation, bringing countless numbers of American citizens into the world with the reckless prodigality of rabbits."

Upon taking office in 1929, President Herbert Hoover had to face the raging debate. He resisted imposing the quotas demanded by Box and others, as Hoover probably feared they would rankle the Mexican government and thus threaten American business interests there. Instead, Hoover, hoping to appease the restrictionists, chose the less-permanent option of virtually eliminating visas for Mexican laborers and by bolstering the Immigration Service, which had grown from a minor government operation to a force that included a border patrol of nearly 800 officers.

After the Depression set in, the removal of foreigners who were taking jobs and services away from cash-strapped, struggling Americans seemed to be a salient solution, perhaps the only tangible recourse to the desperation that had swept the country. Under the direction of William N. Doak, Hoover's newly appointed secretary of labor, immigration officers dredged the country for illegal aliens. They raided union halls, dances, social clubs and other ethnic enclaves where people without papers might be found. Their tactics favored intimidation over legal procedure. Suspects were routinely arrested without warrants. Many were denied counsel, and their deportation "hearings" were often conducted in the confines of a city or county jail. Frightened and ignorant of their rights, many suspects volunteered to leave rather than suffer through deportation.

While Mexicans were not the only target in the drive against illegal aliens, they were often the most visible. This was certainly true in Los Angeles, which, at that time had some 175,000 inhabitants of Mexican descent, second only to Mexico City. In early 1931, Los Angeles newspapers reported on an impending anti-alien sweep led by a ranking immigration officer from Washington, D.C. Walter Carr, the federal Los Angeles district director of immigration, assured the press that no single ethnic group was under siege, but raids in the Mexican communities of El Monte, Pacoima and San Fernando belied that official line. The final show of force occurred with a raid on La Placita, a downtown Los Angeles park that was popular with Mexicans and Mexican-Americans. On February 26, an afternoon idyll on Olivera Street was shattered by an invasion of immigration agents and local police. Agents searched every person on the scene for proof of legal residence. Though hundreds were hauled off for questioning, few were ultimately detained. The message was in the bluster, not the busts.

As recounted in *Decade of Betrayal,* Labor Secretary Doak's efforts proved to be highly successful: Deportees outnumbered those who entered the United States during the first nine months of 1931. There were, however, some detractors. A subcommittee formed by the Los Angeles Bar Association found that Carr's tactics, such as inhibiting a suspect's access to counsel, fell outside the law. Carr dismissed these charges as nothing more than sour grapes over a lost client base and justified the deprivation of counsel on the grounds that lawyers merely sold false hopes in exchange for cash squeezed from needy immigrants.

Immigration officers raided union halls, dances, social clubs and other ethnic enclaves where people without papers might be found.

Investigations into the alleged abuses began on a national level, as well, by the National Commission on Law Observance and Enforcement, which was appointed by President Hoover in 1929. Named for its chairman, former U.S. Attorney General George W. Wickersham, the Wickersham Commission had made front-page news with its investigations into the rackets of Al Capone and others. Like the L.A. Bar Association, the commission also found the methods employed by Doak's underlings to be unconstitutional. Regardless of the legality or illegality of the practices, one thing was clear: Mexican immigrants were departing in great numbers. According to a report by Carr, by May 1931, "There have been approximately forty thousand aliens who left this district during the last eighteen months of which probably twenty percent [were] deportable." Even those who were here legally, he allowed, had been driven out by fear.

A child in 1932, Rubén Jiménez remembers, 'We were not a burden to the U.S. government or anybody.'

In retrospect, other options were available. The Registry Act of 1929, for example, ensured permanent residency status—a version of amnesty—to those who had been in the United States continuously since 1921 and had been "honest, law-abiding aliens." While this surely would have applied to many Mexicans, the act's provisions were utilized mostly by European or Canadian immigrants. In many cases, institutionalized hostility prevailed over legal rights. Anti-Mexican sentiments convinced the father of author Raymond Rodríguez to return to Mexico. His mother met with a local priest, who assured her that, as a mother of five American children and a legal resident, she could not be forced to leave. "So he left and we stayed," says Rodríguez, who never saw his father again.

Instead of driving Mexican aliens underground—as was often the result of raids and other scare tactics—it became apparent to anti-immigrant proponents that it was more expedient simply to assist them out of the country. "Repatriation" became a locally administered alternative to deportation, which was a federal process beyond the purview of the county and municipal officials. "Repatriation is supposed to be voluntary," says Francisco Balderrama, *Decade's* co-author. "That's kind of a whitewash word, a kind of covering up of the whole thing."

Some 350 people departed on the first county-sponsored repatriation train to leave Los Angeles in March 1931. The next month, a second train left with nearly three times as many people, of which roughly one-third paid for their own passage. The repatriates were led to believe that they could return at a later date, observed George F. Clements, manager of agriculture of the Los Angeles Chamber of Commerce. In a memo to the chamber's general manager, Arthur G. Arnoll,

Clements, who wanted to keep the cheap labor, wrote, "I think this is a grave mistake because it is not the truth." Clements went on to state that American-born children leaving without documentation were "American citizens without very much hope of ever coming back into the United States."

Los Angeles later developed a highly efficient repatriation program under the direction of Rex Thomson, an engineer who had impressed members of the Board of Supervisors with his nuts-and-bolts know-how while advising them on the construction of the Los Angeles General Hospital. After the county welfare caseload nearly doubled from 25,913 cases during 1929–30 to 42,124 cases in 1930–31, the board asked the pragmatic Thomson to serve as assistant superintendent of charities. "It was one of the highest paying public jobs in California," Thomson recalled during an interview nearly 40 years later. Having lost a bundle in failed local banks, he continued, "I was interested in a job."

Thomson proved to be a tough administrator who excised bureaucratic fat and made welfare money work for the county. Men dug channels in the Los Angeles River in exchange for room and board. He put the unemployed to work on several local projects: building walls along Elysian Park, grading the grounds around the California State Building. When Thomson visited Congress in Washington, D.C., to seek funding for his public works program, he challenged the feds to "send out people to see if we aren't worthy of this federal help." By the end of the week, he later reported: "I'll be darned if they didn't agree. The government got the idea, and started this Works Progress [Administration], but they didn't always impose the discipline that was necessary."

Along with putting the unemployed to work on government-sponsored projects, repatriation would become another of Thomson's social remedies that would merit emulation. Thomson would later describe his program: "We had thousands of Mexican nationals who were out of work. I went to Mexico City and I told them that we would like to ship these people back—not to the border but to where they came from or where the Mexicans would send them if we agreed it was a proper place. We could ship them back by train and feed them well and decently, for $74 a family. So I employed social workers who were Americans of Mexican descent but fluent in the language, or Mexican nationals, and they would go out and—I want to emphasize—offer repatriation to these people."

A child in 1932, Rubén Jiménez remembers one such social worker, a Mr. Hispana, who convinced Jiménez's father to exchange his two houses in East Los Angeles for 21 acres in Mexicali. "We were not a burden to the U.S. government or anybody," says Jiménez, whose father worked for the gas company and collected rental income on his property. Still, Hispana convinced the man that it was best for him to turn over his bungalow and frame house and depart with his family to Mexico, where their 21 acres awaited them. "We camped under a tree until Dad built a shack out of bamboo," Jiménez recalls. Since there was no electricity available, his parents traded their washing machine and other appliances for chickens, mules, pigs and other necessities for their new life.

In the clutches of the Depression's hard times, families sold their homes at low prices. In some cases, the county placed liens on abandoned property. "While there is no direct authority for selling the effects and applying their proceeds," a county attorney informed Thomson, "we fail to see how the county can be damaged by so doing."

"They are going to a land where the unemployed take all-day siestas in the warm sun," wrote the Los Angeles *Evening Express* in August 1931, which described children "following their parents to a new land of promise, where they may play in green fields without watching out for automobiles." The reality proved to be far less idyllic. Emilia Castañeda first glimpsed Mexican poverty in the tattered shoes on the old train porter who carried her father's trunk. "He was wearing huaraches," she recalled. "Huaraches are sandals worn by poor people. They are made out of old tires and scraps." Along with her father and brother, Castañeda moved to her aunt's place in the state of Durango, where nine relatives were already sharing the one-room domicile. "There was no room for us," she said. "If it rained we couldn't go indoors." She quickly learned that running water and electricity were luxuries left back in Los Angeles. She took baths in a galvanized tub and fetched water from wells. The toilet was a hole in the backyard. "We were living with people who didn't want us there," Castañeda said. "We were imposing on them out of necessity." They left after her father found work. In time her brother would be working also and, to her great dismay, shuffling around in huaraches.

Contrary to what was being propagated, Mexicans in Los Angeles did not impose a disproportionate strain on welfare services during the Depression. This is according to *Decade* and Abraham Hoffman, whose dissertation and subsequent book, *Unwanted Mexican Americans in the Great Depression,* examined repatriation from a Los Angeles perspective. Based on the county's own figures, Mexicans comprised an average of only 10 percent of those on relief. Nonetheless, repatriation was promoted and widely viewed as an effective means of diminishing welfare rolls, and Mexico's proclaimed plans for agricultural expansion conveniently complemented the movement. Indeed, Thomson traveled extensively throughout Mexico to survey proposed work sites and hold negotiations at various levels of the Mexican government, including the ministry of foreign affairs and the presidency. Some Mexican officials were so eager to get Thomson's repatriates, he later recalled, he was personally offered a bounty of land for each. "One time I was met by the governor of Quintaneroo. He offered me 17 and a half hectares (44 acres) for every repatriated individual I sent there to cut sisal and I said 'Absolutely no.'" Thomson claimed repatriates were in high demand across the border. "They brought across skills and industrial discipline," he said. "At that time, if you could repair a Model T Ford, that was quite an art."

Thomson's program—and its seemingly fantastic results—attracted the attention of state and local leaders from around the country, and his practice of engaging the Mexican government

was copied as well. In the fall of 1932, Ignacio Batiza, the Mexican consul in Detroit, urged his compatriots to return home and "accept this opportunity which is offered them." While Batiza may have believed his country's promises of cooperation, others did not. A pamphlet circulated by a group called the International Labor Defense warned that thousands of workers choosing to return to Mexico would die of hunger. This was the end of 1932, and the feasibility of Mexico's grand plans was not yet widely challenged.

With a population of less than 15 million in the early years of the Depression, Mexico needed more workers to attain its goal of land transformation. Even as the Depression took hold, the Mexican government proceeded with its agricultural development plans, which would include repatriated nationals—especially those with farming skills. During that time, "They are proclaiming workers' rights," Balderrama explained. "If they're not accepting of the repatriates, that calls into question what they're all about." In the end, however, the government's post-revolutionary zeal eclipsed a hard reckoning of the facts. The returning mass of impoverished pilgrims from the United States would strain an already fragile economy. Officially, at least, the government welcomed the compatriots from the north, underscoring its proclamation of Mexicanism and support for workers rights.

Mexico struggled to cope with the deluge of new arrivals. Hungry and sick travelers crowded into border towns such as Ciudad Juárez and Nogales, where paltry food and medical supplies ensured a daily death count. There are many accounts of border towns crowded with people, as the train connections were not well organized. One repatriado reported: "Many that come here don't have any place to go. They don't have any idea of where they are going or what they'll do. Some families just stayed down at the railway station."

Forced relocation 'prevented me from completing my education and advancing for better employment.'

In an attempt to manage the crisis, Mexican governmental agencies joined several private organizations to create the National Repatriation Committee in 1933. The first colonization project undertaken by this august assembly was Pinotepa Nacional, located in a fertile tropical area of southern Mexico. Modern farming equipment and mules, along with food and other provisions, were made available to the farmers, who were to earn their equity through produce. And while the crops grew quickly, this highly touted proletarian collective proved to be a disastrous failure beset with complaints about mistreatment and meager food rations. The project's final undoing came from disease, as the land was rife with poisonous insects. Sixty people died within 20 days, according to a settler who had left after one month, taking his three small sons with him. "Some have families and can't leave very well," he told one researcher. "But my boys and I could. We walked to Oaxaca. It took us eight days."

Though the government welcomed repatriates, the general citizenry often did not. "Most of us here in Mexico do not look on these repatriates very favorably," remarked one Mexico City landlady. "They abandoned the country during the revolution, and after getting expelled from the north, they expected their old compatriots . . . to greet them with celebrations of fireworks and brass bands." Castañeda remembers children taunting her as a "repatriada." "The word was very offensive to me," she recalled. "It was an insult, as is calling someone a gringo or a wetback." As one Mexican ranch worker asked a repatriate in Torreón in the northeastern state of Coahuila: "What you doing here for? To eat the little bread we have?"

As news about the harsh conditions in Mexico traveled north, it became more difficult to convince people to leave the United States. President Franklin D. Roosevelt's New Deal provided work for some Mexicans, such as veterans of the U.S. military, and welfare was allotted to those who were barred from the work projects. But, back in Los Angeles, Thomson remained resolute in his efforts to repatriate Mexicans, eventually turning his attention to nursing homes and asylums in his desire to purge what he considered welfare leeches. In some cases, the bedridden were sent out on the back of a truck.

Many American children of repatriates never lost their desire for a true repatriation of their own. Emilia Castañeda, who had relocated 17 times while living in Mexico, decided to return to Los Angeles as her 18th birthday approached, some nine years after that dark morning in 1935. Her godmother in Boyle Heights forwarded Castañeda's birth certificate, along with money for the train ride. Ironically, this American citizen was again subjected to humiliation. At the border crossing, immigration officials asked to see her tourist card. "I had to pay for a tourist card because, according to them, I was a tourist. Can you imagine? Me, a tourist, for nine years." It was 1944, and the train was crowded with soldiers. "I sat on my suitcase in the aisle. The seats were reserved for servicemen, but some were kind and they offered me their seats. I spoke very little English by then. Here was this American girl coming back to the United States."

Castañeda relearned English in the same school she had attended as a child. As she would later admit, her forced relocation "prevented me from completing my education and advancing for better employment." Rubén Jiménez had attended school in Mexico, walking 12 miles a day to a one-room structure where six grades shared one teacher. When he returned to the States, the transition back into Los Angeles schools was difficult. A high school sophomore at age 17, Jiménez dropped out and joined the Army, serving as a radar operator during World War II. After several years, he completed college and eventually retired as a parole investigator.

While many American citizens who were caught up in the repatriation movement returned and struggled to readjust to their native country, thousands who had left without documentation had no legitimate proof of citizenship and were denied reentry. "We talked to one lady, part of her family came back, and part of it, unable to prove their residency, settled along the border so they could get together sometimes," recalls Rodríguez. "But the whole family was not able to make it back. And that was not an unusual circumstance."

In 1972 Hoffman noted that the history of Mexicans in the United States was largely ignored. "A case in point is that of the repatriation phenomenon," he said. "When I started working on it as a dissertation there was really nothing. Historians had neglected it as a topic, as they did essentially everything that today we call ethnic studies. I was interested in the topic because I was born in East L.A., and although I am not a Mexican American, I did have some concerns about what had been going on in an area where I had grown up."

Repatriates often tried to forget the experience, and they did not speak about it to their children. Many saw themselves as victims of local vendettas rather than scapegoats of a national campaign. "They really didn't understand the broad aspects," says Rodríguez. "They thought it was an individual experience. It wasn't something pleasant. It wasn't something they could be proud of."

The silence, however, did not dissuade a new generation from seeking answers. "I knew that my father had spent his childhood in Mexico, despite the fact that he was born in Detroit, and I always had questions about it," says Elena Herrada, a union official and activist in Detroit. While at Wayne State University in the '70s, Herrada and other students began collecting oral histories from elders in the community, a practice she continues today. "All we wanted to do was get the story told in our own families, and in our own communities, so that we would have a better understanding of why we don't vote, why we don't answer the census, why we don't protest in the face of extreme injustice. It just explains so many things for us."

In the summer of 2003, the subject of Mexican repatriation went beyond the confines of family and academic circles and returned to the scrutiny of government. A hearing was held in Sacramento, Calif., presided over by state Senator Joe Dunne, who had been inspired by *Decade of Betrayal*. The book's authors spoke at the session, and Rodríguez's voice faltered as he recalled his own father's flight to Mexico in 1936. Other scholars spoke, as did local politicians and two repatriates. A class action lawsuit on behalf of those who had been unfairly expelled from California was filed in July, with Castañeda as the lead plaintiff. The suit was eventually withdrawn, as two consecutive governors vetoed bills that would have funded research and expanded statutory limitations.

For a time, however, the civil action and the forgotten history behind it were national news. This, in a way, was the beginning of a more lasting restitution: an acknowledgment of the past. "My idea is for it to be in the history books," says Emilia Castañeda, "for children to learn what happened to American citizens."

Critical Thinking

1. What caused the "repatriation" of Mexicans back to Mexico in the 1930s?
2. Is there something to be learned from past mistakes that could help with the immigration issue in the U.S. today? Explain.

Create Central

www.mhhe.com/createcentral

Internet References

Digital History
www.digitalhistory.uh.edu/disp_textbook.cfm?smtid=3&psid=3699

Cal State Fullerton
http://calstate.fullerton.edu/news/2005/valenciana.html

California State University, San Marcos
http://public.csusm.edu/frame004/history.html

Article

A New Deal for the American People

ROGER BILES

Learning Outcomes

After reading this article, you will be able to:

- Explain the purpose and innovations of Roosevelt's New Deal Program.
- Discuss the shortfalls of the New Deal Program and their implications in today's society.

At the close of the Hundred Days, Franklin D. Roosevelt said, "All of the proposals and all of the legislation since the fourth day of March have not been just a collection of haphazard schemes, but rather the orderly component parts of a connected and logical whole." Yet the president later described his approach quite differently. "Take a method and try it. If it fails admit it frankly and try another. But above all, try something." The impetus for New Deal legislation came from a variety of sources, and Roosevelt relied heavily at various times on an ideologically diverse group of aides and allies. His initiatives reflected the contributions of, among others, Robert Wagner, Rexford Tugwell, Raymond Moley, George Norris, Robert LaFollette, Henry Morgenthau, Marriner Eccles, Felix Frankfurter, Henry Wallace, Harry Hopkins, and Eleanor Roosevelt. An initial emphasis on recovery for agriculture and industry gave way within two years to a broader-based program for social reform; entente with the business community yielded to populist rhetoric and a more ambiguous economic program. Roosevelt suffered the opprobrium of both the conservatives, who vilified "that man" in the White House who was leading the country down the sordid road to socialism, and the radicals, who saw the Hyde Park aristocrat as a confidence man peddling piecemeal reform to forestall capitalism's demise. Out of so many contradictory and confusing circumstances, how does one make sense of the five years of legislative reform known as the New Deal? And what has been its impact on a half century of American life?[1]

A better understanding begins with the recognition that little of the New Deal was new, including the use of federal power to effect change. Nor, for all of Roosevelt's famed willingness to experiment, did New Deal programs usually originate from vernal ideas. Governmental aid to increase farmers' income, propounded in the late nineteenth century by the Populists, surfaced in Woodrow Wilson's farm credit acts. The prolonged debates over McNary-Haugenism in the 1920s kept the issue alive, and Herbert Hoover's Agricultural Marketing Act set the stage for further federal involvement. Centralized economic planning, as embodied in the National Industrial Recovery Act, flowed directly from the experiences of Wilson's War Industries Board; not surprisingly, Roosevelt chose Hugh Johnson, a veteran of the board, to head the National Recovery Administration. Well established in England and Germany before the First World War, social insurance appeared in a handful of states—notably Wisconsin—before the federal government became involved. Similarly, New Deal labor reform took its cues from the path-breaking work of state legislatures. Virtually alone in its originality, compensatory fiscal policy seemed revolutionary in the 1930s. Significantly, however, Roosevelt embraced deficit spending quite late after other disappointing economic policies and never to the extent Keynesian economists advised. Congress and the public supported the New Deal, in part, because of its origins in successful initiatives attempted earlier under different conditions.

Innovative or not, the New Deal clearly failed to restore economic prosperity. As late as 1938 unemployment stood at 19.1 percent and two years later at 14.6 percent. Only the Second World War, which generated massive industrial production, put the majority of the American people back to work. To be sure, partial economic recovery occurred. From a high of 13 million unemployed in 1933, the number under Roosevelt's administration fell to 11.4 million in 1934, 10.6 million in 1935, and 9 million in 1936. Farm income and manufacturing wages also rose, and as limited as these achievements may seem in retrospect, they provided sustenance for millions of people and hope for many more. Yet Roosevelt's resistance to Keynesian formulas for pump priming placed immutable barriers in the way of recovery that only war could demolish. At a time calling for drastic inflationary methods, Roosevelt introduced programs effecting the opposite result. The NRA restricted production, elevated prices, and reduced purchasing power, all of which were deflationary in effect. The Social Security Act's payroll taxes took money from consumers and out of circulation. The federal government's $4.43 billion deficit in fiscal year 1936, impressive as it seemed, was not so much greater than Hoover's $2.6 billion shortfall during his last year in office. As economist Robert Lekachman noted, "The 'great spender' was in his heart a true descendant of thrifty Dutch Calvinist forebears." It is not certain that the application of Keynesian formulas would have sufficed by the mid-1930s to restore prosperity, but the president's cautious deflationary policies clearly retarded recovery.[2]

Although New Deal economic policies came up short in the 1930s, they implanted several "stabilizers" that have been more successful in averting another such depression. The Securities and Exchange Act of 1934 established government supervision of the stock market, and the Wheeler-Rayburn Act allowed the Securities and Exchange Commission to do the same with public utilities. Severely embroiled in controversy when adopted, these measures have become mainstays of the American financial system. The Glass-Steagall Banking Act forced the separation of commercial and investment banking and broadened the powers of the Federal Reserve Board to change interest rates and limit loans for speculation. The creation of the Federal Deposit Insurance Corporation (FDIC) increased government supervision of state banks and significantly lowered the number of bank failures. Such safeguards restored confidence in the discredited banking system and established a firm economic foundation that performed well for decades thereafter.

The New Deal was also responsible for numerous other notable changes in American life. Section 7(a) of the NIRA, the Wagner Act, and the Fair Labor Standards Act transformed the relationship between workers and business and breathed life into a troubled labor movement on the verge of total extinction. In the space of a decade government laws eliminated sweatshops, severely curtailed child labor, and established enforceable standards for hours, wages, and working conditions. Further, federal action eliminated the vast majority of company towns in such industries as coal mining. Although Robert Wagner and Frances Perkins dragged Roosevelt into labor's corner, the New Deal made the unions a dynamic force in American society. Moreover, as Nelson Lichtenstein has noted, "by giving so much of the working class an institutional voice, the union movement provided one of the main political bulwarks of the Roosevelt Democratic party and became part of the social bedrock in which the New Deal welfare state was anchored."[3]

Roosevelt's avowed goal of "cradle-to-grave" security for the American people proved elusive, but his administration achieved unprecedented advances in the field of social welfare. In 1938 the president told Congress: "Government has a final responsibility for the well-being of its citizenship. If private co-operative endeavor fails to provide work for willing hands and relief for the unfortunate, those suffering hardship from no fault of their own have a right to call upon the Government for aid; and a government worthy of its name must make fitting response." The New Deal's safety net included low-cost housing; old-age pensions; unemployment insurance; and aid for dependent mothers and children, the disabled, the blind, and public health services. Sometimes disappointing because of limiting eligibility requirements and low benefit levels, these social welfare programs nevertheless firmly established the principle that the government had an obligation to assist the needy. As one scholar wrote of the New Deal, "More progress was made in public welfare and relief than in the three hundred years after this country was first settled."[4]

More and more government programs, inevitably resulting in an enlarged administrative apparatus and requiring additional revenue, added up to a much greater role for the national government in American life. Coming at a time when the only Washington bureaucracy most of the people encountered with any frequency was the U.S. Postal Service, the change seemed all the more remarkable. Although many New Deal programs were temporary emergency measures, others lingered long after the return of prosperity. Suddenly, the national government was supporting farmers, monitoring the economy, operating a welfare system, subsidizing housing, adjudicating labor disputes, managing natural resources, and providing electricity to a growing number of consumers. "What Roosevelt did in a period of a little over 12 years was to change the form of government," argued journalist Richard L. Strout. "Washington had been largely run by big business, by Wall Street. He brought the government to Washington." Not surprisingly, popular attitudes toward government also changed. No longer willing to accept economic deprivation and social dislocation as the vagaries of an uncertain existence, Americans tolerated—indeed, came to expect—the national government's involvement in the problems of everyday life. No longer did "government" mean just "city hall."[5]

The operation of the national government changed as well. For one thing, Roosevelt's strong leadership expanded presidential power, contributing to what historian Arthur Schlesinger, Jr., called the "imperial presidency." Whereas Americans had in previous years instinctively looked first to Capitol Hill, after Roosevelt the White House took center stage in Washington. At the same time, Congress and the president looked at the nation differently. Traditionally attentive only to one group (big business), policymakers in Washington began responding to other constituencies such as labor, farmers, the unemployed, the aged, and to a lesser extent, women, blacks, and other disadvantaged groups. This new "broker state" became more accessible and acted on a growing number of problems, but equity did not always result. The ablest, richest, and most experienced groups fared best during the New Deal. NRA codes favored big business, and AAA benefits aided large landholders; blacks received relief and government jobs but not to the extent their circumstances merited. The long-term result, according to historian John Braeman, has been "a balkanized political system in which private interests scramble, largely successfully, to harness governmental authority and/or draw upon the public treasury to advance their private agendas."[6]

Another legacy of the New Deal has been the Roosevelt revolution in politics. Urbanization and immigration changed the American electorate, and a new generation of voters who resided in the cities during the Great Depression opted for Franklin D. Roosevelt and his party. Before the 1930s the Democrats of the northern big-city machines and the solid South uneasily coexisted and surrendered primacy to the unified Republican party. The New Deal coalition that elected Roosevelt united behind common economic interests. Both urban northerners and rural southerners, as well as blacks, women, and ethnic immigrants, found common cause in government action to shield them from an economic system gone haywire. By the end of the decade the increasing importance of the urban North in the Democratic party had already become apparent. After the economy recovered from the disastrous depression, members of the Roosevelt coalition shared fewer compelling interests. Beginning in the 1960s, tensions mounted within the party as such issues as race, patriotism, and abortion loomed larger. Even so, the Roosevelt coalition retained enough commitment to New Deal principles to keep the Democrats the nation's majority party into the 1980s.[7]

Yet for all the alterations in politics, government, and the economy, the New Deal fell far short of a revolution. The two-party system survived intact, and neither fascism, which attracted so many followers in European states suffering from the same international depression, nor communism attracted much of a following in the United States. Vital government institutions functioned without interruption and if the balance of powers shifted, the nation remained capitalistic; free enterprise and private ownership, not socialism, emerged from the 1930s. A limited welfare state changed the meld of the public and private but left them separate. Roosevelt could be likened to the British conservative Edmund Burke, who advocated measured change to offset drastic alterations—"reform to preserve." The New Deal's great achievement was the application of just enough change to preserve the American political economy.

Indications of Roosevelt's restraint emerged from the very beginning of the New Deal. Rather than assume extraordinary executive powers as Abraham Lincoln had done in the 1861 crisis, the president called Congress into special session. Whatever changes ensued would come through normal governmental activity. Roosevelt declined to assume direct control of the economy, leaving the nation's resources in the hands of private enterprise. Resisting the blandishments of radicals calling for the nationalization of the banks, he provided the means for their rehabilitation and ignored the call for national health insurance and federal contributions to Social Security retirement benefits. The creation of such regulatory agencies as the SEC confirmed his intention to revitalize rather than remake economic institutions. Repeatedly during his presidency Roosevelt responded to congressional pressure to enact bolder reforms, as in the case of the National Labor Relations Act, the Wagner-Steagall Housing Act, and the FDIC. The administration forwarded the NIRA only after Senator Hugo Black's recovery bill mandating 30-hour workweeks seemed on the verge of passage.

As impressive as New Deal relief and social welfare programs were, they never went as far as conditions demanded or many liberals recommended. Fluctuating congressional appropriations, oscillating economic conditions, and Roosevelt's own hesitancy to do too much violence to the federal budget left Harry Hopkins, Harold Ickes, and others only partially equipped to meet the staggering need. The president justified the creation of the costly WPA in 1935 by "ending this business of relief." Unskilled workers, who constituted the greatest number of WPA employees, obtained but 60 to 80 percent of the minimal family income as determined by the government. Roosevelt and Hopkins continued to emphasize work at less than existing wage scales so that the WPA or PWA never

competed with free labor, and they allowed local authorities to modify pay rates. They also continued to make the critical distinction between the "deserving" and "undeserving" poor, making sure that government aided only the former. The New Deal never challenged the values underlying this distinction, instead seeking to provide for the growing number of "deserving" poor created by the Great Depression. Government assumed an expanded role in caring for the disadvantaged, but not at variance with existing societal norms regarding social welfare.

The New Deal effected no substantial redistribution of income. The Wealth Tax Act of 1935 (the famous soak-the-rich tax) produced scant revenue and affected very few taxpayers. Tax alterations in 1936 and 1937 imposed no additional burdens on the rich; the 1938 and 1939 tax laws actually removed a few. By the end of the 1930s less than 5 percent of Americans paid income taxes, and the share of taxes taken from personal and corporate income levies fell below the amount raised in the 1920s. The great change in American taxation policy came during World War II, when the number of income tax payers grew to 74 percent of the population. In 1942 Treasury Secretary Henry Morgenthau noted that "for the first time in our history, the income tax is becoming a people's tax." This the New Deal declined to do.[8]

Finally, the increased importance of the national government exerted remarkably little influence on local institutions. The New Deal seldom dictated and almost always deferred to state and local governments—encouraging, cajoling, bargaining, and wheedling to bring parochial interests in line with national objectives. As Harry Hopkins discovered, governors and mayors angled to obtain as many federal dollars as possible for their constituents but with no strings attached. Community control and local autonomy, conditions thought to be central to American democracy, remained strong, and Roosevelt understood the need for firm ties with politicians at all levels. In his study of the New Deal's impact on federalism, James T. Patterson concludes: "For all the supposed power of the New Deal, it was unable to impose all its guidelines on the autonomous forty-eight states. . . . What could the Roosevelt administration have done to ensure a more profound and lasting impression on state policy and politics? Very little."[9]

Liberal New Dealers longed for more sweeping change and lamented their inability to goad the president into additional action. They envisioned a wholesale purge of the Democratic party and the creation of a new organization embodying fully the principles of liberalism. They could not abide Roosevelt's toleration of the political conservatives and unethical bosses who composed part of the New Deal coalition. They sought racial equality, constraints upon the southern landholding class, and federal intrusion to curb the power of urban real estate interests on behalf of the inveterate poor. Yet to do these things would be to attempt changes well beyond the desires of most Americans. People pursuing remunerative jobs and the economic security of the middle class approved of government aiding the victims of an unfortunate economic crisis but had no interest in an economic system that would limit opportunity. The fear that the New Deal would lead to such thoroughgoing change explains the seemingly irrational hatred of Roosevelt by the economic elite. But, as historian Barry Karl has noted, "it was characteristic of Roosevelt's presidency that he never went as far as his detractors feared or his followers hoped."[10]

The New Deal achieved much that was good and left much undone. Roosevelt's programs were defined by the confluence of forces that circumscribed his admittedly limited reform agenda—hostile judiciary; powerful congressional opponents, some of whom entered into alliances of convenience with New Dealers and some of whom awaited the opportunity to build on their opposition; the political impotence of much of the populace; the pugnacious independence of local and state authorities; the strength of people's attachment to traditional values and institutions; and the basic conservatism of American culture. Obeisance to local custom and the decision to avoid tampering with the fabric of American society allowed much injustice to survive while shortchanging blacks, women, small farmers, and the "unworthy" poor. Those who criticized Franklin Roosevelt for an unwillingness to challenge racial, economic, and gender inequality misunderstood either the nature of his electoral mandate or the difference between reform and revolution—or both.

If the New Deal preserved more than it changed, that is understandable in a society whose people have consistently chosen freedom over equality. Americans traditionally have eschewed expanded government, no matter how efficiently managed or honestly administered, that imposed restraints on personal success—even though such limitations redressed legitimate grievances or righted imbalances. Parity, most Americans believed, should not be purchased with the loss of liberty. But although the American dream has always entailed individual success with a minimum of state interference, the profound shock of capitalism's near demise in the 1930s undermined numerous previously unquestioned beliefs. The inability of capitalism's "invisible hand" to stabilize the market and the failure of the private sector to restore prosperity enhanced the consideration of stronger executive leadership and centralized planning. Yet with the collapse of democratic governments and their replacement by totalitarian regimes, Americans were keenly sensitive to any threats to liberty. New Deal programs, frequently path breaking in their delivery of federal resources outside normal channels, also retained a strong commitment to local government and community control while promising only temporary disruptions prior to the return of economic stability. Reconciling the necessary authority at the federal level to meet nationwide crises with the local autonomy desirable to safeguard freedom has always been one of the salient challenges to American democracy. Even after New Deal refinements, the search for the proper balance continues.

Notes

1. Otis L. Graham, Jr., and Meghan Robinson Wander, eds., *Franklin D. Roosevelt, His Life and Times: An Encyclopedic View* (Boston: G. K. Hall, 1985), p. 285 (first quotation); Harvard Sitkoff, "Introduction," in Sitkoff, *Fifty Years Later*, p. 5 (second quotation).

2. Richard S. Kirkendall, "The New Deal as Watershed: The Recent Literature," *Journal of American History* 54 (March 1968), p. 847 (quotation).

3. Graham and Wander, *Franklin D. Roosevelt, His Life and Times*, p. 228 (quotation).

4. Leuchtenburg, "The Achievement of the New Deal," p. 220 (first quotation); Patterson, *America's Struggle against Poverty, 1900–1980*, p. 56 (second quotation).

5. Louchheim, *The Making of the New Deal: The Insiders Speak*, p. 15 (quotation).

6. John Braeman, "The New Deal: The Collapse of the Liberal Consensus," *Canadian Review of American Studies* 20 (Summer 1989), p. 77.

7. David Burner, *The Politics of Provincialism: The Democratic Party in Transition, 1918–1932* (New York: Alfred A. Knopf, 1968).

8. Mark Leff, *The Limits of Symbolic Reform*, p. 287 (quotation).

9. James T. Patterson, *The New Deal and the States: Federalism in Transition* (Princeton: Princeton University Press, 1969), p. 202.

10. Barry D. Karl, *The Uneasy State: The United States from 1915 to 1945* (Chicago: University of Chicago Press, 1983), p. 124.

Critical Thinking

1. Was the New Deal effective? Explain.
2. How did the New Deal change the federal government?

Create Central

www.mhhe.com/createcentral

Internet References

Library of Congress
www.loc.gov/teachers/classroommaterials/presentationsandactivities/presentations/timeline/depwwii/newdeal

History.com
www.history.com/topics/new-deal

Living New deal, Berkeley
http://livingnewdeal.berkeley.edu/resources/what-was-the-new-deal

USNews.com
www.usnews.com/news/articles/2008/01/17/the-new-deal-sealed-the-deal

Article

Labor Strikes Back

What was good for General Motors wasn't always good for GM workers. Sit-down strikes at the company's Michigan plants sparked a wave of similar actions in workplaces across the country.

ROBERT SHOGAN

Learning Outcomes

After reading this article, you will be able to:

- Describe how the United Auto Workers (UAW) unions sit-down strike in Detroit revitalized the union and propelled sit-downs across the country.
- Discuss the impact of the Wagner Act on union organization.

'Sitting-down has replaced baseball as a national pastime.'

The Detroit News, 1937

It was the height of the Saturday shopping rush in the big F.W. Woolworth's five-and-ten-cent store in the heart of downtown Detroit. Customers thronged the aisles surveying the vast array of hair combs and knitting needles, lampshades and face creams, nearly everything on sale for only a nickel or a dime. The clerks stood by their counters as usual. All seemed normal. But this was February 27, 1937, more than seven years deep into the Great Depression, and what had once passed for normal had long since vanished from the American workplace. Suddenly, the bargain-hunting shoppers were startled by the screech of a whistle blown by a union organizer. The 150 women clerks knew just what to do. All of them, the lunch counter brigade in their white short-sleeved uniforms, and the others in their long, fitted skirts and knitted tops, stepped back from their counters and folded their arms, halting work in unison. "The jangle of cash registers stopped," reported the *Detroit News,* "and bewildered customers found themselves holding out nickels and dimes in vain."

The intrepid Woolworth clerks held their ground day and night for an entire week, taking command of the store. Confounded, the company rewarded the strikers with a 20 percent raise and gave their union a say in hiring.

The locally organized work stoppage in Woolworth's was only one of many examples of the potency of a novel weapon—the sit-down strike—that thousands of workers were taking up and using against their bosses across the land. The strikers demanded and frequently won higher wages, shorter working hours and, most commonly, recognition for their unions. Sparked by the signal triumph of the upstart United Auto Workers' (UAW) sit-down strike against General Motors in December 1936, "sit-downers" were causing Americans to take organized labor more seriously than ever before.

Entrenched corporate interests, the indifference of lawmakers and the outright opposition of the courts had combined to beat back the organizing campaigns of labor unions for years. The Great Depression and the launching of President Franklin Roosevelt's New Deal offered unions hope for contending against big business on a more level playing field. But Roosevelt's key legislative act in support of labor, a federal guarantee of collective bargaining, was torpedoed by the U.S. Supreme Court along with the rest of the National Recovery Administration (NRA), the centerpiece of FDR's reform program. The high court held that the NRA represented an unconstitutional grant of power over the economy to the executive branch of government. Meanwhile, the nation's great corporations continued to use every weapon at their disposal to throttle and disrupt the union movement.

Workers were growing desperate. And nowhere was despair deeper than in the auto industry, particularly at General Motors, then the nation's largest corporation. The pressure of the assembly line had always been a point of contention for autoworkers. But it became even harder to bear when GM stepped up the tempo to take advantage of the boost in the economy achieved by the early New Deal programs. Workers complained about what they considered the assembly line's unbearable pace, which some claimed made them ill or so dizzy that when they left the plant, they could not remember where they had parked their cars.

Well aware that such conditions made its factories a breeding ground for labor unions, GM did all it could to crush any such movement before it could start. Since the beginning of 1934, the automaker had spent about $1 million for private detectives to spy on union activities. A Senate committee, probing interference with union organizing efforts, called GM's espionage operation "a monument to the most colossal super-system of spies yet devised in any American corporation."

Spurred by unrest among the rank and file, UAW leaders on December 16, 1936, sought a meeting with General Motors to discuss working conditions. The company declined to meet with the union. Frustrated and angry, the workers were attracted to the sit-down idea, with its guerrilla war motif. A song composed by a UAW leader caught the mood of the workers:

> When they tie the can to a union man, Sit down! Sit down!
> When they give him the sack they'll take him back, Sit down! Sit down!
> When the speed up comes, just twiddle your thumbs, Sit down! Sit down!
> When the boss won't talk don't take a walk, Sit down! Sit down!

As auto industry national union strategists, led by the head of the Committee of Industrial Organizations (CIO), United Mine Workers president John L. Lewis, were still mulling over when to call a strike, the rank-and-file workers and their local leaders took the decision into their own hands. The catalyst was GM's plan for relocating the dies—the cutting tools used to shape the bodies of Chevrolets and Oldsmobiles—from the Fisher Body plant No. 1 in Flint, Mich., to other plants that were relatively free from UAW penetration.

On the night of December 30, 1936, the local UAW leaders sounded the alarm to their assembled workers at a hastily called lunch break meeting by alerting them to GM's plans for transferring the dies. The response was unanimous and swift. "Them's our jobs!" one worker cried out about the crucial equipment. "Shut her down, shut the goddamn plant down!" another worker shouted. Others took up the call and began sitting down at their machinery, just as the starting whistle was set to blow. Within an hour the production line had shut down. "She's ours!" one striker yelled. For good measure, sit-downers also seized control of the much smaller Fisher Body plant No. 2 nearby.

Sit-downs were by no means a brand-new tactic. As early as 1906, General Electric workers sat down at a Schenectady, N.Y., factory, and European workers staged various forms of sit-ins after World War I. But it was during the hard times and frustration of the Depression years that sit-downs caught on and mushroomed as never before.

As the Flint strike soon proved, the sit-down strategy offered great advantages to labor. It made it possible for a relatively small number of workers to completely shut down a huge factory. No more than 1,000 took over Fisher No. 1, and fewer than half that number controlled the smaller No. 2 plant. But their presence, standing guard at the machinery, was enough to keep management from using strikebreakers to reopen plants.

While companies could get a court injunction against strikers, enforcing the order would mean driving the sit-downers out of the plant they controlled, a move that was hard to do without the violence and bloodshed that politicians wanted to avoid.

Grasping the sit-down's potential, Lewis and the CIO plunged into the fray, hoping to get a foothold in mass production industries such as autos, which had resisted the efforts of the craft-based American Federation of Labor. A hulking figure of a man, with a personality to match, Lewis saw the unplanned sit-down of the Flint UAW as a golden opportunity. On New Year's Eve 1936, barely 24 hours after the Flint sit-downs started, Lewis went on the radio to bolster the strikers' cause and to demand the help of President Roosevelt, to whose reelection the CIO had been a major contributor.

For GM the stakes were just as high as they were for Lewis, the CIO and the New Deal. The automaker could not ignore the fact that the strike was metastasizing across its vast empire.

In the week following the seizure of the Flint plants, UAW sit-downs and walkouts had closed the other GM plants throughout the Midwest. But none of those were as menacing to the company's profit margin as the sit-down at the Flint Fisher Body plants, the biggest producers of bodies and parts for all of GM.

Sit-downs made it possible for a small number of workers to completely shut down a huge factory.

On January 11, 1937, the 12th day of the strike, GM staged an assault on Fisher No. 2, the more lightly held of the two UAW bastions. A platoon of company guards rushed a group of workers handing food in through the main gate of the plant, overpowering them and slamming the gate shut. At the same time, with the outdoor temperature at just 16 degrees above zero, GM turned off the heat in the plant.

Union headquarters was alerted, and hundreds of workers rushed to the scene, reinforcing the union picket line outside the plant. To bolster the outnumbered company guards, Flint police soon arrived, brandishing revolvers and tear gas guns, laying siege to the plant. But the strikers inside dragged fire hoses to the windows and drenched the "bulls," as they called the company agents and police, while bombarding them with tools and hardware, including two-pound car door hinges. To make matters worse for the police, strong winds blew the tear gas they had fired at the strikers back into their faces, forcing them to call off their attack.

Their victory in the "Battle of the Running Bulls," as the union forces dubbed the confrontation, energized the strikers and buttressed their support among autoworkers in Flint and elsewhere. Just as important, the fracas at Fisher No. 2 brought Michigan's newly elected pro-labor Governor Frank Murphy into the picture. His interest carried with it the promise of an even more important development—the potential for increasing involvement on the part of President Roosevelt, Murphy's political patron as well as the beneficiary of union leader Lewis' largesse during his 1936 reelection campaign.

Murphy mobilized the National Guard and vowed to preserve order. But he also made clear that he did not intend to use the Guard to evict the strikers, but only to quell violence that the local police could not control.

For their part, the strikers organized themselves into committees to deal with food, sanitation and health, safety and entertainment. Every worker had a specific duty for six hours a day, which he performed in two three-hour shifts. Every night at 8, the strikers' six-piece band—three guitars, a violin, a mouth organ and a squeezebox—broadcast over a loudspeaker for the strikers and the women and children outside. Spirituals and country tunes made up most of their repertoire, but they always closed with "Solidarity Forever," the anthem of the labor movement, sung to the tune of "The Battle Hymn of the Republic," taking heart from its rousing chorus: "Solidarity forever, for the union makes us strong."

The sit-downers themselves were all men, but women played a major role in the effort. Wives came to the plant windows to distribute food, which went immediately into the general commissary, and clean laundry. Women were not allowed to enter, but children were passed through the windows for brief visits with their fathers.

The tenacity of the strikers and their families made it possible, within a month after the Battle of the Running Bulls, for the UAW to celebrate an even more significant victory. Facing an imminent collapse of its production schedule for the entire year, GM, prodded by Roosevelt and bulldozed by Lewis, came to an agreement with the UAW that paved the way for the long-term, quasi-partnership role the union would ultimately play in the auto industry.

The UAW's triumph inspired an epidemic of sit-down strikes the likes of which neither the United States, nor any other country, had ever seen. Shipyards and textile mills, college campuses and even coffin factories all were hit in one town or another. The number of sit-downs, which had nearly doubled from 25 in January 1937 to 47 in February, made a quantum leap in March to 170. This figure was more than three times the total for 1936, and represented strikes involving nearly 170,000 workers. In Detroit, the center of the storm, "sitting-down has replaced baseball as a national pastime," the *Detroit News* reported, "and sitter-downers clutter the landscape in every direction."

Sit-downs were by no means confined to the workplace. At penitentiaries in Pennsylvania and Illinois, inmates sat down to get better treatment—but failed. In Zanesville, Ohio, housewives occupied the office of the director of public services, protesting against a dusty neighborhood street.

The spree had its lighter side. In the town of Neponset, Ill., schoolchildren sat down in the local drugstore demanding free candy—until a generous resident resolved their grievance with a $5 check to the storeowner. A divorced woman sat down in her ex-husband's apartment demanding that he pay the back alimony he owed her. And in New York's Madison

Square Garden, the New York Rovers amateur hockey team kept 15,000 fans waiting for half an hour while they sat down in their dressing room because they had been denied the free tickets promised them.

But most strikes were in deadly earnest, sometimes accompanied by violence. In the Fansteel Metallurgical Corp. plant south of Waukegan, Ill., a two-hour battle raged with more than 100 sit-downers beating back a like number of police and deputy sheriffs who tried to drive them out of their plant. The police and deputies then besieged the plant, sent for reinforcements and a few days later launched another attack. This time they forced the strikers to evacuate.

Nevertheless, the pace of sit-downs continued to quicken. On one single day, March 8, 1937, 300 members of the United Electrical Workers sat down at the Emerson Electric plant in St. Louis, while in Springfield, Ohio, 300 workers at the Springfield Metallic Casket Company stopped production, and in Pittsburgh 200 workers at the American Trouser Company refused to work. The union demanded a return to the 1929 wage scale of $16 a week for a 40-hour week and intended to organize all 700 pants makers in the city.

Later in the same week, 215 strikers sat down at four stores of the H.L. Green department store chain in New York City. They presented the company with a 22-point program calling for union recognition, a 40-hour workweek and a minimum weekly wage of $20. While negotiations went forward, the union's food distribution system provided workers at the largest of the stores in Manhattan with 85 pounds of veal, which they cheerfully made into goulash. At night a nearby Greek restaurant sent in dinner.

But the major battleground continued to be the starting point for the year's imbroglios—Michigan and the auto industry. This time the principal target of the United Auto Workers was Chrysler, then the second largest of the auto companies. The struggle between the union and Chrysler soon reached the bitter intensity of the previous battle with GM.

The UAW's victory over GM had led to concrete gains—pay raises, the rehiring of fired workers, the retiming of jobs to eliminate the speed-up—all of which helped fuel the UAW drive against Chrysler. The leaders of the Chrysler strike had sent observers to Flint and learned from the sit-down there. But so had Chrysler. When 6,000 strikers took over eight Chrysler plants in the Detroit area, the company lost no time in getting an injunction, giving the workers two days to evacuate.

The UAW's friend, Michigan Governor Murphy, was on the spot. While vowing to support the law, he was reluctant to bring force to bear against the strikers, and with good reason. Neither police nor sheriff's deputies were up to the job, and to call on the National Guard would result in a bloody battle.

So the sit-downs continued, appearing to some to threaten chaos, not only in Detroit but also in other major cities. On March 16, 1937, the same day the Chrysler strikers defied the courts and challenged their governor, taxicab drivers battled strikebreakers and police in the heart of Chicago's Loop as thousands watched from office windows. A mounted policeman who rode into the mob was pulled from his horse and beaten; nearby another officer chased away strikers by leveling a shotgun at them. The strikers stopped cabs driven by scab drivers, threw passengers into the street and in one case set a cab on fire.

In New York City, perhaps inspired by their peers' success with their strike in Detroit, Woolworth clerks caught the sit-down fever. At a downtown Manhattan store of the five-and-ten-cent chain, union supporters clambered up onto a second-story ledge above the store entrance, opened windows and threw food, blankets and other provisions to the strikers inside, while private police tried in vain to stop them. The sit-downers sent a cablegram rebuking the Woolworth heiress Barbara Hutton Mdivani Haugwitz-Reventlow, whose extravagant lifestyle had become an embarrassment to the company's executives. "Babs," as the tabloids called her, had just recently bought $2 million worth of jewelry, two Rolls Royces, a 157-foot yacht and a mansion in London. The strikers condemned her profligacy in the face of the Depression-driven hunger and poverty that prevailed in New York and elsewhere in the country.

In Clifton, N.J., 150 employees of the Pacific Slipper Company sat down to demand higher wages and, among other things, cleaner toilets. The company appealed to the state's governor, Republican Harold Hoffman, who had previously likened sit-down strikers to "gangsters" and vowed to crush any such outbreaks in his state with force. But Hoffman, like Democrat Murphy, was not eager to back up his words with actions. Dealing with sit-down strikes, he declared, was a matter best left to the courts.

But in the U.S. Senate, some decided that the time for dithering had passed. On March 17, 1937, with Chrysler under siege and smaller companies beset everywhere by sit-down strikes, one of the Senate's aging lions, California Republican Hiram Johnson, called the outbreak of sit-downs "the most ominous thing in our national economic life today." If public officials permit the strikes to go on, he declared, "then the warning signals are out, and down that road lays dictatorship." Democrat James Hamilton Lewis of Illinois picked up on that theme, warning, "In every hour such as this there awaits another Hitler and there lurks in the shadows another Mussolini."

Other voices joined the chorus in the chamber until Arkansas' venerable Joseph Robinson, the Democratic majority leader of the Senate, unable to find any other way to silence the critics of the sit-down, adjourned the Senate. But adjournment came too late to erase the impact of the anti–sit-down oratory. The next day's front page of *The New York Times* carried, along with more news of the continued Chrysler strike in Detroit and other sit-downs, a streaming headline that declared "SIT-INS HOTLY DENOUNCED IN SENATE," with even more alarming subheads: "CHAOS IS FORESEEN" and "FASCISM HELD POSSIBLE."

Labor's friends in the Senate tried to counterattack by blaming the U.S. Supreme Court. The high court's conservative majority had bedeviled Roosevelt, leading him to shock the nation with his controversial "court-packing" scheme. This would have allowed FDR to blunt the anti–New Deal thrust of the court by appointing six more justices, one for each of the present justices over age 70. Noting that the court had so far failed to rule on the constitutionality of the Wagner Act,

which had been passed to reestablish the protections for union organizing that had been voided earlier by the Supreme Court, Democratic Senator Sherman Minton of Indiana quipped, "Apparently there is a sit-down strike over there."

But such lame sarcasm was drowned out by the crash of events. In Detroit on March 19, city police broke up sit-down strikes in seven downtown shoe stores, smashing the glass doors to gain entrance when the strikers refused to leave. And as the Chrysler strike dragged on, sit-downers warned that if an attempt were made to evict them, they would meet force with force. Roosevelt privately fretted to his confidant, Interior Secretary Harold Ickes, that the political storm stirred by the sit-down strikes might add to the difficulties facing his already beleaguered plan to overhaul the Supreme Court. He had more reason for anxiety on March 26, when a group of New England civic and business leaders, headed by Harvard University's president emeritus, A. Lawrence Lowell, wired Vice President John Nance Garner demanding an end to what newspaper headlines were now calling the "sit-down revolt." If such defiance of established authority and property rights continued, the distinguished group warned, "then freedom and liberty are at an end, government becomes a mockery, superseded by anarchy, mob rule and ruthless dictatorship."

In Garner, who promised he would present the statement to the Senate at its next session, the Lowell group could not have found a more enthusiastic messenger. Though typically he did not speak out publicly on issues, he made no secret of his views within the administration's inner councils. The sit-down strikes, he told Roosevelt's erstwhile campaign manager, Jim Farley, were "mass lawlessness" and "intolerable" and would lead to "great difficulty if not destruction." Garner was so frustrated about Roosevelt's failure to lambaste the sit-down strikers, as Garner thought he should, that he let his feelings erupt during a Cabinet meeting. The vice president stood behind Labor Secretary Frances Perkins and berated her for being insufficiently rigorous in opposing such outbreaks, causing the nation's first woman Cabinet secretary to weep.

Meanwhile, Lewis and other union leaders were not deaf to the outcry against the sit-downs. Fearful his political allies might desert him, Lewis went along with a compromise offered by Governor Murphy that ultimately led to a union agreement with Chrysler similar to the UAW's landmark deal with General Motors.

In mid-April 1937, the Supreme Court at last handed down its ruling on the Wagner Act, upholding the rights the new law granted to union organizing efforts. The decision was a stunning reversal of the court's previous labor decisions. Writing in his diary, Roosevelt's Attorney General Homer Cummings called the ruling "amazing," and court watchers speculated that the justices, already under pressure from Roosevelt's court-packing scheme, had decided to do what they could to ease the labor turmoil roiling the nation.

By the fall of 1937, 70 percent of Americans disapproved of sit-downs.

That same April, sit-down strikes began to decline for the first time that year. With the backing of the Wagner Act, workers were now finding the drastic action of the sit-down less necessary, and at the same time much riskier because of increased public resentment. Public opinion pollster George Gallup found that by the fall of 1937 about 70 percent of Americans disapproved of sit-downs, a negative view that colored overall public attitudes toward labor unions in general. By December, the sit-downs declined from their all-time high to a mere four, involving only a handful of workers.

In 1939 the Supreme Court put an end to the tactic by finding it illegal. Ruling on a case stemming from the 1937 sit-down at the Fansteel Metallurgical factory in Illinois, the court ruled that although the company had violated provisions of the Wagner Act in dealing with its employees, the sit-down staged by its workers was "a high handed proceeding without shadow of a legal right."

But for labor, it was a great ride while it lasted. In a few stormy months in 1937, the sit-down strikers wrote a new chapter in the annals of American labor. They helped John L. Lewis fulfill his vision of industrial unionism, gaining the opportunity for unions to participate in decision-making within the American economy for decades to come. Just as important, they emboldened individual workers in their struggle for a living wage, the right to organize and a voice in working conditions.

The passion that infused the sit-down strikers faded over the years as the gains they helped to achieve came to be taken for granted by workers. Today some critics blame those gains for contributing to the decline and threatened financial ruin of the great auto giants of the past—GM, Ford and Chrysler. But, as organized labor once again faces stiff challenges from a combination of forces and foes, including a more competitive global economy, others feel that it is time for the union movement to recall the faith expressed in the opening verse of Ralph Chaplin's theme song for the sit-down strikers, "Solidarity Forever":

When the union's inspiration through the workers blood shall run,
There can be no power greater anywhere beneath the sun.
Yet what force on earth is weaker than the feeble strength of one,
But the union makes us strong.

Critical Thinking

1. Why did union workers feel a sit-down strike was necessary?

2. Did workers' union benefits become excessive to the point of causing the decline of the auto industry? Explain.

Create Central

www.mhhe.com/createcentral

Internet References

History.com
www.history.com/this-day-in-history/sit-down-strike-begins-in-flint
UAW.org
www.uaw.org/articles/remembering-iconic-flint-sit-down-strike-1937
workers.org
www.workers.org/2007/us/flint-0308
GenralWatch.com
www.generalwatch.com/editorials/editorial.cfm?EdID=218
SloanLongway.org
www.sloanlongway.org/sloan-museum/exhibits-and-galleries/flint-sit-down-strike

This article is adapted from **ROBERT SHOGAN**'s new book, *Backlash: The Killing of the New Deal*, published by Ivan R. Dee.

Article

Flight of the Wasp

The Women Airforce Service Pilots seemed strange and exotic to World War II America. In fact, not even the military could quite figure out what to do with them.

Victoria Pope

Learning Outcomes

After reading this article, you will be able to:

• Describe the WASP program and its potential impact on future women pilots in the military.

• Discuss the difficulties and biases the women experienced both on and off the base.

Curiosity, patriotism, and even a hint of scandal lured the residents of Sweetwater, Texas, to the outskirts of town one April morning in 1943. The townspeople made a day of it, setting out picnic lunches near the military training base at Avenger Field and searching the sky for incoming aircraft. "Cars lined old Highway 80 for two miles in each direction from the Main Gate," recalled 17-year-old Hershel Whittington.

The first sightings came in mid-afternoon, and then dozens of planes, open cockpit and single propeller, began passing over the rolling plains of tumbleweed and cactus beyond town on the way to the base. "Here comes one," someone shouted. "And here's another!"

The planes belonged to members of the Women Airforce Service Pilots (WASP), a band of roughly 1,000 women flyers that served as a homefront Army auxiliary during World War II. But their program might have come too soon for an Army establishment—and a country—that was still wary about women in the military. From the moment of its creation to its abrupt end two years later, the WASP program met with skepticism despite a stellar record of ferrying B-17s, B-29s, B-26s, and other airplanes. One Pentagon official described the program as "an experiment" to test women's abilities to withstand duress and handle the physical demands of the military.

Some WASP pilots started flying hard-to-handle B-26s and B-29s.

The curious residents of Sweetwater may have had more in common with their high-profile visitors than either group realized. America's entry into war had brought sweeping cultural changes: women took on roles vacated by the men joining the military, leaving their kitchens to work on assembly lines and factory floors. Sweetwater experienced an influx of wartime newcomers, including the high-spirited women pilots, while the women found themselves pushing against the boundaries of society's frontiers.

The newly arrived trainees, outfitted in ill-fitting khaki jumpsuits they called zoot suits, seemed unusual indeed to the people of Sweetwater. "They were aloof, self-contained, self-assured, and self-sufficient; at least so it seemed to me then," remembered Helen Kelly, a young girl when the WASP flyers came to town. She watched them in the women's dressing room at the town pool, where "they stripped and walked around naked, unashamed. We had never seen anyone do that. Every Sweetwater female changed in and out of her bathing suit barricaded behind the firmly locked door of a dressing booth." Even their speech seemed different. "They used words we didn't," Kelly recalled; "some long and fancy words, some short and pungent words. They even cursed openly, something which no proper lady in Sweetwater would do."

Blue Bonnet Hotel's Charles Roberson recalled how they poured in on the weekends to have their shoes shined. Most customers would give a small tip, or perhaps nothing at all; these women arrived with pocketfuls of change. Digging into their pant pockets—they did not carry handbags—they paid him with whatever they pulled out, often a fistful of coins. He remembers looking forward to their weekend visits, not for their extravagance of spending but for the extravagance of their spirit.

That kind of spirit was something they shared with Jacqueline Cochran, the program's guiding light, and a household name in her own right. An accomplished racing pilot, she had earned a victory in 1938's cross-country Bendix flying competition. A striking blonde, Cochran also ran her own cosmetics firm and created such popular products as Wonda-matic mascara. Born Bessie Lee Pittman in the Florida Panhandle, she had escaped poverty by moving to New York City, changing her name, and working in a Fifth Avenue hair salon. Through her well-heeled clients she met and later married Floyd Odlum, a man of great wealth and quiet influence. Odlum bought Cochran her first plane and encouraged her aspirations as a flyer and businesswoman.

Cochran wrote to First Lady Eleanor Roosevelt in 1939 about an idea she had for a corps of women Army reserve pilots. "Should there be a call to arms it is not my thought that women pilots will go and engage in combat, for I'm sure they won't," she wrote. "But every trained male pilot will be needed in active service. The 'lady birds' could do all sorts of helpful back of the lines work. Every woman pilot who can step into the cockpit of an ambulance plane or courier plane or a commercial or transport plane can release a male pilot for more important duty."

Using women pilots, the Pentagon said, was "utterly unfeasible."

The U.S. War Department had already broached the idea of using women pilots as early as 1930. The Pentagon's reply: "utterly unfeasible." Women, as a memo explained, were "too high strung for wartime flying." In 1936 a member of the 99s, a prominent women's aviation organization, suggested women should join the military as pilots, but was promptly rebuffed. In the summer of 1941, Cochran, armed with a letter that the First Lady had helped her extract from President Franklin Roosevelt, made the rounds of the Pentagon. Henry "Hap" Arnold, the commanding general of the U.S. Army Air Forces, turned down her plan, stating that the Army had an adequate number of pilots. He also questioned whether Cochran could assemble enough qualified fliers. And, he asked, what about finding proper facilities for training women? "The use of women pilots presents a difficult situation as to the housing and messing of personnel at Air Corps Stations," he wrote to her.

But with the number of male pilots dwindling further every month, Arnold reversed his position. At roughly the same time, the head of the Army Air Transport Command, Col. William H. Turner, approved the plan of an accomplished flyer, Nancy Harkness Love, to assemble a group of highly experienced women pilots to ferry planes. Cochran, in contrast, sought full military training for her women pilots. She began recruiting women who could compare favorably with the average cadet both in intellect and, as she put it, "coordination." For consideration, applicants could be no shorter than 5 feet 2½ inches tall, no younger than 18 and a half years, and must have flown no fewer than 200 hours. Cochran looked for "clean-cut, stable appearing girls." Conservative in many respects, Cochran wedded her views on female abilities with the conventional views of the period. "A woman, to accomplish all she can, must present herself at an absolute peak of attractiveness, just as she must keep herself in good health and her brain growing and alert," she told *Ladies Home Journal* in 1941. "Her beauty is not a frivolous irrelevancy but a touchstone to a full life." She looked askance at black WASP candidates—there was at least one— because, she argued, they would attract far too much prejudice for them to succeed.

Even in the chaotic atmosphere of wartime America, the recruitment process struck prospective WASP candidates as surprisingly informal. Cochran threw cocktail parties and receptions, sometimes making verbal offers after only short conversations. "How many of you would be willing to fly for your country?" she asked a gathering of women in Washington, D.C. A month after that meeting, Jane Straughan was startled to receive a wire that instructed her to report immediately for duty. While more than qualified, she had not even filled out an application form.

Determined applicants found ways around the physical requirements. At 98 pounds, Caro Bayley was simply too small, but she pinned her father's fishing weights under her clothes to add weight. Her examiner passed her. Called "Little Gear" by her classmates, Bayley had trouble reaching the pedals but nonetheless became one of the best acrobatic pilots in the program with the aid of a small stack of pillows. Some challenged the height requirement by hanging upside down by their heels to stretch themselves out, while others simply begged the examiners to pass them anyway.

The program got under way slowly at Howard Hughes Field in Houston in November of 1942. It was a haphazard start. The 319th Army Air Force Women's Flying Training Detachment (WFTD) lacked classrooms, a cafeteria, and even the military planes to train in, instead relying on ordinary civilian carriers painted olive drab. To eat or use the restrooms, the trainees had to walk to the Houston Municipal Airport a half mile away. Without set uniforms, they dressed in whatever they wanted— cowboy boots, loafers, and saddle shoes. One pilot, Marion Florsheim, wore bedroom slippers with pompoms. The only WFTD-issued item was a hairnet required for flying, because the Washington brass worried that long hair would hinder flight training.

In April the training operation shifted to Avenger Field. By then Sweetwater's residents weren't the only ones who found the fliers unusual. Many of the women pilots themselves felt transformed, noting in diaries and letters that their friends and family might not recognize them because they had grown so rough-and-tumble. Living together in barracks and following a rigorous regimen—beginning with reveille at 6 A.M., followed by Morse code, Link (flight simulation) training, and flight training—did not allow time for primping. Gallows humor became a coping mechanism as well as a form of bonding between the pilots, who sometimes had to withstand slights from bullying instructors. Winifred Wood described how her class grew more confident of its military bearing but felt deflated after performing as the honor guard for visiting generals Barton K. Yount and Barney Giles. After the inspection, Giles had turned to his wife and said, "Aren't they cute!"

The oddity of women in the military made good copy for the American press. In late April 1943 the *Houston Post* ran an Associated Press report on the WASP's move to Sweetwater, dubbing them the "Lipstick Squadron." Reporter Hugh

Williamson described the pilots as "sun-bronzed, trim as the streamlined planes," but also quoted Cochran as saying that the program was hard work with little glamour. Field supervisor Maj. L. E. McConnell told Williamson that "gentler treatment" was the only change required for the instruction of women students. As for fighting in actual combat, McConnell said they could learn gunnery and "take their place in the front if called upon to do it." Cochran shared her worries with Williamson that combat would harden and brutalize the women, who still needed to be wives and mothers after the war. Nonetheless, if events called for it, women could fly combat missions. "When aroused, women make the nastiest fighters," she said.

The WASP pilots that graduated from Avenger fanned out to air bases throughout the United States, where they flew cargo, transported new airplanes from factories, and assumed other aviation roles. One elite group, formed from Cochran's best flyers, received an assignment to tow aerial targets at Camp Davis in South Carolina. Cochran hoped the assignment would serve as a stepping stone to bigger responsibilities, perhaps even overseas. "[Cochran] told us the wonderful news that 25 of us were to be used as an experiment and trained on bigger equipment to see just what women can do," WASP Dora Jean Dougherty wrote in her diary. "Will fly almost everything including B-26s and sounds wonderful. She couldn't tell us everything. . . . None of us could sleep for [we] were too excited."

But at Camp Davis, it almost seemed as though the WASP themselves were the targets. The commanding officer of the 3rd Tow Target Squadron, Lovick Stephenson, made it clear that he did not support women in the military. Male pilots already assigned to tow-target duty felt threatened by the new arrivals. Some enlisted men even requested transfers. Although correspondence plainly stated that the 25 women "would be given every opportunity to demonstrate their ability to replace a proportion of, or all, men tow target pilots," Stephenson instead gave them busy work—administrative paperwork or tracking flights in light planes such as the L-5 Stinson liaison planes and Cubs. It was a big comedown.

In time, the women would fly the big planes they came to fly and win the respect they deserved, but ill will was palpable, as one story in *Flying Magazine* made clear. "Isabel Fenton of West Springfield, Mass. was flying a Vega Ventura about 6,000 feet over the dunes off Camp Davis the other day, hauling an airplane target for a battery to shoot at. In 20 rounds the 90's got the target and the target fell blazing into the sea. There were cries of Ah and Oh and Good Shooting from the gallery of press and radio representatives and officers. But as the Ventura wiggled its wings and swung off for its base, a grizzled colonel mumbled into his moustache, 'Hell, they missed the girl.'"

Cochran did not let the summer's challenges slow her down. She offered the WASP another groundbreaking assignment—a chance to fly the B-26 Marauder "Widowmaker," a twin-engine bomber so named for its proclivity for crashing during takeoff. Soon afterward they began flying the country's newest, biggest bomber—the B-29 Superfortress, another plane with a reputation for being hard to handle. Cochran told General Arnold that her pilots had shown that the concerns about those planes were

overstated. "The obvious conclusion was that if a woman could do it so could a man," Cochran said, with understated irony.

But things were changing for the WASP and for the world at large. By 1944 the war had turned in the Allies' favor. New, long-range fighters could now destroy German Luftwaffe planes on the ground, making the skies even safer for the Allies. The United States required fewer combat pilots in the European theater, so the Army Air Force began shutting down both its War Training Service and its civilian flight training program. The civilian pilots reacted by charging women pilots with stealing their jobs. Columnist Drew Pearson launched a virulent campaign against the WASP program, writing that "Jackie's glamour girls" were benefiting from "a racket." Sen. Harry Truman, the head of a committee investigating war waste, asserted that the cost of training a WASP flyer was a hefty $22,000. It was a wildly inflated figure; a truer estimate for both female and male cadets was $12,000.

In February 1944 Rep. John Costello of California submitted a bill to confer Army Air Force commissions on all on-duty women pilots. It failed a House vote on June 19, with 188 voting against, 169 for, and 73 abstaining. It marked the beginning of the end for the WASP. Congress did approve the necessary appropriation for another year, but Cochran decided to close down the program because full military status—which had been given to the Women's Army Corps (WAC) and other branches of the military—was not forthcoming.

At Avenger Field, the final WASP class learned that its training would be abbreviated. Trainee Peggy Daiger was dispirited by the resulting collapse of general field operations. "Those employed at Avenger Field were draft exempt; they hurried away in droves to find other draft-exempt jobs before the December deadline." The changes became evident immediately. "Maintenance was sloppy; instructors became harried; food declined to the almost inedible. I remember one chill day's evening chow that consisted solely of warmed-over boiled potatoes, gummy macaroni, and milk that had been kept next to something less tasty in the refrigerator. One graduate WASP, on the field for only a day's business, carefully loaded her tray with this mess and then slammed the whole thing against the wall. We applauded mentally but nobody smiled."

More than 100 pilots stationed at bases across the country returned for the final graduation on December 4, 1944, a powerful sign of support for a class of graduates with no base assignments awaiting them, who would receive wings they could not wear in military flight. Cochran predicted that the women would return to more conventional paths: "Their careers will be marriage." And overnight, with the abrupt end of the WASP, that assessment seemed accurate.

At the official ceremony, Cochran stuck to a colorless script, thanking the generals and expressing pride in the program's accomplishments. But then Arnold gave the WASP a meaningful sendoff, saying, "Frankly I didn't know in 1941 whether a slip of a young girl could fly the controls of a B-17 in the heavy weather they would naturally encounter in operational flying." The unusually expansive general concluded, "Well, now in 1944, more than two years since the WASP first started flying with the Air Forces we can come to only one conclusion: It is on the record that women can fly as well as men."

In 1976, the Air Force announced that it would accept women cadets.

Arnold's summation was soon forgotten. The WASP pilots themselves were in a sense responsible, soft pedaling their experience and declining to speak about it when husbands and brothers recalled their supposedly more important wartime experiences. But the women kept in touch, and they eventually launched a campaign for full military recognition. In 1976 the U.S. Air Force announced that it would begin accepting women cadets into their corps, a decision hastened by the end of the draft. Once again women had been invited into the military to counterbalance a shortage of men—but as the WASP alumnae knew, despite media reports, this would not mark the first time women had flown for the U.S. military. Motivated by the new developments, they began a campaign to receive the military status that they had been denied 30 years earlier. Congress finally passed such a bill in 1977 that President Jimmy Carter signed into law. But the law did not make many of the military benefits retroactive. Two years later the secretary of the Air Force announced a further step toward recognition. The members of the WASP program—the women who had served in a service that wasn't ready to accept them—were now considered to be veterans.

Critical Thinking

1. Why did the Air Force refuse to give full military status to the WASPs?

2. Are there discriminatory practices in today's U.S. military?

Create Central

www.mhhe.com/createcentral

Internet References

Texas Woman's University
www.twu.edu/library/wasp.asp

U.S. Army
www.army.mil/women/pilots.html

ABC News
http://abcnews.go.com/Politics/women-airforce-service-pilots-wwii-receive-congressional-gold/story?id=10057074

NPR.org
www.npr.org/2010/03/09/123773525/female-wwii-pilots-the-original-fly-girls

WingsAcrossAmerica.org
www.wingsacrossamerica.org

Article   Prepared by: Larry Madaras, *Howard Community College*

Why Truman Dropped the Bomb

Sixty years after Hiroshima, we now have the secret intercepts that shaped his decision.

RICHARD B. FRANK

Learning Outcomes

After reading this article, you will be able to:

- Determine whether the atomic bombs were dropped for military or political reasons.

- Determine whether the Japanese were ready to surrender if the atomic bombs hadn't been used.

- Determine the importance of intelligence intercepts dubbed "magic" in determining the use of the atomic bombs.

The sixtieth anniversary of Hiroshima seems to be shaping up as a subdued affair—though not for any lack of significance. A survey of news editors in 1999 ranked the dropping of the atomic bomb on August 6, 1945, first among the top one hundred stories of the twentieth century. And any thoughtful list of controversies in American history would place it near the top again. It was not always so.

In 1945, an overwhelming majority of Americans regarded as a matter of course that the United States had used atomic bombs to end the Pacific war. They further believed that those bombs *had* actually ended the war and saved countless lives. This set of beliefs is now sometimes labeled by academic historians the "traditionalist" view. One unkindly dubbed it the "patriotic orthodoxy."

But in the 1960s, what were previously modest and scattered challenges of the decision to use the bombs began to crystallize into a rival canon. The challengers were branded "revisionists," but this is inapt. Any historian who gains possession of significant new evidence has a duty to revise his appreciation of the relevant events. These challengers are better termed critics.

The critics share three fundamental premises. The first is that Japan's situation in 1945 was catastrophically hopeless. The second is that Japan's leaders recognized that fact and were seeking to surrender in the summer of 1945. The third is that thanks to decoded Japanese diplomatic messages, American leaders knew that Japan was about to surrender when they unleashed needless nuclear devastation. The critics divide over what prompted the decision to drop the bombs in spite of the impending surrender, with the most provocative arguments focusing on Washington's desire to intimidate the Kremlin. Among an important stratum of American society—and still more perhaps abroad—the critics' interpretation displaced the traditionalist view.

These rival narratives clashed in a major battle over the exhibition of the Enola Gay, the airplane from which the bomb was dropped on Hiroshima, at the Smithsonian Institution in 1995. That confrontation froze many people's understanding of the competing views. Since then, however, a sheaf of new archival discoveries and publications has expanded our understanding of the events of August 1945. This new evidence requires serious revision of the terms of the debate. What is perhaps the most interesting feature of the new findings is that they make a case President Harry S. Truman deliberately chose not to make publicly in defense of his decision to use the bomb.

When scholars began to examine the archival records in the 1960s, some intuited quite correctly that the accounts of their decision-making that Truman and members of his administration had offered in 1945 were at least incomplete. And if Truman had refused to disclose fully his thinking, these scholars reasoned, it must be because the real basis for his choices would undermine or even delegitimize his decisions. It scarcely seemed plausible to such critics—or to almost anyone else—that there could be any legitimate reason that the U.S. government would have concealed at the time, and would continue to conceal, powerful evidence that supported and explained the president's decisions.

But beginning in the 1970s, we have acquired an array of new evidence from Japan and the United States. By far the most important single body of this new evidence consists of secret radio intelligence material, and what it highlights is the painful dilemma faced by Truman and his administration. In explaining their decisions to the public, they deliberately forfeited their best evidence. They did so because under the stringent security restrictions guarding radio intercepts, recipients of this intelligence up to and including the president were barred from retaining copies of briefing documents, from making any public reference to them whatsoever at the time or in their memoirs, and from retaining any record of what they had seen or what they had concluded from it. With a handful of exceptions, they obeyed these rules, both during the war and thereafter.

Collectively, the missing information is known as *The Ultra Secret* of World War II (after the title of a breakthrough book by Frederick William Winterbotham published in 1974). Ultra was the name given to what became a vast and enormously efficient Allied radio intelligence organization, which secretly unveiled masses of information for senior policymakers. Careful listening posts snatched copies of millions of cryptograms from the air. Code breakers then extracted the true text. The extent of the effort is staggering. By the summer of 1945, Allied radio intelligence was breaking into a million messages a month from the Japanese Imperial Army alone, and many thousands from the Imperial Navy and Japanese diplomats.

All of this effort and expertise would be squandered if the raw intercepts were not properly translated and analyzed and their disclosures distributed to those who needed to know. This is where Pearl Harbor played a role. In the aftermath of that disastrous surprise attack, Secretary of War Henry Stimson recognized that the fruits of radio intelligence were not being properly exploited. He set Alfred McCormack, a top-drawer lawyer with experience in handling complex cases, to the task of formulating a way to manage the distribution of information from Ultra. The system McCormack devised called for funneling all radio intelligence to a handful of extremely bright individuals who would evaluate the flood of messages, correlate them with all other sources, and then write daily summaries for policymakers.

By mid-1942, McCormack's scheme had evolved into a daily ritual that continued to the end of the war—and is in essence the system still in effect today. Every day, analysts prepared three mimeographed newsletters. Official couriers toting locked pouches delivered one copy of each summary to a tiny list of authorized recipients around the Washington area. (They also retrieved the previous day's distribution, which was then destroyed except for a file copy.) Two copies of each summary went to the White House, for the president and his chief of staff. Other copies went to a very select group of officers and civilian officials in the War and Navy Departments, the British Staff Mission, and the State Department. What is almost as interesting is the list of those *not* entitled to these top-level summaries: the vice president, any cabinet official outside the select few in the War, Navy, and State Departments, anyone in the Office of Strategic Services or the Federal Bureau of Investigation, or anyone in the Manhattan Project building the atomic bomb, from Major General Leslie Groves on down.

The three daily summaries were called the *"Magic" Diplomatic Summary*, the *"Magic" Far East Summary*, and the *European Summary*. ("Magic" was a code word coined by the U.S. Army's chief signal officer, who called his code breakers "magicians" and their product "Magic." The term "Ultra" came from the British and has generally prevailed as the preferred term among historians, but in 1945 "Magic" remained the American designation for radio intelligence, particularly that concerning the Japanese.) The *"Magic" Diplomatic Summary* covered intercepts from foreign diplomats all over the world. The *"Magic" Far East Summary* presented information on Japan's military, naval, and air situation. The *European Summary* paralleled the Far East summary in coverage and need not detain us. Each summary read like a newsmagazine. There were headlines and brief articles usually containing extended quotations from intercepts and commentary. The commentary was critical: Since no recipient retained any back issues, it was up to the editors to explain how each day's developments fitted into the broader picture.

When a complete set of the *"Magic" Diplomatic Summary* for the war years was first made public in 1978, the text contained a large number of redacted (literally whited out) passages. The critics reasonably asked whether the blanks concealed devastating revelations. Release of a non-redacted complete set in 1995 disclosed that the redacted areas had indeed contained a devastating revelation—but not about the use of the atomic bombs. Instead, the redacted areas concealed the embarrassing fact that Allied radio intelligence was reading the codes not just of the Axis powers, but also of some 30 other governments, including allies like France.

The diplomatic intercepts included, for example, those of neutral diplomats or attachés stationed in Japan. Critics highlighted a few nuggets from this trove in the 1978 releases, but with the complete release, we learned that there were only 3 or 4 messages suggesting the possibility of a compromise peace, while no fewer than 13 affirmed that Japan fully intended to fight to the bitter end. Another page in the critics' canon emphasized a squad of Japanese diplomats in Europe, from Sweden to the Vatican, who attempted to become peace entrepreneurs in their contacts with American officials. As the editors of the *"Magic" Diplomatic Summary* correctly made clear to American policymakers during the war, however, not a single one of these men (save one we will address shortly) possessed actual authority to act for the Japanese government.

An inner cabinet in Tokyo authorized Japan's only officially sanctioned diplomatic initiative. The Japanese dubbed this inner cabinet the Big Six because it comprised just six men: Prime Minister Kantaro Suzuki, Foreign Minister Shigenori Togo, Army Minister Korechika Anami, Navy Minister Mitsumasa Yonai, and the chiefs of staff of the Imperial Army (General Yoshijiro Umezu) and Imperial Navy (Admiral Soemu Toyoda). In complete secrecy, the Big Six agreed on an approach to the Soviet Union in June 1945. This was not to ask the Soviets to deliver a "We surrender" note; rather, it aimed to enlist the Soviets as mediators to negotiate an end to the war satisfactory to the Big Six—in other words, a peace on terms satisfactory to the dominant militarists. Their minimal goal was not confined to guaranteed retention of the Imperial Institution; they also insisted on preservation of the old militaristic order in Japan, the one in which they ruled.

The conduit for this initiative was Japan's ambassador in Moscow, Naotake Sato. He communicated with Foreign Minister Togo—and, thanks to code breaking, with American policymakers. Ambassador Sato emerges in the intercepts as a devastating cross-examiner ruthlessly unmasking for history the feebleness of the whole enterprise. Sato immediately told Togo that the Soviets would never bestir themselves on behalf of Japan. The foreign minister could only insist that Sato follow his instructions. Sato demanded to know whether the government and the military supported the overture and what its legal basis was—after all, the official Japanese position, adopted in an Imperial Conference in June 1945 with the emperor's sanction, was a fight to the finish. The ambassador also demanded that Japan state concrete terms to end the war, otherwise the effort could not be taken seriously. Togo responded evasively that the "directing powers" and the government had authorized the effort—he did not and could not claim that the military in general supported it or that the fight-to-the-end policy had been replaced. Indeed, Togo added: "Please bear particularly in mind, however, that we are not seeking the Russians' mediation for anything like an unconditional surrender."

This last comment triggered a fateful exchange. Critics have pointed out correctly that both Under Secretary of State Joseph Grew (the former U.S. ambassador to Japan and the leading expert on that nation within the government) and Secretary of War Henry Stimson advised Truman that a guarantee that the Imperial Institution would not be eliminated could prove essential to obtaining Japan's surrender. The critics further have argued that if only the United States had made such a guarantee, Japan would have surrendered. But when Foreign Minister Togo informed Ambassador Sato that Japan was not looking for anything like unconditional surrender, Sato promptly wired back a cable that the editors of the *"Magic" Diplomatic Summary* made clear to American policymakers "advocate[s] unconditional surrender provided the Imperial House is preserved." Togo's reply, quoted in the *"Magic" Diplomatic Summary* of July 22, 1945, was adamant: American policymakers could read for themselves Togo's rejection of Sato's proposal—with not even a hint that a guarantee of the Imperial House would be a step in the right direction. Any rational person following this exchange would conclude that modifying the demand for unconditional surrender to include a promise to preserve the Imperial House would not secure Japan's surrender.

Togo's initial messages—indicating that the emperor himself endorsed the effort to secure Soviet mediation and was prepared to send his own special envoy—elicited immediate attention from the editors of the *"Magic" Diplomatic Summary,* as well as Under Secretary of State Grew. Because of Grew's documented advice to Truman on the importance of the Imperial Institution, critics feature him in the role of the sage counsel. What the intercept evidence discloses is that Grew reviewed the Japanese effort and concurred with the U.S. Army's chief of intelligence, Major General Clayton Bissell, that the effort most likely represented a ploy on American war weariness. They deemed the possibility that it manifested a serious effort by the emperor to end the war "remote." Lest there be any doubt about Grew's mindset, as late as August 7, the day after Hiroshima, Grew drafted a memorandum with an oblique reference to radio intelligence again affirming his view that Tokyo still was not close to peace.

Starting with the publication of excerpts from the diaries of James Forrestal in 1951, the contents of a few of the diplomatic intercepts were revealed, and for decades the critics focused on these. But the release of the complete (unredacted) *"Magic" Far East Summary,* supplementing the *Diplomatic Summary,* in the 1990s revealed that the diplomatic messages amounted to a mere trickle by comparison with the torrent of military intercepts. The intercepts of Japanese Imperial Army and Navy messages disclosed without exception that Japan's armed forces were determined to fight a final Armageddon battle in the homeland against an Allied invasion. The Japanese called this strategy Ketsu Go (Operation Decisive). It was founded on the premise that American morale was brittle and could be shattered by heavy losses in the initial invasion. American politicians would then gladly negotiate an end to the war far more generous than unconditional surrender.

Ultra was even more alarming in what it revealed about Japanese knowledge of American military plans. Intercepts demonstrated that the Japanese had correctly anticipated precisely where U.S. forces intended to land on Southern Kyushu in November 1945 (Operation Olympic). American planning for the Kyushu assault reflected adherence to the military rule of thumb that the attacker should outnumber the defender at least three to one to assure success at a reasonable cost. American estimates projected that on the date of the landings, the Japanese would have only three of their six field divisions on all of Kyushu in the southern target area where nine American divisions would push ashore. The estimates allowed that the Japanese would possess just 2,500 to 3,000 planes total throughout Japan to face Olympic. American aerial strength would be over four times greater.

From mid-July onwards, Ultra intercepts exposed a huge military buildup on Kyushu. Japanese ground forces exceeded prior estimates by a factor of four. Instead of 3 Japanese field divisions deployed in southern Kyushu to meet the 9 U.S. divisions, there were 10 Imperial Army divisions plus additional brigades. Japanese air forces exceeded prior estimates by a factor of two to four. Instead of 2,500 to 3,000 Japanese aircraft, estimates varied between about 6,000 and 10,000. One intelligence officer commented that the Japanese defenses threatened "to grow to [the] point where we attack on a ratio of one (1) to one (1) which is not the recipe for victory."

Concurrent with the publication of the radio intelligence material, additional papers of the Joint Chiefs of Staff have been released in the last decade. From these, it is clear that there was no true consensus among the Joint Chiefs of Staff about an invasion of Japan. The Army, led by General George C. Marshall, believed that the critical factor in achieving American war aims was time. Thus, Marshall and the Army advocated an invasion of the Home Islands as the fastest way to end the war. But the long-held Navy view was that the critical factor in achieving American war aims was casualties. The Navy was convinced that an invasion would be far too costly to sustain the support of the American people, and hence believed that blockade and bombardment were the sound course.

The picture becomes even more complex than previously understood because it emerged that the Navy chose to postpone a final showdown over these two strategies. The commander in chief of the U.S. fleet, Admiral Ernest King, informed his colleagues on the Joint Chiefs of Staff in April 1945 that he did not agree that Japan should be invaded. He concurred only that the Joint Chiefs must issue an invasion order immediately to create that option for the fall. But King predicted that the Joint Chiefs would revisit the issue of whether an invasion was wise in August or September. Meanwhile, two months of horrendous fighting ashore on Okinawa under skies filled with kamikazes convinced the commander in chief of the Pacific Fleet, Admiral Chester Nimitz, that he should withdraw his prior support for at least the invasion of Kyushu. Nimitz informed King of this change in his views in strict confidence.

In August, the Ultra revelations propelled the Army and Navy towards a showdown over the invasion. On August 7 (the day after Hiroshima, which no one expected to prompt a quick surrender), General Marshall reacted to weeks of gathering gloom in the Ultra evidence by asking General Douglas MacArthur, who was to command what promised to be the greatest invasion in history, whether invading Kyushu in November as planned still looked sensible. MacArthur replied, amazingly, that he did not believe the radio intelligence! He vehemently urged the invasion should go forward as planned. (This, incidentally, demolishes later claims that MacArthur thought the Japanese were about to surrender at the time of Hiroshima.)

On August 9 (the day the second bomb was dropped, on Nagasaki), King gathered the two messages in the exchange between Marshall and MacArthur and sent them to Nimitz. King told Nimitz to provide his views on the viability of invading Kyushu, with a copy to MacArthur. Clearly, nothing that had transpired since May would have altered Nimitz's view that Olympic was unwise. Ultra now made the invasion appear foolhardy to everyone but MacArthur. But King had not placed a deadline on Nimitz's response, and the Japanese surrender on August 15 allowed Nimitz to avoid starting what was certain to be one of the most tumultuous interservice battles of the whole war.

What this evidence illuminates is that one central tenet of the traditionalist view is wrong—but with a twist. Even with the full ration of caution that any historian should apply anytime he ventures comments on paths history did not take, in this instance it is now clear that the long-held belief that Operation Olympic loomed as a certainty is mistaken. Truman's reluctant endorsement of the Olympic invasion at a meeting in June 1945 was based in key part on the fact that the Joint Chiefs had presented it as their unanimous recommendation. (King went along with Marshall at the meeting, presumably because he deemed it premature to wage a showdown fight. He did comment to Truman that, of course, any invasion authorized then could be canceled later.) With the Navy's withdrawal of support, the terrible casualties in Okinawa, and the appalling radio-intelligence picture of the

Japanese buildup on Kyushu, Olympic was not going forward as planned and authorized—period. But this evidence also shows that the demise of Olympic came not because it was deemed unnecessary, but because it had become unthinkable. It is hard to imagine anyone who could have been president at the time (a spectrum that includes FDR, Henry Wallace, William O. Douglas, Harry Truman, and Thomas Dewey) failing to authorize use of the atomic bombs in this circumstance.

Japanese historians uncovered another key element of the story. After Hiroshima (August 6), Soviet entry into the war against Japan (August 8), and Nagasaki (August 9), the emperor intervened to break a deadlock within the government and decide that Japan must surrender in the early hours of August 10. The Japanese Foreign Ministry dispatched a message to the United States that day stating that Japan would accept the Potsdam Declaration, "with the understanding that the said declaration does not comprise any demand which prejudices the prerogatives of His Majesty as a Sovereign Ruler." This was not, as critics later asserted, merely a humble request that the emperor retain a modest figurehead role. As Japanese historians writing decades after the war emphasized, the demand that there be no compromise of the "prerogatives of His Majesty as a Sovereign Ruler" as a precondition for the surrender was a demand that the United States grant the emperor veto power over occupation reforms and continue the rule of the old order in Japan. Fortunately, Japan specialists in the State Department immediately realized the actual purpose of this language and briefed Secretary of State James Byrnes, who insisted properly that this maneuver must be defeated. The maneuver further underscores the fact that right to the very end, the Japanese pursued twin goals: not only the preservation of the imperial system, but also preservation of the old order in Japan that had launched a war of aggression that killed 17 million.

This brings us to another aspect of history that now very belatedly has entered the controversy. Several American historians led by Robert Newman have insisted vigorously that any assessment of the end of the Pacific war must include the horrifying consequences of each continued day of the war for the Asian populations trapped within Japan's conquests. Newman calculates that between a quarter million and 400,000 Asians, overwhelmingly noncombatants, were dying each month the war continued. Newman et al. challenge whether an assessment of Truman's decision can highlight only the deaths of noncombatant civilians in the aggressor nation while ignoring much larger death tolls among noncombatant civilians in the victim nations.

There are a good many more points that now extend our understanding beyond the debates of 1995. But it is clear that all three of the critics' central premises are wrong. The Japanese did not see their situation as catastrophically hopeless. They were not seeking to surrender, but pursuing a negotiated end to the war that preserved the old order in Japan, not just a figurehead emperor. Finally, thanks to radio intelligence, American leaders, far from knowing that peace was at hand, understood—as one analytical piece in the *"Magic" Far East Summary* stated in July 1945, after a review of both the military and diplomatic intercepts—that "until the Japanese leaders realize that an invasion can not be repelled, there is little likelihood that they will accept any peace terms satisfactory to the Allies." This cannot be improved upon as a succinct and accurate summary of the military and diplomatic realities of the summer of 1945.

The displacement of the so-called traditionalist view within important segments of American opinion took several decades to accomplish. It will take a similar span of time to displace the critical orthodoxy that arose in the 1960s and prevailed roughly through the 1980s, and replace it with a richer appreciation for the realities of 1945. But the clock is ticking.

Critical Thinking

1. Compare and contrast and critically evaluate whether the decision to drop the atomic bombs were for military or political reasons.
2. Describe how the "magic intercepts" were decoded, translated, distributed, and destroyed. Also explain why they were not declassified partially until 1978 and fully in 1995.
3. Discuss whether you think President Truman would have made a different decision to drop the bomb if he didn't have the intelligence information.

Create Central

www.mhhe.com/createcentral

Internet References

Hiroshima Archive

The Hiroshima Archive was originally set up to join the online effort made by many people all over the world to commemorate the 50th anniversary of the atomic bombing. It is intended to serve as a research and educational guide to those who want to gain and expand their knowledge of the atomic bombing.

www.lclark.edu/~history/HIROSHIMA

The Enola Gay

The official website of Brigadier General Paul W. Tibbets, Jr. (Ret.) offers a wealth of historical analysis and photographs of the events surrounding the use of atomic weapons on Japan in 1945.

www.theenolagay.com/index.html

RICHARD B. FRANK, a historian of World War II is the author of *Downfall: The End of the Imperial Japanese Empire.*

Unit 5

UNIT

From the Cold War to 2010

UNIT

From the Cold War to 2010

President Franklin D. Roosevelt sought to build a working relationship with Soviet leader Josef Stalin throughout World War II. Roosevelt believed that the wartime collaboration had to continue if a lasting peace were to be achieved. At the Yalta Conference of February 1945, a series of agreements were made that FDR hoped would provide the basis for continued cooperation. Subsequent disputes over interpretation of these agreements, particularly with regard to Poland, raised doubts in Roosevelt's mind that Stalin was acting in good faith. Roosevelt died on April 12, 1945, and there is no doubt that he was moving toward a "tougher" position during the last weeks of his life. Harry S Truman assumed the presidency with little knowledge of Roosevelt's thinking. Truman had not been part of the administration's inner circle and had to rely on discussions with the advisers he inherited and his own reading of messages passed between FDR and the Soviets. Aside from an ugly encounter with Soviet Foreign Minister V. M. Molotov at the White House only eleven days after Roosevelt's death, Truman attempted to carry out what he believed were Roosevelt's intentions: be firm with the Soviets, but continue to seek accommodation. He came to believe that Foreign Minister V. M. Molotov was trying to sabotage U.S.–Soviet relations and that the best way to reach agreements was to negotiate directly with Stalin. This he did at the Potsdam Conference during the summer of 1945, and left the talks believing that Stalin was a hard bargainer but one who could be trusted.

Events during the late summer and early autumn eroded Truman's hopes that the Soviets genuinely wanted to get along. Disputes over Poland and other Eastern European countries, the treatment of postwar Germany, and a host of other issues finally persuaded Truman that it was time to stop "babying" the Soviets. A militant public speech by Stalin, which one American referred to as the "declaration of World War III," appeared to confirm this view. Increasingly hostile relations led to what became known as the "Cold War," during which each side increasingly came to regard the other as an enemy rather than merely an adversary. Meanwhile the United States had to cope with the problems of conversion to a peacetime economy. Demobilization of the armed forces proved especially vexing as the public clamored to have service men and women, stationed virtually all over the world, brought home and discharged as quickly as possible. When the administration seemed to be moving too slowly, the threat "no boats, no votes" became popular. Race riots, labor strife, and inflation also marred the postwar period.

Relations with the Soviets continued to deteriorate. Perceived Soviet threats against Greece and Turkey led to promulgation of the "Truman Doctrine" in 1947, which placed the United States on the side of those nations threatened with overt aggression or internal subversion. That same year Secretary of State George C. Marshall sketched the outlines of what would become known as the "Marshall Plan," an even more ambitious effort to prevent economic chaos in Europe. "Dollar Diplomacy" evaluates this program that has been described as "among the most noble experiences in human affairs."

How had things gotten to such a sorry state only a few years after the dragons of fascism and Japanese militarism had been slain? Some people began alleging that, as dangerous as the Soviet Union was, internal subversion was an even greater problem. Opponents of Roosevelt's "New Deal" and Truman's "Fair Deal" cited various allegations of spying on the part of former government officials to bolster their claims that Democrat administrations had been shot-through with subversion. Liberals cried frame up. Some of these allegations have been shown to be true, but what became known as "McCarthysim" (after a Wisconsin senator who was a prominent "Commie hunter") cast a pall of suspicion over the society.

In 1950, a scant five years after the end of World War II, the United States found itself at war again. The North Korean invasion of the South in June of that year appeared to American leaders as a Soviet-inspired probe to test Western resolve. Failure to halt aggression there, many believed, would embolden the Soviets to strike elsewhere just as Hitler had done in the 1930s. President Truman's decision to send American troops to Korea was almost universally applauded at first, but discontent arose as the war dragged on. Americans were not used to fighting "no win" wars.

Domestically, the 1950s offered a mixed bag. Social critics denounced the conformity of those who plodded up the corporate ladder, purchased tract homes that all looked alike, or who had no greater ambition than to sit in front of their television sets every night. Beneath the veneer of tranquility, however, there were stirrings over civil rights and liberties that would erupt into prominence during the 1960s. In 1957, Americans were shocked when the Soviet Union announced that it had launched the first space satellite in history, and how *Sputnik* shattered assumptions about American technological superiority and had grave military implications as well.

The election of John F. Kennedy to the presidency in 1960 appeared to many as a turning point in American history. His charm and good looks, as well as his liberal agenda, provided a marked contrast to the Eisenhower era. Kennedy did sponsor some significant legislation and moved hesitantly on civil rights, but his assassination in 1963 leaves us only to speculate on what he might have accomplished had he served his full term and perhaps a second. Recent historians have given mixed grades to his presidency. They point to the Bay of Pigs fiasco and to the fact that he was the one to first send combat troops to Vietnam.

There was a great deal of social unrest during the latter part of the 1960s. In addition to protests against the war, racism, and social inequities, there were virtual revolutions with regard to sex, music, and to the use of drugs.

Social ferment began to subside during the latter part of the 1970s, causing some observers to regard these years as dull and relatively uneventful. Not so, as others claim that one must look at 1978 to "see the beginnings of the world we live in today."

Public health insurance has been one of the most controversial issues of President Obama's administration. There have been earlier attempts to enact this reform and all have failed for various reasons. American institutions, some claim, make it extremely difficult to achieve heavy reforms.

Article Prepared by: Larry Madaras, _Howard Community College_

Baseball's _Noble_ Experiment

When former Negro Leaguer Jackie Robinson took his place in the Brooklyn Dodgers' starting lineup on April 15, 1947, he initiated a major change not only in sports, but in American society as a whole.

WILLIAM KASHATUS

Learning Outcomes

After reading this article, you will be able to:

- Write a short biographical sketch of Jackie Robinson prior to 1945.
- Write a short biographical sketch of Branch Rickey prior to 1945.
- Examine the racial atmosphere of segregation in American society after World War II had ended.
- Explain why Branch Rickey picked Robinson over better African-American baseball players to integrate the major leagues.
- Examine the hostility faced by Robinson in the 1947 baseball season.

On August 28, 1945, Jackie Robinson, the star shortstop of the Negro Leagues' Kansas City Monarchs, arrived at the executive offices of the Brooklyn Dodgers Baseball Club. Invited on the pretense that Branch Rickey, since 1942 a part owner of the club as well as its president and general manager, was seeking top black talent in order to create a Negro League team of his own, Robinson approached the meeting with great reluctance. Deep down he wanted to break the color barrier that existed in professional baseball, not discuss the possibility of playing for yet another all-black team. Little did he realize that Rickey shared his dream.

A shrewd, talkative man who had dedicated his life to baseball, the 64-year-old Rickey was secretly plotting a sweeping revolution within the national pastime. He believed that integration of the major leagues would be good for the country as well as for the game. Financial gain was only part of his motive—it was also a matter of moral principle. Rickey, a devout Methodist, disdained the bigoted attitudes of the white baseball establishment.

Greeting Robinson with a vigorous handshake, Rickey wasted no time in revealing his true intentions. "The truth is," he confessed, "I'm interested in you as a candidate for the Brooklyn Dodgers. I think you can play in the major leagues. How do you feel about it?"

The young ball player was speechless. He had taught himself to be cynical toward all baseball-club owners, especially white ones, in order to prevent any personal disillusionment.

"What about it? You think you can play for Montreal?" demanded the stocky beetle-browed executive.

Robinson, awestruck, managed to say "yes." He knew that the Montreal Royals was the Dodgers' top minor-league team and that if he made good there, he had an excellent chance to crack the majors. "I just want to be treated fairly," he added. "You will not be treated fairly!" Rickey snapped. "'Nigger' will be a compliment!"

For the next three hours, Rickey interrogated the star shortstop. With great dramatic flair, he role-played every conceivable scenario that would confront the first player to break baseball's color barrier: first he was a bigoted sportswriter who only wrote lies about Robinson's performance; next he was a Southern hotel manager refusing room and board; then, a racist major leaguer looking for a fight; and after that a waiter throwing Robinson out of a "for whites only" diner. In every scenario, Rickey cursed Robinson and threatened him, verbally degrading him in every way imaginable. The Dodger general manager's performance was so convincing, Robinson later said, that "I found myself chain-gripping my fingers behind my back."

When he was through, Rickey told Robinson that he knew he was "a fine ballplayer. But what I need," he added, "is more than a great player. I need a man that will take abuse and insults for his race. And what I don't know is whether you have the guts!"

Robinson struggled to keep his temper. He was insulted by the implication that he was a coward. "Mr. Rickey," he retorted, "do you want a Negro who's afraid to fight back?"

"No!" Rickey barked, "I want a ballplayer with guts enough _not_ to fight back. We can't _fight_ our way through this. There's virtually nobody on our side. No owners, no umpires, virtually no newspapermen. And I'm afraid that many fans will be hostile too. They'll taunt you and goad you. They'll do anything to make you react. They'll try to provoke a race riot in the ball park."

As he listened, Robinson became transfixed by the Dodger president. He felt his sincerity, his deep, quiet strength, and his sense of moral justice. "We can only win," concluded Rickey, "if we can convince the world that I'm doing this because you're a great ballplayer and a fine gentleman. You will symbolize a crucial cause. One incident, just one incident, can set it back twenty years."

"Mr. Rickey," Robinson finally said, "I think I can play ball in Montreal. I think I can play ball in Brooklyn. . . . If you want to take this gamble, I will promise you there will be no incident."

The agreement was sealed by a handshake. Jackie Robinson and Branch Rickey had launched a noble experiment to integrate major-league baseball. Two years later, in 1947, when Robinson actually broke the color barrier, winning rookie-of-the-year honors with the Dodgers, he raised the hopes and expectations of millions of black Americans who believed that deeply rooted patterns of discrimination could be changed.

In 1945, segregation was the most distinguishing characteristic of American race relations. More than half of the nation's 15 million African Americans still lived in the South, amidst a society that sanctioned the principle of "equal but separate." A rigid system of state and local ordinances enforced strict separation of the races in schools, restaurants, movie theaters, and even restrooms. For blacks, these so-called "Jim Crow laws"[1] meant inferior public schools, health care, and public lodging, as well as discriminatory voter registration procedures that kept many of them disenfranchised.

For the nearly one million African Americans who had served in the armed forces during World War II, the contradiction inherent in their fight against totalitarianism abroad while enduring segregation at home was insufferable. No longer willing to knuckle under to Jim Crow this young generation of black Americans was determined to secure full political and social equality. Many migrated to Northern cities, where they found better jobs, better schooling, and freedom from landlord control. Together with their white allies, these Northern blacks would lay the foundations of the momentous civil rights campaign of the 1950s and '60s. And Jackie Robinson became their hero.

To be sure, Robinson's challenge to baseball's whites-only policy was a formidable one. Blacks had been expelled from the major leagues when segregation was established by the 1896 Supreme Court ruling in *Plessy v. Ferguson.*[2] Racist attitudes were reinforced by the significant numbers of white Southerners who played in the majors, as well as by the extensive minor-league system that existed in the South. When blacks established their own Negro Leagues, white journalists, as well as historians, ignored them.

Despite the periodic efforts of some white club owners to circumvent the racist policies and sign exceptional Negro Leaguers, the majors continued to bar blacks through the end of World War II. Baseball Commissioner Judge Kenesaw Mountain Landis ensured the sport's segregationist policies by thwarting all efforts to sign blacks, while publicly stating that "There is no rule, formal or informal, or any understanding—unwritten, subterranean, or sub-anything—against the hiring of Negro players by the teams of organized baseball." Not until Landis died in 1944, however, did baseball open the door for integration.

The new commissioner, Albert "Happy" Chandler, was adamant in defending the "freedom of blacks," especially those who served in the war, to "make it in major league baseball." Chandler's support for integration earned for him the open hostility of the owners of 15 of the 16 major-league clubs, the exception being the Dodgers and Branch Rickey.

Publicly, Rickey never revealed his intentions of breaking the color barrier. Instead, he announced to the baseball world that he was going to organize a team to be known as the "Brown Dodgers" or the "Brown Bombers" as part of a new all-black "United States League." His scouts combed baseball leagues across the country, as well as in Cuba, Mexico, Puerto Rico, and Venezuela, for black prospects. What Rickey really wanted to find was a talented, college-educated ballplayer who would be able to contradict the popular myth of black ignorance. His search narrowed to Jack Roosevelt Robinson, then an infielder for the Kansas City Monarchs.

Born on January 31, 1919, in Cairo, Georgia, Jackie was the grandson of a slave and the fifth child of a sharecropper who deserted his family. Raised by his mother in a white, middle-class neighborhood in Pasadena, California, Jackie and his brothers and sister were verbally ridiculed and frequently pelted with rocks by local children. Rather than endure the humiliation, the boys formed a gang and began to return fire.

What saved the young Jackie from more serious trouble and even crime was his exceptional athletic ability. Robinson's high school career was distinguished by remarkable success in football, baseball, basketball, and track. His versatility earned him an athletic scholarship, first to Pasadena Junior College and later to the University of California at Los Angeles, where he earned varsity letters in four different sports and All American honors in football.

Drafted into the Army in the spring of 1942, Robinson applied to be admitted to Officers' Candidate School, but was denied admission because of his race. His application was eventually approved, however, thanks to the help of boxing champion Joe Louis, who was stationed with Jackie at Fort Riley, Kansas. Commissioned a second lieutenant, Robinson continued during the next few years to defy discriminatory practices within the military. When, in July 1944, he refused to move to the rear of a military bus at Fort Hood, Texas, Robinson was charged with insubordination and court-martialed. But the case against him was weak—the Army had recently issued orders against such segregation—and a good lawyer won his acquittal. Although he received an honorable discharge in November 1944, Robinson's time in the military had left him feeling vulnerable and uncertain about the future.

With Rachel's Support

When Jackie Robinson met with Branch Rickey in August 1945, the Dodgers' general manager asked him if he had a girlfriend, and was pleased when Jackie told him that he was engaged to be married. As he had made abundantly clear to Robinson that day, Rickey was aware that the first black player in the major leagues would face a terrible ordeal, and he clearly believed that he should not face it alone.

In her recent book, *Jackie Robinson: An Intimate Portrait*, Rachel Robinson writes that it was at the start of the '47 season that she and Jackie first realized "how important we were to black America and how much we symbolized its hunger for opportunity and its determination to make dreams long deferred possible." If Jackie failed to make the grade as a player, or if the pressures became so great that he decided to pull out of Rickey's "noble experiment," the hopes of all the nation's blacks would be done enormous, if not irreparable harm. It was a tremendous burden to have to bear, and it belonged not only to Jackie, but also to his family.

Rachel Isum had met her future husband in 1940 while they were both students at UCLA, where she earned a degree in nursing. Engaged in 1941, they endured long separations during World War II, and in 1945, as Jackie traveled with the Kansas City Monarchs. Finally, in February 1946—just before Jackie was due to report to Daytona Beach, Florida, to try to earn a place with the Montreal Royals—they were married. Both Jackie and Rachel had known racial bigotry and discrimination in Southern California, where they grew up, but

they realized that they would face something much more difficult in the institutionalized segregation of the 1940s South. During that first trip to Florida, they experienced repeated humiliations that were, according to Rachel, "merely a foreshadowing of trials to come." As the Royals played exhibition games in other Florida cities, Jackie got a taste of how many Americans viewed his presence in professional baseball.

Following spring training, Jackie joined the Royals in Montreal, where the couple found a much more receptive environment. Although Jackie still faced racism during road trips, the Robinsons' year in Canada was fondly remembered as a respite that helped them prepare for the real test that came when he moved on to the Dodgers in 1947.

As players and fans in cities around the National League tormented Jackie, Rachel was forced to sit "through name calling, jeers, and vicious baiting in a furious silence." For his part, the Dodgers' rookie infielder, who had promised Rickey that he would turn the other cheek, "found that the most powerful form of retaliation against prejudice was his excellent play." But after the '48 season, Robinson called off his deal with Rickey. He would no longer submit quietly to insults, discrimination, and abuses. Able at last to release some of the pent-up pressure and emotion, Robinson became a more confident player; in 1949, he won the National League batting championship with a .349 average and received a trophy ironically named for Kenesaw Mountain Landis, the man who tried to keep blacks out of baseball.

Shortly after his discharge, the Kansas City Monarchs, one of the most talented of baseball's Negro League teams, offered Robinson a contract for four hundred dollars a month. While with the Monarchs, Robinson established himself as a fine defensive shortstop with impressive base stealing and hitting abilities. But he hated barnstorming through the South, with its Jim Crow restaurants and hotels, and frequently allowed his temper to get the better of him.

Some teammates thought Jackie too impatient with the segregationist treatment of blacks. Others admired him for his determination to take a stand against racism. Yet Robinson never saw himself as a crusader for civil rights as much as an athlete who had grown disillusioned with his chosen career. "When I look back at what I had to go through," he recalled years later, "I can only marvel at the many black players who stuck it out for years in the Jim Crow leagues because they had nowhere to go. The black press, some liberal sportswriters and even a few politicians were banging away at those Jim Crow barriers in baseball, but I never expected the walls to come tumbling down in my lifetime. I began to wonder why I should dedicate my life to a career where the boundaries of progress were set by racial discrimination."

There were indications, however, that the tide was turning in favor of integration. On April 16, 1945, Robinson was invited along with two other Negro League stars—Marvin Williams

of the Philadelphia Stars and the Cleveland Buckeyes' Sam Jethroe—to tryout for the Boston Red Sox. Manager Joe Cronin was especially impressed with the Monarchs' shortstop, but still passed on the opportunity to sign him. Nevertheless, the tryout brought Robinson to the attention of Clyde Sukeforth, the chief scout of the Brooklyn Dodgers. Convinced of Robinson's exceptional playing ability and personal determination, Sukeforth set the stage for the memorable August meeting between Robinson and Rickey.

Robinson had no illusions about the purpose of his agreement with the Dodgers. He realized that Rickey's altruism was tempered by a profit motive, and yet he admired the moral courage of the Dodger president. "Mr. Rickey knew that achieving racial equality in baseball would be terribly difficult," Robinson remembered. "There would be deep resentment, determined opposition and perhaps even racial violence. But he was convinced that he was morally right and he shrewdly sensed that making the game a truly national one would have healthy financial results." Rickey was absolutely correct on both counts.

The Dodgers' October 23, 1945, announcement that Robinson had signed a contract for six hundred dollars a month[3] to play for their top minor-league club at Montreal was greeted with great hostility by baseball's white establishment. Rickey was accused of being "a carpetbagger who, under the guise of helping, is in truth using the Negro for his own self-interest." Criticism even came from the Negro League owners who feared, not without reason, that Robinson's signing would lead to declining fan interest in their clubs. The Monarchs were especially angered by the signing and went so far as to threaten a lawsuit against the Dodgers for tampering with a player who was already under contract.

By mid-November the criticism became so hostile that Rickey's own family pleaded with him to abandon his crusade for fear that it would destroy his health. The Dodger president refused, speaking only of the excitement and competitive advantage that black players would bring to Brooklyn baseball, while downplaying the moral significance he attached to integration. "The greatest untapped reservoir of raw material in the history of the game is the black race," he contended. "The Negroes will make us winners for years to come and for that I will happily bear being called a 'bleeding heart' and a 'do-gooder' and all that humanitarian rot."

Robinson's first test came during the 1946 preseason, even before he debuted with the Montreal Royals. Rickey named Mississippian Clay Hopper, who had worked for him since 1929, to manage the Royals. There were reports, probably true, that Hopper begged Rickey to reconsider giving him this assignment. But Rickey's careful handling of Robinson's jump to the big leagues would seem to suggest that he believed that having a Southerner at the helm of the Montreal club would head off some dissension among the players and that he trusted Hopper to handle any situations that might arise.

Throughout the '46 season, Robinson endured racist remarks from fans and opposing players and humiliating treatment in the South. By season's end, the constant pressure and abuse had taken its toll—his hair began to gray, he suffered with chronic stomach trouble, and some thought he was on the brink of a nervous breakdown. Finding himself unable to eat or sleep, he went to a doctor; who concluded that he was suffering from stress. "You're not having a nervous breakdown," the physician told him. "You're under a lot of stress. Stay home and don't read any newspapers, and don't go to the ballpark for a week." Jackie, his wife Rachel remembered, stayed home for one day. The problem, she said, came from his "not being able to fight back." It was, as Rickey had warned him, "the cross that you must bear."

Despite the tension and distractions, Robinson managed to hit for an impressive .349 average and led the Montreal Royals to victory over the Louisville Colonels in the Little World Series. After the final game in that championship series, grateful Royals fans hoisted Robinson onto their shoulders and carried him to the locker room. Hopper shook his shortstop's hand and said: "You're a real ballplayer and a gentleman. It's been wonderful having you on the team." Robinson had made his first convert.

Because Robinson's success with Montreal had been so impressive, Rickey assumed that all the Dodgers would demand his promotion to the majors for the 1947 season. "After all," he reasoned, "Robinson could mean a pennant, and ball players are not averse to cashing World Series checks."

To promote and protect his young black star, Rickey made some additional moves. First, in order to avoid Jim Crow restrictions, he held spring training in Havana, Cuba, instead of Florida. Next, he moved Robinson, an experienced shortstop and second baseman, to first base, where he would be spared physical contact with opposing players who might try to injure him deliberately.

Finally, Rickey scheduled a seven-game series between the Dodgers and the Royals in order to showcase Robinson's talent. "I want you to be a whirling demon against the Dodgers in this series," Rickey told Robinson. "You have to be so good that the Dodger players themselves are going to want you on their club. . . . I want you to hit that ball. I want you to get on base and run wild. Steal their pants off. Be the most conspicuous player on the field. The newspapermen from New York will send good stories back about you and help mold favorable public opinion."

Robinson more than obliged, batting .625 and stealing seven bases in the series. But instead of helping him, the performance served only to alienate him from his future teammates, many of whom were Southerners. Alabamian Dixie Walker drafted a petition stating that the players who signed would prefer to be traded than to play with a black teammate. While the team was playing exhibition games in Panama, Walker proceeded to gather signatures from Dodger teammates. Harold "Pee Wee" Reese, although a Kentuckian, refused to sign. It was a tremendously courageous act on his part because, as the team's shortstop, Reese had more to lose than any other Dodger. "If he can take my job," Reese insisted, "he's entitled to it."

When Dodger manager Leo Durocher learned of the petition, he was furious. He had asked Rickey to bring Robinson up to Brooklyn during the previous year's pennant drive. At a late-night team meeting, according to Harold Parrott, the Dodger road secretary, Durocher told Walker and the other petitioners that "I don't care if the guy is yellow or black, or if he has stripes like a zebra. I'm the manager of this team and I say he plays. What's more, I say he can make us all rich. . . . An' if any of you can't use the money, I'll see that you're traded."[4]

The rebellion squelched, Rickey announced on April 10, 1947, that Jackie Robinson had officially been signed to play first base for the Brooklyn Dodgers. The noble experiment was in full swing.

O f all the major-league cities, Brooklyn, with its ethnically diverse and racially mixed neighborhoods, was just the place to break the color barrier. Despite their reputation as "perennial losers"—since the franchise's establishment in 1883, no Brooklyn team had won a World Series— the Dodgers enjoyed an enduring love affair with their fans. This warm affinity was fostered, in part, by their cramped but colorful ballpark, Ebbets Field, located in the Flatbush section of Brooklyn. The double-decked grandstand stood only along the foul lines, allowing the fans a special intimacy with the players. "If you were in a box seat," said broadcaster Red Barber, "you were so close you were practically an infielder." Aside from the patchwork collection of local advertisements in left field; the large, black scoreboard in right; and the tone-deaf "Dodger Symphony Band" that roamed the grandstand, nothing came between the Dodgers and their die-hard fans.

When Robinson made his first appearance as a Dodger on April 15, 1947, more than 26,000 fans packed Ebbets Field; reportedly some 14,000 of those were African Americans. The afternoon was cold and rainy and Robinson went hitless. Nonetheless, the sight of a black man on a major-league diamond during a regular season game moved the crowd so deeply that they cheered the Dodgers on to a 5–3 victory over the Boston Braves. Every move the 28-year-old rookie made seemed to be greeted with the chant: "Jackie! Jackie! Jackie!" It seemed as if baseball had finally shed its three-quarters of a century of hypocrisy to become truly deserving of the title "national pastime."

When the Philadelphia Phillies arrived in Brooklyn a week later, however, all hopes that integration would come peaceably were shattered. In one of the lowest moments ever in baseball history the Phillies, led by their Southern manager, Ben Chapman, launched a tirade of racial epithets during the pre-game batting practice. And the jeering did not let up throughout the entire three-game series.

Two weeks later, when the Dodgers traveled to the so-called "City of Brotherly Love," Chapman and his Phillies picked up where they had left off, warning the Dodger players that they would contract diseases if they touched Robinson and indulging in even more personal racial slurs. Robinson's less-than-stellar hitting in the series only added to the Phillies' contention that he did not belong in the majors and was a ploy to attract blacks to Dodger games and make more money for Rickey.

After the second game of the series, angry Dodger fans launched a full-scale protest with the National League's president, Ford Frick, who responded by ordering Chapman and the Phillies to stop their verbal assault immediately. In fact, Chapman probably would have lost his job over the incident, if Robinson had not agreed to pose with him for a conciliatory newspaper photograph. Under duress, the Phillies' manager agreed to stand next to the Dodger rookie. "Ben extended his hand," Harold Parrott recalled, "smiling broadly as if they had been buddy-buddy for a lifetime. Robinson reached out and grasped it. The flicker of a smile crept across his face as the photographer snapped away getting several shots."

Years later Robinson admitted that the incessant abuse during those games with the Phillies almost led him to the breaking point. As he described it: "For one wild and rage-crazed minute I thought, 'To hell with Mr. Rickey's noble experiment. It's clear that it won't succeed. . . . What a glorious, cleansing thing it would be to let go.' To hell with the image of the patient black freak I was supposed to create. I could throw down my bat, stride over to the Phillies dugout, grab one of those white sons of bitches and smash his teeth in with my despised black

fist. Then I could walk away from it and I'd never become a sports star. But my son could tell his son some day what his daddy could have been if he hadn't been too much of a man."

The experience with the Phillies revealed the shocking severity of the racism that existed in baseball. At the same time, however, Robinson's tremendous restraint in the face of such ugly prejudice served to rally his teammates around him and the cause of integration. Eddie Stanky one of those who had signed the petition against Robinson joining the team, became so angered by the Phillies' relentless abuse that he challenged them to "yell at somebody who can answer back." Soon after, before a game in Cincinnati, the Reds' players taunted Pee Wee Reese about playing with a black teammate. The Dodger shortstop walked over to Robinson and, in a firm show of support, placed his arm around the first baseman's shoulders.

As the season unfolded, Dodger support for Robinson strengthened in response to the admirable way he handled all the adversity. Opposing pitchers threw at his head and ribs, while infielders would spit in his face if he was involved in a close play on the base paths. And the hate mail was unending. But through it all, Robinson persevered. He even managed to keep a sense of humor. Before one game in Cincinnati, when the Dodgers learned that their first baseman's life had been threatened, one teammate suggested that all the players wear Robinson's uniform number "42" on their backs to confuse the assailant. "Okay with me," responded the rookie. "Paint your faces black and run pigeon-toed too!"

Even the white baseball establishment began to embrace the Dodger infielder. In May of 1947, when Ford Frick learned of the St. Louis Cardinals' intention to instigate a league-wide strike by walking off the ball diamond in a scheduled game against the integrated Dodgers, he vowed to suspend the ring-leaders if they carried out their plan. ". . . I don't care if I wreck the National League for five years," he declared. "This is the United States of America, and one citizen has as much right to play as another. The National League will go down the line with Robinson whatever the consequence." The conspiracy died on the spot.

When the season ended, the *Sporting News,* which had gone on record earlier as opposing the integration of baseball because "There is not a single Negro player with major league possibilities," named Robinson the National League's "Rookie of the Year" for his impressive performance that season—29 stolen bases, 12 home runs, 42 successful bunt hits, and a .297 batting average.

Those efforts helped the Dodgers to capture a pennant, and on September 23, jubilant Brooklyn fans cheered their first baseman with a "Jackie Robinson Day" at Ebbets Field. In addition to a new car and other gifts, Robinson received tributes for his contribution to racial equality. Song-and-dance man Bill "Bojangles" Robinson, one of the guest speakers, told the crowd: "I'm 69 years old but never thought I'd live to see the day when I'd stand face-to-face with Ty Cobb in Technicolor."

The Dodgers forced the New York Yankees to a seventh and deciding game in the World Series. And when all was said and done, no amount of hate mail or verbal and psychological abuse could tarnish the indisputable fact that Jackie Robinson was an exceptional baseball player. He belonged in the major leagues.

Robinson's greatest accomplishment, however, was the inspiration that he provided for other African Americans, both in and out of baseball. Thousands of blacks came to watch him play, setting new attendance records in such cities as Chicago and Pittsburgh. Even in St. Louis, Cincinnati, and Philadelphia, where the opposing teams were the most hostile toward the Dodger rookie, black fans would arrive on chartered buses called "Jackie Robinson Specials," having traveled hundreds of miles just to see him play.

Ed Charles, a black youngster from the Deep South who went on to play in the major leagues himself, remembered the thrill of seeing his childhood hero for the first time. "I sat in the segregated section of the ball park and watched Jackie," he said. "And I finally believed what I read in the papers—that one of us had made it. When the game was over we kids followed Jackie to the train station. When the train pulled out, we ran down the tracks listening for the sounds as far as we could. And when we couldn't hear it any longer, we stopped and put our ears to the track so we could feel the vibrations of that train carrying Jackie Robinson. We wanted to be part of him as long as we could."

Indeed, Robinson had jolted the national consciousness in a profound way. Until 1947 all of baseball's heroes had been white men. Suddenly there was a black baseball star who could hit, bunt, steal, and field with the best of them. His style of play was nothing new in the Negro Leagues, but in the white majors, it was innovative and exciting. Robinson made things happen on the base paths. If he got on first, he stole second. If he could not steal third, he would distract the pitcher by dancing off second in order to advance. And then he would steal home. The name of the game was to score runs without a hit, something quite different from the "power hitting" strategy that had characterized major-league baseball. During the next decade, this new style of play would become known as "Dodger Baseball."

Before the '47 season was over, Branch Rickey had signed 16 additional Negro Leaguers, including catcher and future three-time "Most Valuable Player" Roy Campanella; pitcher Don Newcombe, who in 1956 would win 27 games; and second baseman Jim Gilham, like Robinson always a threat to steal a base. Together with Robinson and such white stars as Pee Wee Reese, Edwin "Duke" Snider, Gil Hodges, and Carl Erskine, these men would form the nucleus of a team that would capture six pennants and, at long last, in 1955, a world championship, before the Dodgers left Brooklyn for the West Coast at the end of the 1957 season. By 1959, every team in major-league baseball was integrated, one of every five players being of African-American descent.

When Rickey talked of trading Robinson to the New York Giants after the '56 season, the pioneering ballplayer chose to retire at the age of 38. His career totals, which included 1,518 hits, more than 200 stolen bases, and a lifetime batting average of .311, earned him a place in the National Baseball Hall of Fame in 1962, the first African American so honored. He continued to fight actively for civil rights long after his baseball career had ended, supporting Dr. Martin Luther King, Jr., and his call for the peaceful integration of American society.

Despite his tremendous accomplishments on and off the baseball field, Jackie Robinson, with characteristic humility never gave himself much credit. A year before his untimely death in 1972, he reflected on his struggle to break baseball's color barrier. "I was proud," Robinson admitted, "yet I was uneasy. Proud to be in the hurricane eye of a significant breakthrough and to be used to prove that a sport can't be called 'national' if blacks are barred from it. But uneasy because I knew that I was still a black man in a white world. And so I continue to ask myself 'what have I really done for my people?'"

The answer was evident to everyone but him; for by appealing to the moral conscience of the nation, Jackie Robinson had given a young generation of blacks a chance at the "American Dream" and in the process taught many white Americans to respect others regardless of the color of their skin.

Notes

1. Originally used in connection with legislation enacted in Southern states during the nineteenth century to separate the races on public transportation, the term "Jim Crow law" eventually applied to all statutes that enforced segregation.

2. The 1896 decision of the Supreme Court in *Plessy v. Ferguson* upheld a Louisiana law that required railroads in that state to provide "equal but separate accommodations for the white and colored races." It was this "equal but separate" doctrine that made the discriminatory practices of this century legal in the United States. The Court essentially reversed itself in its 1954 *Brown v. Board of Education of Topeka, Kansas* decision, effectively ending legal segregation.

3. Robinson also received a bonus of $3,500.

4. Walker, one of a handful of players who asked to be traded, eventually went to the Pittsburgh Pirates, but not until after the '47 season. Durocher, himself, was suspended from baseball before the '47 season and never had the opportunity to manage Robinson.

Create Central

www.mhhe.com/createcentral

Critical Thinking

1. Compare the motivations of Rickey and Robinson in integrating baseball.
2. Critically examine why the other baseball owners were opposed to integrating baseball.
3. Critically examine why Rickey put Robinson on Montreal instead of a southern minor league team and held spring training in Cuba not Florida.
4. Critically examine whether you agree or disagree that Robinson changed not only the game of baseball but also the nation's attitude toward segregation.

Internet References

Library of Congress
http://memory.loc.gov/ammem/collections/robinson/jr1940.html

EyeWitnessToHistory.com
www.eyewitnesstohistory.com/robinson.htm

Oxford University Press Blog
http://blog.oup.com/2013/04/jackie-robinson-branch-rickey-brooklyn-dodgers/

Huffington Post Blog
www.huffingtonpost.com/dan-glickman/jackie-robinson-branch-ri_b_3138246.html

Smithsonianmag.com
www.smithsonianmag.com/history-archaeology/Document-Deep-Dive-The-Heartfelt-Friendship-Between-Jackie-Robinson-and-Branch-Rickey-202533181.html

Remembering Jim Crow
http://americanradioworks.publicradio.org/features/remembering/laws.html

WILLIAM KASHATUS is a school teacher and freelance writer who lives in Philadelphia.

Article

Prepared by: Larry Madaras, *Howard Community College*

The Real Cuban Missile Crisis: Everything You Think You Know Is Wrong

BENJAMIN SCHWARZ

Learning Outcomes

After reading this article, you will be able to:

- State the traditional view of the Cuban missile crisis which makes a hero of President Kennedy.

- List some of the new sources—memoirs of participants in the 1980s and the declassification of the Ex-Comm Committee's tapes in 1997 which give a different view of the crisis.

- List the political and egotistical objectives that both JFK and Kruschev had in the missile crisis.

- Explain how the so-called lessons of the Cuban missile crisis led to our increasing involvement in Vietnam.

O N OCTOBER 16, 1962, *John F. Kennedy and his advisers were stunned to learn that the Soviet Union was, without provocation, installing nuclear-armed medium- and intermediate-range ballistic missiles in Cuba. With these offensive weapons, which represented a new and existential threat to America, Moscow significantly raised the ante in the nuclear rivalry between the superpowers—a gambit that forced the United States and the Soviet Union to the brink of nuclear Armageddon. On October 22, the president, with no other recourse, proclaimed in a televised address that his administration knew of the illegal missiles, and delivered an ultimatum insisting on their removal, announcing an American "quarantine" of Cuba to force compliance with his demands. While carefully avoiding provocative action and coolly calibrating each Soviet countermeasure, Kennedy and his lieutenants brooked no compromise; they held firm, despite Moscow's efforts to link a resolution to extrinsic issues and despite predictable Soviet blustering about American aggression and violation of international law. In the tense 13-day crisis, the Americans and Soviets went eyeball-to-eyeball.*

Thanks to the Kennedy administration's placid resolve and prudent crisis management—thanks to what Kennedy's special assistant Arthur Schlesinger Jr. characterized as the president's "combination of toughness and restraint, of will, nerve, and wisdom, so brilliantly controlled, so matchlessly calibrated, that [it] dazzled the world"—the Soviet leadership blinked: Moscow dismantled the missiles, and a cataclysm was averted.

Every sentence in the above paragraph describing the Cuban missile crisis is misleading or erroneous. But this was the rendition of events that the Kennedy administration fed to a credulous press; this was the history that the participants in Washington promulgated in their memoirs; and this is the story that has insinuated itself into the national memory—as the pundits' commentaries and media coverage marking the 50th anniversary of the crisis attested.

Scholars, however, have long known a very different story: since 1997, they have had access to recordings that Kennedy secretly made of meetings with his top advisers, the Executive Committee of the National Security Council (the "ExComm"). Sheldon M. Stern—who was the historian at the John F. Kennedy Library for 23 years and the first scholar to evaluate the ExComm tapes—is among the numerous historians who have tried to set the record straight. His new book marshals irrefutable evidence to succinctly demolish the mythic version of the crisis. Although there's little reason to believe his effort will be to any avail, it should nevertheless be applauded.

Reached through sober analysis, Stern's conclusion that "John F. Kennedy and his administration, without question, bore a substantial share of the responsibility for the onset of the Cuban missile crisis" would have shocked the American people in 1962, for the simple reason that Kennedy's administration had misled them about the military imbalance between the superpowers and had concealed its campaign of threats, assassination plots, and sabotage designed to overthrow the government in Cuba—an effort well known to Soviet and Cuban officials.

In the 1960 presidential election, Kennedy had cynically attacked Richard Nixon from the right, claiming that the Eisenhower-Nixon administration had allowed a dangerous "missile gap" to grow in the U.S.S.R.'s favor. But in fact, just as Eisenhower and Nixon had suggested—and just as the classified briefings that Kennedy received as a presidential candidate indicated—the missile gap, and the nuclear balance generally, was overwhelmingly to America's advantage. At the time of the missile crisis, the Soviets had 36 intercontinental ballistic missiles (ICBMs), 138 long-range bombers with 392 nuclear warheads, and 72 submarine-launched ballistic-missile warheads (SLBMs). These forces were arrayed against a vastly more powerful U.S. nuclear arsenal of 203 ICBMs, 1,306 long-range bombers with 3,104 nuclear warheads, and 144 SLBMs—all told, about nine times as many nuclear weapons as the U.S.S.R. Nikita Khrushchev was acutely aware of America's huge advantage not just in the number of weapons but in their quality and deployment as well.

Moreover, despite America's overwhelming nuclear preponderance, JFK, in keeping with his avowed aim to pursue a foreign policy characterized by "vigor," had ordered the largest peacetime expansion of America's military power, and specifically the colossal growth of its strategic nuclear forces. This included deploying, beginning in 1961, intermediate-range "Jupiter" nuclear missiles in Italy and Turkey—adjacent to the Soviet Union. From there, the missiles could reach all of the western U.S.S.R., including Moscow and Leningrad (and that doesn't count the nuclear-armed "Thor" missiles that the U.S. already had aimed at the Soviet Union from bases in Britain).

The Jupiter missiles were an exceptionally vexing component of the U.S. nuclear arsenal. Because they sat aboveground, were immobile, and required a long time to prepare for launch, they were extremely vulnerable. Of no value as a deterrent, they appeared to be weapons meant for a disarming first strike—and thus greatly undermined deterrence, because they encouraged a preemptive Soviet strike against them. The Jupiters' destabilizing effect was widely recognized among defense experts within and outside the U.S. government and even by congressional leaders. For instance, Senator Albert Gore Sr., an ally of the administration, told Secretary of State Dean Rusk that they were a "provocation" in a closed session of the Senate Foreign Relations Committee in February 1961 (more than a year and a half before the missile crisis), adding, "I wonder what our attitude would be" if the Soviets deployed nuclear-armed missiles to Cuba. Senator Claiborne Pell raised an identical argument in a memo passed on to Kennedy in May 1961.

Given America's powerful nuclear superiority, as well as the deployment of the Jupiter missiles, Moscow suspected that Washington viewed a nuclear first strike as an attractive option. They were right to be suspicious. The archives reveal that in fact the Kennedy administration had strongly considered this option during the Berlin crisis in 1961.

It's little wonder, then, that, as Stern asserts—drawing on a plethora of scholarship including, most convincingly, the historian Philip Nash's elegant 1997 study, *The Other Missiles of October*—Kennedy's deployment of the Jupiter missiles "was a key reason for Khrushchev's decision to send nuclear missiles to Cuba."

Khrushchev reportedly made that decision in May 1962, declaring to a confidant that the Americans "have surrounded us with bases on all sides" and that missiles in Cuba would help to counter an "intolerable provocation." Keeping the deployment secret in order to present the U.S. with a fait accompli, Khrushchev may very well have assumed America's response would be similar to his reaction to the Jupiter missiles—rhetorical denouncement but no threat or action to thwart the deployment with a military attack, nuclear or otherwise. (In retirement, Khrushchev explained his reasoning to the American journalist Strobe Talbott: Americans "would learn just what it feels like to have enemy missiles pointing at you; we'd be doing nothing more than giving them a little of their own medicine.")

Khrushchev was also motivated by his entirely justifiable belief that the Kennedy administration wanted to destroy the Castro regime. After all, the administration had launched an invasion of Cuba; had followed that with sabotage, paramilitary assaults, and assassination attempts—the largest clandestine operation in the history of the CIA—and had organized large-scale military exercises in the Caribbean clearly meant to rattle the Soviets and their Cuban client. Those actions, as Stern and other scholars have demonstrated, helped compel the Soviets to install the missiles so as to deter "covert or overt US attacks"—in much the same way that the United States had shielded its allies under a nuclear umbrella to deter Soviet subversion or aggression against them.

Remarkably, given the alarmed and confrontational posture that Washington adopted during the missile crisis, the tapes of the ExComm deliberations, which Stern has minutely assessed, reveal that Kennedy and his advisers understood the nuclear situation in much the same way Khrushchev did. On the first day of the crisis, October 16, when pondering Khrushchev's motives for sending the missiles to Cuba, Kennedy made what must be one of the staggeringly absentminded (or sarcastic) observations in the annals of American national-security policy: "Why does he put these in there, though? . . . It's just as if we suddenly began to put a major number of MRBMs [medium-range ballistic missiles] in Turkey. Now that'd be goddamned dangerous, I would think." McGeorge Bundy, the national security adviser, immediately pointed out: "Well we did it, Mr. President."

Once that was straightened out, Kennedy himself declared repeatedly that the Jupiter missiles were "the same" as the Soviet missiles in Cuba. Rusk, in discussing the Soviet motivation for sending missiles to Cuba, cited CIA Director John McCone's view that Khrushchev "knows that we have a substantial nuclear superiority. . . . He also knows that we don't really live under fear of his nuclear weapons to the extent that he has to live under fear of ours. Also, we have nuclear weapons nearby, in Turkey." The chairman of the Joint Chiefs of Staff, Maxwell Taylor, had already acknowledged that the Soviets' primary purpose in installing missiles in Cuba was "to supplement their rather defective ICBM system."

Kennedy and his civilian advisers understood that the missiles in Cuba did not alter the strategic nuclear balance.

Although Kennedy asserted in his October 22 televised address that the missiles were "an explicit threat to the peace and security of all the Americas," he in fact appreciated, as he told the ExComm on the first day of the crisis, that "it doesn't make any difference if you get blown up by an ICBM flying from the Soviet Union or one that was 90 miles away. Geography doesn't mean that much." America's European allies, Kennedy continued, "will argue that *taken at its worst* the presence of these missiles really doesn't change" the nuclear balance.

That the missiles were close to the United States was, as the president conceded, immaterial: the negligible difference in flight times between Soviet Union-based ICBMs and Cuba-based missiles wouldn't change the consequences when the missiles hit their targets, and in any event, the flight times of Soviet SLBMs were already as short as or shorter than the flight times of the missiles in Cuba would be, because those weapons already lurked in submarines off the American coast (as of course did American SLBMs off the Soviet coast). Moreover, unlike Soviet ICBMs, the missiles in Cuba required several hours to be prepared for launch. Given the effectiveness of America's aerial and satellite reconnaissance (amply demonstrated by the images of missiles in the U.S.S.R. and Cuba that they yielded), the U.S. almost certainly would have had far more time to detect and respond to an imminent Soviet missile strike from Cuba than to attacks from Soviet bombers, ICBMs, or SLBMs.

"A missile is a missile," Secretary of Defense Robert McNamara asserted. "It makes no great difference whether you are killed by a missile from the Soviet Union or Cuba." On that first day of the ExComm meetings, Bundy asked directly, "What is the strategic impact on the position of the United States of MRBMs in Cuba? How gravely *does* this *change* the strategic balance?" McNamara answered, "Not at all"—a verdict that Bundy then said he fully supported. The following day, Special Counsel Theodore Sorensen summarized the views of the ExComm in a memorandum to Kennedy. "It is generally agreed," he noted, "that these missiles, even when fully operational, do not significantly alter the balance of power—i.e., they do not significantly increase the potential megatonnage capable of being unleashed on American soil, even after a surprise American nuclear strike."

Sorensen's comment about a surprise attack reminds us that while the missiles in Cuba did not add appreciably to the nuclear menace, they could have somewhat complicated America's planning for a successful first strike—which may well have been part of Khrushchev's rationale for deploying them. If so, the missiles paradoxically could have enhanced deterrence between the superpowers, and thereby reduced the risk of nuclear war.

YET, ALTHOUGH the missiles' military significance was negligible, the Kennedy administration advanced on a perilous course to force their removal. The president issued an ultimatum to a nuclear power—an astonishingly provocative move, which immediately created a crisis that could have led to catastrophe. He ordered a blockade on Cuba,

an act of war that we now know brought the superpowers within a hair's breadth of nuclear confrontation. The beleaguered Cubans willingly accepted their ally's weapons, so the Soviet's deployment of the missiles was fully in accord with international law. But the blockade, even if the administration euphemistically called it a "quarantine," was, the ExComm members acknowledged, illegal. As the State Department's legal adviser recalled, "*Our* legal problem was that their action *wasn't* illegal." Kennedy and his lieutenants intently contemplated an invasion of Cuba and an aerial assault on the Soviet missiles there—acts extremely likely to have provoked a nuclear war. In light of the extreme measures they executed or earnestly entertained to resolve a crisis they had largely created, the American reaction to the missiles requires, in retrospect, as much explanation as the Soviet decision to deploy them—or more.

On that very first day of the ExComm meetings, McNamara provided a wider perspective on the missiles' significance: "I'll be quite frank. I don't think there is a military problem here. . . . This is a domestic, political problem." In a 1987 interview, McNamara explained: "You have to remember that, right from the beginning, it was President Kennedy who said that it was *politically* unacceptable for us to leave those missile sites alone. He didn't say militarily, he said *politically*." What largely made the missiles politically unacceptable was Kennedy's conspicuous and fervent hostility toward the Castro regime—a stance, Kennedy admitted at an ExComm meeting, that America's European allies thought was "a fixation" and "slightly demented."

In his presidential bid, Kennedy had red-baited the Eisenhower-Nixon administration, charging that its policies had "helped make Communism's first Caribbean base." Given that he had defined a tough stance toward Cuba as an important election issue, and given the humiliation he had suffered with the Bay of Pigs debacle, the missiles posed a great political hazard to Kennedy. As the State Department's director of intelligence and research, Roger Hilsman, later put it, "The United States might not be in mortal danger, but . . . the administration most certainly was." Kennedy's friend John Kenneth Galbraith, the ambassador to India, later said: "Once [the missiles] were there, the political needs of the Kennedy administration urged it to take almost any risk to get them out."

But even weightier than the domestic political catastrophe likely to befall the administration if it appeared to be soft on Cuba was what Assistant Secretary of State Edwin Martin called "the psychological factor" that we "sat back and let 'em do it to us." He asserted that this was "more important than the *direct* threat," and Kennedy and his other advisers energetically concurred. Even as Sorensen, in his memorandum to the president, noted the ExComm's consensus that the Cuban missiles didn't alter the nuclear balance, he also observed that the ExComm nevertheless believed that "the United States cannot tolerate the *known* presence" of missiles in Cuba "if our courage and commitments are ever to be believed by either allies or adversaries" (emphasis added). America's European allies (not to mention the Soviets) insisted that Washington should ignore these intangible concerns, but Sorensen was dismissive. Appealing to psychology rather than to the hard calculations of statecraft, he asserted that such arguments "carried some logic but little weight."

Indeed, Washington's self-regard for its credibility was almost certainly the main reason it risked nuclear war over a negligible threat to national security. At the same meeting in which Kennedy and his aides were contemplating military action against Cuba and the U.S.S.R.—action they knew could bring about an apocalyptic war—the president stated, "Last month I said we weren't going to [permit Soviet nuclear missiles in Cuba] and last month I should have said . . . we don't care. But when we said we're *not* going to, and [the Soviets] go ahead and do it, and then we do nothing, then . . . I would think that our . . . risks *increase*."

The risks of such a cave-in, Kennedy and his advisers held, were distinct but related. The first was that America's foes would see Washington as pusillanimous; the known presence of the missiles, Kennedy said, "makes them look like they're coequal with us and that"—here Treasury Secretary Douglas Dillon interrupted: "We're scared of the Cubans." The second risk was that America's friends would suddenly doubt that a country given to appeasement could be relied on to fulfill its obligations.

In fact, America's allies, as Bundy acknowledged, were aghast that the U.S. was threatening nuclear war over a strategically insignificant condition—the presence of intermediate-range missiles in a neighboring country—that those allies (and, for that matter, the Soviets) had been living with for years. In the tense days of October 1962, being allied with the United States potentially amounted to, as Charles de Gaulle had warned, "annihilation without representation." It seems never to have occurred to Kennedy and the ExComm that whatever Washington gained by demonstrating the steadfastness of its commitments, it lost in an erosion of confidence in its judgment.

This approach to foreign policy was guided—and remains guided—by an elaborate theorizing rooted in a school-playground view of world politics rather than the cool appraisal of strategic realities. It put—and still puts—America in the curious position of having to go to war to uphold the very credibility that is supposed to obviate war in the first place.

If the administration's domestic political priorities alone dictated the removal of the Cuban missiles, a solution to Kennedy's problem would have seemed pretty obvious: instead of a public ultimatum demanding that the Soviets withdraw their missiles from Cuba, a private agreement between the superpowers to remove both Moscow's missiles in Cuba and Washington's missiles in Turkey. (Recall that the Kennedy administration discovered the missiles on October 16, but only announced its discovery to the American public and the Soviets and issued its ultimatum on the 22nd.)

The administration, however, did not make such an overture to the Soviets. Instead, by publicly demanding a unilateral Soviet withdrawal and imposing a blockade on Cuba, it precipitated what remains to this day the most dangerous nuclear crisis in history. In the midst of that crisis, the sanest and most sensible observers—among them diplomats at the United

Nations and in Europe, the editorial writers for the *Manchester Guardian,* Walter Lippmann and Adlai Stevenson—saw a missile trade as a fairly simple solution. In an effort to resolve the impasse, Khrushchev himself openly made this proposal on October 27. According to the version of events propagated by the Kennedy administration (and long accepted as historical fact), Washington unequivocally rebuffed Moscow's offer and instead, thanks to Kennedy's resolve, forced a unilateral Soviet withdrawal.

Beginning in the late 1980s, however, the opening of previously classified archives and the decision by a number of participants to finally tell the truth revealed that the crisis was indeed resolved by an explicit but concealed deal to remove both the Jupiter and the Cuban missiles. Kennedy in fact threatened to abrogate if the Soviets disclosed it. He did so for the same reasons that had largely engendered the crisis in the first place—domestic politics and the maintenance of America's image as the indispensable nation. A declassified Soviet cable reveals that Robert Kennedy—whom the president assigned to work out the secret swap with the U.S.S.R.'s ambassador to Washington, Anatoly Dobrynin—insisted on returning to Dobrynin the formal Soviet letter affirming the agreement, explaining that the letter "could cause irreparable harm to my political career in the future."

Only a handful of administration officials knew about the trade; most members of the ExComm, including Vice President Lyndon Johnson, did not. And in their effort to maintain the cover-up, a number of those who did, including McNamara and Rusk, lied to Congress. JFK and others tacitly encouraged the character assassination of Stevenson, allowing him to be portrayed as an appeaser who "wanted a Munich" for suggesting the trade—a deal that they vociferously maintained the administration would never have permitted.

The patient spadework of Stern and other scholars has since led to further revelations. Stern demonstrates that Robert Kennedy hardly inhabited the conciliatory and statesmanlike role during the crisis that his allies described in their hagiographic chronicles and memoirs and that he himself advanced in his posthumously published book, *Thirteen Days.* In fact, he was among the most consistently and recklessly hawkish of the president's advisers, pushing not for a blockade or even air strikes against Cuba but for a full-scale invasion as "the last chance we will have to destroy Castro." Stern authoritatively concludes that "if RFK had been president, and the views he expressed during the ExComm meetings had prevailed, nuclear war would have been the nearly certain outcome." He justifiably excoriates the sycophantic courtier Schlesinger, whose histories "repeatedly manipulated and obscured the facts" and whose accounts—"profoundly misleading if not out-and-out deceptive"—were written to serve not scholarship but the Kennedys.

Although stern and other scholars have upended the panegyrical version of events advanced by Schlesinger and other Kennedy acolytes, the revised chronicle shows that JFK's actions in resolving the crisis—again, a crisis he had largely created—were reasonable, responsible, and courageous. Plainly shaken by the apocalyptic potentialities of the situation, Kennedy advocated, in the face of the bellicose and near-unanimous opposition of his pseudo-tough-guy advisers, accepting the missile swap that Khrushchev had proposed. "To any man at the United Nations, or any other *rational* man, it will look like a very fair trade," he levelheadedly told the ExComm. "Most people think that if you're allowed an even trade you ought to take advantage of it." He clearly understood that history and world opinion would condemn him and his country for going to war—a war almost certain to escalate to a nuclear exchange—after the U.S.S.R. had publicly offered such a reasonable quid pro quo. Khrushchev's proposal, the historian Ronald Steel has noted, "filled the White House advisors with consternation—not least of all because it appeared perfectly fair."

Although Kennedy in fact agreed to the missile swap and, with Khrushchev, helped settle the confrontation maturely, the legacy of that confrontation was nonetheless pernicious. By successfully hiding the deal from the vice president, from a generation of foreign-policy makers and strategists, and from the American public, Kennedy and his team reinforced the dangerous notion that firmness in the face of what the United States construes as aggression, and the graduated escalation of military threats and action in countering that aggression, makes for a successful national-security strategy—really, all but defines it.

The president and his advisers also reinforced the concomitant view that America should define a threat not merely as circumstances and forces that directly jeopardize the safety of the country, but as circumstances and forces that might indirectly compel potential allies or enemies to question America's resolve. This recondite calculation led to the American disaster in Vietnam: in attempting to explain how the loss of the strategically inconsequential country of South Vietnam might weaken American credibility and thereby threaten the country's security, one of McNamara's closest aides, Assistant Secretary of Defense John McNaughton, allowed that "it takes some sophistication to see how Vietnam automatically involves" our vital interests. Kennedy said in his address to the nation during the missile crisis that "aggressive conduct, if allowed to go unchecked and unchallenged, ultimately leads to war." He explained that "if our courage and our commitments are ever to be trusted again by either friend or foe," then the United States could not tolerate such conduct by the Soviets—even though, again, he had privately acknowledged that the deployment of the missiles did not change the nuclear balance.

This notion that standing up to aggression (however loosely and broadly defined) will deter future aggression (however loosely and broadly defined) fails to weather historical scrutiny. After all, America's invasion and occupation of Iraq didn't deter Muammar Qaddafi; America's war against Yugoslavia didn't deter Saddam Hussein in 2003; America's liberation of Kuwait did not deter Slobodan Milošević; America's intervention in Panama did not deter Saddam Hussein in 1991; America's intervention in Grenada did not deter Manuel Noriega; America's war against North Vietnam did not deter Grenada's

strongman, Hudson Austin; and JFK's confrontation with Khrushchev over missiles in Cuba certainly did not deter Ho Chi Minh.

Moreover, the idea that a foreign power's effort to counter the overwhelming strategic supremacy of the United States—a country that spends nearly as much on defense as does the rest of the world combined—ipso facto imperils America's security is profoundly misguided. Just as Kennedy and his advisers perceived a threat in Soviet efforts to offset what was in fact a destabilizing U.S. nuclear hegemony, so today, both liberals and conservatives oxymoronically assert that the safety of the United States demands that the country must "balance" China by maintaining its strategically dominant position in East Asia and the eastern Pacific—that is, in China's backyard. This means that Washington views as a hazard Beijing's attempts to remedy the weakness of its own position, even though policy makers acknowledge that the U.S. has a crushing superiority right up to the edge of the Asian mainland. America's posture, however, reveals more about its own ambitions than it does about China's. Imagine that the situation were reversed, and China's air and naval forces were a dominant and potentially menacing presence on the coastal shelf of North America. Surely the U.S. would want to counteract that preponderance. In a vast part of the globe, stretching from the Canadian Arctic to Tierra del Fuego and from Greenland to Guam, the U.S. will not tolerate another great power's interference. Certainly America's security wouldn't be jeopardized if other great powers enjoy their own (and for that matter, smaller) spheres of influence.

This esoteric strategizing—this misplaced obsession with credibility, this dangerously expansive concept of what constitutes security—which has afflicted both Democratic and Republican administrations, and both liberals and conservatives, is the antithesis of statecraft, which requires discernment based on power, interest, and circumstance. It is a stance toward the world that can easily doom the United States to military commitments and interventions in strategically insignificant places over intrinsically trivial issues. It is a stance that can engender a foreign policy approximating paranoia in an obdurately chaotic world abounding in states, personalities, and ideologies that are unsavory and uncongenial—but not necessarily mortally hazardous.

Critical Thinking

1. Briefly state the traditional view of the Cuban Missile crisis which makes President Kennedy the hero.
2. Analyze the new evidence since the 1990s which refutes the traditional image.
3. Examine whether Kennedy escalated the Cuban missile issue into a crisis for political and egotistical reasons.
4. Should President Kennedy have openly swapped the Jupiter missiles in Turkey for the intermediate missiles in Cuba? Critically analyze.
5. By never informing Vice President Lyndon Johnson of the secret swap, did Kennedy mislead Johnson into believing that by standing up to aggression in Cuba the future President would be able to salvage South Vietnam in the same manner?

Create Central

www.mhhe.com/createcentral

Internet References

CNN and BBC produced a 24-hour documentary on the Cold War in 1998. The website has valuable interviews, documents, and transcripts of the 50-minute videos, as well as some material not included in the films that aired. The work on the Cuban missile crisis was the 10th in this series.

http://cnn.com/SPECIALS/cold.war/episodes/10

Transcripts of Ex Comm meetings in streaming audio.

www.hpol.org//jfk/Cuban

The Cold War History Project, a joint effort of George Washington University and the National Security Archive, has especially good documents on the Cuban missile crisis.

http://cwihp.si.edu/pdj.htm

C-SPAN Online provides RealAudio clips and transcripts from tapes that President Kennedy secretly recorded in the White House, RealAudio newsreels from 1962, an image gallery of the major players and surveillance photos, and RealAudio archives.

www.c-spall.org/guide/society/cuba

The Department of State's definitive volumes relating to the Cuban missile crisis are available online: Foreign Relations of the United States, "Cuba," vol. X, 1961–1963; and Foreign Relations of the United States, "Cuban Missile Crisis and Aftermath," vol. XI, 1961–1963.

www.state.gov

Documents Relating to American Foreign Policy: The Cuban Missile Crisis is a website maintained by Mount Holyoke College. The collection includes documents, links, and other historical materials concerning the Cuban missile crisis.

www.mtholyoke.edu/acad/intrel/cuba.htm

BENJAMIN SCHWARZ is *The Atlantic*'s literary editor and national editor.

Article   Prepared by: Larry Madaras, *Howard Community College*

The Forgotten Radical History of the March on Washington

WILLIAM P. JONES

Learning Outcomes

After reading this article, you will be able to:

- Describe the traditional view of Martin Luther King's "I Have a Dream" speech.
- Describe the forgotten radical speeches that preceded King's speech.

The March on Washington for Jobs and Freedom, which occurred fifty years ago this August 28, remains one of the most successful mobilizations ever created by the American Left. Organized by a coalition of trade unionists, civil rights activists, and feminists—most of them African American and nearly all of them socialists—the protest drew nearly a quarter-million people to the nation's capital. Composed primarily of factory workers, domestic servants, public employees, and farm workers, it was the largest demonstration—and, some argued, the largest gathering of union members—in the history of the United States.

That massive turnout set the stage not only for the passage of the Civil Rights Act of 1964, which President John F. Kennedy had proposed two months before, but also for the addition to that law of a Fair Employment Practices clause, which prohibited employers, unions, and government officials from discriminating against workers on the basis of race, religion, national origin, or sex. And, by linking those egalitarian objectives to a broader agenda of ending poverty and reforming the economy, the protest also forged a political agenda that would inspire liberals and leftists ranging from President Lyndon Johnson to the Black Power movement. After watching organizer Bayard Rustin read the full list of demands, "while every television camera at the disposal of the networks was upon him," left-wing journalist Murray Kempton remarked, "No expression one-tenth so radical has ever been seen or heard by so many Americans."

Yet, despite that success, the Left has largely relinquished its claim to the legacy of the March on Washington. Even before it occurred, Nation of Islam leader Malcolm X leveled the charge—embraced by Black Power and New Left activists in the subsequent decade—that the mobilization had been "taken over by the government" and deprived of its once-radical agenda. Meanwhile, liberals and even conservatives were happy to claim the demonstration as their own—often focusing narrowly on the relatively moderate and conciliatory message of Martin Luther King, Jr.'s "I Have a Dream" speech while overlooking more confrontational statements by A. Philip Randolph, John Lewis, and others.

By the 1980s, a broad consensus had emerged that attributed the success of the protest not to its radicalism but to its narrow focus on, as journalist Juan Williams wrote for the PBS documentary *Eyes on the Prize,* "moral imperatives that had garnered support from the nation's moderates—issues such as the right to vote and the right to a decent education." While conservatives Stephen and Abigail Thernstrom congratulated Randolph, King, and others for suppressing demands for "radical, social, political and economic changes," leftist Manning Marable chided civil rights leaders for failing to "even grapple with [the] social and economic contradictions" of American capitalism. Only in the late 1960s, according to Williams, did the movement expand its agenda to include "issues whose moral rightness was not as readily apparent: job and housing discrimination, Johnson's war on poverty, and affirmative action."

In addition to depriving leftists of a rare success story, this distorted historical memory has reinforced the impression that the racially egalitarian politics of the civil rights movement were somehow incompatible with struggles for economic justice. From Barack Obama to Occupy Wall Street, many liberals and leftists have promoted the belief that Americans can transcend the "racial stalemate" of the post-civil rights era by focusing on their "common hopes" for economic security. Obama succeeded in stabilizing the economy and implementing the most ambitious health reform since the 1960s, and Occupy drew unprecedented attention to the growing gap between the extremely wealthy and the other "99 percent" of our society. Despite those tremendous achievements, however, the nation remains as racially polarized as ever. Neither Obama nor Occupy ignored race completely, but their political framing made it difficult to address persistent racial disparities in wages, unemployment, and incarceration or to respond to the often implicitly racist rhetoric that conservatives employed to restrict immigration, voting rights, and assistance to the poor. Meanwhile, white voters, who had benefited from Obama's economic policies as much or more than others, were less likely to support the president in 2012 than they had been four years earlier. While the Occupy movement faded into the background, Obama was reelected by a coalition of African Americans, Latinos, and women of all races—who were motivated by threats to their civil rights as much as their economic security.

Ironically, the March on Washington was nearly derailed by a similar miscalculation. Contrary to popular mythology, the demonstration was initiated not to break down racial barriers to voting rights, education, and public accommodations in the Jim Crow South but to highlight "the economic subordination of the Negro" and advance a "broad and fundamental program for economic justice." The roots of the protest stretched back to the March on Washington Movement, which Randolph initiated to protest employment discrimination during the Second World War, and it was renewed in the 1960s by the Negro American Labor Council, a nearly forgotten organization that Randolph and other black trade unionists formed to protest segregation and discrimination in organized labor. When Randolph and other trade unionists proposed a "March on Washington for Jobs," however, they faced resistance from other black activists who feared that such mobilization would detract attention and resources away from the campaign that Martin Luther King and others were planning to protest segregation and legal discrimination in the South. Anna Arnold Hedgeman, a black feminist who had directed Randolph's campaign against employment discrimination in the 1940s, convinced him to meet with King and plan a demonstration that could address "both the economic problems and civil rights."

Rather than narrowing their objectives to win support from moderates, Randolph, Hedgeman, King, and others united a broad coalition of radicals behind the slogan "For Jobs and Freedom." The official demands of the protest included passage of Kennedy's civil rights bill, which mandated equal access to public accommodations and voting rights in the South, but marchers also wanted to strengthen the law by requiring all public schools to desegregate by the end of the year, "reducing Congressional representation of states where citizens were disfranchised"; blocking federal funding to discriminatory housing projects, and prohibiting government agencies, unions, and private firms from discriminating against potential employees on the basis of race, religion, color, or national origin. Furthermore, march leaders insisted that such racially egalitarian measures would be ineffective unless coupled with a minimum wage increase, extension of federal labor protections to workers in agriculture, domestic service, and the public sector, and a "massive federal program to train and place all unemployed workers—Negro and white—on meaningful and dignified jobs at decent wages." Countering Malcolm X's charge that the march had been co-opted, journalist Harvey Swados observed that this "merging of two streams of thought and action" produced an agenda "surpassing anything conceived of by white liberals and well-intentioned officialdom."

We have lost sight of that radicalism, but it was hard to miss on the day of the march. "We are the advanced guard of a massive moral revolution for jobs and freedom," Randolph declared in his opening remarks to the rally that would culminate, nearly two hours later, with King's famous speech. While King would challenge the United States to live up to the promises of equality and freedom contained in the Declaration of Independence and the Constitution, Randolph insisted "that real freedom will require many changes in the nation's political and social philosophies and institutions." For example, he explained, ending housing discrimination would require civil rights activists to assert that "the sanctity of private property takes second place to the sanctity of a human personality." Lending a decidedly American flavor to that implicitly socialist ideal, Randolph asserted that the history of slavery placed African Americans at the forefront of the revolution. "It falls to the Negro to reassert this proper priority of values," the seventy-four-year-old trade unionist declared, "because our ancestors were transformed from human personalities into private property."

As the official director of the March on Washington, Randolph set the tone for the other speeches delivered at the Lincoln Memorial. Roy Wilkins, leader of the National Association for the Advancement of Colored People (NAACP), who had initially opposed the mobilization out of fear that it would undermine efforts to pass the civil rights bill, blasted Kennedy's proposal as "so moderate an approach that if it is weakened or eliminated, the remainder will be little more than sugar water." Walter Reuther, of the United Auto Workers union, agreed that the bill needed to be strengthened. "And the job question is crucial," he declared, "because we will not solve education or housing or public accommodations as long as millions of American Negroes are treated as second-class economic citizens and denied jobs."

The most scathing critique of Kennedy's bill came from John Lewis, the twenty-three-year-old representative of the Student Nonviolent Coordinating Committee, who pointed out that the bill did nothing to protect the disfranchised sharecropper, the homeless and hungry, or a domestic servant who earned $5 a week caring for a family that brought in $100,000 a year. "Let us not forget that we are involved in a serious social revolution," Lewis declared, calling on marchers to find alternatives to a system "dominated by politicians who build their careers on immoral compromises and ally themselves with open forms of political, economic and social exploitation."

Moderates objected to the militancy of Lewis' speech, but they failed to restrain him. Randolph and Bayard Rustin convinced the SNCC leader to add a tepid endorsement of Kennedy's bill and to drop a line pledging to "pursue our own 'scorched earth' policy and burn Jim Crow to the ground—non-violently." They pointed out that such statements undermined the legislative objectives and Gandhian principles that had been integral to the March on Washington Movement since the 1940s. Randolph dismissed complaints that Lewis used "communist" language such as "revolution" and "masses," however; stating that he had done so "many times myself."

By the time Martin Luther King came to the podium, there was no need for him to reiterate the specifics of the March on Washington's agenda, which may explain why his speech proved so appealing to moderates. Noting that the other leaders "concentrated on the struggle ahead and spoke in tough, even harsh, language," *The New York Times* reported that "paradoxically it was Dr. King—who had suffered perhaps most of all—who ignited the crowd with words that might have been written by the sad, brooding man enshrined within" the Lincoln Memorial. King began with a prepared text that emphasized the links between racial equality and economic justice, but abandoned it for an optimistic vision of the future that had become a mainstay of his speeches over the previous two years. King had worked references to economic justice into previous versions of his "I Have a Dream" refrain, such as when he told the executive council of the AFL-CIO about his "dream of a land where men will not take necessities from the many to give luxuries to the few." Just two months earlier, at a massive march in Detroit, King looked forward to a day when "Negroes will be able to buy a house or rent a house anywhere that their money will carry them and that they will be able to get a job." He dropped those assertions at the Lincoln Memorial, however, and—caught up in the passion of the moment—focused on the demands of the southern struggles out of which he had emerged. Judging from the applause that followed, he made a wise choice.

King's speech won immediate and widespread praise for its power and eloquence, but only gradually did his emphasis on integration and legal equality come to be seen as the singular expression of the movement's agenda. Ironically, that transformation was initiated by leftists who grew frustrated with their inability to realize the full extent of their goals in the late 1960s. Writing for the liberal journal *Commentary* in 1965, Bayard Rustin urged his relatively moderate readers to take up the calls for full employment, better wages, and increased funding for social services that he and other radicals had called for two years earlier at the Lincoln Memorial. To underline the need for continued struggle toward economic justice, however, he implied that civil rights activists had focused narrowly in the previous decade on racial questions that were "relatively peripheral to both the American socioeconomic order and to the fundamental conditions of life of the Negro people." Stokely Carmichael, who succeeded John Lewis as chairman of SNCC, leveled a similar critique in his 1967 manifesto, *Black Power.* "We must face the fact that, in the past, what we have called the movement has not really questioned the middle-class values and institutions of this country," he charged. Without acknowledging that he was paraphrasing Randolph's address to the March on Washington, Carmichael explained, "Reorientation means an emphasis on the dignity of man, not the sanctity of property."

As suggested by Carmichael's statements, the Left's disowning of the March on Washington depended as much on forgetting other speeches as on elevating King's "I Have a Dream." Drew Hansen points out that many liberals embraced King's legacy only after the civil rights leaders' assassination in 1968, when the optimistic and inherently patriotic message of his 1963 speech offered a soothing alternative to the frustrated and confrontational rhetoric of the Black Power movement and the

New Left. At the same time, many leftists cited the controversy sparked by John Lewis's speech to suggest that he had been censored. Despite Lewis's recollection that he and other SNCC leaders agreed that "our message was not compromised," the incident was cited widely as evidence, as Nicolaus Mills wrote in *Dissent,* of "the compromises the March on Washington's black sponsors had made in order to win over the media and the Kennedy administration."

Even today, that distorted historical memory continues to blind both liberals and leftists to the lessons of the March on Washington. When Obama first ran for president in 2008, he distinguished his own political philosophy from that of the civil rights movement. While he credited Lewis and other members of the "Moses Generation" with defeating Jim Crow and paving the way for him to become the first black president of the United States, the candidate associated his own political beliefs more strongly with "the economic populism of the New Deal—a vision of fair wages and benefits, patronage and public works, and an ever-rising standard of living." Tapping into a widespread nostalgia for the "Greatest Generation," he suggested that the egalitarian politics of "the sixties" destroyed "a sense of common purpose" that was subsequently captured by the Right. A similar narrative is employed by those who praise Occupy Wall Street for salvaging the economic populism of the early-twentieth-century Left from the egalitarian politics of the civil rights and feminist movements. "'We are the 99%' conveys a deeply moral, democratic message that represents a leap beyond what most left activists have been saying since the 1960s," Michael Kazin wrote in *Dissent,* discounting both the lasting appeal of race and gender equality and the degree to which they have been linked to struggles for economic justice.

Meanwhile, the Right remains eager to claim the legacy of the March on Washington. Leftists were outraged in 2010 when conservative pundit Glenn Beck planned a Tea Party rally at the Lincoln Memorial on the forty-seventh anniversary of the March on Washington—but Reverend Al Sharpton and other black leaders were clearly caught off guard as they scrambled to "Reclaim the Dream" by holding an alternative commemoration at a nearby high school. Tens of thousands showed up for the One Nation rally at the Lincoln Memorial, which the NAACP, AFL-CIO, and other groups organized to demand "jobs, justice and education." Organizers claimed to have been planning the protest since April, but they held it four weeks after the anniversary of the historic March on Washington and never shook the perception that they were simply embarrassed by Beck's success.

Let's hope that the Left does not make the same mistake again. The Martin Luther King, Jr. Center and the National Park Service have announced plans to commemorate the fiftieth anniversary of King's speech and the March on Washington (in that order), but they are not likely to challenge the standard narrative of the event and its meaning. King's Southern Christian Leadership Conference is planning to mark the anniversary with a motorcade from Alabama to Washington, with the intention of "talking about jobs as well as freedom," but the group lacks the size and visibility to challenge the tenor of the official commemoration. Larger groups—particularly the NAACP and AFL-CIO—have an opportunity to shift the tone of the anniversary more decisively. Now, more than ever, the Left needs to reclaim the radical legacy of the March on Washington for Jobs and Freedom.

Critical Thinking

1. Describe the groups and the speakers of the radical demands for economic justice that preceded Martin Luther King, Jr.'s "I Have a Dream Speech."
2. Describe the political context explaining why King switched to his extemporaneous "I Have a Dream" that looked forward to a society of political and social equality for all races.
3. Describe why King is remembered today (he has a National holiday in his name) while his radical predecessors are largely forgotten.

Create Central

www.mhhe.com/createcentral

Internet References

The Papers of Martin Luther King, Jr.
Offers online access to the official and personal papers of Martin Luther King, Jr., which include material from the projected 14-volume edition at Stanford University of The Papers of Martin Luther King, Jr., five volumes of which are now published.
  www.kingpapers.org

WILLIAM P. JONES is Associate Professor of History at the University of Wisconsin–Madison. His next book is *The March on Washington: Jobs, Freedom and the Forgotten History of Civil Rights* (W.W. Norton & Company, 2013).

Article

Prepared by: Larry Madaras, *Howard Community College*

The Key to the Warren Report

Seen in its proper historical context—amid the height of the Cold War—the investigation into Kennedy's assassination looks much more impressive and its shortcomings much more understandable.

MAX HOLLAND

Learning Outcomes

After reading this article, you will be able to:

- Explain why President Johnson formed the "Warren Commission" and what its tasks were.

- Describe the political atmosphere in the United States after Kennedy's death.

- Describe the theories that disagreed with the "Warren Commission."

In September 1994, after doggedly repeating a white lie for forty-seven years, the Air Force finally admitted the truth about a mysterious 1947 crash in the New Mexico desert. The debris was not a weather balloon after all but wreckage from Project Mogul, a top-secret high-altitude balloon system for detecting the first Soviet nuclear blasts halfway across the globe.

During the half-century interim, flying-saucer buffs and conspiracy theorists had adorned the incident with mythic significance, weaving wisps of evidence and contradictions in the Air Force's account into fantastic theories: Bodies of extraterrestrial beings had been recovered by the Air Force; the government was hiding live aliens; death threats had been issued to keep knowledgeable people from talking. Such fictions had provided grist for scores of books, articles, and television shows.

In retrospect the Air Force had obviously thought the Cold War prevented it from revealing a project that remained sensitive long after the Soviet Union exploded its first atomic bomb. And such surreptitiousness was certainly not isolated. Might it provide a model even for understanding that greatest alleged government cover-up the assassination of President John F. Kennedy? Indeed our understanding of the assassination and its aftermath may, like so much else, have been clouded by Cold War exigencies. It may be that the suppression of a few embarrassing but not central truths encouraged the spread of myriad farfetched theories.

Admittedly there are Americans who prefer to believe in conspiracies and cover-ups in any situation. H. L. Mencken noted the "virulence of the national appetite for bogus revelation" in 1917, and more than a century after the Lincoln assassination skeptics were still seeking to exhume John Wilkes Booth's remains. The Columbia University historian Richard Hofstadter definitively described this syndrome in his classic 1963 lecture "The Paranoid Style in American Politics," later published as an essay. "Heated exaggeration, suspiciousness, and conspiratorial fantasy" are almost as old as the Republic, Hofstadter observed, as evinced by the anti-Masonic movement of the 1820s, the anti-Catholicism of the 1850s, claims about an international banking cartel in the early 1900s, and Sen. Joe McCarthy's "immense conspiracy" of the 1950s. But a recurring syndrome is not to be confused with a constant one, Hofstadter argued. Paranoia fluctuates according to the rate of change sweeping through society, and varies with affluence and education.

In the case of the Kennedy assassination, unprecedented belief in all kinds of nonsense, coupled with extraordinary disrespect for the Warren Commission, has waxed in good times and bad and flourishes among remarkable numbers of otherwise sober-minded people. Even the highest level of education is not a barrier, to judge from the disregard for the Warren Report that exists in the upper reaches of the academy. In April 1992 the professional historians' most prestigious publication, the *American Historical Review*, published two articles (out of three) in praise of Oliver Stone's movie *JFK*. The lead piece actually asserted that "on the complex question of the Kennedy assassination itself, the film holds its own against the Warren Report." In a similar vein, in 1993, *Deep Politics and the Death of JFK*, by an English professor named Peter Dale Scott, a book conjuring up fantastic paranoid explanations, was published by no less respected an institution than the University of California Press.

The Warren Commission's inquiry occurred at what we now know was the height of the Cold War, and it must be judged in that context. Perhaps with its history understood, the Warren Commission, instead of being an object of derision, can emerge in a different light, battered somewhat but with the essential integrity of its criminal investigation unscathed. The terrible events that began in Dallas are not an overwhelming, unfathomable crossroads; they are another chapter in the history of the Cold War.

In September 1964, when seven lawyers filed into Lyndon Johnson's White House to deliver their 888-page report on the most searing national event since the attack on Pearl Harbor, the transmogrification of the commission into a national joke would have seemed impossible. Collectively the commission represented one hundred and fifty years' experience—at virtually every level of American government, from county judge to director of Central Intelligence. Chief Justice Earl Warren's reputation was nearly impeccable after more than twenty-five years of public service, and the influence of Georgia's senator Richard Russell in Washington, so the cliché went, was exceeded only by the President's, given Russell's power over intelligence matters, the armed forces, and the Senate itself. Two other panel members, Allen W. Dulles and John J. McCloy, were singularly well versed in the most sensitive national matters, Dulles having served as CIA director from 1953 to 1961 and McCloy as an Assistant Secretary of War from 1940 to 1945.

For several months the commission appeared to have accomplished its mission of assuring the public that the truth was known about Kennedy's death. The American people seemed to accept that JFK's sole assassin was Lee Harvey Oswald, and the report won almost universal praise from the news media. Prior to its release, a Gallup poll found that only 29 percent of Americans thought Oswald had acted alone, afterward 87 percent believed so.

L ong before the report came out, of course, nearly everyone had his or her own explanation for the events in Dallas. It was natural to try to invest the tragedy with meaning. And humans being what they are, individual biases determined people's theories. Even as the President was being wheeled into Parkland Memorial Hospital, anguished aides insisted that unspecified right-wingers were responsible, since uppermost in their minds was the rough reception Adlai Stevenson had gotten in Dallas a few weeks earlier, when the U.N. ambassador was booed, jostled, and spat on by right-wing demonstrators. Dallas's longtime reputation as the "Southwest hate capital of Dixie" only reinforced liberals' inclination to blame "refined Nazis." Even Chief Justice Earl Warren, before his appointment to the commission, could not resist issuing a "blunt indictment of the apostles of hate."

But for officials whose instincts were honed by national-security considerations, the Soviet–American rivalry loomed over what had happened and dictated what immediately needed to be done. The overwhelming instant reaction among these officials was to suspect a grab for power, a foreign, Communist-directed conspiracy aimed at overthrowing the U.S. government. The assassination might be the first in a concerted series of attacks on U.S. leaders or the prelude to an all-out attack. Newly installed intercontinental ballistic missiles were capable of reaching their targets in fifteen minutes; whose finger was on the nuclear button now that the President was dead? Both the President and Vice President had traveled to Dallas, and the fact that six senior cabinet members happened to be aboard an airplane headed for Japan suddenly acquired an awful significance. The Washington-area telephone system suffered a breakdown thirty minutes after the shots were fired, and sabotage was suspected. Attention fixed on the Soviet Union, China, and Cuba as the only governments that could possibly undertake and benefit from such a heinous plot.

When Maj. Gen. Chester Clifton, JFK's military aide, arrived at Parkland Hospital, he immediately called the National Military Command Center and then switched to the White House Situation Room to find out if there was any intelligence about a plot to overthrow the government. The Defense Department subsequently issued a flash warning to every U.S. military base in the world and ordered additional strategic bombers into the air. Gen. Maxwell Taylor issued a special alert to all troops in the Washington area, while John McCone, director of Central Intelligence, asked the Watch Committee to convene immediately at the Pentagon. The committee, an interdepartmental group organized to prevent future Pearl Harbors, consisted of the government's best experts on surprise military attacks.

B ack in Dallas, Rufus Youngblood, head of Johnson's Secret Service detail, told the President-to-be, "We don't know what type of conspiracy this is, or who else is marked. The only place we can be sure you are safe is Washington." A compliant LBJ slouched below the windows in an unmarked car on the way to Love Field, where Air Force One was waiting. Despite special security precautions, it seemed possible to those on the tarmac that the presidential jet could be raked by machine-gun fire at any moment. When the plane was finally airborne, it flew unusually high on a zigzag course back to Washington, with fighter pilots poised to intercept hostile aircraft. During the flight, Johnson kept in touch with the Situation Room, manned by the national security adviser, McGeorge Bundy, for any sign that the Communist bloc might be exploiting the situation. Waiting for Johnson at Andrews Air Force Base was JFK's national security team—or as much of it as could be assembled.

As minutes and then hours passed uneventfully and over-burdened telephone exchanges began working again, fears about a surprise attack receded. Conspiracies like the one being imagined rely on surprise and speed for success, and nothing suspicious had occurred after the assassination. Very soon the thought of a master plot seemed irrational, as William Manchester records in *The Death of a President:* "Hindsight began early. Within the next three hours most of those who had considered the possibility began trying to forget it. They felt that they had been absurd." Still, for hours the U.S. military stood poised to deliver an overwhelming counterstrike.

Within hours the Dallas police arrested a twenty-four-year-old Communist sympathizer named Lee Oswald, a bundle of possibilities and seeming contradictions. Now many liberals showed a reluctance to shift the blame from right-wingers to a self-styled Marxist; a liberal President being assassinated by a Marxist seemed to make no sense. Jacqueline Kennedy's reaction upon being told of Oswald's background was to feel sickened because she immediately sensed it robbed JFK's death of a greater meaning. "He didn't even have the satisfaction of being killed for civil rights," she said, according to Manchester. "It's—it had to be some silly little communist."

For security-conscious officials, however, Oswald's arrest meant replacing one Cold War scenario with another, and the second script filled them with no less dread than the first. Undersecretary of State George Ball ordered a search of federal files as soon as the networks broadcast Oswald's capture. Dallas authorities found pro-Soviet and pro-Castro literature in Oswald's boardinghouse room, and frantic searches of FBI, CIA, and State Department records revealed Oswald's defection to the Soviet Union, his recent contacts with the Soviet Embassy in Mexico City, and his one-man Fair Play for Cuba committee in New Orleans. Top officials working through the night to assemble all the pieces had to wonder if the KGB had transformed a onetime defector into an assassin or if Castro had used an overt sympathizer to retaliate against an administration plotting his downfall. As Ball told *The Washington Post* in 1993, "we were just scared to death that this was something bigger than just the act of a madman."

The government's leading experts on the Soviet Union doubted it. Llewellyn Thompson, a well-regarded former ambassador to Moscow, argued that the assassination lacked the earmarks of a Soviet plot. Moscow might kill defectors but not heads of state, he insisted, and would never set such a precedent. Averell Harriman, another experienced Soviet hand, agreed that Oswald was not a likely instrument of the KGB and questioned his professed Marxism. The assassination, utterly inconsistent with recent Soviet behavior, just made no sense. What could the Soviets possibly hope to achieve through such a rash act in a nuclear-tipped world? Nor was there evidence of any effort to advance Soviet interests in the wake of the assassination. As for Cuba, even the mercurial Castro was unlikely to engage in such madness. He had to know that it would put the existence of his regime, if not his revolution, in extreme danger. But past history and common sense were not sufficient to banish all thoughts of Communist complicity. More hard evidence was desperately needed to rule it out.

Over the next two days, while a nation mourned, the entire intelligence community worked to learn everything it could about Oswald and his murky, superficially contradictory activities. New intelligence reports from Mexico City suggested a link between Oswald and the Cuban government. The supersecret National Security Agency and allied eavesdropping agencies went into overdrive to decipher intercepted conversations, cable traffic, radio, and telephone communications at the highest levels of the Soviet and Cuban governments, looking especially for unusual messages between Moscow and the Soviet Embassy in Washington and between Moscow and Havana.

In about forty-eight hours the intercepts showed beyond a reasonable doubt that both the Soviet and Cuban governments had been as shocked as anyone by the news from Dallas. "They were frightened," says one knowledgeable source, "and we knew that." Indeed, Moscow was so uneasy over its remote link to Oswald that the Foreign Ministry voluntarily gave the State Department a KGB account of his every movement inside Russia. Not only was Castro's surprise genuine (he was being interviewed by a French journalist when the news came), he was panic-stricken. He believed that President Johnson would send in the Marines if LBJ decided the Cuban government was connected to the assassination.

That Oswald was not the instrument of a foreign power was an intelligence coup of the first order and of incalculable interest to an unsettled public. Late on Saturday, November 23, the State Department issued a public statement declaring that there was no evidence of a conspiracy involving a foreign country. Yet revealing the intelligence sources and methods that had helped form this determination was out of the question. Cold War–era communications intercepts were as prized as World War II feats of decryption, and the NSA's capabilities were—and are—the most highly guarded of secrets. And because content reveals methodology, certain specifics of what had been learned were equally protected. The American public was told the truth but not the whole truth. It would not be the last time.

With fears of foreign involvement ebbing, a third Cold War worry began to dominate thinking among high officials—that given Oswald's extreme views, the assassination might stir dangerous anti-Communist emotions within the body politic. Anyone who had lived through the McCarthy era knew of the domestic dangers of untrammeled anti-Communism. It could threaten the mild détente achieved since the Cuban missile crisis; indeed, the public might even demand that President Johnson retaliate with a show of force. Already an LBJ aide had squelched language in the original indictment charging Oswald with killing the President "in furtherance of a communist conspiracy." And the U.S. ambassador to Moscow, Foy Kohler, had cabled Washington on Saturday expressing his own concern over the "political repercussions which may develop if undue emphasis is placed on the alleged 'Marxism' of Oswald . . . I would hope, if facts permit, we could deal with the assassin as 'madman' . . . rather than dwell on his professed political convictions."

This mostly domestic problem appeared manageable. But then Jack Ruby, prey to rash impulses and a murderous temper, decided to exact proper revenge. Oswald's death abruptly renewed the note of mystery and suspicion: Had he been killed to suppress something? Top officials considered, but eventually discarded, the notion of an elaborate conspiracy involving Ruby; if there had been one, why was Oswald allowed to live for forty-eight hours, let alone be captured? Meanwhile the need to assuage public anxiety only intensified. Johnson considered releasing detailed results from the FBI investigation ordered the night of November 22, but then dismissed the idea as insufficient. The FBI investigation itself had to be validated, though J. Edgar Hoover fumed at the suggestion. Instead an idea advocated by Nicholas Katzenbach, the deputy Attorney General, gathered support within and without the administration.

Katzenbach, deeply concerned over the appearance of a relationship between the Soviets and Oswald, wanted LBJ to impanel a group of prestigious citizens to investigate the assassination, to develop and control information with possible international repercussions, and ultimately to choke off all talk about a Communist conspiracy. Johnson, keenly aware of the South's sensitivity over states' rights, at first wanted an all-Texas investigation. But long-time Washington hands and friends, including the columnist Joseph Alsop, persuaded him that a state inquiry would be considered tantamount to a whitewash. This argument struck a chord in Johnson; Texas was his home state, and the Soviet-bloc press was charging that a leftist was being made a scapegoat for what was actually a right-wing Texas conspiracy in a decadent, violent country.

The motivation for the formation of the Warren Commission, on November 29, is made clear in transcripts of 275 recently declassified presidential telephone conversations from late 1963. They show that Johnson recruited the members of the panel by repeatedly invoking the need to cut off "explosive" and "dangerous" speculation about a Communist plot. Preventing World War III might have been typical Johnson hyperbole, but the concern was real, and there were still contradictory allegations that needed to be checked out, especially Oswald's mysterious September trip to Mexico City, where he had met a KGB agent doubling as a Soviet consular officer. As Johnson told Chief Justice Warren and Senator Russell—both were reluctant to serve—"This is a question that has a good many more ramifications than on the surface, and we've got to take this out of the arena where they're testifying that Khrushchev and Castro did this and did that and check us into a war that can kill 40 million Americans in an hour."

Even the commission's enlistment of such respected anti-Communists as Russell and Rep. Gerald Ford did not immediately stanch the mischief and pressure Johnson feared from the right. On December 6 the House Republican Policy Committee issued a statement decrying liberals' claims that "hate was the assassin that struck down the President," saying the true criminal was the "teachings of communism." Republican senator Milward Simpson of Wyoming took the floor that same day to attack those who were seeking "political advantage from warping the uncontestable truth." The senator added that the murderer "was a single kill-crazy communist."

When Earl Warren welcomed the assembled commission staff on January 20, he admonished them, "Truth is our only client here," and that phrase became the commission's unofficial motto. Ultimately, the group's massive undertaking yielded two essential conclusions: that Oswald fired all the shots that killed JFK and wounded John Connally and that there was no evidence of a conspiracy. Reaching these simple findings required a prodigious effort by many dedicated people, and it is no small accomplishment that after more than thirty years the first conclusion remains proven beyond a reasonable doubt and the second has never been challenged by any hard, credible evidence.

The only other politically sensitive question facing the commission was that of Oswald's motive and how it might be connected to his Communist beliefs and activities. How did the commission treat Oswald's politics? It's hard to re-create an earlier time and problem, but it is extraordinarily revealing to do so.

The main difficulty in divining Oswald's motive was of course the fact that Jack Ruby had murdered him before he could confess and explain. During twelve hours of questioning Oswald had fallen silent or lied, with that arrogance and air of fantasy peculiar to sociopaths, whenever confronted with hard evidence tying him to the assassination. No, he wasn't the man holding a Mannlicher-Carcano rifle in that picture; someone had altered the photograph to superimpose his face on another body. No, he had never been in Mexico City. No, he was in the lunchroom when Kennedy was shot. Often Oswald appeared to be baiting his interrogators and "was so smug in the way he dealt with the questions," the Dallas assistant district attorney later recalled, that "at times I had to walk out of the room, because in another few minutes I was going to beat the shit out of him myself." One of Oswald's few requests was that he be represented by John J. Abt, a New York lawyer known for his defense of leading Communist-party figures since 1949.

Lacking a confession or hard evidence like a note, the commission ultimately decided not to ascribe to Oswald "any one motive or group of motives." This nonconclusion was sound and sensible for several reasons. First, the commission viewed itself as akin to a judge at a criminal trial, with the job simply of determining Oswald's culpability and the conspiracy issue; motive was less important. Second, the issue seemed a bottomless pit. In a moment of dark humor one staff member, Norman Redlich, wrote a spoof titled the "Washing Machine Theory of the Assassination," describing how Marina Oswald's rejection of her husband's offer to buy her a washing machine had triggered Oswald's sense of failure and his need to prove his mettle by assassinating a President. There was a serious purpose in Redlich's spoof: He wanted to show that there was simply no way to pick one motive from all the possibilities. The chances of achieving unanimity among the commissioners were slim to nil, and anyway a consensus was bound to subject the report to valid, as opposed to irresponsible, criticism. Consequently the report listed a few possibilities and concluded that "others may study Lee Oswald's life and arrive at their own conclusions as to his possible motives."

However reasonable and sound this non-conclusion was, what is striking in retrospect is how a very plausible motive was buried. Ample details about Oswald's extraordinary political activities were provided, but in a detached and clinical manner; the avalanche of facts tended to obscure a salient one. Whenever Oswald actually took violent action, whenever he set free his internal demons, it was on a political stage. This was true when he attempted suicide in 1959, after the Soviets initially refused his defection, and again in April 1963, when he stalked a right-wing retired general named Edwin A. Walker. Walker and Kennedy had one thing in common in Oswald's eyes: their anti-Communism, especially their antipathy to the "purer" Cuban Revolution that had captured Oswald's imagination. (Walker had called for "liquidating the scourge that has descended on Cuba.") The November murder was first of all an act of opportunity by a bent personality, but Kennedy was not in all likelihood a random victim of Oswald.

How did this de-emphasis occur? The most important factor was the cautiousness described above. The commission's task was not to promote speculation and theorizing, no matter how plausible. Another significant, if perhaps less conscious, element was the dominant role lawyers played on the commission and in writing the report. In the most trenchant criticism of the Warren Report ever to appear, a 1965 *Esquire* article, the critic Dwight Macdonald accepted the commission's conclusions but called the report a prosecutor's brief that failed to meet its overarching purpose, which was to produce an objective account of what happened in Dallas. Because the report was written by lawyers, Macdonald said it had a telling defect: "omnivorous inclusiveness. . . . [the] prose is at best workmanlike but too often turgidly legalistic or pompously official. It obscures the strong points of its case, and many are very strong, under a midden-heap of inessential facts. . . . Its tone is that of the advocate, smoothing away or sidestepping objections to his 'case' rather than the impartial judge or the researcher welcoming all data with detached curiosity." Oswald's seriousness about his politics was buried under a "midden-heap" of facts.

Yet there was also a political tinge to the depiction of Oswald. The same Cold War imperative that had led to the formation of the commission persisted as an undercurrent throughout the investigation, and it ultimately detached Oswald from the politics that had animated him. At the commission's first executive session in December, former Director of Central Intelligence Allen Dulles, one of the members most sensitive to Cold War considerations, gave each of his colleagues a book on the history of presidential assassinations in America. Nearly every killer, would-be or successful, had been a lone psychopath. Dulles suggested to his colleagues that Oswald fitted the historical pattern; a disturbed nonentity, in other words, purchased a mail-order rifle and used it to murder the President of the United States. Later Dulles wrote what he hoped would be an appendix to the report on the topic of presidential assassins.

The manner in which the report described Oswald's preferred legal counsel is also revealing. That Oswald had wanted to retain John Abt, or a lawyer who "believes as I believe" and would "understand what this case is all about," was a sure indication that Oswald had intended to exploit his upcoming trial as a megaphone for his peculiar brand of politics. But the report drew no meaning at all from Oswald's clear preference. All three references to Abt simply describe him as a "New York attorney" (or lawyer), not mentioning his ties to

Communist-party figures. The commission's inclination to de-emphasize Oswald's politics was mightily reinforced by another external Cold War imperative. As the staff, to its great chagrin, learned a decade later, the CIA limited its cooperation with the investigation according to its own internal rules. The agency had no intention of volunteering information about American subversion of Castro's regime, including proposed assassination plots that stretched back to the Eisenhower administration, even though Oswald may have suspected the worst about U.S. policy and been motivated by its hostility. And there was no clue that the CIA was holding back, for it did readily share some highly classified secrets, like the communications intercepts. Suspicion of the FBI actually ran far higher, because of J. Edgar Hoover's well-known predilection for holding himself above the law.

When the CIA's omissions were finally revealed in the mid-1970s, the agency was roundly pilloried by Congress and in the news media. Nothing was more devastating to the Warren Commission's reputation, nothing more "weakened the credibility of the Warren Report," CBS's anchorman Walter Cronkite observed. The commission's staff had grown used to bogus "new" revelations by conspiracy buffs, but this genuinely distressed and even angered them. And most Americans, unschooled in the niceties of compartmented information and the need to know, found incomprehensible the notion that the CIA had dissembled in the midst of a national trauma. Could the CIA ever be counted on to tell the whole truth about the assassination? And if the government could so lie to itself—let alone to the public—what wasn't possible?

This revelation made the Warren Commission into a national joke. For a few citizens, of course, the supposed inadequacy of the commission's investigation had been manifest as early as 1966; others had gone through a more gradual disillusionment that reflected their declining faith in government after Vietnam and Watergate. But for most the investigation had never before come under such a cloud, except during a passing controversy over the President's autopsy that had been fairly easily resolved. Now doubts were such that even Congress felt compelled to revisit the entire matter, after fourteen years of self-restraint unprecedented for that publicity-hungry body.

When the House Select Committee on Assassinations issued its final report, in 1979, it castigated the CIA for withholding information. Yet some members of the commission must have pretty well known the CIA wasn't being entirely open. Allen Dulles had extensive knowledge about CIA workings and U.S. efforts to overthrow Castro since March 1960, including proposed assassination plots. John McCloy, chief negotiator during the Cuban missile crisis, was quite familiar with the governmentwide effort to subvert Castro's regime. And two other commissioners, Richard Russell and Gerald Ford, sat in on closed-door, unminuted congressional hearings about CIA budgets, policies, and covert activities. Ford confirmed that in 1963–64 he was aware of agency efforts to subvert Castro, with the exception of proposed assassination plots. And Russell, who dominated congressional involvement in intelligence matters, was a stout believer in covert activities. Far from being an inquisitive, troublesome overseer, "Mr. Senate" acted as the CIA's protector and advocate on Capitol Hill. There is no indication that he viewed his role on the commission any differently. Not one of these four—out of seven—commissioners shared whatever special insight he had with the staff, nor is that really surprising. These men were steeped in the Cold War and in what sometimes had to be done to wage it.

Consider, too, the actions of those officials outside the commission who had the standing and power to bring any relevant information to Warren's attention had they chosen to do so. In particular, consider the role of Attorney General Robert Kennedy. He played a unique part: Not only was he the brother of the slain President, but he had virtually unrivaled knowledge about anti-Castro activities. Indeed, more than any other official, the thirty-eight-year-old Kennedy embodied the harsh political, institutional, and personal dilemmas that existed in the assassination's wake. Any reconsideration of the Warren Commission must address RFK's role directly. His response is a Rosetta stone.

The standard explanation for RFK's seeming uninterest in the commission, as put forward in biographies and memoirs by friends, is that he simply found the subject too painful. Although kept fully apprised of the commission's progress, he emotionally recused himself from the investigation. As RFK told close associates, Jack was dead and nothing he could do would bring him back. In *The Death of a President* William Manchester writes that many of the Kennedy clan who were crushed by the assassination managed to right themselves after the funeral—but not RFK. During the spring of 1964 a "brooding Celtic agony . . . darken[ed] Kennedy's life." He was nonfunctional for hours at a time and to those closest to him seemed almost in physical pain.

What genuinely sent RFK reeling may have been what the historian Robert Jay Lifton calls "survivor guilt," a feeling that he should have died instead of the President. In the end, the raw probability, after all conspiracies were ruled out, was that the administration's obsession with Castro had inadvertently motivated a politicized sociopath. Oswald had seen embodied in President Kennedy all American opposition to Castro, but it was Robert Kennedy, more than his brother, who had played the driving role in the anti-Castro subversion. RFK's involvement had begun just two days after the inauguration, when at the new President's behest the new Attorney General had been included in the first of seven CIA briefings on the plans to invade Cuba. Attorneys General had never before participated in such deliberations, but that was only the beginning.

After the Bay of Pigs debacle, in April 1961, the President ordered RFK to help Gen. Maxwell Taylor poke around the Agency and find out what had gone wrong. Operating with his usual zeal, Robert Kennedy immersed himself in Agency affairs over the next two months, and the more he understood of the CIA's capabilities, the more ardent

a champion he became. Precisely because the Bay of Pigs was such a catastrophe, the Kennedys grew more determined than ever to see Castro deposed.

While Castro erected a sign near the invasion site that read WELCOME TO THE SITE OF THE FIRST DEFEAT OF IMPERIALISM IN THE WESTERN HEMISPHERE, the Kennedy administration resumed plotting against him in earnest. By November 1961 another covert plan, code-named Mongoose, was moving into high gear. This time the operation aimed to destabilize Castro's regime rather than overthrow it. In concert with overtly hostile diplomatic and economic policies, every possible covert tactic would be brought to bear, including sabotage, psychological warfare, and proposed assassination plots; and the President installed his brother as czar over the entire, governmentwide operation. As Sen. Harris Wofford (then a White House aide) wrote in his 1980 memoir, *Of Kennedys & Kings,* "The Attorney General was the driving force behind the clandestine effort to overthrow Castro. From inside accounts of the pressure he was putting on the CIA to 'get Castro,' he seemed like a wild man who was out-CIAing the CIA."

For the first nine months of 1962, Mongoose was the administration's top covert priority, and Castro next to an obsession for Robert Kennedy. RFK's single-minded micromanagement extended to almost daily telephone conversations with Richard Helms, deputy director of the CIA, during which calls the volatile Attorney General applied "white heat" pressure. As Helms told *Newsweek* in 1993, "We had a whip on our backs. If I take off my shirt, I'll show you the scars." It was abundantly clear that Castro was to be gotten rid of.

In 1962 the Attorney General even decided the Mafia could be useful in Mongoose operations. He ordered the CIA to assign a case officer to meet with Mafia figures. "It was Bobby and his secretary (Angie Novello) who called the officer on what used to be called at the Agency a secure line, [to] give him a name, an address, and where he would meet with the Mafia people," recalls Samuel Halpern, a retired CIA official involved in Mongoose. The ensuing conversations contradicted almost every rule for clandestine operations the CIA had, and to add insult to injury, nothing useful ever developed from them. "We thought it was stupid, silly, ineffective, and wasteful," says Halpern. "But we were under orders, and we did it."

The CIA pursued Mongoose with determined vigor until the Cuban missile crisis put the United States and the Soviet Union at the brink of nuclear war. After that some advisers got Kennedy to take tentative steps toward trying to wean Castro from the Soviets, because the Cuban leader was smarting over the Russian "betrayal." But the dominant U.S. policy remained intensely hostile. "Our interest lies in avoiding the kind of commitment that unduly ties our hands in dealing with the Castro regime while it lasts," wrote Secretary of State Dean Rusk in a 1962 document only recently declassified. Ultimately, a more modest program of covert subversion was reintroduced by mid-1963. As before, it included the tactic of "neutralizing" Castro.

Despite the manifest relevance of these activities to the Warren inquiry, Robert Kennedy studiously avoided sharing any information about them with the commission—even when Earl Warren specifically asked him to. As David Belin, a counsel to the Warren Commission, recounts in *Final Disclosure,* Warren informed RFK of the commission's progress, in a letter dated June 11, 1964, and asked him if he was aware of any "additional information relating to the assassination of President John F. Kennedy which has not been sent to the Commission." Warren emphasized in particular the importance of any information suggesting a "domestic or foreign conspiracy."

Kennedy wrote in response that "all information . . . in the possession of the Department of Justice" had been sent to the commission. He added that he had "no suggestions to make at this time regarding any additional investigation which should be undertaken by the Commission prior to the publication of its report."

Several accounts make it clear that Robert Kennedy's immediate instinct after the assassination was to look for a Cuban connection to Oswald, among either pro-Castro elements or Bay of Pigs veterans repatriated from Havana in December 1962. He asked McCone if Agency-connected persons had killed JFK "in a way that [McCone] couldn't lie to me, and [McCone replied] they hadn't." Through close associates, RFK also made other discreet inquires about perceived administration enemies right after the assassination: What was Jimmy Hoffa's reaction? Were Chicago mobsters involved?

Small wonder that in the black months after the murder Robert Kennedy became absorbed by the work of the Greek tragedians. He apparently found solace in one passage from Aeschylus, for he underlined it: "All arrogance will reap a harvest rich in tears. God calls men to a heavy reckoning for overweening pride." Belin also tells of a 1975 conversation he had with McCone after news of the proposed assassination plots finally surfaced along with the fact that Robert Kennedy had overseen those plans. As Belin describes it, "McCone replied that for the first time he could now understand the reactions of Kennedy right after the assassination when the two of them were alone. McCone said he felt there was something troubling Kennedy that he was not disclosing. . . . [It was McCone's] personal belief that Robert Kennedy had personal feelings of guilt because he was directly or indirectly involved with the anti-Castro planning."

In the case of RFK, of course, the national security that dictated silence was reinforced by a very personal imperative. As the reputation of the slain President soared, Robert Kennedy bore the burden of protecting that reputation and carrying its legacy. Already he had sought to insulate his brother from debacles (the Bay of Pigs) and turn near catastrophes into triumphs of calibrated, statesmanlike policy (the Cuban missile crisis). Full disclosure surely would have threatened the emerging Camelot view of the Kennedy Presidency and, it must be said, RFK's fortunes as well. His own political stock was skyrocketing after the assassination.

On the first occasion when he spoke directly about Oswald, Kennedy said exactly what the Warren Commission would eventually report. He told a student questioner in Poland in June 1964, "I believe it was done by a man . . . who was a misfit in society. . . . [He] felt that the only way to take out his strong feelings against life and society was by killing the President of the United States. There is no question that he did it on his own and by himself. He was not a member of a right-wing organization. He was a confessed Communist, but even the Communists would not have anything to do with him."

Even if other officials did not know as much as RFK or share his need to keep the Kennedy image burnished, their personal and institutional loyalties likewise determined the extent of their cooperation with the commission. Anyway, if, as the communications intercepts proved, there was no link between Oswald and the Soviet or Cuban government, then Warren had no need to know about past and ongoing covert operations directed against Cuba, regardless of how relevant they were to Oswald's internal equation. Not a few officials and Cold War operatives had an interest in leaving the assassin a crazed loner, acting on some solitary impulse. To put it another way, officials in the know faced a genuine dilemma only if they had information pointing to someone other than Oswald. The Warren Commission could not deliver to the American people and the world a false conclusion—that might well affect the stability of the government or shake important institutions to their foundations—but there was every reason not to spill secrets that merely echoed the finding that Oswald acted alone. The commission, though denied important supporting information, would still publish the correct conclusion, and the U.S. government could keep its deepest secrets. It was a convenient act of denial and dismissal, but also one perceived as necessary in the midst of the Cold War. Complete candor would not have changed the report's two essential conclusions at all—though it might have done a great deal to prevent its slide into disrepute later.

Full disclosure might have helped the commission explain the political element in Oswald's motive by putting his pro-Castro activities in a new dimension, but the price was considered to be too high. The CIA, especially, had every reason to dread a no-holds-barred investigation into the events of November 22. An uncontrolled investigation would have had serious repercussions for ongoing covert operations. Beyond the inevitable exposure of Mongoose, possibly the largest covert operation that had ever been mounted, the revelations would have given the Communist bloc an undreamed-of propaganda windfall that would have lasted years. There would have followed strong condemnations by the international community and intense investigations of the CIA and administration officials who had directed anti-Castro efforts. Such investigations could conceivably have destroyed the CIA, and it was surely not LBJ's intention to blunt his Cold War weapons when he announced the commission's formation. Altogether, there simply was no contest between these risks and the potential damage that silence might inflict on the Warren Commission's reputation should the withheld information ever leak out.

In time the Warren Commission will be seen for what it truly was. It was not a fiendish cover-up, nor was it designed to anesthetize the country by delivering a political truth at odds with the facts. It was a monumental criminal investigation carried to its utmost limits and designed to burn away a fog of speculation. It did not achieve perfection, and in the rush to print (there was no rush to judgment) the language on pivotal issues, such as the single bullet, was poorly crafted. In retrospect, forensic and scientific experts should have been put on the lawyer-dominated panel. But the commission indisputably achieved its main goal: to determine what happened in Dealey Plaza on November 22, 1963. That was the one thing that needed to and could be proved beyond a reasonable doubt. And the accuracy of the report's essential finding, holding up after three decades, is testimony to the commission's basic integrity. Indeed, as a British reviewer once put it, the best tribute to the solidity of the report is the deviousness of its critics.

The commission did not conduct its work in a political vacuum, nor could it. In fact the Warren Commission reflects a view common during the Cold War, one Gerald Ford explained in general terms during his vice-presidential confirmation hearings in 1973, that government officials have the right, if not the duty, to tell the truth but not necessarily the whole truth when an issue involves national-security matters. Some Americans erroneously believe that secrets per se contradict official verdicts; just as often, if not more often, they buttress conclusions, as the case here shows.

Was parceling out truths an outrageous act or a necessary one during the forty-five years of the Cold War? It depends on one's perspective. There is no doubt it was done here. Secrets considered inessential to the inquiry were kept secret even from the commission. Those considered essential were shared with the commission but not the public. No doubt referring to the communications intercepts, Earl Warren told the press shortly after the report's publication that there were "things that will not be revealed in our lifetime." Or as former President Ford now acknowledges, "Judgments were made back then that seemed rational and reasonable. Today with the totally different atmosphere those judgments might seem improper." The Warren Commission's investigation cut across the entire national-security apparatus during the height of the Cold War, when even a national trauma could not be allowed to disturb the inner workings and unalterable logic of that struggle.

Was this instance of holding back some of the truth one of the great misjudgments in American history? Enduring, perhaps ineradicable controversy over the assassination has helped foster deep alienation and cynicism and a loss of respect among the American people for their government and the citizens who serve in it. That is perhaps the most lasting and grievous wound inflicted by Lee Harvey Oswald.

Critical Thinking

1. Critically examine whether the Warren Commission made a thorough examination of the events of November 22, 1963, in concluding that Oswald acted alone as the president's killer.
2. Critically examine whether the Commission would have reached different conclusions had it known about prior attempts by the CIA to assassinate Castro.
3. Critically examine why the majority of Americans believe that there was a conspiracy involved in the murder of President Kennedy.

Create Central

www.mhhe.com/createcentral

Internet References

John McAdams, "The Kennedy Assassination"
www.kingpapers.org

The Lee Harvey Oswald Page
The purpose of this site, maintained by independent researcher W. Tracy Parnell, is to provide information to researchers and students about Lee Harvey Oswald, accused assassin of President John F. Kennedy, as well as general assassination-related material.
www.madbbs.com/-tracy/lho

National Archives and Records Administration. This site offers access to the "JFK Assassination Records."
www.archives.gov

MAX HOLLAND has written extensively books and articles on *The Warren Commission.*

Holland, Max. From *American Heritage*, November 1995, pp. 50, 52, 54, 56–58, 60, 62, 64. Copyright © 1995 by American Heritage, Inc. Reprinted by permission of American Heritage Publishing and Max Holland.

Article

The Spirit of '78, Stayin' Alive

KENNETH S. BAER

Learning Outcomes

After reading this article, you will be able to:

- Describe the impact certain political and technological events of 1978 have on the world today.

- Explain the ways in which China's plan to become a world power has progressed from 1978 to today.

Everyone seems to be telling us that if you want to understand 2008, you have to look back 40 years to 1968. "It's the year that changed everything," wrote *Newsweek* last November. Seen through tie-dye-tinted glasses, Iraq is the new Vietnam, Barack Obama is the new Bobby Kennedy, and bloggers are the new student activists.

But are we commemorating the right year? If we really want a time that defined the way we live now, we should look back not to the romance and trauma of the '60s but to the gloriously tacky '70s, to the year that made modern America—1978. Look beyond the year's bad disco and worse clothes; if you peer deeply into the polyester soul of 1978, you can see the beginnings of the world we live in today.

Start with politics. Two weeks into that year, on Jan. 13, former vice president Hubert H. Humphrey died, but it took six more months before the big-government liberalism that he embodied was buried. In June, California voters backed Proposition 13, which slashed property taxes and capped tax increases, thereby marking the start of conservatism's rebirth—and the beginning of the long end of New Deal liberalism.

People had good reason to be irked at Washington, too. Voters were fed up with rising tax rates (heavily fueled by inflation) and an inefficient government that was seen as wasting their dollars. The Yankelovich poll found that 78 percent of Americans agreed with the statement, "Government wastes a lot of money we pay in taxes," an 18-point jump from 1968.

This anti-government sentiment propelled successful efforts to limit taxing and spending in 13 states and prompted 23 state legislatures to call for a constitutional convention to consider a balanced-budget amendment to the Constitution. The sour public mood, especially after the passage of Prop 13, triggered a stampede of elected officials to the right, and those who didn't dart quickly enough were run over—such as Massachusetts Gov. Michael S. Dukakis, who lost his party's gubernatorial primary.

In fact, it was in November 1978 that the modern Republican Party—which had been on the verge of extinction after Watergate—was born. In the midterm elections, the GOP gained three Senate seats, 12 House seats and six governorships. The anti-tax, small-government worldview of its right wing was suddenly ascendant—and has dominated American politics until the present day. (Note that, even with President Bush and his party on the ropes, neither Barack Obama nor Hillary Rodham Clinton was willing to back the sort of nationalized health care that every other industrialized democracy enjoys or mention raising taxes to get rid of the massive deficit that Bush is leaving behind.)

Our year also set the contours of today's civil rights battles. In *Regents of the University of California v. Bakke,* the Supreme Court ruled that rigid race quotas for university admissions were unconstitutional but that affirmative action policies designed to ensure a diverse student body were not. Americans have battled over the implications of this decision ever since, but we have come to accept diversity as a virtue in universities, corporations and throughout American life. That began with Bakke in 1978.

Of course, today's most contentious civil rights battles aren't over race but over sexual orientation. Here, too, 1978 was pivotal. As the year began, a handful of communities had ordinances on the books banning discrimination against gays in employment and housing. But as these measures passed, opposition mobilized, often led by the singer Anita Bryant. In 1978, the citizens of Eugene, Ore.; St. Paul, Minn.; and Wichita, Kan., voted overwhelmingly to repeal these gay-friendly laws. Even in liberal New York, Mayor Ed Koch's effort to expand a ban on discrimination on the basis of sexual orientation for municipal hiring never got out of the relevant city council committee.

But the most bizarre and important incident happened, perhaps unsurprisingly, in San Francisco. The city had passed its own anti-discrimination law in March. On Nov. 27, Daniel White, the lone city supervisor to oppose the ordinance, walked into Mayor George Moscone's office and shot him dead, then proceeded to the office of Supervisor Harvey Milk—the country's first openly gay official of any consequence—and killed him, too.

More than 30,000 San Franciscans took to the streets to mourn Milk and Moscone, blaming their deaths on the anti-gay backlash. One person held a sign stating: "Are you happy, Anita?" If this didn't galvanize the gay community, the light sentence that White received did. That year, the gay community's first Washington lobbyist was hired, and its long struggle for equality was underway.

Politics wasn't the only thing that began to change in 1978. Are you reading this article on your BlackBerry? That's only possible because, in 1978, Illinois Bell rolled out the first cellular phone system—a radical new technology that promised to break the 10-year waiting list for mobile phones. That same year, the first computer bulletin-board system was created, and the first piece of e-mail spam was sent over the ARPANET, the forerunner to today's Internet, inviting users to a computer company's product demonstration. (No word on whether it promised to enhance the attendees' virility.)

Computers were quickly becoming more pervasive, too. VisiCalc, an early spreadsheet program, was introduced in 1978 and quickly became the first commercially successful piece of software, giving personal computers mass rather than just geek appeal. "Eventually, the household computer will be as much a part of the home as the kitchen sink," *Time* magazine boldly predicted in February 1978.

E-mail spam went largely unnoticed at the time, but the year's advances in biotechnology certainly did not. Late on the evening of July 25, in the small city of Oldham in northwest England, the first "test-tube baby" was born. Louise Brown's arrival after in vitro fertilization touched off a worldwide ethical debate about whether and how we should be fooling with Mother Nature. Thirty years later, IVF is commonplace, and genetic science has leapt astonishingly forward, but the scope of the debates—now focused on stem cells and cloning—remains the same.

Other eerily familiar issues from today's headlines first appeared three decades ago. Wiretapping and national security? The Foreign Intelligence Surveillance Act—whose overhaul triggered a contentious debate last week on Capitol Hill—was signed into law by President Jimmy Carter in October 1978. Skyrocketing gas prices and national reliance on foreign oil? The country's first comprehensive national energy program was signed into law at the end of 1978—but only after 18 months of contentious logrolling in Congress.

You can find the roots of some of today's biggest foreign policy challenges in 1978, too. A Middle East roiled by Islamist extremism? Nineteen seventy-eight marked the beginning of the end for the shah of Iran, soon to be swept aside by the Shiite radicals led by Ayatollah Ruhollah Khomeini—a man whose example would help pave the way for a new generation of Sunni fanatics also angry about the U.S. role in the Middle East. But while 1978 was a rotten year for U.S. efforts to prop up the shah, it was a far better one for Arab–Israeli peacemaking. Not only did the otherwise hapless Carter help broker the watershed Israeli–Egyptian peace treaty at Camp David, the summit also produced "A Framework for Peace in the Middle East," a much more ambitious document explaining how Israelis, Palestinians and Jordanians would work out their own conflicts over the next five years. That time horizon proved a little ambitious,

but a precedent had been set: Since 1978, Arabs and Israelis have expected the U.S. president to be personally and deeply involved in any painful deal-making.

Then as now, the Middle East got the most headlines, but it was what was happening in the Far East that would most radically shape the world. After years of near-total isolation, China decided to join the rest of the world, setting out on what its rulers called a "New Long March" to become a world power by the end of the century. Under the leadership of Deng Xiaoping, Mao's heir, China ratified a peace and friendship treaty with Japan and reached out to its traditionally wary Asian neighbors. At home, it took momentous early steps toward capitalism by beginning to dismantle its agricultural communes, allowing peasants to sell their crops and pocket the profits.

The most dramatic sign of China's new openness was announced simultaneously in Beijing and Washington in December: The United States formally recognized China, broke its longstanding recognition of Taiwan and normalized relations with the communist titan. This momentous decision helped propel China into the modern world, turn it into a rival—if not an enemy—of the United States and intertwine the two countries' economies. Last year, U.S. trade with China was $386 billion, up from $1 billion in 1978. There is not a person reading this article who doesn't own a Chinese product.

The rise of China may not be as sexy as the student uprisings of 1968, and the passage of Prop 13 may not pack the same emotional punch as the tragic campaign of RFK. But from politics to technology, from civil rights to foreign policy, 1978 marked the start of the age we live in. Thank God, disco didn't survive.

Critical Thinking

1. What had the most impact on U.S. society from 1978 to now? Why?

2. What major factor has played a key role in China's progress?

Create Central

www.mhhe.com/createcentral

Internet References

International-relationships.com
    www.international-relations.com/CM6-2WB/GlobalChinaWB.htm
Stanford Journal of International Relations
    www.stanford.edu/group/sjir/6.1.03_miller.html
wikipedia.org
    http://en.wikipedia.org/wiki/Foreign_Intelligence_Surveillance_Act

KENNETH S. BAER, a former senior speechwriter for Vice President Al Gore, is co-editor of *Democracy: A Journal of Ideas.*

Baer, Kenneth S. From *The Washington Post*, July 13, 2008. Copyright © 2008 by Kenneth S. Baer. Reprinted by permission of the author.

Article

Soft Power
Reagan the Dove

Vladislav M. Zubok

Learning Outcomes

After reading this article, you will be able to:

- Describe Ronald Reagan's contribution toward world peace.
- Discuss the effects of the presence of the SDI on United States security.

Death, not surprisingly, has secured Ronald Reagan's place in history. In recent days, policy veterans, journalists, and scholars have placed him among the top ranks of twentieth-century presidents. In a *New York Times* op-ed written shortly after Reagan's death, Mikhail Gorbachev, the former Soviet leader, acknowledged Reagan's role in bringing about the end of the cold war. Reagan's conservative admirers go even further. They proclaim him the architect of "victory" against the USSR, citing his support of the anti-communist mujahedin in Afghanistan, of the anti-Soviet Solidarity movement in Poland, and, above all, his Strategic Defense Initiative (SDI). Former White House Chief of Staff Donald Regan told CNN seven years ago that Gorbachev's failure to convince President Reagan to give up SDI at the Reykjavik summit in 1986 meant it was "all over for the Soviet Union." A memorial plaque in the court of the Ronald Reagan Presidential Library in Simi Valley, California, flatly states that Reagan's SDI brought down Soviet communism.

Newly released Soviet documents reveal that Reagan indeed played a role in ending the cold war. Yet, it was not so much because of SDI or the support of anti-Soviet forces around the world. Rather, it was the sudden emergence of another Reagan, a peacemaker and supporter of nuclear disarmament—whom conservatives opposed—that rapidly produced a new U.S.–Soviet détente. This détente facilitated Gorbachev's radical overhaul of Soviet domestic and foreign policy—changes that brought the USSR crashing down and that would have been impossible had Reagan remained the hawk conservatives now celebrate.

In retrospect, it's hard to see SDI as anything but a bit player in the final act of the cold war. In 1983, the year Reagan announced the program to stop Soviet missiles in space (immediately dubbed "star wars"), the Soviet leadership convened a panel of prominent scientists to assess whether SDI posed a long-term security threat. The panel's report remains classified, but various leaks point to the main finding (one that mirrored the assessment of independent U.S. scientists): In the next decade or even beyond, SDI would not work. The rumor circulating in politburo circles was that "two containers of nails hurled into space" would be enough to confuse and overwhelm U.S. anti-missile defenses. In a compromise decision between Kremlin leaders and military commanders reached by 1985, a number of R&D labs received limited funds to look into possible countermeasures to SDI. The budget of the Soviet "anti-SDI" program, a fraction of the huge allocations to the Soviet military-industrial complex, remained at the same modest level through the rest of the '80s.

Gorbachev feared SDI less for the military threat it posed to the USSR than for the practical threat it posed to his political agenda. The young general secretary belonged to a generation shaped by the denunciations of Stalinist crimes, the cultural liberalization of the 1960s, and East-West détente; this generation wanted to reform the Soviet Union and end the confrontation with the United States. But the reformists remained a minority and operated in a milieu of anti-American paranoia. As a result, Gorbachev was frustrated by the Reagan administration's hawkish actions—such as increased military assistance to Afghanistan, provocative naval exercises near Soviet coasts, and the CIA's unrelenting "spy war" against the KGB.

The Soviets interpreted SDI as an outgrowth of this renewed American aggressiveness, which made it harder for Gorbachev to push his reforms. As Boris Ponomarev, a Communist apparatchik, grumbled in early 1986, "Let the Americans change their thinking instead. . . . Are you against military strength, which is the only language that imperialism understands?" Gorbachev admitted in his memoirs that he was initially too cautious to resist this pressure. At the politburo, he adopted hard-line language, describing the American president as a "troglodyte" in November 1985.

Still, the early interactions between Gorbachev and Reagan revealed that there might be enough common ground between the two leaders to allow Gorbachev to press ahead: As it happened, both men were closet nuclear abolitionists. For all his outward toughness, Reagan connected nuclear threats to the prophecy of Armageddon and, under the influence of his wife, Nancy, who saw ending the cold war as an opportunity to save the president's legacy from the taint of Iran-Contra, wanted to be remembered as a peacemaker. Gorbachev, likewise, saw eliminating the danger of nuclear confrontation between the superpowers as his top priority. When Gorbachev participated in a strategic game simulating the Soviet response to a nuclear attack shortly after coming to power, he allegedly refused to press the nuclear button "even for training purposes."

Though the continuing U.S.–Soviet confrontation obscured the common anti-nuclear agenda for much of the '80s, the shared goal surfaced suddenly in a dramatic exchange at the Reykjavik summit in October 1986. Gorbachev proposed eliminating all ballistic missiles. When Reagan demurred, Gorbachev raised the ante. Both leaders then began proposing that more and more categories of weapons be abolished until they had agreed upon total disarmament. But Gorbachev refused to cut anything if SDI remained, prompting the frustrated Reagan to interject: "What the hell use will anti-ballistic missiles or anything else be if we eliminate nuclear weapons?" The Soviet leader held firm, at which point the summit collapsed and Reagan returned home feeling angry and cheated.

Though conservatives lauded Reagan for courageously avoiding what they saw as a Soviet trap, administration insiders were furious at the president for even broaching the idea of a nuclear-free world. They were right to be concerned. By the end of 1987, Reagan had begun to distance himself from the extreme hawks who opposed any negotiations (the most prominent of them, Secretary of Defense Caspar Weinberger, left the administration in 1987) and was relying increasingly on the pragmatic advice of Secretary of State George Shultz. In December 1987, the president and Gorbachev met in Washington to sign a treaty eliminating intermediate-range missiles. And, by June 1988, Reagan was kissing Russian babies in Red Square and had nonchalantly dropped the "evil empire" label he had affixed to the Soviet Union in 1983.

For his part, Gorbachev used the increasingly warm encounters with Reagan as capital for domestic reforms. Soviet journalists, as well as the entire international media, covered the summits, transforming Gorbachev into a TV star. Back home, millions of Soviets felt proud of their leader for the first time in years. Reykjavik, in particular, increased Gorbachev's domestic standing; the Soviet audience appreciated his tough talk with Reagan, but not as much as his "struggle for peace." This enhanced stature allowed Gorbachev to make a series of crucial changes in the aftermath of various U.S.–Soviet summits: the release of the Nobel Laureate and political prisoner Andrei Sakharov in December 1986 and the introduction of glasnost came on the heels of Reykjavik; the withdrawal of troops from Afghanistan in January 1988 came just after the Washington summit the previous December; the liberalization of the communist political system began with the announcement of parliamentary elections during the summer of 1988, just after Reagan's visit to Moscow.

It was perhaps inevitable that some of Reagan's former advisers would begin to rewrite his legacy using their hard-line script. Back in the '80s, however, this script produced nothing but new cold war crises, an accelerated arms race, and a huge budget deficit. With the notable exception of the support of Polish Solidarity, U.S. measures to "bleed" the Soviet Union only bred mutual fears of war. The most notorious symbol of U.S. "victory" in the cold war, SDI, still remains an unfulfilled promise 20 years later.

It is not clear how much vision regarding the end of Soviet communism Ronald Reagan had. What Reagan certainly had in abundance was luck and instinct. He was lucky that a new reformist leadership came to power in Moscow looking for a partner to end the cold war. He sensed a historic opportunity in his relationship with Gorbachev and finally seized on it. It was Reagan the peacemaker, not the cold warrior, who made the greatest contribution to history. One only wishes more Americans were aware of this paradox as they pay homage to their fortieth president.

Critical Thinking

1. Do you agree that Reagan himself played a larger role than the SDI in ending the cold war?
2. What did Reagan and Gorbachev have in common? How did this affect their agreeing to the 1987 treaty?

Create Central

www.mhhe.com/createcentral

Internet References

U.S. Department of State
http://history.state.gov/milestones/1981-1989/SDI
http://history.state.gov/milestones/1981-1989/INF
nytimes.com
http://learning.blogs.nytimes.com/2012/03/23/march-23-1983-reagan-proposes-star-wars-missile-defense-system
coldwar.org
www.coldwar.org/articles/80s/SDI-StarWars.asp
BBC
http://news.bbc.co.uk/onthisday/hi/dates/stories/december/8/newsid_3283000/3283817.stm

---

VLADISLAV M. ZUBOK, a professor of history at Temple University, is the author of the forthcoming book *The Enemy That Went Home* (University of North Carolina Press).

Zubok, Vladislav M. From *The New Republic*, June 21, 2004, pp. 11–12. Copyright © 2004 by TNR II, LLC. Reprinted by permission of the New Republic.

Article

The Tragedy of Bill Clinton

GARRY WILLS

Learning Outcomes

After reading this article, you will be able to:

- Describe Bill Clinton's background and the way it impacted his controversial decisions.

- Discuss the ways in which Clinton's personal controversies overshadowed his political success.

So far, most readers of President Clinton's book seem to like the opening pages best, and no wonder. Scenes of childhood glow from many memoirs—by Jean-Jacques Rousseau, Henry Adams, John Ruskin, John Henry Newman, and others. It is hard to dislike people when they are still vulnerable, before they have put on the armor of whatever career or catastrophe lies before them as adults. In fact, Gilbert Chesterton advised those who would love their enemies to imagine them as children. The soundness of this tactic is proved by its reverse, when people become irate at attempts to imagine the childhood or the youth of Hitler—as in protests at the Menna Meyjez film *Max*. So it is hard, even for his foes, to find Clinton objectionable as a child. Yet the roots of the trouble he later had lie there, in the very appeal of his youth.

Another reason we respond to narratives of childhood is that first sensations are widely shared by everyone—the ways we became aware of the world around us, of family, of school, of early friends. One might expect Clinton's pineywood world to be remote from people who did not grow up in the South. But since he experienced neither grinding poverty nor notable privilege, there is an everyman quality to what he is writing about. His relatives were not blue-collar laborers but service providers—as nurse (mother and grandmother), heavy equipment salesman (father), car dealer (first stepfather), hairdresser (second stepfather), food broker (third stepfather). This was no Dogpatch, as one can tell from the number of Clinton's childhood friends who went on to distinguished careers. (The daughters of one of his ministers became, respectively, the president of Wellesley and the ombudsman of *The Washington Post*.)

Admittedly, Clinton's family was notably fissiparous, with a litter of half-relatives filling the landscape—but even that is familiar to us in this time of frequent divorce and divided custodies. It may seem out of the ordinary for Clinton's father to have been married four times by the age of twenty-six, his first stepfather to have been married three times (twice to Clinton's mother), his second stepfather to have been married twice (with twenty-nine months in jail for fraud bridging the two). His mother, because of the mortality rate of her husbands, was married five times (though two of the times were to the same man). Clinton, who has had the gift of empathy throughout his life, remained astonishingly close to all the smashed elements of this marital kaleidoscope—even to his stepfather, whose abuse of his mother Clinton had to stop with physical interventions and calls to the police. He took time from college to give his stepfather loving care at the end of his life. The most recurrent refrain in this book is "I liked him," and it began at home.

Clinton usually looked at the bright side. What the jumble of marriages gave him as a boy was just more relatives to charm and be cosseted by. Later the same people would be a political asset. The first time he ran for office, "I had relatives in five of the district's twenty-one counties." Later still, he could rely on "a big vote in south Arkansas, where I had lots of relatives." One might think he was already preparing for a political career when he got along so well with all his scattered families. But he was, even then, a natural charmer, with an immediate gratification in being liked, not looking (yet) for remoter returns from politics. Clinton won others' affection for a reason Aristotle famously gave—we enjoy doing things that we do well.[1]

Clinton claims that his sunny adaptability as a child was a front, that he lived a secret "parallel life" imposed on a "fat band boy" by his father's violence and alcoholism. He is preparing his explanation of the Monica Lewinsky affair as a product of this secret life. It is true that we all have a public self and several private ones. It is also true that childhood and adolescence prompt dark or lonely moments in most people. But the India-rubber-man resiliency of Clinton makes it hard to believe his explanation-excuse for later aberrations. "Slick Willie," the nickname he says he dislikes most, was always an unlikely brooder. The thing that would impress others about Clinton's later philandering, which long preceded the Monica stuff, was its lack of secrecy, its flamboyant risk-taking.

His attempt at a Dickensian shoe-black-factory childhood is therefore unconvincing. One of the afflictions he says he had to bear in silence was going to church in shoes his mother bought him; "pink and black Hush Puppies, and a matching pink suede belt." But since he shared his mother's idolatry of Elvis, his S-C (sartorially correct) attitude is probably retrospective. In fact, the "fat band boy" was very popular, with a wide circle of friends who stayed true to him (and he to them) ever after. His ability to enthrall others would become legendary, and one of the pleasures of his book is watching him get around obstacles by force of personality and cleverness:

—As a Yale law student organizing New Haven for the nascent McGovern campaign, Clinton goes to the city's Democratic boss, Arthur Barbieri, who tells him he has the money and organization to crush the McGovern insurgency:

> I replied that I didn't have much money, but I did have eight hundred volunteers who would knock on the doors of every house in his stronghold, telling all the Italian mothers that Arthur Barbieri wanted to keep sending their sons to fight and die in Vietnam. "You don't need that grief," I said. "Why do you care who wins the nomination? Endorse McGovern. He was a war hero in World War II. He can make peace and you can keep control of New Haven."

Barbieri is struck by this law student—he and Matty Troy of New York are the only old-line bosses to endorse McGovern in the primary.

—Wanting to take Hillary Rodham to a special exhibit in the Yale art gallery for their first date, he finds the gallery locked, but talks his way in by telling the custodian that he will clean up the litter in the gallery courtyard if he lets them go through the exhibit.

—Fresh from law school, Clinton hears his application for a teaching job is turned down by the dean of the University of Arkansas Law School because he is too young and inexperienced, and he says those qualities are actually a recommendation:

> I'd be good for him, because I'd work hard and teach any courses he wanted. Besides, I wouldn't have tenure, so he could fire me at any time. He chuckled and invited me to Fayetteville for an interview.

He gets the job.

—After doing the whole Lamaze course to assist his wife when their first child is born; he learns that she must have a Caesarean section because the baby is "in breech." No one is allowed in the operating room during surgery. He pleads that Hillary has never been in a hospital before and she needs him. He is allowed to hold her hand during the delivery. Can no one say no to this man?

Persuasiveness on Clinton's scale can be a temptation. The ability to retrieve good will can make a person careless about taking vulnerable steps. Indeed, a certain type will fling himself over a cliff just to prove he can always catch a branch and crawl back up to the top. There is nothing, he begins to feel, for which he cannot win forgiveness. This kind of recklessness followed by self-retrieval is what led Clinton to think of himself as "the comeback kid" (the use of the word "kid" is probably more indicative than he intended). Famous charmers are fun to be around, but they are not people to depend on.

Washington

David Broder at his sniffiest declared that Clinton was a social usurper in Washington: "He came in here and he trashed the place, and it's not his place."[2] Clinton was simply "not one of us." But unlike Broder he had gone to school there. From the time he saw Washington as a high school member of Boys Nation and shook President Kennedy's hand, Clinton wanted to get back there. His college placement counselor, Edith Irons, told me she urged him to apply to several colleges, not just one. But he filled out forms only for Georgetown—not because it was a Jesuit school, or a good school. Because it was in Washington. And so ingratiating was this Southern Baptist in a cosmopolitan Catholic school that he quickly became class president as a freshman and sophomore. He did not run for the office in his third year because by then he was an intern in Arkansas senator William Fulbright's office. He had to be given security clearance because he ran classified documents from place to place on Capitol Hill. Already he was a Washington insider.

Some of the freshest pages in the book register Clinton's impressions of the senators he observed. These were models against which he was measuring his future career, and the images were printed deep in him. He saw Carl Hayden of Arizona, whom a friend called "the only ninety-year-old man in the world who looks twice his age." The senior senator from his own state, John McClellan, had sorrows "drowned in enough whiskey to float the Capitol down the Potomac River." Clinton was especially interested in Senator Robert Kennedy, brother to his own fallen hero:

> He radiated raw energy. He's the only man I ever saw who could walk stoop-shouldered, with his head down, and still look like a coiled spring about to release into the air. He wasn't a great speaker by conventional standards, but he spoke with such intensity and passion it could be mesmerizing. And if he didn't get everyone's attention with his name, countenance, and speech, he had Brumus, a large, shaggy Newfoundland, the biggest dog I ever saw. Brumus often came to work with Senator Kennedy. When Bobby walked from his office in the New Senate Building to the Capitol to vote, Brumus would walk by his side, bounding up the Capitol steps to the revolving door on the rotunda level, then sitting patiently outside until his master returned for the walk back. Anyone who could command the respect of that dog had mine too.

One of Clinton's housemates at Georgetown worked in Robert Kennedy's office, and another was in Henry "Scoop" Jackson's office. A Georgetown girl he was dating hated Kennedy because she was working for his rival, Eugene McCarthy, whose lassitude Clinton compared unfavorably with Kennedy's energy. He especially admired his own boss, Senator Fulbright:

> I'll never forget one night in 1967 or '68. I was walking alone in Georgetown when I saw the Senator and Mrs. Fulbright leaving one of the fashionable homes after a dinner party. When they reached the street, apparently with no one around to see, he took her in his arms and danced a few steps. Standing in the shadows, I saw what a light she was in his life.

Oxford

Clinton not only worked for Fulbright in Washington but drove him around Arkansas. He sincerely admired his opposition to the Vietnam War—among other things it gave him an excuse for avoiding the war. The flap over Clinton's "draft dodging" looks quaint in retrospect. He first tried to do what George W. Bush did, join the National Guard, but he did not have the contacts to be accepted. The differences are that he, unlike Bush, did not support the war, and he is honest in saying that he was trying to avoid combat. He was in his first term as a Rhodes Scholar at Oxford, and a friend and housemate of his (Frank Aller) was defying the draft as a conscientious objector. Aller said Clinton should risk the draft in order to have a political career, though he could not do that himself.

A man much admired by his Oxford contemporaries but tortured by his scruples, Aller later committed suicide. Robert McNamara, who came to know of Aller's anguish, wrote Clinton when he was elected president:

> By their votes, the American people, at long last, recognized that the Allers and the Clintons, when they questioned the wisdom and morality of their government's decisions relating to Vietnam, were no less patriotic than those who served in uniform.

After Clinton failed to get into the National Guard, his uncle tried to get him into a navy program (which would involve less danger, and a delay in enlistment). Clinton's third try was as an ROTC law student at the University of Arkansas in Fayetteville, which would have given him three to four years' delay in actual service—but would have kept him from continuing at Oxford. Only when he drew a low number in the draft did he take his chances on staying in England rather than going to Fayetteville. The famous letter he wrote to explain why he was not going to show up for the ROTC spot was a typical act of ingratiation with the man who had admitted him into the program, Colonel Eugene Holmes. He said that he would "accept" the draft (he did not say he had been given a low number) only "to maintain my political viability within the [political] system." The ingratiation worked, at first. Colonel Holmes, when asked about Clinton's relations with ROTC, said for years that there was nothing abnormal about them. Only in the 1992 campaign did he write a letter denouncing Clinton as a draft dodger. Clinton suggests that Holmes may have had "help" with his memory from his daughter, a Republican activist in the Arkansas Bush campaign. Clinton's best biographer, David Maraniss, goes much further, and says that national officials of the Bush campaign "reviewed the letter before it was made public."[3]

Clinton's time in Oxford led to many silly charges against him. He was said to have been a protester in Arkansas, at a time when he was in England—an accusation that came up in his campaigns for state office. Much was made of his confession that he tried marijuana but "did not inhale." *Could* not inhale would have been more truthful—his allergies had kept him from smoking any kind of cigarette, and

the respected British journalist Martin Walker, who was with Clinton at the time, confirmed that he and others tried to teach Clinton to inhale, but he could not—he would end up "leaning his head out an open window gasping for fresh air." The problem with a reputation for being "slick" is that even the simple truth can look like a ploy.

Clinton's asthma and allergies stood in his way during his first political campaign, but charm overcame the problem when two local figures he wanted to campaign for him in Arkansas took him out from town in a truck, pulled out a pack of Red Man chewing tobacco, and said, "If you're man enough to chew this tobacco, we'll be for you. If not, we'll kick you out and let you walk back to town." Clinton hesitated a moment, then said: "Open the damn door." The two men laughed and became his campaigners for many years.

A more serious charge arising from his two years at Oxford came from his trip to Russia, which would later be called treasonous—a charge that the senior Bush's campaign tried to verify by breaking its own rules on passport and embassy reports. Clinton's interest in Russia came from the fact that his housemate and fellow Rhodes Scholar, Strobe Talbot, was already such an expert on the Russian language and history that he was translating the memoirs of Khrushchev, smuggled out to him by Jerry Schecter, the Moscow correspondent for *Time*. Clinton learned more about America than about either England or Russia during his time at Oxford, where his fellow Rhodes Scholars talked endlessly about their country and the war. Clinton gave up a third year and a degree in England to get back to the Yale Law School and antiwar activities, first in Joseph Duffey's failed Connecticut campaign for senator and then in McGovern's campaign for the presidency. In the latter cause, he had an ally in Hillary Rodham.

Yale

Clinton refers to various women he dated or traveled with in Europe, and he drops some indirect references to his reputation as a ladies' man—as inoculation, I suppose. He says he "had lived a far from perfect life," and carried "more baggage than an ocean liner." "The lies hurt, and the occasional truth hurt more." He even admits that when he proposed to Hillary, "nothing in my background indicated I knew what a stable marriage was all about." With women before Hillary, he was the one not seeking a commitment; but he pursued Hillary relentlessly. As law students, after they began living together, they traveled to Europe and the American West. He first proposed to her in England's Lake Country, but she said no. When she spent the summer of 1968 as an intern for a law firm in Oakland, California, he turned down an offer to organize the McGovern campaign in Miami and went with her to California for the whole summer. He was afraid he would lose her. What their marriage proves is that even a lecherous man can have the one great love affair of his life.

Lechery

In this book Clinton misleads not by equivocation but by omission. He gives a long account of his decision not to run for president in July of 1988—how he summoned friends with wide experience to Little Rock and weighed all the options. He admits that Gary Hart had withdrawn from the race two months earlier, and that "after the Hart affair, those of us who had not led perfect lives had no way of knowing what the press's standards of disclosure were." Clinton had to be paying close attention to the Hart campaign that year. He had worked closely with Hart on the McGovern team—in fact, Hart had rebuked him for paying too much attention to his "girl friend" (Hillary) during the campaign.[4] What Clinton leaves out of the account of his decision in 1988 is the brutal candor of the advice given him by his longtime aide, Betsey Wright. According to David Maraniss,

> Wright met with Clinton at her home on Hill Street. The time had come, she felt, for Clinton to get past what she considered his self-denial tendencies and face the issue squarely. For years, she told friends later, she had been covering up for him. She was convinced that some state troopers were soliciting women for him, and he for them, she said. Sometimes when Clinton was on the road, Wright would call his room in the middle of the night and no one would answer. She hated that part of him, but felt that the other sides of him overshadowed his personal weaknesses.

> . . . She started listing the names of women he had allegedly had affairs with and the places where they were said to have occurred. "Now," she concluded, "I want you to tell me the truth about every one." She went over the list twice with Clinton, according to her later account, the second time trying to determine whether any of the women might tell their stories to the press. At the end of the process, she suggested that he should not get into the race. He owed it to Hillary and Chelsea not to.[5]

No one who has seen Clinton with his daughter can doubt that he loves her deeply, and he does say that concern for her kept him out of the 1988 race, when she was eight years old. "Carl Wagner, who was also the father of an only daughter, told me I'd have to reconcile myself to being away from Chelsea for most of the next sixteen months." The same problem would arise, of course, four years later, when Chelsea would be twelve—yet he would run then. Wagner's advice is given a much different sense in his account to Maraniss. Wagner, who was a friend of Betsey Wright and had been given a job by her when he arrived in Little Rock, knew about her concerns, and shared them. After the conference with advisers, he stayed while the others left, to tell Clinton:

> When you reach the top of the steps, walk into your daughter's bedroom, look at her, and understand that if you do this, your relationship with her will never be the same. I'm not sure if it will be worse or better, but it will never be the same."[6]

Wagner was not worried about Clinton's absence from Chelsea, but about the presence of shadowy women in her young mind.

When Clinton ran in 1992, he admits that he anticipated trouble. A man in George H. W. Bush's White House, Roger Porter—with whom Clinton had worked on the President's "education initiative"—called him to say that "if I ran, they would have to destroy me personally."

> He went on to say the press were elitists who would believe any tales they were told about backwater Arkansas. "We'll spend whatever we have to spend to get whoever we have to get to say whatever they have to say to take you out. And we'll do it early."

Of course, this is Clinton's version of the phone call; it has the ring of a Lee Atwater campaign, although it can even be interpreted as kindly meant. Clinton was being forewarned that he could not expect to get a free pass on his background. Clinton presents his decision to run despite this warning as a brave refusal to be blackmailed: "Ever since I was a little boy I have hated to be threatened."

On Gennifer Flowers, Clinton did resort to equivocation. In the famous post–Super Bowl interview on *60 Minutes,* Steve Kroft asked about "what she calls a twelve-year affair with you." Clinton said, "That allegation is false" (referring to the twelve-year aspect). So, said Kroft, "you're categorically denying that you ever had an affair with Gennifer Flowers?" Clinton answered, "I've said that before, and so has she." Both answers were technically correct, though six years later he would admit that they were "misleading"—he did have an affair. Most people forget that Clinton's trouble with women taping their phone calls did not begin with Monica Lewinsky. In 1992 Flowers was taping him, at a time when she was publicly denying claims of their affair. When he called her after defeating Sheffield Nelson for governor, Clinton mocked Nelson for denying that he had charged Clinton with infidelity: "I knew he lied. I just wanted to make his asshole pucker. But I covered you," Clinton said on a tape that became public.[7]

The Lewinskiad

Clinton claims that he does not offer excuses for his past life in this book. But he now says that he lied because he was confused, fatigued, and angry at being surrounded by bloodhound prosecutors, a hostile Congress, and a barking press: "And if there had been no Kenneth Starr—if we had different kind of people, I would have just said, 'Here are the facts. I'm sorry. Deal with it however you please.'" Here all the contrived contrition is forgotten—it was Ken Starr who made him lie. But what was he lying about? For that he has another excuse, his "parallel life" in which he kept embarrassing things secret. Well, we all do that. But why did he do the reckless things with Lewinsky that he had to keep secret? With both Dan Rather and Charlie Rose he said: "I think I did something for the worst possible reason, just because I could. I think that's the most—just about the most morally indefensible reason that anybody could have for doing anything, when you do something just because you could." Here he is applying to himself what Newt Gingrich said to him when Clinton asked why the Republicans shut down the government in 1995. The answer:

"Because we could." Later Clinton says the prosecutors hunted him "because they could."

As applied to him, the answer is nonsense. First of all, he *couldn't* do it, if that meant doing it with impunity—as he found out. Moreover, that is not the worst possible reason for doing anything. There are far worse reasons—hatred, revenge, religious fanaticism, sadism. He avoids saying that he did it because he wanted to, but that is the only honest answer. He did it from lechery. And the absurdity of it, the risk, just spiced the matter with danger. He was not withdrawing into a secret self but throwing himself outward in flamboyant bravado. Clinton, like his mother, is a gambler. He does not, as she did, play the ponies. He dares the lightning. He knew he had numerous hunters and trackers circling him about. He knew that he already had to cope with Gennifer Flowers, Paula Jones, and Kathleen Willey. The young woman he was adding to the list was not likely to be discreet—she boasted of earning her presidential kneepads, and wangled thirty-seven entrances to the White House, and snapped her thong, and preserved the candied semen. (DNA technology is still a comparatively young discipline, but it is not likely for some time to get a stranger exercise than testing the effluvia of presidential fellation.)

Flirting with ever greater peril, he repeatedly telephoned Lewinsky. He sent her presents (*Leaves of Grass* as Seducer's Assistant). He wore her present. He lied in risky forums. He put in jeopardy political efforts he cared about, as well as the respect and love of his wife and daughter. It was such a crazy thing to do that many of us could not, for a long time, believe he had done it. But Betsey Wright, from her long experience of the man, knew at once: "I was miserably furious with him, and completely unable to communicate with him from the time the Lewinsky stuff was unfolded on the national scene. This was a guy I had given thirteen years of my life to."[8]

Starr

Though Clinton's conduct was inexcusable, it does pale next to the deep and vast abuses of power that Kenneth Starr sponsored and protected. He is a deceptively sweet-looking fellow, a dimpled, flutily warbling Pillsbury Doughboy. But he lent himself to the schemes of people with an almost total disregard for the law. A man of honor would not have accepted his appointment by a right-wing judge to replace Robert Fiske, a Republican general counsel who was a distinguished prosecutor. Not only did Starr have no prosecutorial experience; he had already lent support to Paula Jones's suit against the President. He continued private practice for right-wing causes with right-wing funding. Five former presidents of the American Bar Association said that he had conflicts of interest for which he should recuse himself. At one point in his investigation, a *New York Times* editorial said he should resign. His own chosen ethics adviser, Sam Dash, left him in protest at his tactics. The American Civil Liberties Union had to bring an end to the "barbaric" conditions he imposed on the imprisoned Susan McDougal.[9]

Starr raised again the suspicion that Vince Foster was murdered, after his predecessor had disposed of that claim. This was a favorite cause of the man funding much of the right-wing

pursuit of Clinton, Richard Mellon Scaife, who is a principal donor to Pepperdine College, where Starr now holds a chair. The list of Starr's offenses is long and dark. Congressman Barney Frank questioned him about the fact that he released his damning "sex report" on Clinton before the 1998 elections though he held findings that cleared Clinton of other charges—findings reached months earlier—until after the election. After Starr made several attempts at evading the question, Frank said, "In other words, you don't have anything to say [before an election] unless you have something bad to say."[10]

Starr prolonged his investigations as charge after charge was lengthily discredited, until the right-wing Rutherford Institute's lawyers, representing Paula Jones, could trap Clinton in a confession of his contacts with Monica Lewinsky, to which Starr then devoted his frenzied attention. The wonder is that Starr got away with all his offenses. For that he needed a complicit press, which disgraced itself in this period, gobbling up the illegal leaks that flowed from his office. The sniffy Washingtonians went so berserk over the fact that Clinton was Not One of Us that they bestowed on Starr an honorary Oneness with Usness. Sally Quinn wrote in *The Washington Post* that "Beltway Insiders" were humiliated by Clinton, and that "Starr is a Washington insider, too."[11]

Starr was one thing that made some people stay with Clinton, who says Starr's unfairness helped bring Hillary back to his side. Paul Begala admitted he was disgusted by what Clinton had done, but determined that he would not let Starr accomplish a "coup d'état." That does not describe what a Starr success would have meant. Conviction on impeachment charges would not have brought in a Republican administration. Succession would have gone to Vice President Al Gore in Clinton's own administration. But Clinton agrees with Begala. He presents his fight with Starr as a defense of all the things the right wing disliked about him—his championship of blacks, and gays, and the poor. He works himself up to such a righteous pitch that he says his impeachment trial was a "badge of honor."

Honor

Actually, the honorable thing for Clinton would have been to resign. I argued for that in a *Time* magazine article as soon as he revealed that he had lied to the nation.[12] I knew, of course, that he wouldn't. He had thrown himself off the highest cliff ever, and he had to prove he could catch a last-minute branch and pull himself, improbably, back up. And damned if he didn't. He ended his time as president with high poll numbers and some new accomplishments, the greatest of the Kid's comebacks—so great that I have been asked if I still feel he should have resigned. Well, I do. Why? Partly because what Ross Perot said in 1996 was partly true—that Clinton would be "totally occupied for the next two years in staying out of jail." That meant he would probably go on lying. He tried for as long as possible to "mislead" the nation on Gennifer Flowers. He still claims that Paula Jones and Kathleen Willey made false charges. Perhaps they did, but he became unbelievable about personal behavior after lying about Flowers and Lewinsky. I at first disbelieved the story Paula Jones told because it seemed too bizarre; but the cigar-dildo described by Monica Lewinsky considerably extended the vistas of the bizarre.

Though Clinton accomplished things in his second term, he did so in a constant struggle to survive. Unlike the current president, his administration found in Sudan the presence of a weapon of mass destruction (the nerve gas precursor Empta) and bombed the place where it had existed—but many, including Senator Arlen Specter and the journalist Seymour Hersh, said that Clinton was just bombing another country to distract people from his scandal.[13] "That reaction," according to Richard Clarke, "made it more difficult to get approval for follow-up attacks on al Qaeda."[14] Even when Clinton was doing things, the appearance of his vulnerability made people doubt it. It was said in the Pentagon that he was afraid to seize terrorists because of his troubles; but Clarke rebuts those claims—he says that every proposal to seize a terrorist leader; whether it came from the CIA or the Pentagon, was approved by Clinton "during my tenure as CSG [Counterterrorism Security Group] chairman, from 1992 to 2001."

We shall never know what was not done, or not successfully done, because of Clinton's being politically crippled. He has been criticized for his insufficient response to the ethnic cleansing in Kosovo. Michael Walzer said of the bombing raids Clinton finally authorized that "our faith in airpower is . . . a kind of idolatry."[15] But Clinton was limited in what he could do by the fact that the House of Representatives passed a resolution exactly the opposite of the war authorization that would be given George W. Bush—it voted to deny the President the power to commit troops. Walzer says that Clinton should have prodded the UN to take action; but a Republican Congress was not going to follow a man it distrusted when he called on an institution it distrusted.

At the very end of Clinton's regime, did Arafat feel he was not strong enough in his own country to pressure him into the reasonable agreement Clinton had worked out and Ehud Barak had accepted? Clinton suggests as much when he says that Arafat called him a great man, and he had to reply: "I am not a great man. I am a failure, and you have made me one."

Clinton had a wise foreign policy. But in an Oval Office interview, shortly before he admitted lying to the nation, he admitted that he had not been able to make it clear to the American people. His vision had so little hold upon the public that Bush was able to discard it instantly when he came in. Clinton summed up the difference between his and Bush's approach for Charlie Rose by saying that the latter thinks we should "do what we want whenever we can, and then we cooperate when we have to," whereas his policy was that "we were cooperating whenever we could and we acted alone only when we had to." The Bush people are learning the difference between the two policies as their preemptive unilateralism fails.

Clinton claims that he was not hampered in his political activity by scandals. He even said, to Charlie Rose, that "I probably was more attentive to my work for several months just because I didn't want to tend to anything else." That is improbable a priori and it conflicts with what he told Dan Rather about

the atmosphere caused by the scandal: "The moment was so crazy. It was a zoo. It was an unr—it was—it was like living in a madhouse." Even if he were not distracted, the press and the nation were. His staff was demoralized. The Democrats on the Hill were defensive, doubtful, absorbed in either defending Clinton or deflecting criticism from themselves. His freedom to make policy was hobbled.

Clinton likes to talk now of his "legacy." That legacy should include partial responsibility for the disabling of the Democratic Party. There were things to be said against the Democratic Leadership Council (Mario Cuomo said them well) and the "triangulation" scheme of Dick Morris, by which Clinton would take positions to the right of most congressional Democrats and to the left of the Republican Party. But Clinton, as a Southerner, knew that the party had to expand its base back into sources of support eroded by the New Right. This was a defensible (in fact a shrewd) strategy as Clinton originally shaped it. He could have made it a tactical adjunct to important strategic goals. But after the scandals, all his maneuvering looked desperate—a swerving away from blows, a flurried scrambling to find solid footing. His very success made Democrats think their only path to success was to concede, cajole, and pander. Al Gore began his 2000 campaign unhappy about his association with Clinton but trying to outpander him when he opposed the return of the Cuban boy Elian Gonzalez to his father. There is a kind of rude justice to the fact that the election was stolen from Gore in the state where he truckled to the Cubans.

Clinton bequeathed to his party not a clear call to high goals but an omnidirectional proneness to pusillanimity and collapse. This was signaled at the very outset of the new presidency. The Democrats, still in control of the Senate, facing a president not even strong enough to win the popular vote, a man brought into office by linked chicaneries and chance (Kathleen Harris, Ralph Nader, Antonin Scalia), nonetheless helped to confirm John Ashcroft as attorney general. The senators knew Ashcroft well; they were surely not impressed by his acumen or wisdom.

A whole series of capitulations followed. While still holding a majority in the Senate, the Democrats did not use subpoenas and investigative powers to challenge Dick Cheney's secret drafting of energy policy with Enron and other companies. A portion of the Democrats would support the welfare-to-billionaires tax cut. They fairly stampeded to support the Patriot Act and the presidential war authorization—with John Kerry, John Edwards, and Hillary Clinton at the front of the pack. The party had become so neutered that Al From and others from the Democratic Leadership Council called Howard Dean an extremist for daring to say what everyone is now saying about the war with Iraq—that it was precipitate, overhyped, and underprepared, more likely to separate us from the friends needed to fight terrorists than to end terrorism.

What would have happened had Clinton resigned? Gore would have been given a "honeymoon" in which he could have played with a stronger hand all the initiatives Clinton had begun, unashamed of them and able to bring them fresh energy. That is what happened when

Lyndon Johnson succeeded John Kennedy. Clinton himself may have reaped a redeeming admiration for what he had sacrificed to recover his honor. Before him would have lain all the opportunities he has now, and more. Hillary Clinton's support of him in this act of real contrition would have looked nobler. Clinton's followers were claiming that it was all and only about sex. Clinton could have said, "Since that is what it is about, I'll step aside so more important things can be addressed." All the other phony issues Starr had raised would have fallen of their own insubstantiality.

Of course, this is just one of many what-ifs about the Clinton presidency. By chance I saw a revival of Leonard Bernstein's musical *Wonderful Town,* just before getting my copy of the Clinton book. All through the 957 pages of it, a song from the show kept running through my head: "What a waste! What a waste!"

Notes

1. Aristotle, *Nichomachean Ethics,* 1097–1098.
2. Sally Quinn, "Not in Their Backyard: In Washington, That Let Down Feeling," *The Washington Post,* November 2, 1998.
3. David Maraniss, *First in His Class: A Biography of Bill Clinton* (Simon and Schuster, 1995), p. 205.
4. Garry Wills, "Lightning Rod," *The New York Review,* August 14, 2003.
5. Maraniss, *First in His Class,* pp. 440–441.
6. Maraniss, *First in His Class,* p. 441.
7. Maraniss, *First in His Class,* p. 457.
8. Interview in the Harry Thomason and Nicholas Perry film *The Hunting of the President* (Regent Entertainment, 2004).
9. The despicable treatment of Susan McDougal is movingly presented in *The Hunting of the President,* a film that has many trivializing touches (like intercut clips of old Hollywood melodramas). McDougal's story is backed up by a very impressive woman, Claudia Riley, the wife of Bob Riley, the former Arkansas governor and college president, who stayed with McDougal through her ordeal and describes the bullying tactics she witnessed.
10. Sidney Blumenthal, *The Clinton Wars* (Farrar, Straus and Giroux, 2003), p. 512.
11. Quinn, "Not in Their Backyard: In Washington, That Let Down Feeling."
12. Garry Wills, "Leading by Leaving," *Time,* August 31, 1998.
13. See the important work by two former National Security Council antiterrorist directors, Daniel Benjamin and Steven Simon, *The Age of Sacred Terror: Radical Islam's War Against America* (Random House, 2002), pp. 352–360. See also Richard Clarke, *Against All Enemies: Inside America's War on Terror* (Free Press, 2004), pp. 146–147.
14. Clarke, *Against All Enemies,* p. 189.
15. Michael Walzer, *Arguing About War* (Yale University Press, 2004), p. 99.

Critical Thinking

1. Is Bill Clinton partially responsible for damaging the Democratic Party? Why or why not?
2. Do you think Clinton should have resigned? Why or why not?

Create Central

www.mhhe.com/createcentral

Internet References

Millercenter.org
http://millercenter.org/president/clinton/essays/biography/9
Huffington Post Blog
www.huffingtonpost.com/robert-scheer/bill-clintons-legacy-of-d_b_881916.html
PBS.org
www.pbs.org/wgbh/americanexperience/features/biography/clinton-bill

Article

The Rove Presidency

Karl Rove had the plan, the power, and the historic chance to remake American politics. What went wrong?

JOSHUA GREEN

Learning Outcomes

After reading this article, you will be able to:

- Identify Karl Rove's key strategies and objectives during the Bush administration.
- Understand how 9/11 became a turning point for the Bush administration.
- Discuss the political relationship between George W. Bush and Karl Rove.

The Early Birds

At dawn they start again, the early birds, as if they'd left some bitter things unsaid the day before. The sharp notes rise in thirds. I wake up knowing that I'll soon be dead, and that's no worse than justice, as is just. The kindest words are almost never meant. Most fond endearments fill us with disgust. To lie is sometimes all too eloquent; but, as I stumble toward that unknown date, even the lies may be inadequate.

—William Logan

William Logan's most recent book of essays and reviews, *The Undiscovered Country,* received the 2005 National Book Critics Circle Award in Criticism. His most recent book of poetry is *The Whispering Gallery* (2005).

With more than a year left in the fading Bush presidency, Karl Rove's worst days in the White House may still lie ahead of him. I met Rove on one of his best days, a week after Bush's reelection. The occasion was a reporters' lunch hosted by *The Christian Science Monitor* at the St. Regis Hotel in Washington, a customary stop for the winning and losing campaign teams to offer battle assessments and answer questions.

Kerry's team had glumly passed through a few days earlier. Afterward his chief strategist, Bob Shrum, boarded a plane and left the country. Rove had endured a heart-stopping Election Day (early exit polls indicated a Kerry landslide) but had prevailed, and plainly wasn't hurrying off anywhere. "The Architect," as Bush had just dubbed him, had spent the week collecting praise and had now arrived—vindicated, secure of his place in history—to hold court before the political press corps.

When Rove entered the room, everyone stood up to congratulate him and shake his hand. Washington journalism has become a kind of Cult of the Consultant, so the energy in the room was a lot like it might have been if Mickey Mantle had come striding into the clubhouse after knocking in the game-winning run in the World Series. Rove was pumped.

Before taking questions, he removed a folded piece of paper from his pocket and rattled off a series of numbers that made clear how he wanted the election to be seen: not as a squeaker but a rout. "This was an extraordinary election," Rove said. "[Bush won] 59.7 million votes, and we still have about 250,000 ballots to count. Think about that—*nearly 60 million votes!*

The previous largest number was Ronald Reagan in 1984, sweeping the country with 49 states. We won 81 percent of all the counties in America. We gained a percentage of the vote in 87 percent of the counties in America. In Florida, we received nearly a million votes more in this election than in the last one." Rove was officially there to talk about the campaign, but it was clear he had something much bigger in mind. So no one missed his point, he invoked Franklin Roosevelt's supremacy in the 1930s and suggested that something similar was at hand: "We've laid out an agenda, we've laid out a vision, and now people want to see results."

One of the goals of any ambitious president is to create a governing coalition just as Roosevelt did, one that long outlasts your presidency. It's the biggest thing you can aim for, and only a few presidents have achieved it. As the person with the long-term vision in the Bush administration, and with no lack of ambition either, Rove had thought long and hard about achieving this goal before ever arriving in the White House, and he has pursued it more aggressively than anyone else.

Rove has always cast himself not merely as a campaign manager but as someone with a mind for policy and for history's deeper currents—as someone, in other words, with the wherewithal not just to exploit the political landscape but to reshape it. At *The Christian Science Monitor* lunch, he appeared poised to do just that. It was already clear that Social Security privatization, a longtime Rove enthusiasm, was the first thing Bush would pursue in his second term. When things are going well for Rove, he adopts a towel-snapping jocularity. He looked supremely sure of his prospects for success.

But within a year the administration was crumbling. Social Security had gone nowhere. Hurricane Katrina, the worsening war in Iraq, and the disastrous nomination of Harriet Miers to the Supreme Court shattered the illusion of stern competence that had helped reelect Bush. What surprised everybody was how suddenly it happened; for a while, many devotees of the Cult of Rove seemed not to accept that it had. As recently as last fall, serious journalists were churning out soaring encomiums to Rove and his methods with titles like *One Party Country* and *The Way to Win.* In retrospect, everyone should have been focusing less on how those methods were used to win elections and more on why they couldn't deliver once the elections were over.

The story of why an ambitious Republican president working with a Republican Congress failed to achieve most of what he set out to do finds Rove at center stage. A big paradox of Bush's presidency is that Rove, who had maybe the best purely political mind in a generation and almost limitless opportunities to apply it from the very outset, managed to steer the administration toward disaster.

Years from now, when the major figures in the Bush administration publish their memoirs, historians may have a clearer idea of what went wrong than we do today. As an exercise in not waiting that long, I spent several months reading the early memoirs and talking to people inside and outside the administration (granting anonymity as necessary), in Congress, and in lobbying and political-consulting firms that dealt directly with Rove in the White House. (Rove declined requests for an interview.) The idea was to look at the Bush years and make a first pass at explaining the consequential figure in the vortex—to answer the question, How should history understand Karl Rove, and with him, this administration?

Fifty years ago, political scientists developed what is known as realignment theory—the idea that a handful of elections in the nation's history mattered more than the others because they created "sharp and durable" changes in the polity that lasted for decades. Roosevelt's election in 1932, which brought on the New Deal and three decades of Democratic dominance in Washington, is often held up as the classic example. Modern American historians generally see five elections as realigning: 1800, when Thomas Jefferson's victory all but finished off the Federalist Party and reoriented power from the North to the agrarian South; 1828, when Andrew Jackson's victory gave rise to the modern two-party system and two decades of Jacksonian influence; 1860, when Abraham Lincoln's election marked the ascendance of the Republican Party and of the secessionist impulse that led to the Civil War; 1896, when the effects of industrialization affirmed an increasingly urban political order that brought William McKinley to power; and Roosevelt's election in 1932, during the Great Depression.

Academics debate many aspects of this theory, such as whether realignment comes in regular cycles, and whether it is driven by voter intensity or disillusionment. But historians have shown that two major preconditions typically must be in place for realignment to occur. First, party loyalty must be sufficiently weak to allow for a major shift—the electorate, as the political scientist Paul Allen Beck has put it, must be "ripe for realignment." The other condition is that the nation must undergo some sort of triggering event, often what Beck calls a "societal trauma"—the ravaging depressions of the 1890s and 1930s, for instance, or the North–South conflict of the 1850s and '60s that ended in civil war. It's important to have both. Depressions and wars throughout American history have had no realigning consequence because the electorate wasn't primed for one, just as periods of electoral unrest have passed without a realignment for lack of a catalyzing event.

Before he ever came to the White House, Rove fervently believed that the country was on the verge of another great shift. His faith derived from his reading of the presidency of a man most historians regard as a mediocrity. Anyone on the campaign trail in 2000 probably heard him cite the pivotal importance of William McKinley's election in 1896. Rove thought there were important similarities.

"Everything you know about William McKinley and Mark Hanna"—McKinley's Rove—"is wrong," he told Nicholas Lemann of *The New Yorker* in early 2000. "The country was in a period of change. McKinley's the guy who figured it out. Politics were changing. The economy was changing. We're at the same point now: weak allegiances to parties, a rising new economy." Rove was suggesting that the electorate in 2000, as in 1896, was ripe for realignment, and implying, somewhat immodestly, that he was the guy who had figured it out. What was missing was an obvious trigger. With the economy soaring (the stock-market collapse in the spring of 2000 was still months away) and the nation at peace, there was no reason to expect that a realignment was about to happen.

Instead, Rove's idea was to use the levers of government to create an effect that ordinarily occurs only in the most tumultuous periods in American history. He believed he could force a realignment himself through a series of far-reaching policies. Rove's plan had five major components: establish education standards, pass a "faith-based initiative" directing government funds to religious organizations, partially privatize Social Security, offer private health-savings accounts as an alternative to Medicare, and reform immigration laws to appeal to the growing Hispanic population. Each of these, if enacted, would weaken the Democratic Party by drawing some of its core supporters into the Republican column. His plan would lead, he believed, to a period of Republican dominance like the one that followed McKinley's election.

Rove's vision had a certain abstract conceptual logic to it, much like the administration's plan to spread democracy by force in the Middle East. If you could invade and pacify Iraq and Afghanistan, the thinking went, democracy would spread across the region. Likewise, if you could recast major government programs to make them more susceptible to market forces, broader support for the Republican Party would ensue.

But in both cases the visionaries ignored the enormous difficulty of carrying off such seismic changes.

The Middle East failure is all too well-known—the vaulting ambition coupled with the utter inability of top administration figures to bring about their grand idea. What is less appreciated is how Rove set out to do something every bit as audacious with domestic policy. Earlier political realignments resulted from historical accidents or anomalies, conditions that were recognized and exploited after the fact by talented politicians. Nobody ever planned one. Rove didn't wait for history to happen to him—he tried to create it on his own. "It's hard to think of any analogue in American history," says David Mayhew, a Yale political scientist who has written a book on electoral realignments, "to what Karl Rove was trying to do."

Rove's style as a campaign consultant was to plot out well in advance of a race exactly what he would do and to stick with it no matter what. But he arrived in the White House carrying ambitions at striking variance with those of a president whose stated aims were modest and who had lost the popular vote. The prevailing view of Bush at the time seems impossibly remote today. But the notion that he wanted nothing more than "to do a few things, and do them well," as he claimed, seemed sensible enough. Nothing suggested that radical change was possible, much less likely, and the narrow margins in Congress meant that any controversial measure would require nearly flawless execution to prevail.

And yet at first it appeared that Bush might be capable of achieving big things. His first initiative, the No Child Left Behind Act, unfolded as a model of how to operate in a narrowly divided environment. Bush had made education a central theme of his campaign, an unlikely choice given that the issue strongly favors Democrats. Accountability standards had been one of his signature accomplishments as governor of Texas, and he made a persuasive pitch for them on the campaign trail. Rove likes to point out that people who named education as their top issue voted for the Democrat over the Republican 76–16 percent in the 1996 presidential election, but just 52–44 in 2000. His point is that Bush moved the electorate.

As the top political adviser in the White House, Rove orchestrated the rollout of Bush's legislative agenda. In December, even before the inauguration, he put together a conference in Austin that included key Democrats who went on to support the education bills that sailed through Congress and became the first piece of Rove's realignment. At the time, everybody assumed this was how Bush would operate—"as a uniter, not a divider," his method in Texas, where he left behind a permanent-seeming Republican majority.

In retrospect, everyone should have been focusing less on how Rove's methods were used to win elections and more on why they couldn't deliver once the elections were over.

It's not clear why Bush abandoned the moderate style that worked with No Child Left Behind. One of the big what-ifs of his presidency is how things might have turned out had he stuck with it (education remains the one element of Rove's realignment project that was successfully enacted). What did become clear is that Rove's tendency, like Bush's, is always to choose the most ambitious option in a list and then pursue it by the most aggressive means possible—an approach that generally works better in campaigns than in governing. Instead of modest bipartisanship, the administration's preferred style of governing became something much closer to the way Rove runs campaigns: Steamroll the opposition whenever possible, and reach across the aisle only in the rare cases, like No Child Left Behind, when it is absolutely necessary. The large tax cut that Bush pursued and won on an almost party-line vote just afterward is a model of this confrontational style. Its limitations would become apparent.

By late summer of his first year, the early burst of achievement had slowed and Bush's approval ratings were beginning to sag. Ronald Brownstein of *The Los Angeles Times* dubbed him the "A4 president," unable even to make the front page of the newspaper. He did not seem the likely leader of a realignment.

That September 11 was both a turning point for the Bush administration and an event that would change the course of American history was immediately clear. It was also clear, if less widely appreciated, that the attacks were the type of event that can instantly set off a great shifting of the geological strata of American politics. In a coincidence of epic dimensions, 9/11 provided, just when Rove needed it, the historical lever missing until then. He had been presented with exactly the sort of "societal trauma" that makes realignment possible, and with it a fresh chance to pursue his goal. Bob Woodward's trilogy on the Bush White House makes clear how neoconservatives in the administration recognized that 9/11 gave them the opening they'd long desired to forcefully remake the Middle East. Rove recognized the same opening.

After 9/11, any pretense of shared sacrifice or of reaching across the aisle was abandoned. The administration could demand—and get—almost anything it wanted, easily flattening Democratic opposition, which it did with increasing frequency on issues like the Patriot Act and the right of Department of Homeland Security workers to unionize. The crisis atmosphere allowed the White House to ignore what normally would have been some of its most basic duties—working with Republicans in Congress (let alone Democrats) and laying the groundwork in Congress and with the American public for what it hoped to achieve. At the time, however, this didn't seem to matter.

Rove's systematic policy of sharply contrasting Republican and Democratic positions on national security was a brilliant campaign strategy and the critical mechanism of Republican victory in the 2002 midterms. But he could not foresee how this mode of operating would ultimately work at cross-purposes with his larger goal. "What Bush went out and did in 2002," a former administration official told me, "clearly at Karl's behest, with an eye toward the permanent Republican majority, was very aggressively attack those Democrats who voted with him and were for him. There's no question that the president helped pick up seats. But all of that goodwill was squandered."

From the outset, Rove's style of pursuing realignment—through division—was in stark contrast to the way it had happened the last time. In *Franklin D. Roosevelt and the New Deal*, the historian William E. Leuchtenburg notes that Roosevelt mentioned the Democratic Party by name only three times in his entire 1936 reelection campaign. Throughout his presidency, Roosevelt had large Democratic majorities in Congress but operated in a nonpartisan fashion, as though he didn't. Bush, with razor-thin majorities—and for a time, a divided Congress—operated as though his margins were insurmountable, and sowed interparty divisions as an electoral strategy.

Rove never graduated from college. He dropped out of the University of Utah and campaigned for the chairmanship of the College Republicans, a national student organization whose leaders often go on to important positions in the party. He won, placing himself on a fast track to a career in politics. But he was and remains an autodidact, and a large part of his self-image depends on showing that his command of history and politics is an order of magnitude greater than other people's. Rove has a need to outdo everybody else that seems to inform his sometimes contrarian views of history. It's not enough for him to have read everything; he needs to have read everything and arrived at insights that others missed.

This aspect of Rove was on fuller-than-usual display during a speech he gave at the University of Utah, titled "What Makes a Great President," just after the Republicans swept the 2002 elections. The incumbent presidential party typically loses seats in the off-year election, so winning was a big deal to Rove, who actively involved himself in many of the campaigns. Overcoming historical precedent seemed to feed his oracular sense of himself, and during his speech and the question-and-answer period that followed he revealed a lot about how he thinks and where he imagined his party was going.

In his speech, he described a visit to the White House by the revisionist historian Forrest McDonald, who spoke about presidential greatness. Rove expressed delight at discovering a fellow McKinley enthusiast, and said that McDonald had explained in his talk, "Nobody knows McKinley is great, because history demanded little of him. He modernized the presidency, he modernized the Treasury to deal with the modern economy, he changed dramatically the policies of his party by creating a durable governing coalition for 40 years"—this last part clearly excited Rove—"and he attempted deliberately to break with the Gilded Age politics. He was inclusive, and he was the first Republican candidate for president to be endorsed by a leader in the Catholic hierarchy. The Protestant Anglo-Saxon Republicans were scandalized by his 1896 campaign, in which he paraded Portuguese fishermen and Slovak coal miners and Serbian iron workers to Canton, Ohio, to meet him. He just absolutely scandalized the country."

In this way of telling it, McKinley alone understood what everybody else was missing: A political realignment was under way, and by harnessing it, though it might "scandalize" conventional thinking, McKinley would not only carry the presidency but also bring about an unprecedented period of dominance for his party. The subtext seemed to be that Rove, too, recognized something everybody else had missed—the chance for a Republican realignment—just as he recognized the overlooked genius of William McKinley. He joked to the audience, "This tripled the size of the McKinley caucus in Washington—it was Bob Novak, me, and now Forrest McDonald."

After the speech a member of the audience asked a question that took as its premise the notion that America was evenly divided between Republicans and Democrats. Rove insisted this was not the case, pouring forth a barrage of numbers from the recent midterm elections that seemed to lay waste to the notion. "Something is going on out there," Rove insisted. "Something else more fundamental . . . But we will only know it retrospectively. In two years or four years or six years, [we may] look back and say the dam began to break in 2002."

Like his hero McKinley, he alone was the true visionary. Everyone else looked at the political landscape and saw a nation at rough parity. Rove looked at the same thing and saw an emerging Republican majority.

From Rove's vantage point after the 2002 elections, everything seemed to be on track. He had a clear strategy for achieving realignment and the historical conditions necessary to enact it. His already considerable influence within the administration was growing with the Republican Party's rising fortunes, which were credited to his strategy of aggressive divisiveness on the issues of war and terrorism. But what Rove took to be the catalyst for realignment turned out to be the catalyst for his fall.

September 11 temporarily displaced much of what was going on in Washington at the time. The ease with which Republicans were able to operate in the aftermath of the attacks was misleading, and it imbued Rove, in particular, with false confidence that what he was doing would continue to work. In reality, it masked problems—bad relationships with Congress, a lack of support for Bush's broader agenda—that either went unseen or were consciously ignored. Hubris and a selective understanding of history led Rove into a series of errors and misjudgments that compounded to devastating effect.

He never appreciated that his success would ultimately depend on the sustained cooperation of congressional Republicans, and he developed a dysfunctional relationship with many of them. This wasn't clear at first. Several of the administration's early moves looked particularly shrewd, one of them being to place the White House congressional liaisons in the office suite of the majority whip, Tom DeLay of Texas. At the time, DeLay was officially third in the Republican House leadership hierarchy, but as everyone knew, he was the capo of House Republicans and the man to see if you wanted to get something done.

Things never clicked. Republicans on the Hill say that Rove and DeLay, both formidable men who had known each other in Texas, had a less-than-amiable relationship. When I asked

XYZ

The cross the fork the zigzag—a few straight lines
For pain, quandary and evasion, the last of signs.
—Robert Pinsky

Robert Pinsky's new collection of poems, *Gulf Music*, will be published this fall. He served three terms as the United States poet laureate and currently teaches at Boston University.

DeLay about their history, he let out a malevolent chuckle and told me that his very first race had pitted him against one of Rove's candidates. "They were nasty to me," DeLay recalled. "I had some payroll tax liens against me, as most small businessmen do, and I was driving a red Eldorado at the time. The taxes were paid, but they were running radio ads saying I was a deadbeat who didn't pay my taxes." DeLay still remembered the ad: "He wants to drive his red Cadillac to Washington on the backs of the taxpayers."

DeLay made a point of saying he didn't hold a grudge. ("That wouldn't be Christian of me.") But he did allow that Rove had been extremely aggressive in trying to impose his ideas on Congress. "Karl and I are sort of the same personality," he explained, "so we end up screaming at each other. But in the end you walk out of the room with an agenda." DeLay insists he didn't mind Rove's screaming, but if that's true, he belongs to a truly Christian group.

Rove's behavior toward Congress stood out. "Every once in a while Rove would come to leadership meetings, and he definitely considered himself at least an equal with the leaders in the room," a Republican aide told me. "But you have to understand that Congress is a place where a certain decorum is expected. Even in private, staff is still staff. Rove would come and chime in as if he were equal to the speaker. Cheney sometimes came, too, and was far more deferential than Rove—and he was the vice president." Other aides say Rove was notorious for interrupting congressional leaders and calling them by their first name.

Dick Armey, the House Republican majority leader when Bush took office (and no more a shrinking violet than DeLay), told me a story that captures the exquisite pettiness of most members of Congress and the arrogance that made Bush and Rove so inept at handling them. "For all the years he was president," Armey told me, "Bill Clinton and I had a little thing we'd do where every time I went to the White House, I would take the little name tag they give you and pass it to the president, who, without saying a word, would sign and date it. Bill Clinton and I didn't like each other. He said I was his least-favorite member of Congress. But he knew that when I left his office, the first schoolkid I came across would be given that card, and some kid who had come to Washington with his mama would go home with the president's autograph. I think Clinton thought it was a nice thing to do for some kid, and he was happy to do it." Armey said that when he went to his first meeting in the White House with President Bush, he explained the tradition with Clinton and asked the president if he would care to continue it. "Bush refused to sign the card. Rove, who was sitting across the table, said, 'It would probably wind up on eBay,'" Armey continued.

"Do I give a damn? No. But can you imagine refusing a simple request like that with an insult? It's stupid. From the point of view of your own self-interest, it's stupid. I was from Texas, and I was the majority leader. If my expectations of civility and collegiality were disappointed, what do you think it was like for the rest of the congressmen they dealt with? The Bush White House was tone-deaf to the normal courtesies of the office."

Winning the 2002 elections earned Rove further distinction as an electoral strategist. But it didn't change the basic dynamic between the White House and Congress, and Rove drew exactly the wrong lesson from the experience, bringing the steamroller approach from the campaign trail into his work in government. Emboldened by triumph, he grew more imperious, worsening his relations with the Hill. With both houses now in Republican hands, he pressed immigration reform and Social Security privatization. A congressional aide described a Republican leadership retreat after the midterms where Rove whipped out a chart and a sheaf of poll numbers and insisted to Republican leaders that they pursue a Social Security overhaul at once. Making wholesale changes to a beloved entitlement program in the run-up to a presidential election would have been a difficult sell under the best of circumstances. Lacking goodwill in Congress and having laid no groundwork for such an undertaking, Rove didn't get a serious hearing on the issue—or on immigration, either.

A revealing pattern of behavior emerged from my interviews. Rove plainly viewed his standing as equal to or exceeding that of the party's leaders in Congress and demanded what he deemed his due. Yet he was also apparently annoyed at what came with his White House eminence, complaining to colleagues when members of Congress called him to consult about routine matters he thought were beneath his standing—something that couldn't have endeared him to the legislature.

When Bush revived immigration reform this past spring and let it be known that Rove would not take part in the negotiations, the president seemed to have belatedly grasped a basic truth about congressional relations that Armey summed up for me like this: "You can't call her ugly all year and expect her to go to the prom with you."

Another important misjudgment by Bush, prodded by Rove, was giving Rove too much power within the administration. This was partly a function of Rove's desire to control policy as well as politics. His prize for winning the reelection campaign was a formal role and the title of deputy chief of staff for policy. But his power also grew because the senior policy staff in the White House was inept.

In an early scene in Ron Suskind's book *The Price of Loyalty*, Treasury Secretary Paul O'Neill, not yet alive to the futility of his endeavor, warns Dick Cheney that the White House policy process is so ineffectual that it is tantamount to "kids rolling around on the lawn." Had O'Neill lasted longer than he did (he resigned in 2002), he might have lowered his assessment. Before she left the White House in humiliation after conservatives blocked her nomination to the Supreme Court, White House Counsel Harriet Miers had also served as deputy chief of staff for policy. The president's Domestic Policy Council was run by Claude Alien, until he, too, resigned, after he was caught shoplifting at Target.

Rove was and remains an autodidact, and a large part of his self-image depends on showing that his command of history and politics is an order of magnitude greater than other people's.

The weakness of the White House policy staff demanded Rove's constant involvement. For all his shortcomings, he had clear ideas about where the administration should go, and the ability to maneuver. "Where the bureaucracy was failing and broken, Karl got stuff done," says a White House colleague. "Harriet was no more capable of producing policy out of the policy office she directed than you or I are capable of jumping off the roof of a building and flying to Minneapolis."

As a result, Rove not only ran the reelection campaign, he plotted much of Bush's second-term agenda, using the opportunity to push long-standing pet issues—health-savings accounts, Social Security privatization—that promised to weaken support for Democrats, by dismantling Medicare and Social Security. But this also meant committing the president to sweeping domestic changes that had no public favor and had not been a focus of the 2004 campaign, which had centered almost exclusively on the war.

Bush's reelection and Rove's assumption of a formal policy role had a bigger effect than most of Washington realized at the time. It is commonly assumed (as I assumed) that Rove exercised a major influence on White House policy before he had the title, all the time that he had it, and even after it was taken away from him in the staff shake-up last year that saw Josh Bolten succeed Andrew Card as chief of staff.

Insiders don't disagree, but say that Rove's becoming deputy chief of staff for policy was still an important development. For the purposes of comparison, a former Bush official cited the productiveness of the first two years of Bush's presidency, the period that generated not just No Child Left Behind but three tax cuts and the Medicare prescription-drug benefit. At the time, Bolten was deputy chief of staff for policy, and relations with Congress had not yet soured. "Josh was not an equal of Karl's with regard to access to the president or stature," says the official. "But he was a strong enough intellect and a strong enough presence that he was able to create a deliberative process that led to a better outcome." When Bolten left to run the Office of Management and Budget, in 2003, the balance shifted in Rove's favor, and then shifted further after the reelection. "Formalizing [Rove's policy role] was the final choke-off of any internal debate or deliberative process," says the official. "There was no offset to Karl."

Rove's greatest shortcoming was not in conceptualizing policies but in failing to understand the process of getting them implemented, a weakness he never seems to have recognized in himself. It's startling that someone who gave so much thought to redirecting the powers of government evinced so little interest in understanding how it operates. Perhaps because he had never worked in government—or maybe because his standing rested upon his relationship with a single superior—he was often ineffective at bringing into being anything that required more than a presidential signature.

As the September 11 mind-set began to lose its power over Washington, Rove still faced the task of getting the more difficult parts of his realignment schema through Congress. But his lack of fluency in the art of moving policy and his tendency to see the world through the divisive lens of a political campaign were great handicaps. There was an important difference between the administration's first-term achievements and the entitlement overhauls (Social Security and Medicare) and volatile cultural issues (immigration) that Rove wanted to push through next. Cutting taxes and furnishing new benefits may generate some controversy in Washington, but few lawmakers who support them face serious political risk. (Tax cuts get Republicans elected!) So it's possible, with will and numbers alone, to pass them with the barest of majorities. Rove's mistake was to believe that this would work with everything.

Entitlement reform is a different animal. More important than reaching a majority is offering political cover to those willing to accept the risk of tampering with cherished programs, and the way to do this is by enlisting the other side. So the fact that Republicans controlled the White House and both houses of Congress after 2002—to Rove, a clinching argument for confrontation—actually *lessened* the likelihood of entitlement reform. Congressional Republicans didn't support Rove's plan in 2003 to tackle Social Security or immigration reform because they didn't *want* to pass such things on a party-line vote. History suggested they'd pay a steep price at election time.

Rove's idea was to use the levers of government to create a realignment—to force an effect that ordinarily occurs only in the most tumultuous periods in American history.

To understand this, Rove need not have looked back any farther than the last Republican president who had attempted something on this order. Before he was president, Ronald Reagan talked about letting people opt out of the Social Security system, a precursor of the plan Rove favors. In 1981, in the full tide of victory, Reagan proposed large cuts—and the Republican Senate refused even to take them up. The mere fact that they had been put forward, however, was enough to imperil Republicans, who took significant losses in 1982.

The following year, Reagan tried again, this time cooperating with the Democratic speaker of the House, Tip O'Neill. He now understood that the only way to attain any serious change on such a sensitive issue was for both parties to hold hands and jump together. To afford each side deniability if things fell apart, the two leaders negotiated by proxy. O'Neill chose Robert Ball, a widely respected Social Security commissioner under three presidents, while Reagan picked Alan Greenspan, the future chairman of the Federal Reserve. Key senators in both parties were looped in.

As Ball and Greenspan made headway, it was really O'Neill and Reagan who were agreeing. To assure both sides political cover, the negotiations were an all-or-nothing process. The plan that was eventually settled on addressed the solvency problem by raising the retirement age (which pleased Republicans) and taxing Social Security benefits for the first time (which pleased Democrats). Unlike in 1981, Republicans in Congress weren't left exposed. Democrats couldn't attack them for raising the retirement age, because Tip O'Neill had signed on. Republicans couldn't complain about higher taxes, because Democrats had supported Ronald Reagan's plan.

At *The Christian Science Monitor* lunch just after the reelection, Rove, then at the apogee of his power, had no time for nostrums like bipartisanship or negotiation. Armed with his policy title and the aura of political genius, he pressed for the Social Security changes so far denied him. In many ways, this decision was the fulcrum of the Bush presidency. Had Bush decided not to pursue Social Security or had he somehow managed to pursue it in a way that included Democrats, his presidency might still have ended up in failure, because of Iraq. But the dramatic collapse of Rove's Social Security push foreclosed any other possibility. It left Bush all but dead in the water for what looks to be the remainder of his time in office.

Rove pursued his plan with characteristic intensity, running it out of the White House from the top down, like a political campaign, and seeking to enlist the network of grassroots activists that had carried the Bush-Cheney ticket to a second term. Bush gave Social Security prominence in his State of the Union address, then set out on a national road show to sell the idea. But after an election fought over the war, Social Security drew little interest, and in contrast to the effect Bush achieved on education in the 2000 campaign, public support didn't budge. (It actually worsened during his tour.)

Unlike Reagan, Bush did not produce a bill that could have served as a basis for negotiation—nor did he seriously consult any Democrats with whom he might have negotiated. Instead, Rove expected a bill to emerge from Congress. The strategy of a president's outlining broad principles of what he'd like in a bill and calling on Congress to draft it has worked many times in the past. But Rove had no allies in Congress, had built no support with the American public, and had chosen to undertake the most significant entitlement reform since Reagan by having Bush barnstorm the country speaking before handpicked Republican audiences with the same partisan fervor he'd brought to the presidential campaign trail—all of which must have scared the living daylights out of the very Republicans in Congress Rove foolishly counted upon to do his bidding. The problems buried for years under the war and then the presidential race came roaring back, and Bush got no meaningful support from the Hill. He was left with a flawed, unpopular concept whose motive—political gain—was all too apparent.

Within months it was clear that the Social Security offensive was in deep trouble and, worse, was dragging down Bush's popularity at a time when he needed all the support he could muster for Iraq. Every week, the political brain trust in the Bush White House gathers under Rove for what is known as the "Strategery Meeting" (an ironic nod to Bush's frequent malapropisms) to plot the course ahead. What transpires is usually a closely held secret. But two former Bush officials provided an account of one meeting in the late spring of 2005, in the middle of the Social Security push, that affords a remarkable glimpse of Rove's singularity of purpose.

He opened the meeting by acknowledging that the Social Security initiative was struggling and hurting the president's approval ratings, and then announced that, despite this, they would stay the course through the summer. He admitted that the numbers would probably continue to fall. But come September, the president would hit Democrats hard on the issue of national security and pull his numbers back up again. Winning on Social Security was so important to Rove that he was evidently willing to gamble the effectiveness of Bush's second term on what most people in the White House and Congress thought were very long odds to begin with. The gamble didn't pay off. Even before Hurricane Katrina hit New Orleans on the morning of August 29, what slim hope might have remained for Social Security was gone.

Hurricane Katrina clearly changed the public perception of Bush's presidency. Less examined is the role Rove played in the defining moment of the administration's response: when Air Force One flew over Louisiana and Bush gazed down from on high at the wreckage without ordering his plane down. Bush advisers Matthew Dowd and Dan Bartlett wanted the president on the ground immediately, one Bush official told me, but were overruled by Rove for reasons that are still unclear: "Karl did not want the plane to land in Louisiana." Rove's political acumen seemed to be deserting him altogether.

An important theme of future Bush administration memoirs will be the opportunity cost of leading off the second term with the misguided plan to overhaul Social Security. "The great cost of the Social Security misadventure was lost support for the war," says a former Bush official. "When you send troops to war, you have no higher responsibility as president than to keep the American people engaged and maintain popular support. But for months and months after it became obvious that Social Security was not going to happen, nobody—because of Karl's stature in the White House—could be intellectually honest in a meeting and say, 'This is not going to happen, and we need an exit strategy to get back onto winning ground.' It was a catastrophic mistake."

It strains belief to think that someone as highly attuned as Rove to all that goes on in politics could have missed the reason for Bush's reelection: He persuaded just enough people that he was the better man to manage the war. But it's also hard to fathom how the master strategist could leave his president and his party as vulnerable as they proved to be six months into the second term. The Republican pollster Tony Fabrizio says, "People who were concerned about the war, we lost. People who were concerned about the economy, we lost. People who were concerned about health care, we lost. It goes on and on. Any of those things would have helped refocus the debate or at least put something else out there besides the war. We came out of the election and what was our agenda for the next term?

Social Security. There was nothing else that we were doing. We allowed ourselves as a party to be defined by—in effect, to live and die by—the war in Iraq."

That Rove ignored a political reality so clear to everyone else can be explained only by the immutable nature of his ambition: Social Security was vital for a realignment, however unlikely its success now appeared. At the peak of his influence, the only person who could have stopped him was the one person he answered to—but the president was just as fixated on his place in history as Rove was on his own.

Moments of precise reckoning in politics are rare outside of elections. Snapshot polls don't tell you much about whole epochs. Even voter identification can be a misleading indicator. In 1976, the post-Watergate Republican Party would have appeared to be in existential peril, when in fact it was on the verge of setting the agenda for a generation. So the question of where exactly things stand right now is more complicated than it might appear.

As he nears the end of his time in government, Rove has been campaigning for the notion that Bush has been more successful than he's being credited for. But the necessity of adopting history's longer perspective to make his argument says a great deal. Of the five policies in his realignment vision, Social Security and immigration failed outright; medical-savings accounts and the faith-based program wound up as small, face-saving initiatives after the original ambitions collapsed; and the lone success, No Child Left Behind, looks increasingly jeopardized as it comes up for renewal in Congress this year, a victim of Bush's unpopularity. Rove no longer talks about realignment—though the topic is now very popular with Democrats, who have a good shot at controlling both houses of Congress and the presidency after the next election. On the face of things, the Republican Party is in trouble. In a representative example, voters in a recent NBC-*Wall Street Journal* poll preferred that the next president be a Democrat by 52–31 percent, and delivered the most negative assessment of the Republican Party in the surveys two-decade history. In 2002, Americans were equally split along partisan lines. A recent Pew study shows that 50 percent of the public identifies as Democratic or leaning that way, while just 35 percent identifies with the GOP.

Rove is a great devotee of the historian Robert H. Wiebe, who also emphasizes the pivotal quality of the 1896 election. Wiebe thought industrialization had launched a great sorting-out process in the 1880s and '90s that reached a dramatic culmination in 1896. He argues in his book *The Search for Order, 1877–1920* that "a decade's accumulated bitterness ultimately flowed into a single national election."

It seems highly unlikely, though not impossible, that historians will one day view 2000 or 2004 as the kind of realigning election that Rove so badly wanted. Ken Mehlman, a protégé of Rove's and one of the sharper minds in the Republican Party, is adamant that the analysis that led Rove to believe realignment was at hand remains fundamentally correct. "If you look back over the last few decades, an era of politics has run its course," Mehlman told me. "Both parties achieved some of their highest goals. Democrats got civil rights, women's rights, the New Deal, and recognition of the need for a cleaner environment.

Republicans got the defeat of the Soviet Union, less violent crime, lower tax rates, and welfare reform. The public agrees on this. So the issues now become: How do you deal with the terrorist threat? How do you deal with the retirement of the Baby Boomers? How do you deliver health care with people changing jobs? How do you make sure America retains its economic strength with the rise of China and India? How that plays out is something we don't know yet." As far as what's happened since 2000, Mehlman says, "the conditions remain where they were." In this view, America is still in the period of great churn, and the 1896 election hasn't happened yet.

Rove has no antecedent in modern American politics, because no president before Bush thought it wise to give a political adviser so much influence.

Premised as it is on the notion that the past seven years have been a wash, Mehlman's analysis has a self-justifying tinge. At least for now, Republicans have measurably fallen behind where they were in 2000. It's hard to sift underlying political views from temporary rage against Bush, or to anticipate what effect his presidency will have on the Republican Party's fortunes once he's gone. But the effect does seem certain to be less pronounced—less disastrous—than it is now. Considered in that context, Mehlman's analysis rings true.

When I asked Mark Gersh, one of the Democrats' best electoral analysts, for his view of how the political landscape has shifted, he basically agreed with Mehlman, and offered his own perspective on Rove's vision of realignment. "September 11 is what made them, and Iraq is what undermined them, and the truth lies in between the two—and that is that both parties are at parity," Gersh told me. "There was never any indication that the Republicans were emerging as the majority party. What was happening was that partisanship was actually hardening. Fewer people in both parties were voting for candidates of the other party." Gersh added that he doesn't believe Democrats are the majority party, and he gives Republicans "at worst a 4-in-10 chance" of holding the presidency in 2008. Even if Rove didn't create a generational shift to the Republican Party, so far at least he does not appear to have ushered in a Democratic one, either.

Nonetheless, certain painful, striking parallels between the presidencies of George Bush and William McKinley can't have been lost on Rove, even if he would be the last to admit them. Both originally campaigned almost exclusively on domestic issues, only to have their presidencies dominated by foreign affairs. Neither distinguished himself. *Policy inertia* is the term the historian Richard L. McCormick uses to characterize McKinley's presidency. David Mayhew, the political scientist, writes in his skeptical study *Electoral Realignments,* "Policy innovations under McKinley during 1897–1901 [McKinley was assassinated in 1901] probably rank in the bottom quartile among all presidential terms in American history." Both sentiments could be applied to Bush.

Perhaps the strangest irony is the foreign adventure that consumed much of McKinley's presidency. Though he lacked Bush's storm-the-barricades temperament, McKinley launched the Spanish-American War partly at the urging of his future vice president, Teddy Roosevelt, and other hawks. As the historian Eric Rauchway has pointed out, after American forces defeated the Spanish navy in the Philippines, the U.S. occupation encountered a bloody postwar insurgency and allegations of torture committed by U.S. troops. Roosevelt, who succeeded McKinley, was hampered by questions about improper force size and commitment of troops and eventually came to rue his plight. "While I have never varied in my feeling that we had to hold the Philippines," he wrote in 1901, "I have varied very much in my feelings whether we were to be considered fortunate or unfortunate in having to hold them."

To understand Rove's record, it's useful to think of the disaster as being divided into foreign and domestic components. Rove had little say in foreign policy. Dick Cheney understood from decades of government experience how to engineer a war he'd pressed for, and still the administration failed to reshape the Middle East. More than anyone outside the Oval Office, Rove was responsible for much of what went wrong on the domestic front—partly because he had never served in government, and he lacked Cheney's skill at manipulating it. Both men came in believing they had superior insights into history and theoretical underpinnings so strong that their ideas would prevail. But neither man understood how to see them through, and so both failed.

Rove has proved a better analyst of history than agent of historical change, showing far greater aptitude for envisioning sweeping change than for pulling it off. Cheney, through a combination of stealth and nuance, was responsible for steering the Bush administration's policy in many controversial areas: redirecting foreign policy, winning a series of tax cuts, weakening environmental regulations, asserting the primacy of the executive branch. But his interests seldom coincided with Rove's overarching goal of realignment. And Rove, forever in thrall to the mechanics of winning by dividing, consistently lacked the ability to transcend the campaign mind-set and see beyond the struggle nearest at hand. In a world made new by September 11, he put terrorism and war to work in an electoral rather than a historical context, and used them as wedge issues instead of as the unifying basis for the new political order he sought.

Why did so many people get Rove so wrong? One reason is that notwithstanding his pretensions to being a world-historic figure, Rove excelled at winning elections, which is, finally, how Washington keeps score. This leads to another reason: Journalists tend to admire tactics above all else. The books on Rove from last year dwell at length on his techniques and accept the premise of Republican dominance practically on tactical skill alone. A corollary to the Cult of the Consultant is the belief that winning an election—especially a tough one you weren't expected to win—is proof of the ability to govern. But the two are wholly distinct enterprises.

Rove's vindictiveness has also cowed his critics, at least for the time being. One reason his standing has not yet sunk as low as that of the rest of the Bush administration is his continuing ability to intimidate many of those in a position to criticize him. A Republican consultant who works downtown agreed to talk candidly for this article, but suggested that we have lunch across the river in Pentagon City, Virginia. He didn't want to be overheard. Working with Rove, he explained, was difficult enough already: "You're constantly confronting the big, booming voice of Oz."

In ways small and large, Rove has long betrayed his lack of understanding of Washington's institutional subtleties and the effective application of policy, even for the rawest political objectives. The classic example is Rove's persuading the president in 2002 to impose steep tariffs on foreign steel—a ploy he believed would win over union workers in Rust Belt swing states, ordinarily faithful Democrats, in the next presidential election. This was celebrated as a political masterstroke at the time. But within a year the tariffs were declared illegal by the World Trade Organization and nearly caused a trade war. The uproar precipitated their premature and embarrassing removal.

"It is a dangerous distraction to know as much about politics as Karl Rove knows," Bruce Reed, the domestic-policy chief in Bill Clinton's administration, told me. "If you know every single poll number on every single issue and every interest group's objection and every political factor, it can be paralyzing to try to make an honest policy decision. I think the larger, deeper problem was that they never fully appreciated that long-term success depended on making sure your policies worked."

Rove has no antecedent in modern American politics, because no president before Bush thought it wise to give a political adviser so much influence. Rove wouldn't be Rove, in other words, were Bush not Bush. That Vice President Cheney also hit a historic high-water mark for influence says a lot about how the actual president sees fit to govern. All rhetoric about "leadership" aside, Bush will be viewed as a weak executive who ceded far too much authority. Rove's failures are ultimately his.

Bush will leave behind a legacy long on ambition and short on positive results. History will draw many lessons from his presidency—about the danger of concentrating too much power in the hands of too few, about the risk of commingling politics and policy beyond a certain point, about the cost of constricting the channels of information to the Oval Office. More broadly, as the next group of presidential candidates and their gurus eases the current crew from the stage, Rove's example should serve as a caution to politicians and journalists.

The Bush administration made a virtual religion of the belief that if you act boldly, others will follow in your wake. That certainly proved to be the case with Karl Rove, for a time. But for all the fascination with what Rove was doing and thinking, little attention was given to whether or not it was working and why. This neglect encompasses many people, though one person with far greater consequences than all the others. In the end, the verdict on George W. Bush may be as simple as this: He never questioned the big, booming voice of Oz, so he never saw the little man behind the curtain.

Critical Thinking

1. In what specific ways did Karl Rove influence the political agenda of George W. Bush?

2. Did the Bush administration and the Republican Party become too defined by the Iraq war? Explain.

3. Was Rove given too much authority and influence over the Bush administration? Explain.

Create Central

www.mhhe.com/createcentral

Internet References

George W. Bush Presidential Library
www.georgewbushlibrary.gov/white-house

The New York Times
www.nytimes.com/2007/08/13/world/americas/13iht-rove.2.7098038
.html?pagewanted=all&_r=0

The Iran Primer
http://iranprimer.usip.org/resource/george-w-bush-administration

---

JOSHUA GREEN is a senior editor of *The Atlantic*.

Article

Good Health for America?

America has struggled to reform public health care for over 100 years and now has a byzantine, costly system controlled by powerful, money-hungry interest groups. Martin Gorsky wonders whether President Obama can deliver reform.

MARTIN GORSKY

Learning Outcomes

After reading this article, you will be able to:

- Discuss the challenges and obstacles to health care reform in America.
- Explain how current economic hardships and government debt are hindering Obama's efforts.

When Barack Obama swept to power in November 2008, he seemed to promise a new start for domestic politics in the United States. High on his agenda was reform of the health care system, widely considered to be expensive, underperforming and unfair. America was spending a huge proportion of its national wealth on medical care—15 per cent in 2005, compared with eight per cent in Britain and 11 per cent in France. Yet unlike European countries with universal coverage, around 46 million US citizens lacked any health insurance. With Obama's thumping majority and a tide of goodwill towards him, expectations of change were high.

Since then reform politics have been a rollercoaster ride. The president's proposals had three basic goals: regulation of the private insurance market, a 'public option' of a state-run health insurance scheme and more compulsion on employers and individuals to purchase coverage. However, the plan quickly generated huge controversy with opponents saying it was tantamount to Soviet-style Communism. For European observers, long accustomed to tax-funded national health services or state-mandated social insurance, this is rather baffling. Why should so many Americans believe universal health coverage poses a fundamental threat to their liberty and why has it been so hard for Obama to deliver his legislation?

History can help us understand the choices which led the US to such a different approach to that of Europe. A useful concept in thinking about this is 'path dependency', the idea that decisions taken early on can significantly constrain possibilities for change later in time. With this in mind, we can look at why

national health insurance was rejected by Americans from the early 20th century onwards.

Statutory sickness insurance originated in Germany in 1883, devised by civil servant Theodor Lohmann and implemented by the 'Iron Chancellor' Otto von Bismarck. The principle was that health coverage became obligatory for particular groups of waged workers, financed by employer contributions and employee payroll deductions. Bismarck's goals in delivering welfare benefits were partly to enhance the efficiency with which 'human capital' was managed in an era of dynamic industrial expansion and partly to head off the appeal of socialism. As the system proved broadly successful, other countries began to consider their own versions of it. In Britain it was adopted in 1911 as part of the Liberal welfare reforms, which also included unemployment insurance and old age pensions.

In America, proposals for blue-collar health insurance were made in the 1910s by the American Association for Labor Legislation (AALL), a group typifying the 'progressive' strand in US politics which held that social intervention was needed to ameliorate the damage inflicted by untrammelled capitalism. The market, they suggested, had failed to protect the health of the workforce and American industrial productivity was suffering. But their strategy of presenting a model insurance law for state governments was rejected. Organised labour withheld support for the proposals, arguing that it was nothing but a ploy to avoid paying fair wages. Recent scholarship has also shown that the AALL underestimated the extent to which private insurance schemes were already providing sick pay coverage in many industries. Moreover, American wages were high and many workers could pay their medical bills. However, this 'labour rejection' analysis ignores the fact that trade unions in Britain and Germany had also been unenthusiastic, yet their opposition did not stop determined governments imposing such welfare laws.

So why not in America? Opinion is divided. Marxist historians emphasise that ruling classes used welfare legislation to wean proletarian loyalties away from the lure of socialism, represented in Germany by the Social Democrats and in Britain by the Labour Party. In America, however, socialist politics never took hold so there was no imperative for governments to undercut the left by advancing welfare entitlements.

Perhaps a better explanation lies with political structures and the power of pressure groups to influence law-making. In the US, there were various interests which stood to lose from state intervention. Doctors feared the loss of their freedom to treat and charge patients as they saw fit and their trade body, the American Medical Association (AMA), provided powerful opposition. Employers worried that expenditure on health insurance premiums might undermine competitiveness, while private insurers and pharmaceutical manufacturers anticipated a loss of business. These groups argued that the introduction of statutory health insurance would lead to dependency and to what economists now call 'moral hazard': unwarranted claims and high absenteeism. Such criticisms reached a head after America's entry into the First World War, with health insurance depicted as an insidious German innovation fundamentally at odds with the American way.

After America's entry into the First World War, health insurance was depicted as an insidious German innovation at odds with the American way.

The failure of the AALL meant that between the wars most working Americans relied instead on private and voluntary approaches to their health care needs. Public hospitals and asylums remained for the very poor. This system was tested by the Depression of the 1930s, when the medical marketplace was hit hard. Hospital income was rescued by locally-based non-profit insurance schemes called Blue Cross, while the associated Blue Shield provided cover for medical care. Meanwhile, industry-based pre-payment plans became more established. In 1938 the industrialist Henry Kaiser established a fund to provide medical care for workers building the Grand Coulee Dam in Washington State, which led to the birth of Kaiser Permanente, the forerunner of the later Health Maintenance Organisations (HMOs).

However, no progress was made in implementing statutory insurance despite growing support in the New Deal era of the 1930s. This was when the Democratic Party established key elements of America's welfare state, put in place to tackle the distress that followed the Wall Street Crash of 1929. President Franklin Roosevelt briefly considered whether national health insurance should be an element of his 1935 Social Security Bill, which introduced pension provisions and unemployment insurance. However, fearing that it might imperil the bill, he decided against including it. Pro-reform senators brought forward unsuccessful bills in 1939, 1943 and finally 1945, when President Truman lent his support. These repeated congressional defeats meant that, like FDR before him, Truman retreated from the reform agenda. Once again, America put its faith in a private and voluntary sector route towards universal and comprehensive health care.

At this point, the 'path dependency' explanation comes into play. In western Europe politicians and people were already

accustomed to compulsory health insurance. Moreover, the resistance of groups such as doctors had been partly overcome. It was therefore not such a big leap to legislate in the 1940s for a larger state role, whether through the tax-funded NHS devised by Britain's Aneurin Bevan, or through extending the reach of insurance, as under France's Sécurité Sociale, introduced by President de Gaulle. In the US, by contrast, there was no prior popular acceptance and the fears of opponents were undimmed. Nor, unlike in Europe, had the political left entirely embraced the goal of a bigger welfare state. Instead, American trade unions had accommodated themselves to the market by demanding that employers provide health benefits within remuneration packages. Thus the favourable labour market conditions of wartime had seen a huge expansion of voluntary coverage, so that by 1945 there were 15.7 million people enrolled in Blue Cross schemes.

That said, path dependency does not really explain why popular, competent politicians failed to overcome the odds against them. Why, despite Democratic electoral successes and the trauma of depression and war, could Roosevelt and Truman not assert their wills? A fuller explanation demands the 'institutionalist' and 'pressure group' explanations.

The key point is that the political institutions of the US tend to impede deep and contentious reforms. Indeed, the separation of powers between the executive, Congress and the Supreme Court was designed to provide checks and balances on over-mighty presidents. Nor can US presidents always count on the support of their own members in Congress. Meanwhile pressure groups wield considerable influence over decision-making, with contributions to campaign funds giving politicians an incentive to block reform. Contrast this with Britain where the 'first past the post' system frequently delivers governments with clear working majorities.

In the 1930s and 1940s congressional opposition to the US president came from conservative Southern Democrats, who were expressing the political wishes of a range of interest groups, notably those of the AMA. National health insurance, US doctors worried, would curtail their medical autonomy and reduce them to the status of salaried employees. They launched a series of propaganda drives, a favourite theme being that national health insurance was 'un-American', the contrast drawn first with German medicine under Nazism then, as the Cold War began, with Soviet Communism.

In the 1960s, however, the US state finally extended its role through the Medicare and Medicaid programmes. Once again the Democrats were in power and once again a president, Lyndon B. Johnson, backed the proposals. This time, though, various factors undermined the capacity of interest groups to block change. First, demographic and scientific factors combined to expose the limits of markets as providers of health care: the elderly population was booming and technological and pharmaceutical innovation both increased costs and raised expectations about what medicine could deliver. The problem of health cover had therefore returned to the political limelight. The intellectual mood had also changed in the era of Kennedy progressives: President Eisenhower's Great Society of the 1950s, founded on industrial prosperity and mass consumerism, had not, they argued, solved all America's social problems. This time the reformers adopted a more subtle strategy, pressing not for universalism, but rather for incremental changes that would be politically more palatable. The economic context was also favourable with America enjoying a golden age of growth before the burden of Vietnam and the oil crisis of the 1970s. Finally, doctors were won round because the organisation of Medicare seemed to promise a fillip for their incomes, since the state would reimburse them according to their 'customary' fees.

So with this benign combination of factors, America had arrived by the mid-1970s at a mixed economy of health care which apparently satisfied all citizens: the poor through Medicaid and public hospitals, the elderly through the respectable channel of Medicare, the working and middle classes through HMOs (developed under legislation passed by President Nixon) and workplace-related insurance, and the wealthy through private insurance or direct payment. Unfortunately, the cracks in the system soon began to appear. Public expenditure shot up to meet Medicare payments as both hospitals and physicians increased their activities. Meanwhile the structure of the private health care industry changed, with small institutions superseded by large, profit-hungry corporations running hospital chains. This was the point at which US health spending began its relentless upwards course, rising from 5.6 per cent of GDP in 1966 to 8.1 per cent in 1976 and reaching 13.2 per cent in 1996. Medicaid, meanwhile, remained an incomplete solution as the right of states to determine eligibility could lead to the exclusion of groups such as two-parent families, childless couples and widows. President Reagan acted in 1983 to stem the Medicare/Medicaid budgets, introducing the 'Prospective Payment System', which pegged costs of reimbursement to doctors. But this was only a partial brake.

The next attempt at a solution was the Clinton Plan of 1993, with its 'third way' goal of 'managed competition'. A more tightly regulated private health insurance sector would remain dominant, supplemented by new state-level 'health purchasing alliances', while mandatory employer contributions would ensure universal coverage. Once again though, the absence of party unity undermined support in Congress with conservative Democrats too ready to concede to the interests of employers on whom they depended for funding. The labour movement, bruised by the president's embrace of free trade, was also unsupportive and other groups which stood to gain, such as senior citizens, hung back for fear that Medicare might be cut to pay for the reform. Without a pro-reform coalition to foster support at the grassroots, public sentiment was easily swayed by the opposition which, true to historical form, swiftly entered the political arena with well-funded campaigning. Four other factors were in play: first, the level of government debt meant this was not an economically propitious moment for anything which might raise public expenditure; second, the detail of the plan was complicated and the president was slow to start explaining it to the people; third, he delegated the framing of the plan to Hillary Clinton and an inner circle of advisers rather than to Congress and thereby failed to forge a broader consensus; and fourth, the Republican Party seized on the health issue as a platform for a personal attack on Clinton, charging him with secretive policy-making and with imposing 'big government' on Americans.

President Obama has learnt enough from history to dodge some of Clinton's errors on health reform.

Where does all this leave Obama's America? The path dependency analysis tells us why health care reform is such a challenge. At each fork in the road the private health insurance industry emerged stronger and now forms a huge opposition lobby. This means that pro-reform politicians now regard a European-style NHS or social insurance scheme as unfeasible. The institutional structure still means the president can't count on party unity, which encourages the hostile propaganda of interest groups and Republican adversaries. They, in time-honoured fashion, maintain that a state plan would be un-American. Meanwhile the government debt racked up from bailing out the banks makes this, once again, an inopportune economic moment to propose a 'public option'. However, Obama has learnt enough from history to dodge some of Clinton's errors. He has set broad policy goals and then left it to congressional committees to work out the detail while actively selling his plan to voters. Then, with astute political management, he has swayed enough Democratic opponents to make a modified health care bill in 2010 a real possibility. Will this be the year that America finally breaks with the trajectory of the 20th century?

Critical Thinking

1. How has the private health insurance industry hindered Obama's progress in health care reform?

2. In what ways has the economy and government deficit affected Obama's health care plan?

Create Central

www.mhhe.com/createcentral

Internet References

The Huffington Post
    www.huffingtonpost.com/news/obama-health-care-reform
nytimes.com
    http://topics.nytimes.com/top/news/health/diseasesconditionsandhealthtopics/
    health_insurance_and_managed_care/health_care_reform/index.html
USnews.com
    www.usnews.com/topics/subjects/health_care_reform

MARTIN GORSKY is Senior Lecturer in the History of Public Health at the London School of Hygiene and Tropical Medicine. For more articles on this subject visit www.historytoday.com/medicine.

Gorsky, Martin. From *History Today*, February 2010, pp. 49–51. Copyright © 2010 by History Today, Ltd. Reprinted by permission.

Unit 6

UNIT

New Directions for American History

The breakup of the Soviet Union and the end of the Cold War could only be welcomed by those who feared a great power confrontation might mean all-out nuclear conflict. One scholar proclaimed that the collapse of Communism as a viable way of organizing society (only a few small Communist states remain, and China is Communist in name only) in effect signaled "the end of history." By that he meant that liberal democracy has remained as the only political system with universal appeal. Not so, argued another scholar. He predicted that the "clash of cultures" would engender ongoing struggles in the post-Cold War era. At the time of this writing, the United States is at war in both Iran and Afghanistan.

The treatment of minorities is reflected in the recorded activities of a new generation of educated Indians who used the courts to get redress from the hundreds of treaties that were broken or ignored. In addition, immigration in our history has alarmed people who felt that the newcomers might somehow taint our culture. The recent controversy over Mexican immigration has been no exception. Finally, there is the question of paying reparations to black people for their centuries under the yoke of slavery. Some argue that even if one accepts the idea of reparations, the question of who should be responsible for paying them is enormously complex.

Despite controversy over some irregularities in reports on global warming, most scientists in the field believe it constitutes a very real threat. Some argue that it could cause a broad-based disruption of the global economy unparalleled by any event since World War II.

Article

What Do We Owe the Indians?

For starters, a new generation of courthouse-savvy warriors insists we honor the solemn promises made in 371 active treaties, some of which predate the Constitution.

PAUL VANDEVELDER

Learning Outcomes

After reading this article, you will be able to:

- Describe the ways in which the government continued to take land from the Indians after treaties were signed in the early 1800s.
- Discuss the changes brought about by Nixon's American Indian Self-Determination and Education Assistance Act in 1975.

The Yellowtail ranch, tucked into a narrow valley of soft-rock geology that separates the Big Horn Mountains from the surrounding plains on the southern border of Montana, is not the easiest place to find. Hang a right at Wyola, population 100, the home of the "Mighty Few" as Wyolians are known to their fellow Crow Indians, and head straight for the mountains. This is the rolling rangeland where Montana got its famous moniker, Big Sky Country. Eventually a red sandstone road will take you to a small log cabin on Lodge Grass Creek, 26 miles from the nearest telephone.

The Crow Indian Nation once stretched for hundreds of miles across this high plains grassland without a single road, fencepost or strand of barbed wire to mar the view. Then, in 1887, the federal government cast aside its treaty obligations to the Crow and other tribes and opened up their homelands to white settlers. Cattle soon replaced buffalo, and a hundred years later, about the same time the economics of the cattle industry began circling the drain, geologists discovered that the Big Horn Mountains are floating on a huge lake of crude oil. It wasn't long before guys in blue suits and shiny black cars were cruising the back roads of Crow country and gobbling up land and mineral rights for pennies on the dollar. By hook and crook, the Yellowtails managed to keep their 7,000-acre chunk of that petrochemical dream puzzle. "We just barely hung on to this ranch in the '80s," says Bill Yellowtail, who, in addition to

being a cattleman, has been a state legislator, a college professor, a fishing guide and a regional administrator for the Environmental Protection Agency. "It was dumb luck, I guess. And stubbornness."

At 6 feet 2 inches tall and 250 pounds, Yellowtail is a prepossessing figure, and no matter where his life mission takes him, his spirit will always inhabit this place. When his eyes take in the 360-degree view of soaring rock and jack-pine forest and endless blue sky, he sees a wintering valley of 10,000 bones that has been home to his clan for nearly a millennium. And because his inner senses were shaped by this land, by this scale of things, his vision of the future is a big picture. "The battle of the 21st century will be to save this planet," he says, "and there's no doubt in my mind that the battle will be fought by native people. For us it is a spiritual duty," says Yellowtail, sweeping his hand across the thunderous silence of the surrounding plains from the top of a sandstone bluff, "and this is where we will meet."

What Yellowtail describes with the sweep of his hand is not so much a physical place as a metaphorical landscape where epic legal battles over the allocation and distribution of rapidly diminishing natural resources are destined to be fought. Tacitly, those looming battles echo a question that Americans have finessed, deflected or avoided answering ever since the colonial era: What do we owe the Indian? Long before the United States became an independent nation, European monarchs recognized the sovereignty of Indian nations. They made nation-to-nation treaties with many of the Eastern tribes, and our Founders, in turn, acknowledged the validity of these compacts in Article VI, Clause 2 of the U.S. Constitution, which describes treaties as "the supreme law of the land." Once the Constitution was ratified, the new republic joined a pre-existing community of sovereign nations that already existed within its borders. Today, the United States recognizes 562 sovereign Indian nations, and much of what we owe them is written in the fine print of 371 treaties.

Indian lands hold 65 percent of the nation's uranium, 20 percent of its fresh water, millions of barrels of oil and a treasure chest of copper and zinc.

In 2009, Indians comprise about 1 percent of the population, and irony of ironies, the outback real estate they were forced to accept as their new homelands in the 19th century holds 40 percent of the nation's coal reserves. And that's just for openers. At a time when the nation's industrial machinery and extractive industries are running out of critical mineral resources, Indian lands hold 65 percent of the nation's uranium, untold ounces of gold, silver, cadmium, platinum and manganese, and billions of board feet of virgin timber. In the ground beneath that timber are billions of cubic feet of natural gas, millions of barrels of oil and a treasure chest of copper and zinc. Perhaps even more critically, Indian lands contain 20 percent of the nation's fresh water.

Tribal councils are well aware of the treasures in the ground beneath their boots and are determined to protect them. Fifteen hundred miles southwest of Yellowtail Ranch, Fort Mojave tribe lawyers thwarted a government nuclear waste facility in Ward Valley, Calif. Eight hundred miles east of Ward Valley, Isleta Pueblo attorneys recently won a U.S. Supreme Court contest that forced the city of Albuquerque to spend $400 million to clean up the Rio Grande River. Northwest tribes won the right to half of the commercial salmon catch in their ancestral waterways, including the Columbia and Snake rivers. And, after a 20-year-long legal battle, the Potawatomi and Chippewa tribes of Wisconsin prevented the Exxon Corporation from opening a copper mine at Crandon Lake, a battle Indian lawyers won by enforcing Indian water rights and invoking provisions in the Environmental Protection Agency's Clean Air Act.

The Indian Wars of the 19th century were largely fought over land because the federal government refused to uphold its various treaty obligations. The spoils in the 21st-century battles will be natural resources, and underlying those battles will be the familiar thorn of sovereignty. "Back in the old days," says Tom Goldtooth, the national director for the Indigenous Environmental Network, "we used bows and arrows to protect our rights and our resources. That didn't work out so well. Today we use science and the law. They work much better."

Back in the old days, we used bows and arrows to protect our rights and resources. Today we use science and the law.

None of our laws are more deeply anchored to our national origin than those that bind the fate of the Indian nations to the fate of the republic. And none of our Founding Fathers viewed the nation's debt to the Indians with greater clarity than George Washington. "Indians being the prior occupants [of the continent] possess the right to the Soil," he told Congress soon after he was elected president. "To dispossess them . . . would be a gross violation of the fundamental Laws of Nature and of that distributive Justice which is the glory of the nation." In Washington's opinion, the young war-depleted nation was in no condition to provoke wars with the Indians. Furthermore, he warned Congress that no harm could be done to Indian treaties without undermining the American house of democracy.

The country had no sooner pushed west over the Allegheny Mountains than problems began to emerge with the Constitution itself. The simple model of federalism envisioned by the Founders was proving unequal to the task of managing westward migration. Nothing in the Constitution explained how the new federal government and the states were going to share power with the hundreds of sovereign Indian nations within the republic's borders. The Constitution's commerce clause was designed to neutralize the jealousy of states by giving the federal government exclusive legal authority over treaties and commerce with the tribes, but when Georgia thumbed its nose at Cherokee sovereignty in 1802 by demanding that the entire nation be removed from its territory, the invisible fault line in federalism suddenly opened into a chasm.

The Indians found themselves entangled in a fierce jurisdictional battle that they had no part in starting. It was not their fight, but when the smoke and dust finally settled four decades later, the resolution would be paid for in Indian blood. Georgia's scheme was to bring the issue of states' rights to a national crisis point, and it worked. Bewailing the arrogance of "southern tyrants," President John Quincy Adams declared that Georgia's defiance of federal law had put "the Union in the most imminent danger of dissolution. . . . The ship is about to founder." Short of declaring war against Georgia and its sympathetic neighbors, the nation finally turned in desperation to the Supreme Court.

When the concept of Indian sovereignty was put to the test, Chief Justice John Marshall offered up a series of judgments that infuriated Southern states' rights advocates, including his cousin and bitter rival Thomas Jefferson. In three landmark decisions, known as the Marshall Trilogy issued between 1823 and 1832, the court laid the groundwork for all subsequent federal Indian law. In *Johnson v. McIntosh,* Marshall affirmed that under the Constitution, Indian tribes are "domestically dependent nations" entitled to all the privileges of sovereignty with the exception of making treaties with foreign governments. He explained in *Cherokee Nation v. Georgia* and *Worcester v. Georgia* that the federal government and the Indian nations are inextricably bound together as trustee to obligee, a concept now referred to as the federal trust doctrine. He also ruled that treaties are a granting of rights *from* the Indians *to* the federal government, not the other way around, and all rights not granted by the Indians are presumed to be reserved by the Indians. This came to be known as the reserved rights doctrine.

The federal trust doctrine and the reserved rights doctrine placed the government and the tribes in a legally binding partnership, leaving Congress and the courts with a practical problem—guaranteeing tribes that American society would expand across the continent in an orderly and lawful fashion. Inevitably, as disorderly and unlawful expansion became the norm—by common citizens, presidents, state legislators, governors and lawmakers alike—the conflict of interest embedded in federalism gradually eclipsed the rights of the tribes.

For their part, President Andrew Jackson and the state of Georgia scoffed at Marshall's rulings and accelerated their plans to remove all Indians residing in the Southeast to Oklahoma Territory. Thousands of Cherokee, Choctaw, Creek and Chickasaw Indians died in forced marches from their homelands. Eyewitness reports from the "trail of tears" were so horrific that Congress called for an investigation. The inquiry—conducted by Ethan Allen Hitchcock, the grandson of his revolutionary era namesake—revealed a "cold-blooded, cynical disregard for human suffering and the destruction of human life." Hitchcock's final report, along with supporting evidence, was filed with President John Tyler's secretary of war, John C. Spencer. When Congress demanded a copy, Spencer replied with a curt refusal: "The House should not have the report without my heart's blood." No trace of Hitchcock's final report has ever been found.

By 1840 America's first Indian "removal era" was completed, and within a decade a second removal era would begin. Massive land grabs in the West commenced when Congress passed the Kansas-Nebraska Act of 1854, opening treaty-protected Indian lands to white settlement. While the act is most often remembered as a failed attempt to ease rapidly growing tensions between the North and South by giving settlers the right to determine whether to allow slavery in the new territories, it also embodied a brazen disregard by Washington lawmakers of their trust obligations to Western tribes.

Three decades later, the federal government ignored its trust obligations yet again when the 1887 Dawes Act gave the president the authority to partition tribal lands into allotments for individual Indian families. "Surplus" Indian land was opened up to settlement by white homesteaders, and soon 100 million acres of land once protected by treaties had been wrested from Indian control. Euphemistically known as the Allotments Era, this period lasted until 1934, when Franklin Delano Roosevelt and Congress finally put an end to the land grabs. Meanwhile, federal courts began relying on Marshall's century-old legal precedents in a series of controversial decisions that forcefully reminded Washington lawmakers of their binding obligations to the tribes. The decisions also prompted jealous state governments to resume their adversarial relationship with tribes, and to treat the tribes' partner, the federal government, as a heavy-handed interloper.

Surplus land was opened up to white settlement and soon 100 million acres of land once protected by treaties had been wrested from Indian control.

Although many Allotment Era executive orders were eventually ruled illegal by federal courts, the genie was out of the bottle. There was no way to return the land that had been taken to its rightful owners, and besides, the powerless remnants of once great Indian tribes were lucky to survive from one year to the next. Ironically, the turning point for Indians came decades later, courtesy of Richard Nixon.

On July 8, 1970, in the first major speech ever delivered by an American president on behalf of the American Indian, Nixon told Congress that federal Indian policy was a black mark on the nation's character. "The American Indians have been oppressed and brutalized, deprived of their ancestral lands, and denied the opportunity to control their own destiny." Through it all, said Nixon, who credited his high school football coach, a Cherokee, with teaching him lessons on the gridiron that gave him the fortitude to be president, "the story of the Indian is a record of endurance and survival, of adaptation and creativity in the face of overwhelming obstacles."

In Nixon's view, the paternalism of the federal government had turned into an "evil" that held the Indian down for 150 years. Henceforth, he said, federal Indian policy should "operate on the premise that Indian tribes are permanent, sovereign governmental institutions in this society." With the assistance of Sen. James Abourezk of South Dakota, Nixon's staff set about writing the American Indian Self-Determination and Education Assistance Act, which gave tribes more direct control over federal programs that affected their members. By the time Congress got around to passing the law, in 1975, Nixon had left the White House in disgrace. But for the 1.5 million native citizens of the United States, the Nixon presidency was a great success that heralded an end to their "century-of-long-time-sleeping."

Word of Nixon's initiatives rumbled like summer thunder through the canyon lands and valleys of Indian Country. While the American Indian Movement grabbed national attention by staging a violent siege of the town of Wounded Knee, S.D., in 1973, thousands of young Indian men and women began attending colleges and universities for the first time. According to Carnegie Foundation records, in November 1968 fewer than 500 Indian students were enrolled in schools of higher education. Ten years later, that number had jumped tenfold.

Among the first to benefit from Nixon-era policies was a generation of determined young Indians with names like Bill Yellowtail, Tom Goldtooth and Raymond Cross. "For the first time in living history, Indian tribes began developing legal personalities," says Cross, a Yale-educated Mandan attorney and law school professor who has made two successful trips to the U.S. Supreme Court to argue the merits of Indian sovereignty. "They realized that federal Indian policies had been a disaster for well over a hundred years. The time had come to change all that."

As various tribes slowly developed their political power, young college educated Indians came to view efforts to wrest away their natural resources as extensions of 19th-century assaults on sovereignty and treaty rights. Mineral corporations, federal agencies and state governments—emboldened by 160 years of neglect of the government's trust responsibilities—were accustomed to having their way with Indian Country.

In places like Lodge Grass, Shiprock and Mandaree, long-term neglect of treaty rights had translated into widespread poverty and a 70 percent unemployment rate. In New Town, Yankton and Second Mesa, that neglect meant a proliferation of kidney dialysis clinics and infant mortality rates that would be scandalous in Ghana. In Crow Agency, Lame Deer and Gallup, neglect looked like a whirlpool of dependency on booze and methamphetamines that spat Indian youth out into a night so dark that wet brain, self-inflicted gunshot wounds, cirrhotic livers and the all too familiar jalopy crashes, marked by a blizzard of little white crosses on wind-scoured reservation byways, read like a cure for living. Indians, no less than their counterparts in white society, found themselves prisoners of the pictures in their own heads.

Neglect spat Indian youth out into a night so dark that gunshot wounds and cirrhotic livers read like a cure for living.

Two hundred and thirty-one years after the new United States signed its first treaty with the Delaware Indians, there is too much money on the table, and too many resources in the ground, for either the Indians or the industrialized world to walk away from Indian Country without a fight. There may be occasional celebrations of mutual understanding and reconciliation, but no one is fooling anybody. The contest of wills will be just as fierce as it was in the Alleghenies in the 1790s, in Georgia in the 1820s, and on the Great Plains in the 1850s. "From the beginning, the Europeans' Man versus Nature argument was a contrived dichotomy," says Cross. "The minute you tame nature, you've destroyed the garden you idealized. The question that confronts the dominant society today is 'Now what?' After you destroy Eden, where do you go from here?"

Meanwhile, on a late Sunday evening inside a cabin on Lodge Grass Creek at Yellowtail Ranch, the weighty matters of the world are at bay. Friends and family have gathered around a half moon table in the kitchen for an evening of community fellowship. No radio. No cell phones. Wide-eyed children lie curled like punctuation marks under star quilts in the living room, listening to grown-ups absorbing each other's lives. Mostly, the grown-ups dream out loud over cherry pie and homemade strawberry ice cream. Gallons of coffee flow from a blue speckled pot on the stove. At peak moments all seven voices soar and collide in clouds of laughter.

Outside, the Milky Way glows overhead as brightly as a Christmas ribbon. The surrounding countryside is held by a silence so pure, so absolute, that individual stars seem to sizzle. Laughter, happy voices and a shriek of disbelief drift into the night where far overhead a jet's turbines pull at the primordial silence with a whisper. From 35,000 feet in the night sky, soaring toward tomorrow near the speed of sound, a transcontinental traveler glances out his window and sees a single light burning in an ocean of darkness. He wonders: Who lives down there? Who are those people? What are their lives like?

Far below, that light marks the spot where the Indians' future meets the Indians' past, where the enduring ethics of self-sufficiency and interdependence, cooperation and decency, community and spirit are held in trust for unborn generations of Crow and Comanche, Pueblo and Cheyenne, Hidatsa and Cherokee—where people who know who they are gather around half moon kitchen tables to make laughter and share grief. Still there after the storms.

Critical Thinking

1. What was the purpose of the 1887 Dawes Act?
2. What was the main reason for the 19th century Indian Wars?

Create Central

www.mhhe.com/createcentral

Internet References

wikipedia.org
http://en.wikipedia.org/wiki/Indian_Self-Determination_and_Education_Assistance_Act_of_1975

epa.gov
www.epa.gov/tp/pdf/president-nixon70.pdf

nativetimes.com
www.nativetimes.com/life/people/7232-nixons-role-in-self-determination-focus-of-talk

U.S. National Library of Medicine
www.nlm.nih.gov/nativevoices/timeline/539.html

PAUL VANDEVELDER is an author and documentary filmmaker based in Oregon. His book *Coyote Warrior: One Man, Three Tribes, and the Trial That Forged a Nation* was nominated for both the Pulitzer Prize and the National Book Award in 2004.

VanDevelder, Paul. From *American History*, June 2009, pp. 31–32, 35–36, 39. Copyright © 2009 by Weider History Group. Reprinted by permission.

Becoming Us

ALAN EHRENHALT

Learning Outcomes

After reading this article, you will be able to:

- Describe the immigration issues in the United States today.
- Discuss the problem of assimilation.

O f all the maddening complexities that make it hard for the American people to decide what should be done about immigrants, the problem of assimilation may carry the most emotional impact. All those people who look different, speak a different language and eat different food—will they ever blend into American society the way previous immigrant groups have? Or will they be a quasi-alien presence down through the decades of the coming century?

How long does it take for immigrants to assimilate into American society?

One way or another, we have been arguing about this question in America for the past 170 years, since Germans and Irish began arriving in our largest cities in massive numbers. We were an Anglo-Saxon Protestant society: The Irish and many of the Germans were Catholics. Would they be taking orders from the Pope rather than the institutions of American authority? Much of the elite thought so. It turned out to be a ludicrous concern.

Half a century later, the issue was immigration from Italy and from the Pale of Jewish settlement in Russia. The question then was generally not religion per se but the adaptability of the poor from Southern and Eastern Europe to the modern United States. The Jews, Poles and Italians dressed, spoke and behaved so exotically on the streets of New York, Philadelphia and Chicago. How could they represent the future of American society? This wasn't a concern that dwelt mainly on the fringes of American politics. To a remarkable extent, these were the beliefs of the country's best-educated, most affluent and most influential citizens.

The odd thing about these arguments over immigration was that they tended to be self-contradictory. On the one hand, nativists argued that immigrants would never assimilate and

would remain aliens in every important way—religion, culture, politics, the fundamental values of Western democracy. On the other hand, it was feared with equal vehemence that these millions of newcomers would intermarry with native-born Americans, dilute the quality of the nation's genetic stock and produce what was referred to frequently as "a mongrel race." This was more than a little crazy. If foreigners couldn't assimilate to Anglo-Saxon culture, why would Anglo-Saxons want to marry them? Still, both of these ideas remained current in national political debate on into the 1920s, and in large part led to the exclusionist immigration bill that was passed by Congress in 1924 and remained in effect for more than 40 years.

Today, at a time when Jews are essentially treated as WASPs when they apply to elite private colleges, and Irish-, Italian- and Polish-Americans have become overwhelmingly middle-class, all of this sounds like the quaint mythology of an unrecognizable time. And to a great extent, it is. But the dilemma of assimilation never really went away, and in the past decade, it has re-emerged as powerfully as ever.

W e all know the reason why. The foreign-born population of the United States was less than 10 million when the nation's borders were opened up by law in 1965; today it is nearly 40 million. About a quarter of this immigrant cohort has arrived from Asia; to a great extent, that portion is middle-class and upwardly mobile and has attracted comparatively little controversy. It is the 20 million immigrants from Latin America, a majority from Mexico and many of them in this country illegally, who have returned the question of assimilation to the forefront of public debate.

And it was no less a figure than Harvard University political scientist Samuel Huntington, by no means a proponent of crude racism, who raised the issue most bluntly in his 2004 book *Who Are We: The Challenges to America's National Identity.*

Well aware that the assimilation issue had been a red herring for most of the nation's history, Huntington nevertheless insisted that it was relevant in dealing with Mexican immigrants in the past couple of decades. He offered some provocative numbers: Rates of high-school graduation for the Mexican-born in America were roughly half those of the foreign-born population as a whole. Poverty rates for Mexican immigrants in 1998 were more than double those of any Asian group and considerably higher than the rates for other Hispanic newcomers. Mexicans were much more likely to marry within their own ethnic enclave than any other immigrant population, and more likely to identify emotionally with their country of origin than with their adopted home.

In short, Huntington insisted, the massive Mexican immigration of the 1980s and '90s constituted "a major potential threat to the cultural and possibly political integrity of the United States." Nativists may have cried wolf over and over again in earlier centuries, but now the nation was faced with the genuine prospect of a large alien enclave likely to plague it for decades. In his view, the Mexican influx was simply so large that historical comparisons suggesting more rapid assimilation were irrelevant. Mexicans in America were generating such a large in-group that they had relatively little incentive to venture out of it.

Huntington's analysis was vulnerable to challenge on several counts—and "challenge" may be too mild a word for the response it attracted—but Huntington did perform one valuable service. He refocused interest in the seemingly eternal question of assimilation. How important is it, and how might we begin to measure it?

Four years later, some interesting answers have begun to emerge. They are coming mostly from the work of Jacob Vigdor, a professor of economics at Duke University who has spent the past year developing a statistical index of immigrant assimilation, in collaboration with the Manhattan Institute in New York.

Vigdor believes that we will never understand assimilation as long as we continue to assume that it is a simple, unitary idea: that people either are assimilated or they aren't. He makes the plausible point that there are at least three distinct forms of immigrant assimilation that one might be interested in and want to measure. There is economic assimilation—the pace at which newcomers reach middle-class salary levels and acquire their own homes. There's cultural assimilation—the rate at which they learn English and marry native-born Americans rather than fellow-immigrants. And there is civic assimilation, measured by such things as naturalization and military service.

The conclusion of Vigdor's study is that each of these brands of assimilation operates on its own schedule and applies to different ethnic groups in strikingly different ways. Asian immigrants are very quick to assimilate economically. They learn English easily, graduate from high school at impressive rates and launch and successfully operate small businesses of their own. On the other hand, they are relatively slow to assimilate culturally, at least according to the criteria that Vigdor uses. They cling to traditional religious practices and look for marriage partners within their own tight-knit immigrant cohort, rather than marrying into other ethnic groups. One's view of Asians as more or less assimilated depends to a great extent on which of these categories one considers most important.

Mexicans are very weak on the index of civic assimilation. They are far less likely to vote than other immigrants, or even to take out naturalization papers. They maintain political ties to Mexico, just as Huntington noticed, and in many cases

return there to live after a period of years in the United States. The numbers on voting and naturalization aren't exactly a surprise: Millions of Mexicans are in this country illegally—they couldn't become citizens or vote even if they wanted to.

But Vigdor argues that the tendency of many new arrivals to tune out from American politics doesn't necessarily imply much about prospects for long-term civic assimilation. The data for Italians who came to America early in the 20th century are actually rather similar to the data for Mexicans now. They were slow to become American citizens and traveled back and forth to Italy on a regular basis. It's been estimated that roughly one-third of those who came here from Italy in the wave of migration a hundred years ago ended up returning for good. But those who remained here did eventually become citizens and vote in numbers roughly comparable to the national average. It just took them a while.

A careful reading of Vigdor's research suggests to me that panic at this point about a permanent enclave of alien foreigners in our midst is about as misguided as it was a century ago, however different the ethnic details might be. What it doesn't suggest is that we ought to throw the borders wide open and welcome another 10 million as soon as they want to move here. Communities that are heavily affected by the most recent immigration have legitimate concerns: schools that can't handle the overflow and inadequate housing stock that invites dangerous living conditions and the flouting of local codes. Long-time residents of any community have a right to be concerned about those things—and not to be derided as racists every time they bring them up.

Panic about a permanent enclave of alien foreigners in our midst is about as misguided as it was a century ago.

This is the moment, if there ever was one, to bring our borders under control and slow down the pace of immigration for a little while. Once we do that, we may be in a position to ponder the implications of Jacob Vigdor's research, and reassure ourselves that, in the long run, the American economy, polity and culture are not going to be destroyed by immigrants from south of the border, any more than they were by immigrants from across the ocean a century ago.

Critical Thinking

1. What are some causes for concern for communities with the most recent immigration?
2. Should the United States close its borders while determining its immigration reform policy? Why or why not?

Create Central

www.mhhe.com/createcentral

Internet References

Washingtonpost.com
www.washingtonpost.com/blogs/wonkblog/wp/2013/01/28/hispanic
-immigrants-are-assimilating-just-as-quickly-as-earlier-groups/

Politico.com
www.politico.com/story/2013/06/assimilation-a-flash-point-in
-immigration-debate-92469.html

nytimes.com
www.nytimes.com/2013/04/28/opinion/sunday/douthat-when-the
-assimilation-of-immigrants-stalls.html?_r=0

americanprogress.org
www.americanprogress.org/issues/2010/09/pdf/immigrant_assimilation.pdf

Article

Prepared by: Larry Madaras, *Howard Community College*

Losing Streak: The Democratic Ascendancy and Why It Happened

JEFFREY BELL

Learning Outcomes

After reading this article, you will be able to:

- Explain how Reagan destroyed the New Deal Coalition (1932–1964) and kept it going from (1968–1988).

- Explain how Barack Obama was able to regain the popular vote majority for the Democratic Party (1992–2012) in the two most recent presidential elections (2008–2012).

In the six presidential elections between 1992 and 2012, the Democratic party has regained the solid popular-vote majority it enjoyed during the New Deal/Great Society era (1932–64) but relinquished in the six elections between 1968 and 1988.

Since losing in 1988, Democrats have carried the popular vote in five of six elections and won the Electoral College in four. Of the two close elections in the current era (2000 and 2004), Republicans won the presidency in both. The four Democratic victories, by contrast, came by comfortable popular margins of 5.6, 8.5, 7.3, and 3.9 percentage points (in order, the two Clinton and two Obama wins). These Democratic showings were good for 370, 379, 365, and 332 electoral votes, while George W. Bush's two wins featured 271 and 286 electoral votes, just slightly above the 270 needed for election. In 2012 Barack Obama became the first president since Ronald Reagan to win two popular majorities (52.9 percent in 2008 and 51.1 percent on November 6).

Republicans cannot take much comfort in their 234-seat majority in the House of Representatives. For one thing, Democrats won the 2012 House popular vote by 1.2 percentage points, a sharp improvement from their 6.6-point deficit in 2010. More important, since ticket-splitting achieved mass proportions in the 1950s, greatly aiding House and Senate incumbents seeking reelection, congressional dominance has been on a different track from presidential dominance. It has arguably become something of a lagging indicator. The fact that Republicans never came close to a House majority between 1968 and

1988 was small consolation to Democratic nominees who lost the presidency time after time. More recently, Republican congressional landslides in 1994 and 2010 did nothing to prevent the subsequent reelection of Democratic presidents.

In the midst of these recent losses, Republican analysts (including me) became adept at finding one-off, "special" circumstances to account for supposedly anomalous Democratic wins. Bill Clinton ran as a moderate or even a conservative on selected issues like crime and welfare reform. Ross Perot's independent candidacy confused the electorate and divided the Republican vote in 1992 and 1996. Barack Obama in 2008 benefited from bipartisan goodwill as the first minority nominee for president. A mediocre or bad economy wrecked Republican chances in 1992 and 2008.

But Obama's reelection makes the GOP's minority status in presidential politics impossible to analyze away. Economic conditions—stagnant growth and high unemployment—seemed to fulfill the classic conditions for a "referendum" election that would very likely result in the ouster of the incumbent. The president's signature domestic accomplishment, Obamacare, was rejected by majorities in poll after poll. The charisma and voter euphoria that marked Obama's election in 2008 had seemingly long since dissipated.

When most polls during 2012 showed Obama with a slender lead over Mitt Romney, Republican elites questioned the pollsters' methodology. Some samples projected a bigger Democratic share of total turnout than in the banner Democratic year of 2008, which seemed implausible given the close national numbers. Many polls showed Romney leading among independents, in past elections a harbinger of victory. Moreover, the Romney-Ryan ticket made no game-changing mistakes, and in the judgment of both sides, Romney dominated the first presidential debate, invariably in earlier cycles the most important.

But when all the votes were counted, the election was not very close. Obama's victory margin was a hair under 5 million votes. Of the 28 states he had won in 2008, he held 26. Of the 12 "battleground" states, Obama won 11—8 of them by a margin of more than 5 percentage points. Remarkably, this meant that if there had been a uniform 5-point swing toward the Republicans in the national popular-vote margin—that is, had Romney won the popular vote by 1.1 percentage points instead of losing it by 3.9—Obama would still have prevailed in the Electoral College, winning 23 states and 272 electoral votes.

In the last two decades of Democratic dominance, 18 states and the District of Columbia have voted Democratic six out of six times. These currently have 242 electoral votes, which is quite close to the 270 needed to win the presidency. There are 13 states that have voted Republican in every election since 1992, but they total just 102 electoral votes. This means that to win, a Republican nominee must either break a generation-long Democratic winning streak in one or more states, or carry 168 of 194 electoral votes among the "purple" states that have gone both ways since 1992. Not for nothing have political insiders taken to calling the GOP path to an Electoral College majority the equivalent of drawing to an inside straight.

If the next two decades are anything like the last two, the presidential outlook for Republicans is pretty bleak. Yet even while digesting some earlier defeats, conservatives could take a bit of comfort from the notion that Democrats had been forced to move toward the center to become competitive again after their disastrous showings in the presidential elections of the 1980s. In the elections from 1992 to 2000, and even to a degree in 2004, the term "New Democrat" was often heard in the land. After 1984 Democrats seldom campaigned for broad-based tax increases or deep cuts in defense spending. Far more Democratic senators voted for the authorization of war against Iraq under George W. Bush than had voted to authorize the Persian Gulf war against Iraq a decade earlier under his father. More Democrats were talking tough on crime, many became supporters of the death penalty, and in the late 1990s and early 2000s, the party pretty much dropped its decades-long campaign for federal gun control. In 1996 President Clinton made good on his 1992 campaign promise to "end welfare as we know it" and in 1997 signed a good-sized tax cut as part of a deficit-reduction deal with a Republican Congress. Even on the core Democratic commitment to unlimited abortion rights, New Democrat rhetoric was to make the procedure "safe, legal, and rare."

Things began to change in the last decade and a half with the rise on the Democratic left of what came to be called the "Netroots." At first it seemed possible this was a reaction to high-profile events that infuriated the left, especially the impeachment and trial of Bill Clinton in 1998 and the election of George W. Bush, who in December 2000 was in effect declared the winner of the Electoral College by a 5–4 vote of the U.S. Supreme Court in an election carried by Al Gore in the popular vote. MoveOn.org, a trendsetting militant left organization, got its name from opposition to 1998's impeachment process, and there is no doubt that the resolution of the 2000 election was a traumatic event for the left. Bush's unusual status as an elected president who had lost the popular vote contributed to making Democrats far more confrontational toward him than they had been toward his father.

But when Howard Dean saw his presidential fundraising go through the roof in 2003, it was clear something much deeper was happening in the Democratic party. By 2008, all three Democratic candidates for the presidential nomination—Obama, Hillary Clinton, and John Edwards—were running to the left of earlier primary candidates and (in the case of Clinton and Edwards) well to the left of where their own Senate voting records had been just a few years earlier. Obama's nomination was correctly considered a victory for the left, and Clinton clearly benefited from her husband's centrist aura in the more conservative primary states, yet it is difficult to remember a single issue where either Clinton or Edwards was to the right of Obama's stated positions. Today the term "New Democrat" is the equivalent of a curse among the party's political and policy elites.

The Democrats' sharp move to the left since 1998 is the most recent leap forward in polarization, which has been the underlying trend of American politics since the 1960s. What few could foresee is how well the Democrats' decision to embrace the left would work politically. Political polarization involves a rallying of popular forces behind or against a worldview. In the late 1960s and early 1970s, Nixon rallied what he called the Silent Majority against the left-led cultural and political upheavals of the 1960s. Reagan did something similar in California when he took office as governor in 1967 in the wake of unprecedented campus upheavals and urban rioting that had erupted there in 1964 and 1965.

Reagan was also increasingly involved in the American conservative movement, which had unexpectedly prevailed over the Eastern establishment in the epic Republican nomination struggle of 1964. In becoming its preeminent figure following the landslide defeat of Barry Goldwater and his own election as governor, Reagan inherited a grassroots state-by-state infrastructure that helped him battle an incumbent president to a near-standstill in the primaries of 1976, laying the groundwork for his nomination and election in 1980.

Reagan did more than benefit from an existing conservative movement. He transformed it and brought it to maturity. Influenced by Jack Kemp, between his 1976 and 1980 campaigns he embraced supply-side economics, adding an important pro-growth component to Goldwater's advocacy of limited government. In foreign policy, he fully identified with the anti-Communist forward strategy of Goldwater and *National Review* but placed increased emphasis on America's commitment to spreading our founding principles and democratic values around the world. He directly challenged the realism of Secretary of State Henry Kissinger and became an advocate of "morality in foreign policy" (the title of a Reaganite plank added unanimously to the 1976 platform). On social and cultural issues, which in an earlier form had been key to his election as governor, he had a pro-life conversion and added the first militantly anti-abortion plank to the Republican platform in 1980. In his first term Reagan became such a central figure in the debate about the right of people of faith to advance their beliefs in the public square that during the 1984 campaign, Democratic nominee Walter Mondale accused him of being an "ayatollah."

All of this proved effective in pushing previously Democratic voting streams toward the Republican presidential coalition between 1976 and 1984. But the most striking thing about Reagan as a political leader was his integrated worldview and his determination to advance it on a broad range of policy fronts. None of Reagan's five successors as GOP nominee fully shared his integrated worldview, but the momentum of his positive polarization continued in 1988 when Lee Atwater and Roger Ailes, both high-level alumni of the 1984 campaign, turned the race against Democratic nominee Michael Dukakis into a debate about the Massachusetts governor's social liberalism on such issues as prison furloughs and his veto of saying the Pledge of Allegiance in public schools. Nonetheless, before the end of his first and only term, George H. W. Bush had turned against supply-side economics and embraced a "big tent" on the abortion issue—ironically via a speech delivered by Atwater—which was designed to play down polarization on behalf of a "kinder and gentler" society and presidency.

Barack Obama, of course, openly models himself not on Reagan's Republican successors or on his own pragmatic Democratic predecessor Bill Clinton, but on Reagan, whom he has recognized as transformational. In the context of his first term, his reelection campaign, and (especially) the weeks since, Obama is proving effective in pushing an ideologically comprehensive, consistent, and unapologetic left agenda. By its nature, this involves polarization. And in our age of polarization, aided by the comeback of the left that began to gain momentum after 1998, this has already made him a more consequential president than Bill Clinton, for all his popularity, could ever dream of being.

Since the 1960s, two social trends have laid the groundwork for the revitalization of the American left. The earlier and more significant one is the left's reorientation toward social and sexual liberation, rather than government ownership of business, as its center of gravity. This was not so much an innovation as a return to the origins of the left in late 18th-century France. It then took the form of an assault on organized religion and the traditional family, formulated by Rousseau and first executed politically by Robespierre and the Jacobins in the 1790s, when the left was first named.

The second is the steady increase as a share of the electorate—about 1 percent per year for the last 10 years or so, as measured by surveys of the Pew Charitable Trust, among others—of voters who list "none" as their religious affiliation. In an era marked by frequency of religious observance as the single most important factor in determining Republican/conservative allegiance, the rise of the "seculars" has added

several percentage points to the share of self-described liberals in the composition of voter turnout, though by no means bringing them close to parity with conservatives. The Obama campaign of 2012 was well aware of this trend in a reelection effort heavily dependent on turning out its existing ideological base, and this explains much of its in-your-face pursuit of social issues like same-sex marriage, support for Planned Parenthood, and imposition of contraceptive and early-term abortion mandates on the Catholic church and other traditional religions.

In taking a passive position in response to left-inspired polarization on these issues, the Romney campaign was pursuing an economics-only strategy fully supported by the Republican establishment. It even extended, with establishment approval, to Romney's decision not to bring up the Obama administration's Benghazi fiasco in the presidential debate on foreign policy. One can be confident of this full establishment agreement from the fact that Karl Rove and his associates, with close to a billion dollars of completely independent advertising money, did not run a single ad critical of the administration on social issues or any aspect of foreign and defense policy, including Benghazi. Instead their ads limited themselves to echoing the Romney campaign theme that the U.S. economy was not vibrant and had continued high unemployment.

There is little evidence that for all this advertising, Republicans achieved much of a net benefit even on economic issues. When Bill Clinton in his convention speech asked rhetorically why, with some progress being made, we would want to return to the policies that brought us the financial crisis in the first place, the Romney campaign and other Republicans offered zero rebuttal. The lack of a persuasive economic narrative is still haunting Republicans in the polarized economic debate pursued by the president since the election.

So why is the left winning, and in particular why did it prevail in 2012? In the words of Christopher Caldwell's post-election article ("Values Voters Prevail Again," *The Weekly Standard,* November 19, 2012): "[S]tructurally the outcome was the same one that we have seen decade after decade. Where two candidates argue over values, the public may prefer one to the other. But where only one candidate has values, he wins, whatever those values happen to be." This is particularly true in our age of polarization, and Republicans need to relearn the lesson taught by both Ronald Reagan and Barack Obama before their party drops completely off the charts.

Critical Thinking

1. Critically analyze what Bell means when he calls both Ronald Regan and Barack Obama transformational presidents.

2. When Reagan lost control of the Senate in 1986 and Obama lost the House of Representatives in 2010, why, according to Bell, did this not affect their transformational presidencies?

3. Explain why Romney did not beat Obama in the 2012 presidential election considering the unemployment rate was over 87 percent and the economy was still in recession.
4. Explain (look elsewhere if necessary) the importance of Obama's use of email, Twitter, and the computer analysis of raw data in organizing his campaign.
5. Explain (look elsewhere if necessary) why the traditional pollsters such as Gallup were way off in their predictions.

Create Central

www.mhhe.com/createcentral

Internet References

The Gallup Organization

Open this Gallup Organization home page to access an extensive archive of public opinion poll results and special reports on a huge variety of topics related to American society, politics, and government.
www.gallup.com

JEFFREY BELL is policy director of the *American Principles Project* and author of *The Case for Polarized Politics: Why America Needs Social Conservatism* (Encounter Books, 2012).

Article

Global Warming
Who Loses—and Who Wins?

**Climate change in the next century (and beyond) could be
enormously disruptive, spreading disease, and sparking wars.
It could also be a windfall for some people, businesses, and nations.
A guide to how we all might get along in a warming world.**

GREGG EASTERBROOK

Learning Outcomes

After reading this article, you will be able to:

- Describe the potential effects, beyond environmental, of global warming on world societies.

- Discuss the impact climate change may have on industry.

C oastal cities inundated, farming regions parched, ocean currents disrupted, tropical diseases spreading, glaciers melting—an artificial greenhouse effect could generate countless tribulations. If Earth's climate changes meaningfully—and the National Academy of Sciences, previously skeptical, said in 2005 that signs of climate change have become significant—there could be broadbased disruption of the global economy unparalleled by any event other than World War II.

Economic change means winners as well as losers. Huge sums will be made and lost if the global climate changes. Everyone wonders what warming might do to the environment—but what might it do to the global distribution of money and power?

Whether mainly natural or mainly artificial, climate change could bring different regions of the world tremendous benefits as well as drastic problems. The world had been mostly warming for thousands of years before the industrial era began, and that warming has been indisputably favorable to the spread of civilization. The trouble is that the world's economic geography is today organized according to a climate that has largely prevailed since the Middle Ages—runaway climate change would force big changes in the physical ordering of society. In the past, small climate changes have had substantial impact on agriculture, trade routes, and the types of products and commodities that sell. Larger climate shifts have catalyzed the rise and fall of whole societies. The Mayan Empire, for instance,

did not disappear "mysteriously"; it likely fell into decline owing to decades of drought that ruined its agricultural base and deprived its cities of drinking water. On the other side of the coin, Europe's Medieval Warm Period, which lasted from around 1000 to 1400, was essential to the rise of Spain, France, and England: Those clement centuries allowed the expansion of farm production, population, cities, and universities, which in turn set the stage for the Industrial Revolution. Unless greenhouse-effect theory is completely wrong—and science increasingly supports the idea that it is right—21st-century climate change means that sweeping social and economic changes are in the works.

To date the greenhouse-effect debate has been largely carried out in abstractions—arguments about the distant past (what *do* those 100,000-year-old ice cores in Greenland really tell us about ancient temperatures, anyway?) coupled to computer-model conjecture regarding the 22nd century, with the occasional Hollywood disaster movie thrown in. Soon, both abstraction and post-apocalyptic fantasy could be pushed aside by the economic and political realities of a warming world. If the global climate continues changing, many people and nations will find themselves in possession of land and resources of rising value, while others will suffer dire losses—and these winners and losers could start appearing faster than you might imagine. Add artificially triggered climate change to the volatility already initiated by globalization, and the next few decades may see previously unthinkable levels of economic upheaval, in which fortunes are won and lost based as much on the physical climate as on the business climate.

It may sound odd to ask of global warming, What's in it for me? But the question is neither crass nor tongue-in-cheek. The ways in which climate change could skew the world's distribution of wealth should help us appreciate just how profoundly an artificial greenhouse effect might shake our lives. Moreover, some of the lasting effects of climate change are likely to come not so much from the warming itself but from how we react to it: If the world warms appreciably, men and women will not sit by idly, eating bonbons and reading weather reports; there will be instead what economists call "adaptive response," most likely a great deal of it. Some aspects of this response may inflame tensions between those who are winning and those who are losing. How people, the global economy, and the international power structure adapt to climate change may influence how we live for generations. If the world warms, who will win? Who will lose? And what's in it for you?

Land

Real estate might be expected to appreciate steadily in value during the 21st century, given that both the global population and global prosperity are rising. The supply of land is fixed, and if there's a fixed supply of something but a growing demand, appreciation should be automatic. That's unless climate change increases the supply of land by warming currently frosty areas while throwing the amount of *desirable* land into tremendous flux. My hometown of Buffalo, New York, for example, is today so déclassé that some of its stately Beaux-Arts homes, built during the Gilded Age and overlooking a park designed by Frederick Law Olmsted, sell for about the price of one-bedroom condos in Boston or San Francisco. If a warming world makes the area less cold and snowy, Buffalo might become one of the country's desirable addresses.

At the same time, Arizona and Nevada, blazing growth markets today, might become unbearably hot and see their real-estate markets crash. If the oceans rise, Florida's rapid growth could be, well, swamped by an increase in its perilously high groundwater table. Houston could decline, made insufferable by worsened summertime humidity, while the splendid, rustic Laurentide Mountains region north of Montreal, if warmed up a bit, might transmogrify into the new Poconos.

These are just a few of many possible examples. Climate change could upset the applecarts of real-estate values all over the world, with low-latitude properties tanking while high latitudes become the Sun Belt of the mid-21st century.

Local changes in housing demand are only small beer. To consider the big picture, examine a Mercator projection of our planet, and observe how the Earth's landmasses spread from the equator to the poles. Assume global warming is reasonably uniform. (Some computer models suggest that warming will vary widely by region; for the purposes of this article, suffice it to say that all predictions regarding an artificial greenhouse effect are extremely uncertain.) The equatorial and low-latitude areas of the world presumably will become hotter and less desirable as places of habitation, plus less valuable in economic terms; with a few exceptions, these areas are home to developing nations where living standards are already low.

So where is the high-latitude landmass that might grow more valuable in a warming world? By accident of geography, except for Antarctica nearly all such land is in the Northern Hemisphere, whose continents are broad west-to-east. Only a relatively small portion of South America, which narrows as one

travels south, is high latitude, and none of Africa or Australia is. (Cape Town is roughly the same distance from the equator as Cape Hatteras; Melbourne is about the same distance from the equator as Manhattan.) More specifically, nearly all the added land-value benefits of a warming world might accrue to Alaska, Canada, Greenland, Russia, and Scandinavia.

This raises the possibility that an artificial greenhouse effect could harm nations that are already hard pressed and benefit nations that are already affluent. If Alaska turned temperate, it would drive conservationists to distraction, but it would also open for development an area more than twice the size of Texas. Rising world temperatures might throw Indonesia, Mexico, Nigeria, and other low-latitude nations into generations of misery, while causing Canada, Greenland, and Scandinavia to experience a rip-roarin' economic boom. Many Greenlanders are already cheering the retreat of glaciers, since this melting stands to make their vast island far more valuable. Last July, *The Wall Street Journal* reported that the growing season in the portion of Greenland open to cultivation is already two weeks longer than it was in the 1970s.

And Russia! For generations poets have bemoaned this realm as cursed by enormous, foreboding, harsh Siberia. What if the region in question were instead enormous, temperate, inviting Siberia? Climate change could place Russia in possession of the largest new region of pristine, exploitable land since the sailing ships of Europe first spied the shores of what would be called North America. The snows of Siberia cover soils that have never been depleted by controlled agriculture. What's more, beneath Siberia's snow may lie geologic formations that hold vast deposits of fossil fuels, as well as mineral resources. When considering ratification of the Kyoto Protocol to regulate greenhouse gases, the Moscow government dragged its feet, though the treaty was worded to offer the Russians extensive favors. Why might this have happened? Perhaps because Russia might be much better off in a warming world: Warming's benefits to Russia could exceed those to all other nations combined.

Of course, it could be argued that politicians seldom give much thought—one way or the other—to actions whose value will become clear only after they leave office, so perhaps Moscow does not have a grand strategy to warm the world for its own good. But a warmer world may be much to Russia's liking, whether it comes by strategy or accident. And how long until high-latitude nations realize global warming might be in their interests? In recent years, Canada has increased its greenhouse-gas output more rapidly than most other rich countries. Maybe this is a result of prosperity and oil-field development—or maybe those wily Canadians have a master plan for their huge expanse of currently uninhabitable land.

Global warming might do more for the North, however, than just opening up new land. Temperatures are rising on average, but *when* are they rising? Daytime? Nighttime? Winter? Summer? One fear about artificially triggered climate change has been that global warming would lead to scorching summer-afternoon highs, which would kill crops and brown out the electric power grid. Instead, so far a good share of the warming—especially in North America—has come in the form of nighttime and winter lows that are less low. Higher lows reduce the harshness of winter in northern climes and moderate the demand for energy. And fewer freezes allow extended growing seasons, boosting farm production. In North America, spring comes ever earlier—in recent years, trees have flowered in Washington, D.C., almost a week earlier on average than a generation ago. People may find this creepy, but earlier springs and milder winters can have economic value to agriculture—and lest we forget, all modern societies, including the United States, are grounded in agriculture.

If a primary impact of an artificially warmed world is to make land in Canada, Greenland, Russia, Scandinavia, and the United States more valuable, this could have three powerful effects on the 21st-century global situation.

First, historically privileged northern societies might not decline geopolitically, as many commentators have predicted. Indeed, the great age of northern power may lie ahead, if Earth's very climate is on the verge of conferring boons to that part of the world. Should it turn out that headlong fossil-fuel combustion by northern nations has set in motion climate change that strengthens the relative world position of those same nations, future essayists will have a field day. But the prospect is serious. By the middle of the 21st century, a new global balance of power may emerge in which Russia and America are once again the world's paired superpowers—only this time during a Warming War instead of a Cold War.

Second, if northern societies find that climate change makes them more wealthy, the quest for world equity could be dealt a huge setback. Despite the popular misconception, globalized economies have been a positive force for increased equity. As the Indian economist Surjit Bhalla has shown, the developing world produced 29 percent of the globe's income in 1950; by 2000 that share had risen to 42 percent, while the developing world's share of population rose at a slower rate. All other things being equal, we might expect continued economic globalization to distribute wealth more widely. But if climate change increases the value of northern land and resources, while leaving nations near the equator hotter and wracked by storms or droughts, all other things would not be equal.

That brings us to the third great concern: If climate change causes developing nations to falter, and social conditions within them deteriorate, many millions of jobless or hungry refugees may come to the borders of the favored North, demanding to be let in. If the very Earth itself turns against poor nations, punishing them with heat and storms, how could the United States morally deny the refugees succor?

Shifts in the relative values of places and resources have often led to war, and it is all too imaginable that climate change will cause nations to envy each other's territory. This envy is likely to run both north–south and up–down. North–south? Suppose climate change made Brazil less habitable, while bringing an agreeable mild clime to the vast and fertile Argentinean pampas to Brazil's south. São Paulo is already one of the world's largest cities. Would a desperate, overheated Brazil of the year 2037—its population exploding—hesitate to attack Argentina for cool, inviting land? Now consider the up–down prospect: the desire to leave low-lying areas for altitude. Here's

an example: Since its independence, in 1947, Pakistan has kept a hand in the internal affairs of Afghanistan. Today Americans view this issue through the lens of the Taliban and al-Qaeda, but from Islamabad's perspective, the goal has always been to keep Afghanistan available as a place for retreat, should Pakistan lose a war with India. What if the climate warms, rendering much of Pakistan unbearable to its citizens? (Temperatures of 100-plus degrees are already common in the Punjab.) Afghanistan's high plateaus, dry and rocky as they are, might start looking pleasingly temperate as Pakistan warms, and the Afghans might see yet another army headed their way.

A warming climate could cause other landgrabs on a national scale. Today Greenland is a largely self-governing territory of Denmark that the world leaves in peace because no nation covets its shivering expanse. Should the Earth warm, Copenhagen might assert greater jurisdiction over Greenland, or stronger governments might scheme to seize this dwarf continent, which is roughly three times the size of Texas. Today Antarctica is under international administration, and this arrangement is generally accepted because the continent has no value beyond scientific research. If the world warmed for a long time—and it would likely take centuries for the Antarctic ice sheet to melt completely—international jockeying to seize or conquer Antarctica might become intense. Some geologists believe large oil deposits are under the Antarctic crust: In earlier epochs, the austral pole was densely vegetated and had conditions suitable for the formation of fossil fuels.

And though I've said to this point that Canada would stand to become more valuable in a warming world, actually, Canada and Nunavut would. For centuries, Europeans drove the indigenous peoples of what is now Canada farther and farther north. In 1993, Canada agreed to grant a degree of independence to the primarily Inuit population of Nunavut, and this large, cold region in the country's northeast has been mainly self-governing since 1999. The Inuit believe they are ensconced in the one place in this hemisphere that the descendants of Europe will never, ever want. This could turn out to be wrong.

For investors, finding attractive land to buy and hold for a warming world is fraught with difficulties, particularly when looking abroad. If considering plots on the pampas, for example, should one negotiate with the current Argentinian owners or the future Brazilian ones? Perhaps a safer route would be the contrarian one, focused on the likelihood of falling land values in places people may leave. If strict carbon-dioxide regulations are enacted, corporations will shop for "offsets," including projects that absorb carbon dioxide from the sky. Growing trees is a potential greenhouse-gas offset, and can be done comparatively cheaply in parts of the developing world, even on land that people may stop wanting. If you jump into the greenhouse-offset business, what you might plant is leucaena, a rapidly growing tree species suited to the tropics that metabolizes carbon dioxide faster than most trees. But you'll want to own the land in order to control the sale of the credits. Consider a possible sequence of events: First, climate change makes parts of the developing world even less habitable than they are today; then, refugees flee these areas; finally, land can be snapped up at Filene's Basement prices—and used to grow leucaena trees.

Water

If Al Gore's movie, *An Inconvenient Truth,* is to be believed, you should start selling coastal real estate now. Gore's film maintains that an artificial greenhouse effect could raise sea levels 20 feet in the near future, flooding Manhattan, San Francisco, and dozens of other cities; Micronesia would simply disappear below the waves. Gore's is the doomsday number, but the scientific consensus is worrisome enough: In 2005, the National Academy of Sciences warned that oceans may rise between four inches and three feet by the year 2100. Four inches may not sound like a lot, but it would imperil parts of coastal Florida and the Carolinas, among other places. A three-foot sea-level rise would flood significant portions of Bangladesh, threaten the national survival of the Netherlands, and damage many coastal cities, while submerging pretty much all of the world's trendy beach destinations to boot. And the Asian Tigers? Shanghai and Hong Kong sit right on the water. Raise the deep a few feet, and these Tiger cities would be abandoned.

The global temperature increase of the last century—about one degree Fahrenheit—was modest and did not cause any dangerous sea-level rise. Sea-level worries turn on the possibility that there is some nonlinear aspect of the climate system, a "tipping point" that could cause the rate of global warming to accelerate markedly. One reason global warming has not happened as fast as expected appears to be that the oceans have absorbed much of the carbon dioxide emitted by human activity. Studies suggest, however, that the ability of the oceans to absorb carbon dioxide may be slowing; as the absorption rate declines, atmospheric buildup will happen faster, and climate change could speed up. At the first sign of an increase in the rate of global warming: Sell, sell, sell your coastal properties. Unload those London and Seattle waterfront holdings. Buy land and real property in Omaha or Ontario.

The Inuit believe they are ensconced in the one place in this hemisphere that the descendants of Europe will never, ever want. This could turn out to be wrong.

An artificial greenhouse effect may also alter ocean currents in unpredictable ways. Already there is some evidence that the arctic currents are changing, while the major North Atlantic current that moves warm water north from the equator may be losing energy. If the North Atlantic current falters, temperatures could fall in Europe even as the world overall warms. Most of Europe lies to the north of Maine yet is temperate because the North Atlantic current carries huge volumes of warm water to the seas off Scotland; that warm water is Europe's weathermaker. Geological studies show that the North Atlantic current has stopped in the past. If this current stops again because of artificial climate change, Europe might take on the climate of present-day Newfoundland. As a result, it might depopulate, while the economic value of everything within its icy expanse declines. The European Union makes approximately the same contribution to the global economy as the United States makes: Significantly falling temperatures in Europe could trigger a worldwide recession.

While staying ready to sell your holdings in Europe, look for purchase opportunities near the waters of the Arctic Circle. In 2005, a Russian research ship became the first surface vessel ever to reach the North Pole without the aid of an icebreaker. If arctic sea ice melts, shipping traffic will begin transiting the North Pole. Andrew Revkin's 2006 book, *The North Pole Was Here,* profiles Pat Broe, who in 1997 bought the isolated far-north port of Churchill, Manitoba, from the Canadian government for $7. Assuming arctic ice continues to melt, the world's cargo vessels may begin sailing due north to shave thousands of miles off their trips, and the port of Churchill may be bustling. If arctic polar ice disappears and container vessels course the North Pole seas, shipping costs may decline—to the benefit of consumers. Asian manufacturers, especially, should see their costs of shipping to the United States and the European Union fall. At the same time, heavily trafficked southern shipping routes linking East Asia to Europe and to America's East Coast could see less traffic, and port cities along that route—such as Singapore—might decline. Concurrently, good relations with Nunavut could become of interest to the world's corporations.

Oh, and there may be oil under the arctic waters. Who would own that oil? The United States, Russia, Canada, Norway, and Denmark already assert legally complex claims to parts of the North Pole seas—including portions that other nations consider open waters not subject to sovereign control. Today it seems absurd to imagine the governments of the world fighting over the North Pole seas, but in the past many causes of battle have seemed absurd before the artillery fire began. Canada is already conducting naval exercises in the arctic waters, and making no secret of this.

Then again, perhaps ownership of these waters will go in an entirely different direction. The 21st century is likely to see a movement to create private-property rights in the ocean (ocean property rights are the most promising solution to overfishing of the open seas). Private-property rights in the North Pole seas, should they come into existence, might generate a rush to rival the Sooners' settlement of Oklahoma in the late 1800s.

Whatever happens to our oceans, climate change might also cause economic turmoil by affecting freshwater supplies. Today nearly all primary commodities, including petroleum, appear in ample supply. Freshwater is an exception: China is depleting aquifers at an alarming rate in order to produce enough rice to feed itself, while freshwater is scarce in much of the Middle East and parts of Africa. Freshwater depletion is especially worrisome in Egypt, Libya, and several Persian Gulf states. Greenhouse-effect science is so uncertain that researchers have little idea whether a warming world would experience more or less precipitation. If it turns out that rain and snow decline as the world warms, dwindling supplies of drinking water and freshwater for agriculture may be the next resource emergency. For investors this would suggest a cautious view of the booms in China and Dubai, as both places may soon face freshwater-supply problems. (Cost-effective desalinization continues to elude engineers.) On the other hand, where water rights are available in these areas, grab them.

A 401(k) for a Warming World

Climate change could have a broad impact on industrial sectors, and thus help or hurt your stock investments and retirement funds. What types of equity might you want to favor or avoid?

Big Pharma.   Rising temperatures might extend the range of tropical diseases such as malaria and dengue fever. A 2005 World Health Organization report suggested that global warming may already cause 150,000 deaths annually, mainly by spreading illnesses common to hot nations. If diseases of the poor, low-latitude regions of the world began to reach developed countries, large amounts of capital would flow into the Pharmaceuticals sector as the affluent began to demand protection—so it could prove profitable to be holding pharmaceutical stocks, although exactly which shares to buy would be influenced by laboratory discoveries that are impossible to predict. But consider the social upside: If malaria threatened the United States, this scourge might finally be cured.

Health-Care Service Providers.   The contrarian view is that a warming world would, on balance, improve public health in high-latitude areas. Though hot regions in the developing world experience high rates of communicable diseases that scare us, people are still far more likely to die from the cold than from heat—overall death rates in winter are much higher than those in summer. Retirees living in Florida, for instance, have less reason to fear a hot summer than those living in Vermont have to fear a cold winter. If the cold areas of affluent nations became less cold, we would expect longevity to increase. That would be good for society, and also a reason to hold health-care (and pharmaceutical) stocks, since the elderly require far more in the way of hospital services and drugs. The assisted-care industry might also be in for a long bullish run.

Electricity Producers.   The World Energy Council has estimated that global demand for electricity will triple by 2050. The lion's share of the increased demand will be in developing nations, but the United States and the European Union nations will need more megawatts too—and that's even assuming increases in energy efficiency. It is all but certain that some form of greenhouse-gas regulation will come to the United States; many Fortune 500 CEOs already assume this. The result will be an electricity sector that's much more technology- and knowledge-sensitive than today's. Lots of brainpower and skill will be required to increase electricity generation and reduce greenhouse-gas emissions at the same time. It's reasonable to guess that power-production firms with a track record of innovation, such as Duke Energy (which pioneered many techniques to improve the efficiency of nuclear-power plants), will be the kind of energy-sector stocks to own. Don't be surprised if nuclear energy, which is nearly greenhouse-gas-free, enjoys a boom in coming decades. General Electric, Westinghouse, and Siemens are some of the leading producers of new "inherently safe" power reactors designed so they can't melt down even if all safety systems are turned off.

"Green" Energy.   Renewable-energy industries—such as solar energy and biofuels—might seem like a promising place for 401(k) chips, but bear in mind that no form of green energy is yet cost-competitive with fossil energy, and no one knows which may eventually win in the marketplace. Solar-cell production, for example, is an expanding sector, but nearly all large solar cells for residential and commercial applications are currently sold in California, Japan, or Germany, which heavily subsidize the installation of solar power. Many investors today are racing to ethanol, but wariness seems advisable. Bill Gates has already invested $84 million in a start-up called Pacific Ethanol; venture-capital firms have moved into the ethanol "space." If the smart money is already there, you're too late. Besides, BP and DuPont are now looking past ethanol to bet on butanol, a crop-derived petroleum substitute with superior technical properties.

Agriculture.   Should growing seasons and rainfall patterns change quickly, genetic engineering of crop plants might become essential to society's future. DuPont, Monsanto, Syngenta, and other firms that are perfecting genetic improvement of crops—either through gene splicing or via natural crossbreeding aided by genetic analysis—could become even bigger players if there is significant climate change.

The Deus Ex Machina Industry.   Be wary of start-ups and venture capitalists who may soon talk up "geoengineering." In theory, it could be possible to cause the seas to absorb more greenhouse gases, if oceans were fertilized with substances that encourage the growth of marine organisms that need carbon dioxide. In theory, the upper atmosphere could be seeded with shiny fleck-sized particles that bounce sunlight back into space, cooling the Earth. In theory, if volcanoes could be made more active, their emissions also would reduce global temperature by blocking some sunlight. (The sole exception to the last two decades of warm years resulted from the 1991 eruption of Mount Pinatubo, in the Philippines, which caused cool weather worldwide.) It's likely that some investors will be tempted by offers of early stakes in geoengineering enterprises. But it's unlikely that any government will ever approve an experiment involving the entire planet.

Want the profile of what seems the perfect large firm of the future? Think General Electric. The company builds nuclear-power reactors and is ready to build extremely efficient coal-fired power plants, which are likely to become more commonplace than nuclear reactors owing to lower cost and less political opposition. George W. Bush talks grandly of Future-Gen, a billion-dollar federal initiative for a prototype coal-fired power plant that emits hardly any greenhouse gases. But the FutureGen crash program doesn't even break ground until 2009. Meanwhile, GE has already completed the engineering work for an advanced coal-fired power plant able to operate with negligible greenhouse-gas emissions. If greenhouse-gas regulations are enacted, GE may be swamped with orders for its new coal-fired generating station. GE has also recently engineered jet engines, power turbines, and diesel locomotives that require less fuel, and hence release less greenhouse gas, than those now in use. The company has also made serious investments in wind turbines, photovoltaic cells, and other zero-emission energy forms. This big, profit-conscious corporation is at the cutting edge of preparation for a greenhouse world—which is likely to keep GE big and profitable.

—Gregg Easterbrook

Much of the effect that global warming will have on our water is speculative, so water-related climate change will be a high-risk/high-reward matter for investors and societies alike. The biggest fear is that artificially triggered climate change will shift rainfall away from today's productive breadbasket areas and toward what are now deserts or, worse, toward the oceans. (From the human perspective, all ocean rain represents wasted freshwater.) The reason Malthusian catastrophes have not occurred as humanity has grown is that for most of the last half century, farm yields have increased faster than population. But the global agricultural system is perilously poised on the assumption that growing conditions will continue to be good in the breadbasket areas of the United States, India, China, and South America. If rainfall shifts away from those areas, there could be significant human suffering for many, many years, even if, say, Siberian agriculture eventually replaces lost production elsewhere. By reducing farm yield, rainfall changes could also cause skyrocketing prices for commodity crops, something the global economy has rarely observed in the last 30 years.

Recent studies show that in the last few decades, precipitation in North America is increasingly the result of a few downpours rather than lots of showers. Downpours cause flooding and property damage, while being of less use to agriculture than frequent soft rains. Because the relationship between artificially triggered climate change and rainfall is conjectural, investors presently have no way to avoid buying land in places that someday might be hit with frequent downpours. But this concern surely raises a red flag about investments in India, Bangladesh, and Indonesia, where monsoon rains are already a leading social problem.

Water-related investments might be attractive in another way: for hydropower. Zero-emission hydropower might become a premium energy form if greenhouse gases are strictly regulated. Quebec is the Saudi Arabia of roaring water. Already the hydropower complex around James Bay is one of the world's leading sources of water-generated electricity. For 30 years, environmentalists and some Cree activists opposed plans to construct a grand hydropower complex that essentially would dam all large rivers flowing into the James and Hudson bays. But it's not hard to imagine Canada completing the reengineering of northern Quebec for hydropower, if demand from New England and the Midwest becomes strong enough. Similarly, there is hydropower potential in the Chilean portions of Patagonia. This is a wild and beautiful region little touched by human activity—and an intriguing place to snap up land for hydropower reservoirs.

Adaptation

Last October, the treasury office of the United Kingdom estimated that unless we adapt, global warming could eventually subtract as much as 20 percent of the gross domestic product from the world economy. Needless to say, if that happens, not even the cleverest portfolio will help you. This estimate is worst-case, however, and has many economists skeptical.

Optimists think dangerous global warming might be averted at surprisingly low cost (see "Some Convenient Truths," September 2006). Once regulations create a profit incentive for the invention of greenhouse-gas-reducing technology, an outpouring of innovation is likely. Some of those who formulate greenhouse-gas-control ideas will become rich; everyone will benefit from the environmental safeguards the ideas confer.

Enactment of some form of binding greenhouse-gas rules is now essential both to slow the rate of greenhouse-gas accumulation and to create an incentive for inventors, engineers, and businesspeople to devise the ideas that will push society beyond the fossil-fuel age. *The New York Times* recently groused that George W. Bush's fiscal 2007 budget includes only $4.2 billion for federal research that might cut greenhouse-gas emissions. This is the wrong concern: Progress would be faster if the federal government spent nothing at all on greenhouse-gas-reduction research—but enacted regulations that gave the private sector a significant profit motive to find solutions that work in actual use, as opposed to on paper in government studies. The market has caused the greenhouse-gas problem, and the market is the best hope of solving it. Offering market incentives for the development of greenhouse-gas controls—indeed, encouraging profit making in greenhouse-gas controls—is the most promising path to avoiding the harm that could befall the dispossessed of developing nations as the global climate changes.

Yet if global-warming theory is right, higher global temperatures are already inevitable. Even the most optimistic scenario for reform envisions decades of additional greenhouse-gas accumulation in the atmosphere, and that in turn means a warming world. The warming may be manageable, but it is probably unstoppable in the short term. This suggests that a major investment sector of the near future will be climate-change adaptation. Crops that grow in high temperatures, homes and buildings designed to stay cool during heat waves, vehicles that run on far less fuel, waterfront structures that can resist stronger storms—the list of needed adaptations will be long, and all involve producing, buying, and selling. Environmentalists don't like talk of adaptation, as it implies making our peace with a warmer world. That peace, though, must be made—and the sooner businesses, investors, and entrepreneurs get to work, the better.

Why, ultimately, should nations act to control greenhouse gases, rather than just letting climate turmoil happen and seeing who profits? One reason is that the cost of controls is likely to be much lower than the cost of rebuilding the world. Coastal cities could be abandoned and rebuilt inland, for instance, but improving energy efficiency and reducing greenhouse-gas emissions in order to stave off rising sea levels should be far more cost-effective. Reforms that prevent major economic and social disruption from climate change are likely to be less expensive, across the board, than reacting to the change. The history of antipollution programs shows that it is always cheaper to prevent emissions than to reverse any damage they cause.

For the United States, there's another argument that is particularly keen. The present ordering of the world favors the United States in nearly every respect—political, economic, even natural, considering America's excellent balance of land and resources. Maybe a warming world would favor the United States more; this is certainly possible. But when the global order already places America at No. 1, why would we want to run the risk of climate change that alters that order? Keeping the world economic system and the global balance of power the way they are seems very strongly in the U.S. national interest—and keeping things the way they are requires prevention of significant climate change. That, in the end, is what's in it for us.

Critical Thinking

1. What potential economic impacts could global warming have on countries around the world?
2. Why is controlling greenhouse gases a critical component in addressing global warming?

Create Central

www.mhhe.com/createcentral

Internet References

nytimes.com
http://topics.nytimes.com/top/news/science/topics/globalwarming/index.html

Union of Concerned Scientists
www.climatehotmap.org/global-warming-effects/economy.html

americanprogress.org
www.americanprogress.org/issues/green/news/2007/09/17/3515/global-warmings-toll-on-the-economy

Regents Earth Science
www.regentsearthscience.com/index.php?option=com_content&task=view&id=1001&Itemid=119

heritage.org
www.heritage.org/research/reports/2013/05/a-cure-worse-than-the-disease-global-economic-impact-of-global-warming-policy

GREGG EASTERBROOK is an *Atlantic* contributing editor, a visiting fellow at the Brookings Institution, and the author of *The Progress Paradox* (2003).

Article

Prepared by: Larry Madaras, *Howard Community College*

It's Hard to Make It In America: How the United States Stopped Being the Land of Opportunity

Lane Kenworthy

Learning Outcomes

After reading this article, you will be able to:

- Explain how the income gap, which has widened since the 1970s, limits economic opportunities for the middle and lower classes.

- Explain the roles the government can play in narrowing the gap.

- List some solutions, according to the author, that might create more economic opportunities.

For all the differences between Democrats and Republicans that were laid bare during the 2012 U.S. presidential campaign, the parties' standard-bearers, Barack Obama and Mitt Romney, do seem to have agreed on one thing: the importance of equal opportunity. In remarks in Chicago in August, Obama called for an "America where no matter who you are, no matter what you look like, no matter where you come from, no matter what your last name is, no matter who you love, you can make it here if you try." The same month, he urged the Supreme Court to uphold affirmative action in public universities, putting his weight behind what has been a mainstay of U.S. equal opportunity legislation since the 1960s. Days later, the Republican vice presidential nominee, Paul Ryan, echoed Obama's sentiment, saying, "We promise equal opportunity, not equal outcomes." Romney, too, argued that whereas Obama "wants to turn America into a European-style entitlement society," his administration would "ensure that we remain a free and prosperous land of opportunity."

It is no accident that both campaigns chose to emphasize equality of opportunity. It has long been at the center of the American ethos. And one of the United States' major successes in the last half century has been its progress toward ensuring that its citizens get roughly the same basic chances in life, regardless of gender or race. Today, women are more likely to graduate from college than men and are catching up in employment and earnings, too. The gap between whites and nonwhites has narrowed as well, albeit less dramatically.

Yet this achievement has been double edged. As gender and race have become less significant barriers to advancement, family background, an obstacle considered more relevant in earlier eras, has reemerged. Today, people who were born worse off tend to have fewer opportunities in life.

Of course, there is no perfect way to measure opportunities. The best method devised thus far is to look at outcomes: college completion, gainful employment, and sufficient income. If the average outcome for one group far outpaces that for another, social scientists conclude that the first group had greater opportunities. Comparing outcomes is not foolproof, as differences in outcomes can result from differences in effort. But a person's effort is itself shaped by the circumstances he or she encounters.

To assess equality of opportunity among people from different family backgrounds, the measure of outcome that social scientists look at is relative intergenerational mobility—a person's position on the income ladder relative to his or her parents' position. Social scientists don't have as much information as they would like about the extent of relative intergenerational mobility, its movement over time, and its causes. The data requirements are stiff; analysts need a survey that collects information about citizens' incomes and other aspects of their life circumstances, then does the same for their children, and for their children's children, and so on. The best assessment of this type in the United States, the Panel Study of Income Dynamics, has been around only since the late 1960s.

Even so, there is general consensus among social scientists on a few basic points. First, an American born into a family in the bottom fifth of incomes between the mid-1960s and the mid-1980s has roughly a 30 percent chance of reaching the middle fifth or higher in adulthood, whereas an American born into the top fifth has an 80 percent chance of ending up in the middle fifth or higher. (In a society with perfectly equal opportunity, every person would have the same chance—20 percent—of landing on each of the five rungs of the income ladder and a 60 percent chance of landing on the middle rung or a higher one.) This discrepancy means that there is considerable inequality of opportunity among Americans from different family backgrounds.

Second, inequality of opportunity has increased in recent decades. The data do not permit airtight conclusions. Still, available compilations of test scores, years of schooling completed, occupations, and incomes of parents and their children strongly suggest that the opportunity gap, which was narrowing until the 1970s, is now widening.

Third, in a sharp reversal of historical trends, there is now less equality of opportunity in the United States than in most other wealthy democratic nations. Data exist for ten of the United States' peer countries (rich long-standing democracies). The United States has less relative intergenerational mobility than eight of them; Australia, Canada, Denmark, Finland, Germany, Norway, Sweden, and the United Kingdom all do better. The United States is on par with France and Italy.

So how did the United States get here? Why did it falter where other nations have not? And how can it fix the problem? On the right, a standard proposal is to strengthen families. On the left, a recent favorite is to reduce income inequality. And everyone supports improving education. To know which proposals would work best, it helps to understand the roots of the new opportunity gap.

The Lost Opportunity Cost

Between the mid-1800s and the 1970s, differences in opportunity based on family circumstances declined steadily. As the formerly farming-based U.S. labor force shifted to manufacturing, many Americans joined the paid labor force, allowing an increasing share of them to move onto and up the income ladder. Elementary education became universal, and secondary education expanded. Then, in the 1960s and 1970s, school desegregation, the outlawing of discrimination in college admissions and hiring, and the introduction of affirmative action programs helped open economic doors for an even wider swath of Americans.

But since the 1970s, the United States has been moving in the opposite direction. A host of economic and social shifts seem to have widened the opportunity gap between Americans from low-income families and those from high-income families. First, family life has changed, at least for some. The share of poorer children growing up with both biological parents has fallen sharply, whereas there has been less change among the wealthy. About 88 percent of children from high-income homes grow up with married parents. That is down from 96 percent four decades ago. Meanwhile, only 41 percent of poorer children grow up in homes with married parents, down from 77 percent four decades ago. That has hurt poorer children's chances of success, since children who live with both of their parents are more likely, even accounting for income, to fare better in school, stay out of trouble with the law, maintain lasting relationships, and earn higher incomes as adults.

The modern culture of intensive parenting—a largely middle- and upper-class phenomenon—adds to the gap. Low-income parents are not able to spend as much on goods and services aimed at enriching their children, such as music lessons, travel, and summer camp. Low-income parents also tend to read less to their children and provide less help with schoolwork. They are less likely to set and enforce clear rules and routines for their children. And they are less likely to encourage their children to aspire to high achievement in school and at work.

Furthermore, a generation ago, most preschool-aged children stayed at home with their mothers. Now, many are enrolled in some sort of child care. But the quality of their experiences varies. Affluent parents can send their children to nationally recognized education-oriented preschools. Poorer parents might have little choice but to leave their children with a neighborhood babysitter who plops them in front of the television. Research by the economist James Heckman and others finds that much of the gap in cognitive and noncognitive skills between children from poor homes and those from affluent homes is already present by the time they enter kindergarten.

Things don't improve once children reach grade school. Funding for public K–12 schools, which used to vary sharply across school districts, has become more even in recent decades. Nevertheless, a large difference remains in the quality of education between the best and the worst schools, and the poorest neighborhoods often have the weakest schools. According to data compiled by Sean Reardon of Stanford University's School of Education, the gap in average test scores between elementary- and secondary-school children from high-income families and those from low-income families has risen steadily in recent decades. Among children born in 1970, those from high-income homes scored, on average, about three-quarters of a standard deviation higher on math and reading tests than those from low-income homes. Among children born in 2000, the gap has grown to one and a quarter standard deviations. That is much larger than the gap between white and black children.

Partly because they tend to be far behind at the end of high school, and partly because college has gotten so expensive, children from poor backgrounds are less likely than others to enter and complete college. The economists Martha Bailey and Susan Dynarski have compared the college completion rates of Americans who grew up in the 1960s and 1970s to the rates of those who grew up in the 1980s and 1990s. The share of young adults from high-income homes that got a four-year college degree rose from 36 percent in the first group to 54 percent in the second group. The share from low-income homes, however, stayed almost flat, rising only from five percent to nine percent.

When it comes time to get a job, the story is no better. Low-income parents tend to have fewer valuable connections to help their children find good jobs. Some people from poor homes are further hampered by a lack of English-language skills. Another disadvantage for the lower-income population is that in the 1970s and 1980s, the United States began incarcerating a lot more young men, including many for minor offenses. Having a criminal record makes it all the more difficult to get a stable job with decent pay—if, that is, good jobs still exist. A number of developments, including technological advances, globalization, a loss of manufacturing employment, and the decline of unions, have reduced the number of jobs that require limited skills but pay a middle-class wage—the very kind of jobs that once moved poorer Americans into the middle class.

Finally, changes in partner selection have also widened the opportunity gap. Not only do those from better-off families tend to end up with more schooling and higher-paying jobs; they are more likely than ever to marry (or cohabit with) others like themselves, according to research by the sociologists Christine Schwartz and Robert Mare.

For all these reasons, the gap in opportunity between the United States' rich and poor has expanded in recent decades. Left unchecked, the trend threatens not only to offset the progress the United States has made on gender and racial equality but also to usher in a future of deep and hardened class divisions.

It might be tempting to shrug and conclude that the high and increasing opportunity gap in the United States is an unfortunate but inevitable consequence of economic and social shifts. The problem with this reaction is that other affluent democracies do better. The United States has lost its historical distinction as the land of opportunity. Yet there is at least some good news: the fact that other countries are more successful in this area suggests that with the right policies, the United States could do better, too.

Valuable Families

One simple, straightforward solution would be to get more money into the hands of low-income families with children. The education policy experts Greg Duncan, Ariel Kalil, and Kathleen Ziol-Guest have found that for children who grew up in the United States in the 1970s and 1980s, an increase in family income of a mere $3,000 during a person's first five years of life was associated with nearly 20 percent higher earnings later in life. The finding suggests that government cash transfers of just a few thousand dollars could give a significant lifelong boost to the children who need it most. Most other affluent countries, including those that do better on equality of opportunity, offer a universal "child allowance" that does exactly this. In Canada, for instance, a family with two children receives an annual allowance of around $3,000, and low-income families with two children might receive more than $6,000. The United States has only a weaker version of the benefit, the Child Tax Credit, which doles out a maximum of just $1,000 a year per child. Moreover, receipt of the money is contingent on filing a federal tax return, which not all low-income families do.

Other solutions involve Washington getting involved in home life. Fewer children in the United States grow up with both biological parents than in any other affluent country for which data are available. To remedy this, some, such as Barbara Dafoe Whitehead and David Popenoe, co-directors of the National Marriage Project at Rutgers, favor efforts to promote marriage. But research by the sociologists Kathryn Edin, Sara McLanahan, and Paula England and others suggests that this strategy is misplaced. Since women today need

less from marriage and expect more from it than they used to, those who are better educated and better off tend to take more time to get established in their jobs and find good partners, which enhances the likelihood of a lasting marriage (or cohabitation). They delay childbearing as well. Among poorer and less-educated women, who see little prospect of a fulfilling and lucrative career, having a child in their teens or early 20s remains common. These women are less likely to stay with a partner: they have had less time to mature personally and to find a person with whom they are compatible, their partners are more likely to have weak financial prospects and a preference for traditional gender roles, and the presence of a child heightens financial and interpersonal tensions. Given all this, convincing more young low-income couples who get pregnant to marry is unlikely to produce many lasting relationships.

Genuine progress probably hinges on poor or less-educated women delaying childbirth. Eventually, this will happen; the teen birthrate has already been dropping for nearly two decades, albeit slowly. For its part, Washington (or any other government) has only limited tools to speed it up. The best might be an education campaign, as Ron Haskins and Isabelle Sawhill, policy experts at the Brookings Institution, have suggested, that focuses on the benefits of the "success sequence": first education, then a stable job, then marriage, and then children.

What about parenting practices, which have a clear effect on childhood development? Although few Americans support extensive government intrusion into home life, one potentially acceptable way that Washington and state governments could try to improve parenting is by paying for home visits by nurses or counselors and providing free or low-cost parenting classes. Getting people to change their behavior and routines is very difficult, so the benefits of such programs are inevitably modest. Nonetheless, in a recent review of existing research, the sociologist Frank Furstenberg found evidence that programs aimed at teaching better practices to parents of children at middle-school age or younger yield some improvements in school readiness and school performance.

Making the Grade

Given the difficulties of altering home life, improving schools remains the United States' main tool for assisting less-advantaged children. For all their inadequacies, public schools do help equalize opportunity by improving students' cognitive abilities. During summer vacation, the cognitive abilities of children in low-income families tend to regress, relative to those of their more advantaged peers. In other words, these children would lag even further behind if they never attended school.

A universal system of affordable, educational child care and preschool could help close the capability gap that opens up during the early years of life. Additionally, it would facilitate parents' employment and thereby boost household incomes, making it doubly helpful for children in low-income families. The Nordic countries offer some lessons: in the 1960s and 1970s, these countries introduced paid maternity leave and publicly funded child care. Today, early education teachers there have training and pay comparable to those of elementary school teachers. The cost of early education is capped at around ten percent of household income. In all these countries, a person's cognitive abilities, likelihood of completing high school and college, and eventual success in the job market tend to be less heavily determined by his or her family's wealth and makeup than in the United States.

There has been some movement to expand the United States' child-care and educational systems at the state level in the past two decades. Most states now have full-day public kindergarten, and some have added public preschool for four-year-olds. But the progress has been very slow, and in recent years, it has been set back by state revenue shortfalls. Assistance from Washington would be of considerable help.

The equalizing effects of college, too, cannot be overstated. Among Americans whose family incomes at birth are in the bottom fifth but who get four-year college degrees, 53 percent end up in the middle fifth or higher. That is pretty close to the 60 percent chance they would have with perfectly equal opportunity. Washington needs to do better at helping people from less-advantaged homes afford college. The average in-state tuition at an American four-year public university exceeds $8,000. In Norway, Sweden, Denmark, and Finland, attending four-year public universities is free. According to data from the Organization for Economic Cooperation and Development, in those nations, the odds that a person whose parents did not complete high school will attend college are between 40 and 60 percent, compared with just 30 percent in the United States.

Working on Labor

Employment is the next challenge. First, the low-hanging fruit: since a prison record impedes labor-market success, the United States should rethink its approach to punishment for nonviolent drug offenders. According to the sociologist Bruce Western, states that have reduced imprisonment over the past decade, instead turning to alternative punishments, such as fines and community corrections programs, have experienced drops in crime similar to states that have increased imprisonment. If other states were to follow suit, the United States could avoid needlessly undermining the employment opportunities of a significant number of young men from less-advantaged homes.

Broader trends in the labor market since the 1970s present a stickier problem. Hourly wages at the median and below have not budged in inflation-adjusted terms. In the 1980s and 1990s, the United States created a lot of new jobs. These facilitated the movement of women into the work force and thereby helped many households enjoy rising incomes despite the stagnation in wages. But in the early years of this century, employment growth stopped, and the subsequent recession and slow recovery have dealt a crushing blow to the less skilled. The employment rate among men aged 25–54 who did not finish high school dropped by ten percentage points between 2007 and 2010.

Eventually, the U.S. economy will get back on track, but that will not automatically lead to more jobs and higher wages. The lone period of sustained wage growth at the middle rung and below occurred in the late 1990s. What distinguishes that period is that the Federal Reserve allowed the unemployment rate to drop to four percent, well below what many economists believed to be the level at which inflation would accelerate. If and when the United States returns to low unemployment, it will need the Federal Reserve to again be willing to allow wages to rise significantly before stepping on the brakes.

It would be foolish to count on this, though, so the United States would do well to consider alternative strategies. One useful tool might be the Earned Income Tax Credit. At the moment, the EITC provides an annual subsidy of up to $6,000 to households with less than $50,000 in earnings. That is helpful, but for a person with no children, the credit amounts to less than $500. That group—young adults with low earnings and no children—includes many Americans who grew up in disadvantaged circumstances. If the economy is growing but wages are not, the United States can and should offer a bigger boost to these people's incomes.

In the past year, a number of commentators, most notably Alan Krueger, chair of the White House Council of Economic Advisers, have suggested that reversing the rise in income inequality could improve economic mobility in the United States. After all, among the countries for which there are comparable data, those with less income inequality tend to have higher relative intergenerational mobility. The United States was already on the high end of the income-inequality scale a generation ago, and since then it has moved even further in that direction.

Yet general calls to reduce income inequality offer little help in identifying which policies to pursue. Consider three possibilities. First, imagine that Washington legislated a radical reduction in the pay differentials for various types of jobs. (Narrower pay differentials account for part of the smaller opportunity gaps in the Nordic countries.) This certainly would reduce income inequality. It would also reduce opportunity inequality: at least in the first generation, even if someone's capabilities matched perfectly those of his or her parents, his or her income would not. But such a drastic step is not likely to happen, in part because few Americans would support it. Second, suppose the United States were to raise income tax rates for the top one percent of households and lower them for middle-class households. Such a move would reduce income inequality, but it would do little to improve the opportunities of children in low-income families. Third, suppose the United States increased tax rates for all households and used the revenue to fund universal early education. (As the political scientist Andrea Campbell recently wrote, most other advanced democracies devote far more tax revenue to social programs.) That step would do little to counter income inequality, but it could substantially expand opportunity. A reduction in income inequality, in short, is neither necessary nor sufficient for achieving a reduction in inequality of opportunity.

Land of Opportunity

For all that other countries' experiences can teach the United States, there are also lessons the United States should take from its own history. The most direct way that Washington has made opportunity more equal in the past has been through affirmative action. Affirmative action is not a strategy that many other affluent countries have embraced, but it has a proven track record in the United States. Since the late 1960s, affirmative action programs for college admissions and for hiring have expanded opportunities for women and various minority groups.

Now, a number of observers from across the partisan spectrum, from Richard Kahlenberg, a senior fellow at the left-leaning Century Foundation, to Charles Murray, a fellow at the right-leaning American Enterprise Institute, favor shifting the focus of affirmative action efforts from race and gender to family background. Emphasizing family background would continue to disproportionately help African American and Latino children, since they are more likely to come from families with low incomes and other disadvantages. Indeed, it would do more to help poor black and Latino children than traditional race-based affirmative action programs, which have mainly benefited middle-class members of such minority groups.

In response to court rulings and ballot initiatives outlawing consideration of race in admissions decisions, some public university systems, including those of California and Texas, have already moved in this direction. One approach guarantees the top ten percent of students graduating from any public high school in a state automatic admission to a public university in that state. Sometimes, this is helpful; in schools where almost all the students are from poor families, the top ten percent of the graduating class will inevitably include low-income students. A more direct strategy would be for colleges and universities to consider family background as one of several kinds of disadvantages that applicants may have faced and to include that among the criteria by which applicants are ranked.

How might employers be persuaded to use this direct approach? Half a century ago, the federal government mandated the use of affirmative action in public agencies and in firms with which it contracted. It could do the same now in order to address the nation's new opportunity gap.

In the last half century, the United States has taken long strides toward equalizing economic opportunity. That progress did not happen on its own; it took place with a push from the government. In recent decades, however, the opportunity gap for Americans from different family backgrounds has started to grow. Fortunately, the United States' experience and that of other affluent nations suggest that the country is not helpless in the face of economic and social changes. There is no silver bullet; a genuine solution is likely to include an array of shifts in policy and society. Even so, a fix is not beyond the United States' reach.

Critical Thinking

1. Critically analyze why the changing post-industrial economy has reduced economic opportunities for the middle and lower classes since the 1970s.
2. Explain why eight Western European countries have created more economic opportunities for its citizens than America has.
3. Critically analyze whether Kenworthy's solutions to the income gap problem are realistic politically. Furthermore, will they solve the problem?

Create Central

www.mhhe.com/createcentral

Internet References

Georgetown University, American Studies Web

This eclectic site provides links to a wealth of Internet resources for research in American studies, from agriculture and rural development, to history and government, to race and ethnicity.

www.georgetown.edu/crossroads/asw

National Center for Policy Analysis

Through this site, click onto links to read discussions on an array of topics that are of major interest in the study of American history, from regulatory policy and privatization to economy and income.

www.public-policy.org/web.public-policy.org/index.php

LANE KENWORTHY is Professor of Sociology and Political Science at the University of Arizona.

Kenworthy, Lane. From *Foreign Affairs*, vol. 91, no. 6, November/December, 2012. Copyright © 2012 by Council on Foreign Relations, Inc. Reprinted by permission of Foreign Affairs. www.ForeignAffairs.com.